Law for Forensic Scientists

Law for Forensic Scientists fills a significant gap by providing an accessible and comprehensive textbook for forensic science students, practitioners, and attorneys working with forensic evidence. While numerous books cover criminal law, criminal procedure, and expert testimony separately – often tailored for law students and criminal defense attorneys – this book uniquely integrates these key areas for forensic scientists.

Designed to build a broad understanding of the legal landscape, this book covers essential topics such as criminal offenses, criminal procedures, Fourth Amendment search and seizure law, forensic evidence collection, the treatment of science in Anglo-American jurisprudence, and expert testimony. Each chapter presents content in a structured and digestible format, featuring case studies, key terms, thought-provoking questions, chapter summaries, and references for further reading. Significant case law is incorporated throughout that illustrate real-world applications. To support both students and instructors, this book includes a full subject, case, and statutory index, as well as a glossary for quick reference. Additionally, online instructor resources provide supplementary materials, including a proposed syllabus and test questions, making it a valuable resource for forensic science and legal studies courses.

Law for Forensic Scientists is an accessible textbook appropriate for students in forensic science programs taking a course on criminal law.

Law for Forensic Scientists

Victor W. Weedn and Kenneth E. Melson

CRC Press
Taylor & Francis Group
Boca Raton London New York

CRC Press is an imprint of the
Taylor & Francis Group, an **informa** business
AN AUERBACH BOOK

Designed cover image: Shutterstock

First edition published 2026
by CRC Press
2385 NW Executive Center Drive, Suite 320, Boca Raton FL 33431

and by CRC Press
4 Park Square, Milton Park, Abingdon, Oxon, OX14 4RN

CRC Press is an imprint of Taylor & Francis Group, LLC

ISBN: 9781498777964 (hbk)
ISBN: 9781041066675 (pbk)
ISBN: 9780429272455 (ebk)

DOI: 10.4324/9780429272455

Typeset in Minion
by codeMantra

Access the Support Material: www.routledge.com/9781498777964

Contents

About the Authors . . . xv

Preface . . . xvii

Acknowledgments . . . xix

CHAPTER 1 — **Introduction to the Law** . . . 1

Introduction . . . 1
Historical Background . . . 2
Natural Law . . . 2
Rule of Law . . . 5
Common Law versus Civil Law . . . 6
Anglo-American Common Law and Precedent . . . 7
Ignorance of the Law . . . 9
Federalism . . . 9
The Federal Government . . . 10
State Governments . . . 10
Federal Preemption . . . 11
Comity . . . 13
Branches of the Federal Government . . . 13

Judicial Review of Legislation . . . 14
Sources of Law . . . 16
International Law . . . 18
Conflict of Law . . . 18
Branches of Law . . . 19
Summary . . . 21
Terms . . . 22
Cases . . . 22
Statutes . . . 23
Thought Questions . . . 23

CHAPTER 2 — **Due Process** . . . **25**

Introduction . . . 25
Historical Background . . . 26
The American Constitution . . . 27
Civil War Reconstruction Amendments . . . 29
Two Due Process Clauses . . . 30
The Selective Incorporation Doctrine . . . 30
Procedural and Substantive Due Process . . . 36
Summary . . . 41
Terms . . . 42
Cases . . . 42
Statutes . . . 42
Reference Material . . . 43
Thought Questions . . . 43

CHAPTER 3 — **Judicial Apparatus** . . . **44**

Introduction . . . 44
Historical Background . . . 45
Case Names . . . 45
Reporter Services . . . 45
Court Structure . . . 47
Judges and Magistrates . . . 48
Jurisdiction . . . 48
Federal Jurisdiction . . . 50
Judicial Process . . . 51
Appeals . . . 52
The U.S. Supreme Court . . . 55
Habeas Corpus . . . 57

Judicial Activism versus Judicial Restraint 57
Summary 60
Terms. 61
Cases 61
Statutes 62
Thought Questions 62

CHAPTER 4 — Civil Law. 63

Introduction. 63
Historical Background 64
Civil versus Criminal Law 64
Civil Remedies. 65
Vicarious Liability. 66
Statutes of Limitations and Statutes of Repose 67
Torts 67
Contracts 73
Violations of Civil Rights 78
Governmental Immunity. 80
Summary 83
Terms. 83
Cases 84
Statutes 84
Thought Questions 85

CHAPTER 5 — Crimes and Defenses. 86

Introduction. 86
Historical Background 87
Criminal Law Philosophy. 87
Classification and Criminal Statistics. 88
Elements of a Crime 90
Inchoate Crimes 93
Homicide 94
Sexual Offenses 97
Assault. 97
Property Crimes 98
Federal Crimes. 98
Other Crimes. 100
Defenses 101
Summary 105

Terms.......... 105
Cases.......... 106
Statutes.......... 106
Thought Questions.......... 107

CHAPTER 6 — Criminal Procedure.......... 108

Introduction.......... 108
Historical Background.......... 109
Criminal Procedure Mechanics.......... 110
Criminal Procedure Constitutional Control.......... 119
Summary.......... 123
Terms.......... 124
Cases.......... 125
Statutes and Other Authorities.......... 125
Thought Questions.......... 125

CHAPTER 7 — Search and Seizure I: Reasonableness.......... 126

Introduction.......... 126
Historical Background.......... 127
Fourth Amendment.......... 127
Scope of the Fourth Amendment.......... 128
What Is a Search?.......... 132
Summary.......... 144
Terms.......... 145
Cases.......... 145
Statutes.......... 146
Thought Questions.......... 146

CHAPTER 8 — Search and Seizure II: Warrant Searches.......... 147

Introduction.......... 147
Judicial Approval.......... 148
Targets of Search Warrants.......... 149
Elements of Valid Search Warrants.......... 149
Probable Cause.......... 150
Confidential and Anonymous Informants.......... 151
Particularity.......... 153
Staleness.......... 154

Anticipatory Warrants . . . 154
Sneak and Peak Warrants . . . 155
Defective Warrants . . . 155
Execution Requirements . . . 156
Return of the Warrant . . . 158
Good Faith . . . 158
FISA Warrants . . . 164
Administrative Warrants . . . 166
Summary . . . 167
Terms . . . 168
Cases . . . 168
Statutes . . . 169
Thought Questions . . . 170

CHAPTER 9 — **Search and Seizure III: Warrantless Searches** . . . **171**

Introduction . . . 171
Well-Recognized Exceptions . . . 172
Plain View . . . 172
Consent . . . 175
Stop and Frisk (Terry Stop) . . . 177
Search Incident to Arrest . . . 179
Automobile Exception . . . 184
Exigency/Emergency . . . 185
Hot Pursuit . . . 187
Special Needs . . . 188
General Reasonableness . . . 189
Administrative Searches . . . 189
Summary . . . 190
Terms . . . 190
Cases . . . 191
Thought Questions . . . 195

CHAPTER 10 — **Forensic Evidence I: Collection** . . . **196**

Introduction . . . 196
Searches of Places . . . 196
Searches of Persons . . . 201
DNA Collection and Database Searching . . . 215
Summary . . . 217
Terms . . . 217

Cases ... 218
Statutes ... 219
Thought Questions ... 219

CHAPTER 11 — Forensic Evidence II: Integrity and Preservation ... 221

Introduction ... 221
Chain-of-Custody ... 221
Spoliation of Potentially Exculpatory Evidence ... 223
Biological Evidence ... 227
Sample Consumption ... 228
Summary ... 229
Terms ... 229
Cases ... 229
Statutes ... 230
Thought Questions ... 230

CHAPTER 12 — Scientific Evidence I: The Science ... 231

Introduction ... 231
Historical Background ... 231
Science ... 232
General Sciences ... 234
Forensic Science ... 236
NAS Report ... 239
PCAST Report ... 240
Historicity ... 244
Wrongful Convictions ... 244
Statistical Interpretation ... 246
Funding ... 248
Summary ... 249
Terms ... 250
Cases ... 250
Other Authorities ... 250
Thought Questions ... 251

CHAPTER 13 — Scientific Evidence II: Admissibility ... 253

Introduction ... 253
Frye Standard for Admission of Novel Scientific Evidence ... 253

Federal Rules of Evidence. 256
Daubert Standard for Admission of Scientific Evidence 258
Daubert Trilogy 262
Daubert Aftermath 263
PCAST. 266
Summary 266
Terms. 266
Cases 267
Other Authorities 267
Thought Questions 267

CHAPTER 14 — **Scientific Evidence III: Weight** **269**

Introduction. 269
Historical Background 269
Proving Reliability. 270
Pattern-Matching Examinations. 272
Laboratory Test Validation. 273
Standards 273
Personnel Qualifications 274
Laboratory Qualifications 277
Forensic Science Boards and Commissions 279
Regulation of Reports and Testimony 280
Court Treatment of Forensic Science Irregularities 280
Cognitive Bias 282
Reasonable Scientific Certainty. 282
Harmless versus Harmful Error 283
"New Evidence" 283
Summary 285
Terms. 285
Cases 286
Other Authorities 286
Thought Questions 287

CHAPTER 15 — **Sixth Amendment Confrontation** **288**

Introduction. 288
Historical Background 289
Hearsay Rule 290
Unavailability of a Witness. 293
Remote Video Testimony. 296

U.S. Supreme Court Case Law 296
Testimonial Statements 307
Independent Expert Opinion 308
Supervisor-Assistant/Teacher-Student 310
Practical Implications of Confrontation 310
Summary 310
Terms 310
Cases 311
Statutes and Other Authorities 311
Thought Questions 312

CHAPTER 16 — Pretrial, Trial, and Appellate Procedures 313

Introduction 313
Historical Background 314
Modern Court Procedures 315
Pretrial Procedures 315
Trial Procedures 321
Post-Trial Motions 328
Appeals 328
Process Crimes 329
Summary 330
Terms 330
Cases 331
Statutes and Other Authorities 331
Thought Questions 332

CHAPTER 17 — Expert Testimony 333

Introduction 333
Historical Background 334
Ordinary and Expert Witnesses 335
Expert Witnesses 336
Bases of an Expert 338
Qualifying an Expert Witness 339
Examining an Expert Witness 341
Refreshing Memory 342
Objections 343
Challenges to the Testimony 344
Opinion on the Ultimate Issue 344
Introducing Physical Evidence 345

Jury Evaluation of Witnesses 347
Effective Testimony 349
Courtroom Etiquette 351
Summary 353
Terms 353
Cases 354
Other Authorities 354
Thought Questions 355

Glossary 357

Case Index 365

Statutory Authorities 372

Subject Index 374

About the Authors

Kenneth E. Melson, JD, is a graduate of Denison University and the George Washington University Law School. He has been a county prosecutor, an Assistant U.S. Attorney, a court-appointed U.S. Attorney, the Director of the Executive Office for U.S. Attorneys, an acting Director of the ATF, and an attorney in an Inspector General's office. He has been an Adjunct Professor at the GWU School of Law for over 35 years and taught criminal law in the Department of Forensic Sciences. He has served as the Senior Advisor on Forensic Science in the Office of Legal Policy at the US Department of Justice. He was a co-chair of the Subcommittee on Forensic Science in the Office of Science and Technology Policy within the Executive Office of the President. He was the President of the American Academy of Forensic Sciences in 2003–2004.

Victor W. Weedn, MD, JD, is a graduate of the University of Texas at Austin, South Texas College of Law, and the Southwestern Medical School. He has been employed as a medical examiner, crime lab director, research scientist, and forensic science and law professor. He has taught forensic science and law courses at various institutions. He founded the DNA identification program for the U.S. military, where he helped to pioneer STR and mtDNA technologies. He developed the current NAME Inspection and Accreditation program. He has twice testified to the U.S. Congress, drafted legislation that was later enacted, and drafted several amicus briefs for NAME for state and federal courts that proved persuasive. He was the President of the American Academy of Forensic Sciences from 2015 to 2016. He served as the Senior Forensic Advisor to U.S. Deputy Attorney General Sally Yates from late 2016 to 2017. He participated on the Scientific Advisory Board of the International Criminal Court Office of the Prosecutor in 2017 and 2018.

Preface

This book is intended to be a readable textbook for law or criminal law courses taken by forensic science students in the United States. It summarizes the broad topic areas and is not an exhaustive reference textbook. Furthermore, readers should understand that no book on the law is a substitute for sound professional legal advice as the law changes over time, by jurisdiction, and according to circumstance. The law varies from jurisdiction to jurisdiction and changes over time.

This book will cover the basics of law that forensic scientists need to know. Forensic scientists work in both the criminal and civil legal arenas, and while we cover both, our emphasis is on criminal law. Still, we do not cover all aspects of criminal law – such as the law of arrests or interrogation. Crime scene and medicolegal death investigators must focus on Fourth Amendment search and seizure law. In contrast, forensic scientists working in the laboratories (forensic chemists, forensic molecular biologists, and toxicologists) need an emphasis on scientific evidence and expert testimony. All practitioners should benefit from knowledge of the law on evidence handling. All practitioners will need to know how to give testimony. This book attempts to put everything together in an accessible and readable form.

Acknowledgments

We wish to thank John Morgan for review and comments on Chapter 12 and Brad Putnam for review and comments on Chapter 14.

The material in this book is presented for educational purposes and is not a replacement for legal advice by a licensed attorney of the jurisdiction.

Chapter 1

Introduction to the Law

Learning Objectives

After reading this chapter, students are expected to be able to:

- define *the law*
- describe the origins of American jurisprudence
- explain the dual sovereignty nature of the United States government
- articulate federal preemption
- discuss judicial review
- list sources of law
- recognize various branches of law.

Introduction

"The Law" is a term with concrete and vague notional elements that defies a crisp definition everyone will accept. Generally, the law is a society's official set of enforceable rules. Many modern languages, unlike English, distinguish between written laws (French *lois*) and law generally (French *droit*). Jurisprudence is the theory or philosophy of law.

The law functions to keep the peace, restrain wickedness, and protect the weak. The law determines rights and obligations. The law is a framework

DOI: 10.4324/9780429272455-1

for human relations and family interests. The law allows for settlement of disputes. The law embraces customs and morality and promotes justice. The law can also be considered a form of social control, providing the mechanisms of intrusion and governance. Others might say "the law" *is* the government. The legal system purports to be a coherent yet haphazard and often contradictory system of social regulation that punishes wrongdoers and helps make social life more predictable.

Historical Background

Legal governance in ancient Egypt dates to at least 3000 BCE. There is physical evidence for a legal code in the Syrian city of Ebla from 2400 BCE. Still, the first significant recorded law is *Hammurabi's Code* that is from about 1754 BCE. It covered topics such as civil disputes, domestic affairs, and criminal prosecutions. The Code is famous for its statement of punishments: "An eye for an eye, a tooth for a tooth." Hammurabi, the sixth Babylonian King, made and administered the laws; he was essentially "the judge, jury, and executioner," as well as the legislature. Thus, "the law" predated courts, police, and prisons by millennia but included methods of adjudication and enforcement from the outset. Of course, the world is vastly more complicated, and "the law" has evolved such that every nation, territory, and jurisdiction on Earth now has an elaborate and sophisticated legal system and set of institutions to govern.

Natural Law

Laws attempt to maintain social welfare through a reasonable balance between governmental control to press collective rights against individual rights of liberty and freedom – what Justice Benjamin Cardozo in *Palko v. Connecticut* (1937) referred to as "a scheme of ordered liberty." Modern societies recognize limits on the power of governments over people, such as fundamental human rights and religious freedoms. Thomas Hobbes and John Locke conceived a social contract in which individuals give up some liberties for protection by the state.

Natural law is an unwritten, "God-given" law that always applies to everyone. It is what Thomas Jefferson is referring to in the Declaration of Independence when he declares:

> …for one people…to assume among the powers of the earth, the separate and equal station to which the Laws of Nature and of Nature's God entitle them… We hold these truths to be self-evident, that all men are created equal, that they are endowed by their Creator with certain unalienable Rights, that among these are Life, Liberty, and the pursuit of Happiness.

BOX 1.1 DEFINITIONS OF LAW

Law as defined by the Merriam-Webster Dictionary

1.a (1): a binding custom or practice of a community : a rule of conduct or action prescribed (see prescribe sense 1a) or formally recognized as binding or enforced by a controlling authority

(2): the whole body of such customs, practices, or rules

// The courts exist to uphold, interpret, and apply the *law*.

(3): Common Law

b (1): the control brought about by the existence or enforcement of such *law*

// preserved law and order in the town

(2): the action of laws considered as a means of redressing wrongs

also: litigation

// developed the habit of going to law over the slightest provocation —H. A. Overstreet

(3): the agency of or an agent of established law

// When he saw that the fighting was escalating, he called in the law.

c: a rule or order that it is advisable or obligatory to observe

// a law of self-preservation

d: something compatible with or enforceable by established law

// The decrees were judged not to be law and were therefore rescinded.

e: control, authority

// The child submits to no law.

2.a *often capitalized*: the revelation of the will of God set forth in the Old Testament

b *capitalized*: the first part of the Jewish scriptures : pentateuch, torah

3: a rule of construction or procedure

// the *laws* of poetry

4: the whole body of laws relating to one subject

// criminal *law*

// probate *law*

5.a: the legal profession

// studied for a career in *law*

b: law as a department of knowledge : jurisprudence

c: legal knowledge

// a man with much history but little *law*

6.a: a statement of an order or relation of phenomena that so far as is known is invariable under the given conditions

// a *law* of thermodynamics

// Boyle's law

b: a general relation proved or assumed to hold between mathematical or logical expressions

Source: https://merriam-webster.com/dictionary/law

Law as defined by the Black's Law Dictionary

1. That which is laid down, ordained, or established. A rule or method according to which phenomena or actions coexist or follow each other.

2. A system of principles and rules of human conduct, being the aggregate of those commandments and principles which are either prescribed or recognized by the governing power in an organized jural society as its will in relation to the

conduct of the members of such society, and which it undertakes to maintain and sanction and to use as the criteria of the actions of such members.

"Law" is a solemn expression of legislative will. It orders and permits and forbids. It announces rewards and punishments. Its provisions generally relate not to solitary or singular cases, but to what passes in the ordinary course of affairs.

"Law," without an Article, properly implies a science or system of principles or rules of human conduct, answering to the Latin "jus"; as when it is spoken of as a subject of study or practice. In this sense, it includes the decisions of courts of justice, as well as acts of the legislature. The judgment of a competent, court, until reversed or otherwise superseded, is law, as much as any statute. Indeed, it may happen that a statute may be passed in violation of law, that is, of the fundamental law or Constitution of a state; that it is the prerogative of courts in such cases to declare it void, or, in other words, to declare it not to be law.

3. A rule of civil conduct prescribed by the supreme power in a, state.

Source: https://thelawdictionary.org/law/

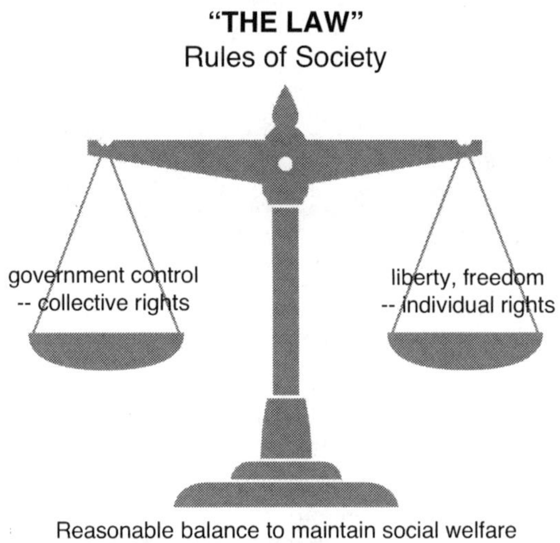

FIGURE 1.1 Balancing Public Good and Private Rights.

Natural law and fundamental human rights are ethical and moral imperatives. Natural law is the basis of the Universal Declaration of Human Rights (UDHR) adopted by the United Nations in 1948.

Positive law, in contrast to natural law, is the law written by humans for governance. It is not universal and changes with time. When discussing "The Law," most people think about positive law. Unlike the Declaration of Independence, the U.S. Constitution is an example of positive law. This book is about the positive law of the United States.

Positive law imperfectly overlaps with natural law. Although many laws regulate conduct without any moral connotations (e.g., speed limits), in other cases, the law often attempts to control behavior in conformance with ethical principles (e.g., homicide). Not all unethical behavior is illegal (e.g., infidelity). Some would argue that morality cannot be legislated and point to prohibition as an example. Regardless, courts dispense equitable notions of fairness and justice through punishment of offenders and *restitution* of victims, placing them back in the position they were in before they were wronged.

Rule of Law

The United States of America is a nation under *the rule of law*, the principle that all people and institutions are subject to a set of laws that are applied fairly and enforced equally. Other countries may have dictators that are "above the law" as potentates. The American Revolution was fought to free the colonies from the yoke of the English king and establish a democracy.

In the representative democracy of the United States, "the people" establish the laws through their elected legislative representatives. Moreover, trials are ruled by the juries of our peers. The Constitution of the United States begins:

> We the People of the United States, in Order to form a more perfect Union, establish Justice, insure domestic Tranquility, provide for the common defense, promote the general Welfare, and secure the Blessings of Liberty to ourselves and our Posterity, do ordain and establish this Constitution for the United States of America.

President Lincoln, in his Gettysburg address, spoke of "…that government of the people, by the people, for the people…"

All federal government officials are bound by an oath or affirmation to uphold and obey the Constitution and the laws of the United States.

In *Trump v. U.S.* (2024), Chief Justice Roberts, writing for the majority, declared, "The President is not above the law" but then decided that the President enjoys absolute immunity for acts of core constitutional power and at least presumptive immunity for all other official acts but none for unofficial acts. He argues this is needed to allow the President to take "bold and unhesitating action." In writing for the dissent, Justice Sotomayor wrote the majority's grant of immunity means, "the President is now a king above the law," and she fears for our democracy. Justice Jackson observes that the decision removes some of the legislative branch's checks on the executive branch.

Common Law versus Civil Law

Most modern nation-states have adopted either *Civil Law* or *Common Law* as their system of jurisprudence. Customary law and religious law, or some combination, are alternatives to these systems (e.g., Sharia or Islamic law for Muslim countries, Catholic canon law for the Vatican, customary law for international law, and bijural system for Canada). Of course, the individual law of each nation-state varies according to its own unique history, customs, culture, and local needs. The study of these different systems of jurisprudence is called comparative law.

The term *Civil Law* is used here as a system of jurisprudence, as opposed to its use as a term for the non-criminal branch of law as described later in this textbook.

Civil Law emerged from ancient Roman law (*Corpus Juris Civilis*) and has been adopted by approximately 150 countries worldwide, primarily in continental Europe. Civil Law is codified law – it has been reduced to written legal codes. The most influential of these codes, often used as a basis for other codes, is the Napoleonic Code promulgated in 1804, but the three main traditions are the French Civil Law, the German Civil Law, and the Scandinavian Civil Law. Only legislative enactments, not prior decisions, are binding on judges, and thus, law is interpreted, rather than developed, by judges. Civil Law legal proceedings are *inquisitorial* in nature and are directed and adjudicated by judges, who are often described as investigators.

Common Law emerged in England and has been adopted in approximately 80 countries, primarily the Commonwealth countries. The term originated from the law common to all the King's courts across England following their establishment by Henry II after the Norman Conquest of 1066. However, it developed fundamentally from Anglo-Saxon law. The Common Law is judge-made law, known as *case law*, originating from decisions in individual cases that act as precedents for future cases. Over time, legal principles emerge. This is unlike Civil Law, where the facts of a case are judged against the written code without reference to determinations in other cases. Although scattered legislation is also a part of this system, the Common Law was initially generally uncodified. Proceedings are *accusatory* and *adversarial* in nature, directed by lawyers and adjudicated by juries. Judges act primarily as umpires.

Today, in practice, Civil Law and Common Law are converging. Common Law countries are increasingly codifying their laws, and Civil Law countries are adopting some of the trial procedures of Common Law countries. European Union law has been codified in treaties but develops through the precedent set by the European Court of Justice. In the United States, statutory law largely replaced Common Law traditions by the early 20th century, but courts still interpret statutes and build new case laws after statutes are enacted. Oliver Wendell Holmes, Jr., who served on the U.S. Supreme Court from 1902 to 1932, is said to be the last great Common Law justice, and Louis Brandeis, who served on the U.S. Supreme Court from 1916 to 1939, is said to be the first modern statutory justice.

Anglo-American Common Law and Precedent

Anglo-American jurisprudence is a Common Law system; all U.S. States are Common Law jurisdictions, except Louisiana. Due to its French heritage, Louisiana has a Civil Law tradition blended with American jurisprudence. When there is no prior law on a subject, then Common Law applies.

Unlike Civil Law jurisdictions, prior judicial decisions in English and American courts act as *binding precedents* for later cases, so a judge must defer to previous decisions. The American colonies had been using English law when they declared independence and continued using the legal apparatus established after that. The former British colonies formally adopted English Common Law through *reception statutes*, by which former British colonies, upon gaining their independence, adopted the English Common Law that was not explicitly rejected by the new nation's laws. Accordingly, Anglo-American law goes back to the early English courts from centuries before the existence of America as a nation.

This doctrine of precedent, which developed in England during the 12th and 13th centuries, is known as *stare decisis*, "to stand by things decided." Thus, the law builds on itself and becomes more sophisticated and intricate. It creates uniformity across a jurisdiction and consistency and stability over time. Moreover, it creates predictability, permitting citizens to know the established law. However, as Justice Oliver Wendell Holmes wrote:

> It is revolting to have no better reason for a rule of law than that so it was laid down in the time of Henry IV. It is still more revolting if the grounds on which it was laid down have vanished long since, and the rule simply persists from blind imitation of the past.

Only published appellate court holdings will bind lower courts and courts at the same level within the same jurisdiction, unless they can be distinguished legally or factually. Although non-published cases and cases from other jurisdictions may not be binding on a court, they may still be *persuasive* arguments and relied on by the court. Furthermore, only the core holding of the case (*ratio decidendi*) is *binding precedent*; the extraneous *dicta*, in the judge's opinion, are not binding but nonetheless may be persuasive. Likewise, dissenting judicial opinions, although not the court's holding, may later become law if, in a subsequent case, the court finds the dissent persuasive and overturns its previous decision.

A lawyer may like a prior case holding and thus argue that the prior case applies because the case fact pattern and legal issues are sufficiently similar. In contrast, the lawyer may not like the prior case holding and will argue that the prior case does not apply because the fact pattern is distinguishable. The judge must decide whether the prior case is a precedent in the current case. The doctrinal argument may still be persuasive even if the case is not a binding precedent. This discretion to use the precedent based on the facts permits flexibility to adapt to changes. Consequently, the case law becomes ever more refined and nuanced to fact patterns while broad legal doctrine develops.

A case brought to court without prior case law is called "a case of first impression."

BOX 1.2 *PLANNED PARENTHOOD V. CASEY* (1992) – UPHOLDING ROE

The U.S. Supreme Court considered whether to overrule its *Roe v. Wade* opinion 19 years earlier. The Court, in a plurality decision, declined to completely overrule *Roe*, upholding the essential holding of the right to an abortion, but substituted a viability analysis for a trimester framework. Justice Sandra Day O'Connor, who was personally against abortions, wrote:

> Liberty finds no refuge in a jurisprudence of doubt. ...
>
> The obligation to follow precedent begins with necessity, and a contrary necessity marks its outer limit. ...we recognize that no judicial system could do society's work if it eyed each issue afresh in every case that raised it. Indeed, the very concept of the rule of law underlying our own Constitution requires such continuity over time that a respect for precedent is, by definition, indispensable. At the other extreme, a different necessity would make itself felt if a prior judicial ruling should come to be seen so clearly as error that its enforcement was for that very reason doomed.
>
> Even when the decision to overrule a prior case is not, ...virtually foreordained, it is common wisdom that the rule of stare decisis is not an "inexorable command," certainly, it is not such in every constitutional case. Rather, when this Court reexamines a prior holding, its judgment is customarily informed by a series of prudential and pragmatic considerations designed to test the consistency of overruling a prior decision with the ideal of the rule of law and to gauge the respective costs of reaffirming and overruling a prior case. Thus, for example, we may ask whether the rule has proven to be intolerable simply in defying practical workability; whether the rule is subject to a kind of reliance that would lend a special hardship to the consequences of overruling and add inequity to the cost of repudiation; whether related principles of law have so far developed as to have left the old rule no more than a remnant of abandoned doctrine; or whether facts have so changed, or come to be seen so differently, as to have robbed the old rule of significant application or justification.
>
> Although *Roe* has engendered opposition, it has in no sense proven "unworkable," representing as it does a simple limitation beyond which a state law is unenforceable. ...
>
> The inquiry into reliance counts the cost of a rule's repudiation as it would fall on those who have relied reasonably on the rule's continued application. ...

BOX 1.3 *DOBBS V. JACKSON WOMEN'S HEALTH ORGANIZATION* (2022) – OVERTURNING ROE

The U.S. Supreme Court reconsidered whether to overrule its *Roe v. Wade* opinion 30 years after *Planned Parenthood*. This time, the Court overruled

Roe and *Planned Parenthood*, with five justices holding that abortion was not a constitutional right and not deeply rooted in the country's history, leaving states to decide the issue for themselves. Justice Samuel Alito wrote:

> *Roe* was egregiously wrong from the start. Its reasoning was exceptionally weak, and the decision has had damaging consequences. And far from bringing about a national settlement of the abortion issue, *Roe* and *Casey* have enflamed debate and deepened division.

The reaction to the *Dobbs's* overruling of long-established law was immediate and robust. Polls revealed that 55%–60% of the population disapproved of the decision. Polls also showed a sudden loss of confidence in the court and the impression that the court had become political. Post-*Dobbs* state and federal elections were heavily influenced by abortion politics. Laws for and against abortion rights were passed. Oral contraceptive use rose. Maternal and infant death rates increased in states that banned or restricted abortions.

Ignorance of the Law

For citizens to follow the law, they must know it. Thus, laws must be accessible and provide "fair warning" – they must be sufficiently definite to give persons of ordinary intelligence reasonable certainty that a given action or conduct is illegal and subject him or her to punishment (*McBoyle v. U.S.*, 1931). Ignorance of the law is no excuse. You generally cannot say "Well, I did not know that was the law!" and expect not to be held accountable. In some rare cases of arcane, highly technical, and complex regulatory law or recent laws that have not been adequately publicized, ignorance may be found to be a mitigation or an excuse.

Nonetheless, it is impossible to know all the laws. Furthermore, the laws change. The U.S. Congress passes 2–3 million words of law each year. Statutes promulgated at different times for different purposes may conflict, such that to follow one law is to break the other. Furthermore, most laws are often nuanced and subject to interpretation. Moreover, applying the law to a particular case may not be clear. Thus, getting advice from a competent licensed attorney familiar with the law is necessary for all these reasons. By law, only attorneys who are licensed in your jurisdiction are allowed to give their legal advice to you and represent you. This book is not a substitute for legal counsel!

Federalism

As its name indicates, the United States of America's governmental structure involves a *dual sovereignty* of federal and state governments. The Fourteenth Amendment declares explicitly, "All persons born or naturalized in the United States, and subject to the jurisdiction thereof, are citizens of the United

States and of the state wherein they reside." In this dual context, the nearly 90,000 county and local governments are part of the states in which they are located and not independent sovereignties, although "home rule" grants some autonomy of subunits of states in some states.

Upon entering the Union, states surrendered some of their sovereignty to the national government, a sovereign that does not have plenary power over them but that is more than their coequal. The Founding Fathers vigorously debated how much power should be taken from the states and given to the central government. After secession from England, the original 13 states existed and operated as independent nation-states when they came together to decide how to form a federal government. The promulgation of the Articles of Confederation was an initial attempt to create the central government, but it failed to grant sufficient powers to the federal government. Federalists wanted a strong central government to provide strong leadership in times of crisis. However, anti-federalists opposed a strong government because they thought the federal government would threaten the sovereignty and prestige of state and local governments, which are closer to the people. Regardless, this dual sovereignty system allows for greater public participation, and the various state governments act as laboratories, which enables the federal government to adopt best practices.

The Federal Government

The U.S. Constitution describes the federal government's framework and governs its basic operations. Since the Constitution is a grant of power from the states, the federal government's powers are specifically *enumerated* in the Constitution's text.

The federal government's powers include the authority and responsibility to make treaties, establish and regulate the postal system, regulate foreign and interstate commerce, tax imports and exports, declare war, maintain a military, coin money, and grant and protect copyrights and patents, among others. Moreover, the *Necessary and Proper Clause* grants the federal government the power to make all laws "necessary and proper" to meet its responsibilities. The scope of the federal government has significantly increased with time.

State Governments

The federal government's enumerated powers, those expressly stated in the Constitution, include exclusive federal powers and concurrent powers shared with the states.

The federal government shares concurrent powers with the states to collect taxes, regulate banks, establish and administrate courts, borrow money, make and enforce laws, regulate intrastate commerce, provide for public education, conduct elections, protect public health and safety, regulate marriage and divorce, and confer professional licensure, among others.

Any non-enumerated powers not delegated to the federal government or denied to the states by the U.S. Constitution are residual powers reserved exclusively for the states – the so-called states' rights. The Tenth Amendment defines the residual powers of the States:

> The [express and implied] powers not delegated to the United States by the Constitution, nor prohibited by it to the states, are reserved to the States respectively, or to the people.

The Founding Fathers expressly reserved to the states the general power to act in the best interests of their citizens, the so-called *police power* (constitutional term), to regulate and enforce the health, safety, morals, and general welfare of their inhabitants. Police power should not be confused with *police authority*, which allows law enforcement to carry out their duties. Police power allows the states to create generally applicable criminal laws. The federal government, by contrast, may make a criminal law only if it is within the scope of a federal power under the Constitution as a federal power enumerated in the Constitution involves governance of a federal place (i.e., Washington, D.C.) or for the protection of the government itself, its institutions, and its employees. The police power of the states is limited only by (1) the rights guaranteed by the Constitution, (2) the necessity of the legitimate public purpose, and (3) a reasonable exercise of that power (*President Riverboat Casino, Inc. v. Missouri Gaming Commission*, 13 S.W.3d 635, Mo. 2000). Police power may also be limited by state constitutions.

Federal Preemption

Federal preemption occurs when Congress intends for federal law to supersede state law. The *Supremacy Clause* (Article VI, Paragraph 2) of the U.S. Constitution reads:

> This Constitution, and the Laws of the United States which shall be made in Pursuance thereof; and all Treaties made, or which shall be made, under the Authority of the United States, shall be the Supreme law of the land; and the Judges in every State shall be bound thereby, any Thing in the Constitution or Laws of any State to the Contrary notwithstanding.

Thus, Congress can promulgate new laws within its enumerated powers that supersede state laws, but states cannot enact laws that infringe on the federal government's laws. However, the states are free to impose stricter laws or greater protections than the federal government, but they cannot contradict federal law.

The Constitution's *Commerce Clause* (Article I, Section 8, Clause 3) is an enumerated federal government power, giving the U.S. Congress the power: "To regulate Commerce with foreign Nations, and among the several States, and with the Indian Tribes." During the Presidency of Franklin Roosevelt, as the nation was overcoming economic depression, in the case of *Wickard v. Filburn* (1942), the Supreme Court held that the *Commerce Clause* empowers the U.S. Congress to set and enforce production quotas on individual farmers because their actions have a collective substantial economic effect, albeit indirect, on interstate commerce. Thus, the Supreme Court extended this power over intrastate affairs that economically impact interstate commerce, effectively expanding federal jurisdiction over all commercial and most non-commercial activities. Particularly, when combined with the *Necessary and Proper Clause*, the federal government has virtually unlimited power to act, despite the fears of the Founding Fathers and those who advocate states' rights.

The growth of the federal government and increasing encroachment over state activities have spawned a States' Rights movement but to minor effect. However, there are limits to what the federal government can do. In *Murphy v. NCAA* (2018), the U.S. Supreme Court concluded that Congress could not "commandeer" the authority of state legislatures and struck down a statute prohibiting states from authorizing sports gambling.

In some areas, the federal government may adopt state law. The Assimilative Crimes Act (ACA) adopts state criminal laws for areas of exclusive or concurrent federal jurisdiction if no specific federal crime exists. In other words, when a crime has been committed in a building or land owned or operated by the federal government, federal prosecutors will incorporate the relevant state law through the ACA and use the state criminal code unless a federal law is controlling. An example is the George Washington Memorial Parkway on federal property in Virginia, where the state's motor vehicle laws are assimilated into federal law since there is no universal federal motor vehicle law.

The U.S. federal government recognizes indigenous Native American tribal nations as "domestic dependent nations." Thus, Indian reservations are treated more like foreign countries than states (*Worcester v. Georgia*, 1832). The inherent sovereign authority of indigenous tribes to rule themselves is to be respected. The U.S. Constitution mentions Indian tribes three times in Article I regarding representation and taxation. Three principles dominate Indian law:

1. Territorial sovereignty is primal and not granted by the states.
2. Plenary power is invested in Congress, not the executive branch, to address matters affecting Indian tribes.
3. A trust relationship is maintained through the federal government's duty to protect Indian tribes.

In *McGirt v. Oklahoma* (2020), the U.S. Supreme Court, in a 5–4 decision, held that much of Eastern Oklahoma is still a Muscogee (Creek) Indian Reservation and that Jimcy McGirt, a Seminole man, cannot be convicted by Oklahoman courts for the alleged sex crimes that occurred within the historical Indian boundaries. McGirt had filed a *habeas corpus* petition in federal court, claiming that only the federal government had the right to convict and hold him because Congress had created the reservation and had not taken away the sovereignty of the Creek Nation over the area. The Major Crimes Act grants jurisdiction to federal courts, exclusive of the states, over Native Americans who commit certain offenses, regardless of whether the victim is an Indian or non-Indian. *Oklahoma v. Castro-Huerta* (2022) clarified that both states and the federal government may prosecute non-Native Americans who commit crimes on tribal lands because, in such cases, jurisdiction is held jointly by both the federal and state governments.

Comity

Comity is the notion that governments will respect each other. It implies an obligation of reciprocity. The Comity Clause of the U.S. Constitution, also known as the *Privileges and Immunities Clause* (Article IV, Section 2, Clause 2), ensures that "The Citizens of each State shall be entitled to all Privileges and Immunities of Citizens in the several States." For example, the Sixth Amendment proscription against double jeopardy does not prohibit prosecution in both federal and state courts (*Gamble v. U.S.*, 2019) – thus, states and the federal government respect each other's sovereignty. Where the use of marijuana is permitted by state law, the federal government may still prosecute for illegal use under federal law, but the federal government has chosen not to enforce minor marijuana use. Comity also applies in many international situations.

Branches of the Federal Government

The U.S. Constitution establishes three branches of the federal government:

1. Article I. the legislative branch – to make the laws – headed by Congress
2. Article II. the executive branch – to carry out the laws – headed by the President of the United States (POTUS)
3. Article III. the judiciary branch – to interpret the laws – headed by the Supreme Court of the United States (SCOTUS)

Our national legislature, composed of the House of Representatives and the Senate, promulgates statutes. The executive branch comprises the Presidency, the Vice Presidency, and the various federal agencies implementing and executing the statutory will. The judiciary, composed of the Supreme Court and other federal courts, interprets the statutes.

A "checks and balances" system exists to limit excesses of any one branch. The President may veto a law passed by the legislature, but Congress may override the veto. The legislature may pass laws to bind the President. The judiciary interprets the statutory laws and may rule them unconstitutional or void. The legislature, Congress – the House of Representatives and the Senate, promulgates statutes. The executive branch comprises the Presidency, the Vice Presidency, and the various federal agencies implementing and executing the statutory will. The judiciary, composed of the Supreme Court and other federal courts, interprets the statutes.

Judicial Review of Legislation

Chief Justice John Marshall established the principle of judicial review in the early U.S. Supreme Court case *Marbury v. Madison* (1803). In *Marbury*, the Judiciary Act of 1789 was struck down because Congress had expanded the judiciary beyond what was allowed in Article 3 of the Constitution. This unanimous landmark decision is the single weightiest decision in American constitutional law. This case firmly established judicial review of executive and legislative actions; courts can interpret laws, say what the law is, and strike down legislation inconsistent with the Constitution.

Courts may strike down enacted legislation, rendering them void and unenforceable, for constitutional and non-constitutional reasons, including that they are against public policy, arbitrary or capricious, overly vague, overly broad, or *ex post facto* (laws enacted after the fact). The *principle of legality* holds that no liberty or right can be taken away or diminished without the legislature making its intention known through promulgating unmistakably clear and unambiguous language.

Laws are presumed to be constitutional. The usual standard of constitutional judicial review is the *rational basis test*, in which a law must be rationally related to a legitimate government interest. When a substantial liberty or property interest is involved, an *undue burden test* is applied; the government restriction must not be overly burdensome on individual citizens. An even higher standard of review, *strict scrutiny*, is used when a fundamental constitutional right, particularly those in the Bill of Rights, is infringed or involves a *suspect class*, e.g., classifications based upon race or national origin. The law will be struck down unless the government can show it is necessary to a *compelling state interest*, the law is *narrowly tailored* to achieving that compelling purpose, and the law is the *least restrictive means* to achieve that purpose (*U.S. v. Carolene Products* [footnote 4], 1938; *Skinner v. Oklahoma*, 1942; *Village of Arlington Heights v. Metropolitan Housing Development Corp.*, 1977).

Judicial interpretation of legislation will vary by approach, perspective, and emphasis of the judges involved. Courts may look to the statutory language, history, tradition, precedents, purposes, and consequences of the enacted legislation. In general, conservative justices tend to look to the text's plain meaning (textualism) and its original intent (originalism). In contrast, liberal justices view the Constitution as a "living document" that permits a pragmatic and changing interpretation as society changes (Justice Breyer's "active liberty"). An example of the importance of judicial interpretation is demonstrated in *District of Columbia v. Heller* (2008), where the Court majority and dissent came to different conclusions on the meaning of the Second Amendment to civilians – whether it applied strictly to state militias only or to individual citizens for self-defense purposes.

Recently, the U.S. Supreme Court has challenged the rulemaking authority of federal agencies. In *West Virginia v. E.P.A.* (2022), the Court most clearly established the *Major Questions Doctrine* that an agency regulation is unconstitutional if it presents a major economic or political question where Congress has not provided a clear statement authorizing the agency's action. In Loper Bright *Enterprises v. Raimondo* (2024), the Court declared that courts must review an agency rule using two questions: (1) what authority, if any, did Congress delegate to the agency? If the statute expressly delegated to an agency authority to interpret and enact regulations, the court will decide whether the agency action reasonably falls within that delegation. If not, (2) what constitutes the best interpretation of the statute? A court may rely on agency interpretations but is not bound to do so. This ruling overturns the Court's prior ruling in *Chevron U.S.A, Inc. v. Natural Resources Defense Council* (1984), which directed judges, when interpreting ambiguous federal statutes, to defer to federal agency officials, who were familiar with the technicalities of the regulations and the technical and scientific matters regulated. The new ruling reflects a skepticism of governmental power and a bloated "administrative state." In her dissent, Justice Kagan claimed it to be a "breathtaking change" that is a "judicial power grab" and warned that the courts would become clogged with filings for courts to make interpretations. Although *Loper Bright* struck down the Chevron doctrine, giving deference to administrative agencies' interpretation of ambiguous statutes, the Auer rule giving deference to administrative agencies for interpretation of their own regulations may still be intact (see *Kisor v. Wilkie*, 2019). Just one day before *Loper Bright*, the Court struck down the use of internal tribunals by the Securities and Exchange Commission (SEC) to resolve securities fraud cases, holding that the Seventh Amendment right to a jury trial applied and the "public rights" exception to Article III courts did not apply (*S.E.C. v. Jarkesy*, 2024).

BOX 1.4 *SKILLING V. UNITED STATES* (2010) – "HONEST SERVICES" VAGUE

The Enron scandal, which broke out in 2001, involved unethical corporate behavior and improper accounting practices. After an SEC investigation, Enron executives Jeffrey Skilling, Conrad Black, and Bruce Weyhrauch were prosecuted for crimes, including the federal mail and wire fraud statute's honest services fraud provision, which makes a scheme or artifice to deprive someone of "the intangible right of honest services" a criminal fraud. Prosecutors apply the provision in cases of public corruption and cases in which private individuals breached a fiduciary duty to another. Skilling was convicted of 19 counts, including the honest services fraud conspiracy charge. The U.S. Supreme Court unanimously overturned the honest services conviction and found the statute overly broad and vague because the term "honest services" did not have a known or specific meaning. The Court noted that "to satisfy due process, a penal statute must define the criminal offense [1] with sufficient definiteness that ordinary people can understand what conduct is prohibited and [2] in a manner that does not encourage arbitrary and discriminatory enforcement." The Court found the law to be impermissibly vague. The Court did not invalidate the statute entirely but interpreted it to criminalize only schemes to defraud that involve bribes or kickbacks. Ultimately, Skilling's sentence was reduced by ten years as a result. In a concurring opinion, Justice Scalia found the law was so vague that the defendants did not know they were acting illegally – it "simply failed to convey the requisite consciousness of wrongdoing" – and would have struck down the entire statute.

BOX 1.5 *UNITED STATES V. DAVIS* (2019) – "CRIME OF VIOLENCE" VAGUE

The defendants were convicted of robbery and conspiracy. During the robbery, they had brandished shotguns with short barrels. The Hobbs Act applies enhanced punishment to the use of a firearm for any federal "crime of violence," which is then defined in a residual clause as a felony "that by its nature, involves a substantial risk that physical force against the person or property of another may be used in the course of committing the offense." The court held the language in the residual clause unconstitutionally vague and stated, "In our constitutional order, a vague law is no law at all."

Sources of Law

U.S. law is embodied in several sources. These sources have a hierarchical rank order: constitutions, treaties, statutes, regulations, and case law. Each source has a formal authority that empowers it to make law. Articles in law reviews may be influential, but they do not have the force of law.

Sources of Law (In Hierarchical Rank Order)

- Constitutions
- International Treaties
- State Compacts
- Statutes
- Regulations
- Ordinances
- Case law

Constitutions: constitutions are founding documents that establish a government's basic organization and framework, the basic procedures for its operation, and the ability to change it. The U.S. Constitution is the federal government's founding document and supreme law. Each state also has its own Constitution. As foundational documents, constitutions do not contain specific details but rather use broad language. Amendments to constitutions can be made, but they are difficult to pass. There have been only 27 amendments made to the U.S. Constitution, of which the first ten, the Bill of Rights, were proposed as the Constitution was being ratified.

Treaties and Compacts: to become law, international treaties must be signed by the President and ratified by the Senate by a two-thirds (2/3) supermajority. Compacts are agreements between States, analogous to international treaties between nations, e.g., compacts between states of a region for mutual disaster aid.

Statutes: statutory law (legislation) is enacted by legislative bodies composed of representatives of the citizenry – "policymakers" (often attorneys). Congress or state legislatures pass acts that create new laws, amend old laws, or both. Federal legislation can be tracked on Congress.gov. Statutes cannot go beyond the bounds of what their state and federal constitutions allow. Statutes are more detailed and specific than constitutional provisions and more easily amended than constitutions (hence the colloquial phrase "It takes an act of Congress"). Codes are systematic compilations of laws covering a specific area or an entire legal system. Annotated codes include information beyond the statutory text. When they cover a specific area, they may attempt to organize it rationally. Criminal law is now set in criminal (penal) codes. Uniform laws are identical or nearly identical statutes enacted in all states. Commercial law has been made uniform by promulgating the Uniform Commercial Code (UCC). In contrast to uniform laws, model laws are guides that are adopted by the various states with modifications for their local needs. Federal statutes are compiled in the United States Code (U.S.C.) that in 2024 is >60,000 pages [https://www.govinfo.gov/app/collection/uscode].

Ordinances: ordinances are rules or decrees enacted by a county, municipal, or other local authority. They are the equivalent of statutes but promulgated at a level below the state.

Regulations: regulations are rules issued by an executive authority or regulatory agency having the force of law. The executive branch promulgates the regulations and implements the statutory guidance of the legislatures. The official or agency must have "rulemaking" authority to issue regulations. Regulations are more specific and detailed than statutes and can be amended more easily than statutes. The federal government makes announcements and publishes proposed regulations in the Federal Register [https://www.federalregister.gov/], and when promulgated, they become part of the Code of Federal Regulations (CFR) that in 2024 is >180,000 pages [https://www.govinfo.gov/app/collection/CFR].

Case law: case law is the body of law established by judicial decisions of appellate courts, which have interpreted the statutes and precedents in the cases brought before them. As legislatures promulgate new statutes and agencies promulgate regulations, courts will review and interpret these as cases involving them are brought before them. Case law builds from the precedential value of cases decided previously and made into legal doctrine.

International Law

International law developed from European mercantile and maritime trade in the 1600s. International law has traditionally been based upon custom, but international treaties are increasingly dominating international law in the same way that statutory law has come to dominate over Common Law. As noted above, international treaties, signed by the executive and ratified by the legislative branch, hold a near constitutional authority as a supreme law of the land. Countries may also join international organizations (IOs), e.g., North American Treaty Organization, as members; some nations must accede some of their own authority to the organization's rules. In general, smaller countries liberally give up their rights to IOs, whereas the larger and more powerful countries are reluctant to do so. The United Nations induced larger countries to join by establishing a National Security Council comprised primarily of large countries with veto power. The United States has not joined the International Criminal Court precisely not to relinquish sovereignty to that body.

Conflict of Law

The laws of different countries and different states may not agree. Similarly, the profusion of statutes, even within the same jurisdiction, inevitably contains contradictory provisions. *Conflict of law* is the technical legal term for these real and apparent clashes. Courts may distinguish apparent conflicts by finding that they involve different actors or operate with different purposes and contexts. At other times, courts must rule which law is superior and preempts the other.

Branches of Law

The law covers a broad and diverse array of activities across society. Branches of law are specialized areas of law devoted to a given area. Examples of branches of law include family law, labor law, torts, administrative law, constitutional law, international law, appellate law, regulatory law, etc. The American Bar Association (ABA) lists 19 specialty areas of legal practice.

ABA Practice Specialties

Administrative law	Commerce, environment	Real estate
Alternative dispute resolution	Family, health	Solo practice
Antitrust	Intellectual property	Taxation
Business and corporate	International law	Tort
Corporate compliance	Labor and employment	Trial practice
Criminal	Mergers and acquisitions	Trusts and estates
Cybersecurity		

Criminal law: criminal law is the body of law that relates to crime. Crimes are offenses against society, and the people are represented by government prosecutors in criminal courts. Government prosecutors prosecute defendants for breaking the laws and seek punishment by fines, probation, incarceration, or death.

Civil Law: civil law is the body of law (non-criminal law) that refers to "civil wrongs." As plaintiffs, private citizens, businesses, and other entities sue for damages or other remedies. Sub-branches of civil law include torts (personal injury suits), contracts (breaches of agreements), family law (divorce, child custody), labor law, etc. Wrongful death actions by families are the civil equivalent of homicide cases in criminal courts.

Administrative Law: administrative law is the body of law that deals with government agencies of the executive branch of the federal and state governments and the regulations they promulgate. These typically involve administrative hearings rather than trials and do not necessarily involve lawyers.

Alternative Dispute Resolution (ADR): ADR involves processes and techniques to avoid going to court. The primary methods are:

- Negotiation – a discussion between the parties to reach a resolution
- Mediation – an informal negotiation to reach a resolution involving a third party
- Arbitration – a formal mediation process involving a third party to reach a resolution

If the parties fail to negotiate a settlement or otherwise reach an acceptable resolution, they may seek a final resolution in court if the ADR is not final.

BOX 1.6 *ENTICK V. CARRINGTON* (1765) – LEGAL AUTHORITY FOR STATE ACTION

Lord Halifax, the new Secretary of State for the Northern District of England, ordered Nathan Carrington and three other King's messengers "to make strict and diligent search for… the author, or one concerned in the writing of several weekly very seditious papers entitled, *The Monitor*, or *British Freeholder*." They broke into the home of the Grub Street writer, John Entick, with force and arms. They ransacked the house and broke open locks and doors before carrying away 100 charts and 100 pamphlets and causing £2,000 in damage. Entick sued the messengers for trespassing on his land. At trial, Carrington and his accomplices claimed that they acted on Halifax's warrant, which gave them legal authority for the search, and thus were not liable for the tort. Lord Camden, Chief Justice of the Common Pleas, held that Halifax had no right under any statute or case law to issue such a warrant and, therefore, found in Entick's favor, writing:

> The great end, for which men entered into society, was to secure their property. That right is preserved sacred and incommunicable in all instances, where it has not been taken away or abridged by some public law for the good of the whole. The cases where this right of property is set aside by private law, are various. Distresses, executions, forfeitures, taxes etc. are all of this description; wherein every man by common consent gives up that right, for the sake of justice and the general good. By the laws of England, every invasion of private property, be it ever so minute, is a trespass. No man can set his foot upon my ground without my licence, but he is liable to an action, though the damage be nothing, which is proved by every declaration in trespass, where the defendant is called upon to answer for bruising the grass and even treading upon the soil. If he admits the fact, he is bound to show by way of justification, that some positive law has empowered or excused him. The justification is submitted to the judges, who are to look into the books; and if such a justification can be maintained by the text of the statute law, or by the principles of common law. If no excuse can be found or produced, the silence of the books is an authority against the defendant, and the plaintiff must have judgment.

The case is a landmark case in English law, establishing civil liberties and limiting executive power. The most famous line is: "If it is law, it will be found in our books. If it not be found there, it is not law." The case has come to stand for the general principle that the state cannot do anything which is not expressly authorized by law, while the individual may do anything except that which is forbidden by law. The case is considered an important motivation for the Fourth Amendment of the U.S. Constitution.

BOX 1.7 *DESHANEY V. WINNEBAGO COUNTY DEPARTMENT OF SOCIAL SERVICES* (1989) – STATE ACTION, POSITIVE RIGHTS

A Wyoming divorce decree gave custody of infant Joshua DeShaney to his father, Randy DeShaney, who moved to Winnebago County, Wisconsin. A report of child abuse prompted the Wisconsin Department of Social Services (DSS) to request that the hospital keep Joshua in custody, but three days later, the child protection team recommended he be returned to his father. Over the next year, the DSS visited five times and recorded suspicion of child abuse, but the DSS took no action. A hospital reported a suspicion of child abuse to the DSS, but they still took no action. In the two subsequent visits, the social worker was told that Joshua was too ill to be seen, and again, the DSS took no action. Then, the father beat four-year-old Joshua so severely that he became comatose. The surgery revealed chronic traumatic brain damage. He remained alive in a persistent vegetative state. Joshua's mother filed a lawsuit against Winnebago County DSS on Joshua's behalf, claiming that they failed to intervene and protect him from his father and thus deprived him of his due process rights. In a 6–3 ruling, the U.S. Supreme Court found that the DSS did not violate his constitutional rights. The Court held that due process protects individuals against state action. The child abuse was the private action of Randy DeShaney. Furthermore, the Constitution only protects against negative civil liabilities – actions that the state must not do, but not positive liabilities – actions that the state must do. Joshua was not in the custody of the DSS, and the DSS was not required to protect him from harm in his own home. The Constitution cannot be interpreted to mean that the government is responsible for all ills in society.

Notes: Joshua eventually died at the age of 36 years. His father, Randy DeShaney, was tried and convicted of child abuse and served less than two years in jail.

Summary

The law provides enforceable rules for society. Natural laws are fundamental human values of fairness, whereas societies set forth positive laws. The United States is under the rule of law.

The United States adopted the Common Law jurisprudence from England. It differs from the Roman-based Civil Law of continental Europe through the notion of *stare decisis*, in which cases can become binding precedents for other cases and lead to the development of the case law.

American jurisprudence is a dual sovereignty system consisting of state and federal law. The federal government has certain enumerated powers. The states have concurrent and residual powers, including the *police powers* to regulate and enforce their inhabitants' health, safety, morals, and general welfare. Federal law preempts state law. Comity is a notion of respecting the laws of other sovereignties. Both federal and state governments have legislative, judicial, and executive branches of government to make, interpret, and enforce laws.

The U.S. Constitution and international treaties are the supreme law of the land. Legal frameworks are defined in federal and state constitutions. Legislative bodies promulgate statutory law. Administrative agencies of the executive branch promulgate rules with the force of law that refine and implement the statutory law. Case law is another source of law.

There are many branches of law, such as civil and criminal law.

Terms

Binding precedent – prior published opinions of appellate judges controlling the present case.

Branches of law – areas of legal specialization.

Case Law – legal doctrine developed through judicial decisions rather than law based on constitutions, statutes, or regulations.

Civil Law – the system of jurisprudence derived from Roman law and based on legal codes; it is also used as a term for non-criminal branches of law.

Code of Federal Regulations – the compilation of federal regulations.

Common Law – legal doctrine developed in early English case law.*Federal Preemption* – the supremacy of federal statutes over state laws.

Federal Register – a daily publication of Presidential documents, proposed federal regulations, and other information of the federal government to be made public.

Judicial Review – the power of the courts to interpret, enforce, and strike down legislation.

Law – the set of rules promulgated by competent authorities and enforceable by the government.

Police Power – the constitutional power reserved to the states to regulate and enforce their inhabitants' health, safety, morals, and general welfare.

Sources of Law – the various methods by which law is promulgated.

Stare Decisis – the doctrine of legal precedent.

United States Code – the compilation of federal statutes.

Cases

Chevron v. Natural Resources Defense Council, 467 U.S. 837 (1984)

DeShaney v. Winnebago County Department of Social Services, 489 U.S. 189 (1989)

District of Columbia v. Heller, 554 U.S. 570 (2008)

Dobbs v. Jackson Women's Health Organization, 597 U.S. 215 (2022)

Entick v. Carrington, 95 Eng. Rep. 807 (C.P. 1765)
Gamble v. United States, 587 U.S. 678 (2019)
Kisor v. Wilkie, 588 U.S. 558 (2019)
Loper Bright Enterprises v. Raimondo, 603 U.S. ___ (2024)
Marbury v. Madison, 5 U.S. (1 Cranch) 137 (1803)
McBoyle v. United States, 283 U.S. 25 (1931)
McGirt v. Oklahoma, 591 U.S. ___ (2020)
Murphy v. National Collegiate Athletic Association, 584 U.S. 453 (2018)
Oklahoma v. Castro-Huerta, 597 U.S. 629 (2022)
Palko v. Connecticut, 302 U.S. 319 (1937)
Planned Parenthood of Southeastern Pennsylvania v. Casey, 505 U.S. 833 (1992)
President Riverboat Casino, Inc. v. Missouri Gaming Commission, 13 S.W.3d 635 (MO. 2000)
Securities and Exchange Commission v. Jarkesy, 603 U.S. ___ (2024)
Skilling v. United States, 561 U.S. 358 (2010)
Skinner v. Oklahoma, 316 U.S. 535 (1942)
Trump v. United States, 603 U.S. ___ (2024)
United States v. Carolene Products, 304 U.S. 144 (1938)
United States v. Davis, 588 U.S. 445 (2019)
Village of Arlington Heights v. Metropolitan Housing Development Corp., 429 U.S. 252 (1977)
West Virginia v. Environmental Protection Agency, 597 U.S. 697 (2022)
Wickard v. Filburn, 317 U.S. 111 (1942)
Worcester v. Georgia, 31 U.S. 515 (1832)

Statutes

Assimilative Crimes Act (ACA), 18 U.S.C. §13 (1825)
Code of Federal Regulations (C.F.R.), https://www.govinfo.gov/app/collection/CFR
Hobbs Act, 18 U.S.C. §924(c) (1951)
Honest Services Fraud, 18 U.S.C. §1346 (1988) [voided]
Major Crimes Act, 18 U.S.C. §1153 (1885)
United States Code (U.S.C.), https://www.govinfo.gov/app/collection/uscode

Thought Questions

1. To what extent does the law embody ethics and morality?
2. To what extent does the positive law embody natural law?
3. Does U.S. law reflect the will of the people?
4. The famous German writer Goethe was said to favor injustice over lawlessness. Why might this be?

5. What should we make of conflicts in law, and how best are they resolved?
6. Why is judicial review sometimes thought of as anti-democratic?

Further Reading

Fletcher GP, Sheppard S, *American Law in a Global Context: The Basics*, Oxford Univ Press, Oxford, 2005.

Forsyth A, *Common Law and Natural Law in America: From the Puritans to the Legal Realists,* Cambridge University Press, Cambridge, 2019.

Holmes OW, Childress SA, *The Annotated Common Law: With 2010 Foreword and Explanatory Notes,* Quid Pro Books, New Orleans, LA, 2010.

Holmes OW, The Path of the Law, *Harvard Law Review* 10:457, 1897.

Maine HS, *Ancient Law*, Routledge, New York, 2002.

Roberson C, Das DK, *An Introduction to Comparative Legal Models of Criminal Justice,* 2d ed, CRC Press, Boca Raton, 2016.

The Declaration of Independence (U.S. 1776).

The Universal Declaration of Human Rights (UN 1948).

United States Constitution (U.S. 1787)

Chapter 2
Due Process

Learning Objectives

After reading this chapter, students are expected to be able to:

- explain the origins of the Due Process Clauses.
- recognize the applicability of the Fifth and Fourteenth Amendment Due Process Clauses.
- discuss the Civil War Amendments.
- recount the Scottsboro Boys case.
- describe the defendants' rights revolution.
- explain the difference between substantive and procedural due process.

Introduction

Due Process of Law is a fundamental notion of constitutional law. Due Process Clauses are written into both the Fourth and Fourteenth Amendments of the U.S. Constitution. Due process encompasses the principle of *fundamental fairness* and the notion of the *rule of law*. It embodies both procedural safeguards and liberty interests that statutes and regulations must not infringe. At its core, due process was included in the Bill of Rights as a reaction to English governmental abuse and is a constitutional guarantee that the government must follow.

DOI: 10.4324/9780429272455-2

Due process began in Clause 39 of the Magna Carta of 1215. It gives a freeman the right to a jury of his peers:

> No freeman shall be taken, or imprisoned, disseised, outlawed, banished, or exiled, or in any way destroyed, nor will We proceed against or prosecute him, except by the lawful judgement of his peers and by the law of the land.

In subsequent English law, the phrases "the lawful judgment of his peers" and "law of the land" were treated as substantially synonymous. However, the phrase "by the law of the land" was changed to "by due process of law" in a 1354 statute of King Edward III that restated Magna Carta's guarantee of the subject's liberty. The notion of due process has received even greater attention from American courts.

The U.S. Constitution does not define the phrase *due process.* Taken literally, it refers to the legal rights and procedures that you are owed or entitled to, but this is a tautology – you have a right to the procedures you are entitled to! Thus, it provides fertile ground for continuous reinterpretation by the courts. When John Bingham drafted the first section of the Fourteenth Amendment, he specifically intended not to write a legal code but to use broad language that would last for ages.

Historical Background

The roots of our Anglo-American jurisprudence began in the east and progressed westward from Babylonia to Athens, to Rome, to France, to England, before its growth here in America. The earliest legal codes were simplistic, but laws have become ever more complex. Despite societal upheavals, continuity and progression in the law were maintained by insulated legal faculty members of autonomous university-based law schools since the 12th century and the canon law scholars of the Papacy since the 4th century. Laws have been transformed from their draconian origins to more liberal laws that increasingly recognize individuals' rights. The major reforms to legal systems have been mainly reactions provoked by overly harsh and heavy-handed governments. These legal reforms establish protections of individual rights manifest in the *due process of law* owed to citizens. Thus, modern legal systems attempt to strike a reasonable balance between government efficiency and collective societal rights on one side and liberty, freedom, and individual rights on the other.

BOX 2.1 MILEPOSTS IN LEGAL HISTORY

1754 BCE	Babylonian Code of Hammurabi
621 BCE	Athenian Code of Draco

594 BCE	Athenian Code of Solon
450 BCE	Roman Twelve Tables
400	Apostolic Constitutions
534	Roman Justinian Code
1215	Magna Carta
1788	U.S. Constitution ratified
1804	French Napoleonic Code

The American Constitution

The American Revolution was itself a response to perceived oppressive governmental intrusion. The Founding Fathers rejected autocratic monarchy and had an overriding suspicion of strong central governments. In the Declaration of Independence, Thomas Jefferson referred to "... certain unalienable rights, among these, life, liberty, and the pursuit of happiness." Then, James Madison wrote in the Bill of Rights, "No person shall be ...deprived of life, liberty, or property, without due process of law."

When the American Revolution formally ended with the Treaty of Paris in 1783, the colonies became nation-states, but no United States of America yet existed. Each state had independent operational governments in place for many years that continued without English oversight. The first attempt at forming a union was the 1777 Articles of Confederation, but its failure to form a sufficiently authoritative central government was immediately apparent. A Constitutional Convention was convened in Philadelphia from May to September 1787 to write a constitution that addressed the weaknesses of the Articles of Confederation. The final draft, written primarily by James Madison, was sent to the States but was not immediately ratified because of opposition over the lack of enumerated rights and sufficient protections for the citizens from the new central government. Delaware was the first to ratify the new Constitution on December 1, 1787, and the requisite ninth state ratified it on June 22, 1788, understanding that it would be immediately amended; by 1790, all states had ratified it. Congress began on March 9, 1789. Madison submitted a list of 20 amendments on June 8, 1789; the House passed 17 amendments, but only 12 were passed by the Senate. By December 15, 1791, three-fourths of the states had ratified ten, now known as the "Bill of Rights."

BOX 2.2 BILL OF RIGHTS

Amendment I	Freedom of religion
	Free exercise of religion
	Freedom of speech
	Freedom of the press
	Freedom of assembly
	Right to petition for redress of grievances
Amendment II	Right to keep and bear arms
Amendment III	Freedom from quartering soldiers
Amendment IV	No unreasonable search and seizure
	Warrant requirement
Amendment V	Due process of law
	Right to grand jury
	No double jeopardy
	Privilege against self-incrimination
	No taking of private property without just compensation
Amendment VI	Right to speedy trial in criminal cases
	Right to a jury trial where the crime occurred
	Notice of accusations
	Right to confront witnesses
	Right to subpoena
	Right to the assistance of counsel
Amendment VII	Jury trial in civil case
	No re-examination of cases
Amendment VIII	No excessive bail
	No excessive fines
	No cruel and unusual punishments
Amendment IX	Non-exclusion of other rights
Amendment X	Powers not delegated to the federal government and not prohibited are reserved to the States

The concern of the Founding Fathers was abuse by an overly powerful federal government. When the Bill of Rights became law, they were intended as limitations only on the federal government, not the states, as was confirmed in *Barron v. Baltimore* (1833). Most of the protections involved civil rights, but the rights of the criminally accused are found in the Fourth, Fifth, Sixth, and Eighth Amendments – originally, these only referred to federal criminal prosecutions.

Civil War Reconstruction Amendments

As time went by, citizens needed protection against abuses from state governments more than from the federal government, particularly from racial discrimination by the states of the Deep South. The division in society over slavery that had been brewing since before the Constitution spilled out into a bloody Civil War (1861–1865). During and after the war, the "Radical Republicans" then in Congress began reconstruction efforts in preparation for the emancipation of the 4 million African-American inhabitants. Specifically, constitutional amendments were needed to force the abolition of slavery on the slave-holding states and limit their ability to harm their citizens. The Thirteenth, Fourteenth, and Fifteenth Amendments are collectively known as the *Civil War* or *Reconstruction Amendments*. The Thirteenth Amendment, ratified in 1864, abolished slavery and declared that "Congress shall have the power to enforce this article by appropriate legislation." The Fourteenth Amendment, ratified in 1868, imparts citizenship rights to formerly enslaved people and mandates equal protection and due process of law for all citizens. The Fifteenth Amendment, ratified in 1870, ensured voting rights for all male citizens, including formerly enslaved people. The Fifteenth Amendment does not refer to gender, as women were not yet allowed to vote following English Common Law and social customs.

BOX 2.3 CIVIL WAR (RECONSTRUCTION) AMENDMENTS

Amendment XIII	Abolished slavery
	Enforcement power is given to Congress
Amendment XIV	Made citizens of nation and of the state
	States cannot abridge privileges and immunities
	States owe equal protection of the law
	Representatives apportioned by whole numbers
	Representatives not been engaged in rebellion
	Debts to be paid, except if in support of rebellion
	Enforcement power is given to Congress
Amendment XV	Right of freemen to vote
	Enforcement power is given to Congress

A few years after the passage of the Civil War Amendments, the U.S. Supreme Court considered the *Slaughter-House Cases* (1872). Those consolidated cases involved the Privileges or Immunities Clause of the Fourteenth

Amendment, which states, "No State shall make or enforce any law which shall abridge the privileges or immunities of citizens of the United States…." The drafters intended it to protect newly freed Black slaves from states' oppressions by granting them the various fundamental rights of national citizenship. This could and perhaps should have been interpreted to apply the Bill of Rights to the states, but the Court was not ready to make such a sweeping change. Instead, the Court interpreted this clause narrowly, holding that the clause only pertains to rights of federal citizenship (e.g., protection on high seas), not state citizenship. However, the holding did not speak to the Due Process Clause of the Fourteenth Amendment, which continued as a potential future option for the Court to ensure state citizens' rights and protections.

Two Due Process Clauses

Congress incorporated Due Process Clauses in the Fifth Amendment of the 1789 Bill of Rights and the 1868 Reconstruction Fourteenth Amendment. The Due Process Clause in the Fifth Amendment applies to the federal government:

> No person shall be… deprived of life, liberty, or property, without due process of law…

The Due Process Clause in the Fourteenth Amendment applies to the states:

> … nor shall any State deprive any person of life, liberty, or property, without due process of law;…

Thus, the Fourteenth Amendment entrusted the Supreme Court with the responsibility of constitutional oversight of the states' judicial processes.

The Selective Incorporation Doctrine

The interpretation of *due process* evolved over time. For over a century, "due process" was taken to mean whatever the applicable state's legal process was. Then, after cases of egregious examples of failures of state legal processes, the Supreme Court began applying "fundamental fairness" as the lynchpin of due process scrutiny – defined as whether it conformed to the historical principles of the Magna Carta or Declaration of Independence or otherwise "shocked the conscience" of the Court.

Eventually, the Court turned to the Bill of Rights for due process guidance. The Supreme Court began a process of *selective incorporation*, in which the provisions of the Bill of Rights were incorporated under the Due Process Clause of the Fourteenth Amendment. First Amendment rights

BOX 2.4 *BROWN V. MISSISSIPPI* (1936) – FUNDAMENTAL FAIRNESS

Stuart, a White planter, was murdered. Three Black tenant farmers were blamed for his death and convicted based on their confessions.

> ...defendants were made to strip and they were laid over chairs and their backs were cut to pieces with a leather strap with buckles on it, and they were likewise made by the said deputy definitely to understand that the whipping would be continued unless and until they confessed, and not only confessed, but confessed in every matter of detail as demanded... the transcript reads more like pages torn from some medieval account than a record made within the confines of a modern civilization...

The Court ruled that constitutional due process limits a State when it "offends some principle of justice so rooted in the traditions and conscience of our people as to be ranked as fundamental."

were the first of the Bill of Rights to be incorporated, beginning with *Gitlow v. New York* in 1925, which established free speech as a substantive due process right of individuals that the States could not abridge. After several provisions had been haphazardly incorporated, Justice Benjamin Cardozo formally articulated the process of selective incorporation in *Palko v. Connecticut* (1937). The Court held that the Due Process Clause protected only those rights that were "of the very essence of a scheme of ordered liberty and that the Court should, therefore, incorporate the Bill of Rights onto the States gradually, as justiciable violations arose, based on whether the infringed right met that test." Thus, through selective incorporation under the Fourteenth Amendment the Bill of Rights became "federalized."

The Court turned to the criminal provisions of the Bill of Rights beginning in the 1932 case of *Powell v. Alabama*, which involved the infamous case of racial injustice known as the Scottsboro Boys case. In this case, the Sixth Amendment right to counsel for criminal defendants was incorporated into the Fourteenth Amendment Due Process Clause as a matter of fundamental fairness, and thus, the right was imposed on the states. Later, in *Gideon v. Wainwright* (1962), the right to counsel included free counsel to indigents. In *Strickland v. Washington* (1984), the right to counsel was extended to mean the right to effective assistance of counsel. In *Wolf v. Colorado* (1949), the U.S. Supreme Court applied the Fourth Amendment to the states.

BOX 2.5 *POWELL V. ALABAMA* (1932) – SCOTTSBORO BOYS CASE

In 1931, two dozen Blacks and Whites were "hoboing" on a freight train between Chattanooga and Memphis, Tennessee. A group of seven White teenagers attempted to push a Black teenager off the train, declaring it was "a White man's train." A fight ensued, and all but one of the seven Whites were forced off the train near Scottsboro, Alabama. The evicted Whites reported to the local sheriff that a group of Black teenagers had attacked them. The sheriff formed a posse that stopped the train and arrested nine illiterate Black teenagers, who were constantly referred to as "the boys" (Scottsboro Boys).

Two young White women from the train accused the Black teenagers of rape while onboard the train. Alabama law held that the rape of White women by Blacks was a capital offense punishable by death. News of the rapes created a tense and hostile public atmosphere, and a large hostile mob formed, requiring a military guard for the defendants.

The youths were from outside Alabama, without family or friends in the area, and had no significant opportunity to communicate with their families or to obtain counsel. Indictments were returned six days later; the defendants were arraigned and pled not guilty that same day. A lawyer from Tennessee arrived the morning of the trials. He had not been employed to represent any of the defendants and was unfamiliar with the case or Alabama laws – he had merely hoped to assist appointed counsel. When the court called the first case and inquired whether the parties were ready for trial, the prosecutor replied that he was ready to proceed, but no one answered for the defendants. Each of the trials was completed within a single day. The all-White juries found the defendants guilty and imposed the death penalty upon them all, except the 13-year-old, which ended in a hung jury and mistrial after one juror favored life imprisonment to death. The trial court overruled motions for new trials, and the state Supreme Court affirmed seven of the eight convictions but granted the 13-year-old a new trial.

In *Powell v. Alabama*, the U.S. Supreme Court declared that their constitutional right to counsel violated the Fourteenth Amendment Due Process Clause and remanded the cases for new trials. During the retrials, one woman admitted to fabricating the story and that neither woman was ever touched. Charges were eventually dropped against four, but the other five were again found guilty and received sentences from 75 years to death; nonetheless, by 1946, all had been released or escaped from prison or never served time.

BOX 2.6 *MAPP V. OHIO* (1961) – EXCLUSIONARY RULE

Dollree Mapp was a worker in the illegal gambling racket of Cleveland kingpin Shondor Birns. A rival of Birns informed the police that Mapp was hiding gambling paraphernalia as well as her boyfriend, Virgil Ogletree, who was wanted for questioning in connection with a recent bombing. Three police arrived at the two-family residence where she and her daughter lived on the top floor. The officers knocked on the door and demanded entrance, but Mapp refused to admit them without a search warrant.

Later, when additional officers arrived, they forced their way in. Miss Mapp demanded to see the warrant. A piece of paper, said to be a warrant, was held up by one of the officers, and she snatched it away and tucked it into her dress. A struggle ensued in which the officers recovered the piece of paper, and she was placed in handcuffs. After searching the entire building, the police found some betting slips in a footlocker in the basement, as well as a pistol and a small number of pornography that Mapp claimed were left behind by a previous tenant; they also found Ogletree in the apartment below Mapp's apartment.

Mapp was arrested and charged with possession of gambling paraphernalia but then cleared. However, after she refused to testify against Birns and others, she was then prosecuted and convicted of possession of pornographic material and sentenced to prison. During the trial, the search warrant was not produced, nor was its absence explained; there is considerable doubt that there was ever a warrant. The Supreme Court of Ohio found that her conviction was valid, though based primarily upon the introduction of evidence of lewd and lascivious books and pictures unlawfully seized during an unlawful search of the defendant's home.

Mapp appealed to the U.S. Supreme Court because the police had no probable cause to suspect her of having such materials, that the search was unreasonable under the Fourth Amendment, and that the evidence should be excluded. During an oral argument in the Supreme Court, a justice asked about the piece of paper. The Cleveland prosecutor dodged the question, and the Court did not press the issue. In a 6–3 vote, the Court doubted the existence of the search warrant and reversed the conviction.

The Court held the evidence was illegally obtained because the search and the seizures were unlawful. Moreover, the Court overturned the prior precedent in *Wolf v. Colorado* (1949), holding that the exclusionary rule does apply to impermissible state searches and seizures. The Court held that the exclusionary rule had applied to the federal government since 1914, and many states, by the time of *Mapp*, had adopted the rule. Justice Clark viewed the freedom from state invasions of privacy as implicit in the concept of ordered liberty and declared:

> ...in extending the substantive protections of due process to all constitutionally unreasonable searches – state or federal – it was logically and constitutionally necessary that the exclusion doctrine – an essential part of the right to privacy – be also insisted upon as an essential ingredient of the right newly recognized by the *Wolf* case. In short, the admission of the new constitutional right by *Wolf* could not consistently tolerate denial of its most important constitutional privilege, namely, the exclusion of the evidence which an accused had been forced to give by reason of the unlawful seizure. To hold otherwise is to grant the right, but in reality, to withhold its privilege and enjoyment... our holding that the exclusionary rule is an essential part of both the Fourth and Fourteenth Amendments... makes very good sense.

President Eisenhower appointed Earl Warren Chief Justice in 1953, and he led the court for the next 16 years. His liberal activist court is credited for what has come to be known as the *defendants' rights revolution* that transformed the legal landscape. This can be considered part of the *civil rights movement* of the 1960s (the Civil Rights Act was promulgated in 1964). The first case that Warren presided over was *Brown v. Board of Education* (1954), which overruled the segregation doctrine of *separate but equal*, citing the Equal Protection Clause of the Fourteenth Amendment. However, most of the significant cases of the Warren court involved the selective incorporation of the various Bill of Rights protections through the Fourteenth Amendment to criminal defendants in state courts. Many of these cases are discussed elsewhere in this book.

Today, all rights of the Bill of Rights have been incorporated through the Fourteenth Amendment to the States, except:

- Third Amendment – freedom from quartering of soldiers
- Fifth Amendment – requirement of a Grand Jury
- Sixth Amendment – right to a jury of residents from the district where the crime occurred
- Seventh Amendment – right to a jury trial in civil cases

BOX 2.7 SELECT LANDMARK WARREN COURT RULINGS

Case	Citation	Year	Ruling
Brown v. Board of Education	347 U.S. 483	1954	End racial segregation
Mapp v. Ohio	367 U.S. 643	1961	Fourth Amendment search and seizure exclusionary rule enforcement
Robinson v. California	370 U.S. 660	1962	Eighth Amendment ban of punishment for being a drug addict
Gideon v. Wainwright	372 U.S. 335	1963	Sixth Amendment right to counsel
Malloy v. Hogan	378 U.S. 1	1964	Fifth Amendment right against self-incrimination
Aguilar v. Texas	378 U.S. 108	1964	Fourth Amendment probable cause requirement for warrants based on confidential informants
Escobedo v. Illinois	378 U.S. 478	1964	Sixth Amendment right to counsel during police interrogation

Griffin v. California	380 U.S. 609	1965	Fifth Amendment right to remain silent
Pointer v. Texas	380 U.S. 609	1965	Sixth Amendment right to confront witnesses
Griswold v. Connecticut	381 U.S. 479	1965	Fourteenth Amendment right to marital privacy
Parker v. Gladden	385 U.S. 252	1966	Sixth Amendment right to an impartial jury
Miranda v. Arizona	384 U.S. 436	1966	Fifth Amendment right to remain silent while in custody
Schmerber v. California	384 U.S. 757	1966	Fourth and Fifth Amendment clarification with respect to human body intrusions
Katz v. United States	389 U.S. 347	1967	Fourteenth Amendment right to privacy
Klopfer v. North Carolina	386 U.S. 213	1967	Sixth Amendment right to a speedy trial
In re Gault	387 U.S. 1	1967	Fourteenth Amendment due process (Fifth and Sixth) applies to juvenile defendants
Washington v. Texas	388 U.S. 14	1967	Sixth Amendment right to compulsory process for obtaining witnesses
Duncan v. Louisiana	391 U.S. 145	1968	Sixth Amendment right to a jury trial
Terry v. Ohio	382 U.S. 1	1968	Fourth Amendment allowance of stop and frisk on reasonable suspicion may be armed and dangerous
Spinelli v. United States	393 U.S. 410	1969	Fourth Amendment probably causes requirement for warrants based on confidential informants
Chimel v. California	395 U.S. 752	1969	Fourth Amendment limitation on search incident to an arrest
Benton v. Maryland	395 U.S. 784	1969	Fifth Amendment right against double jeopardy

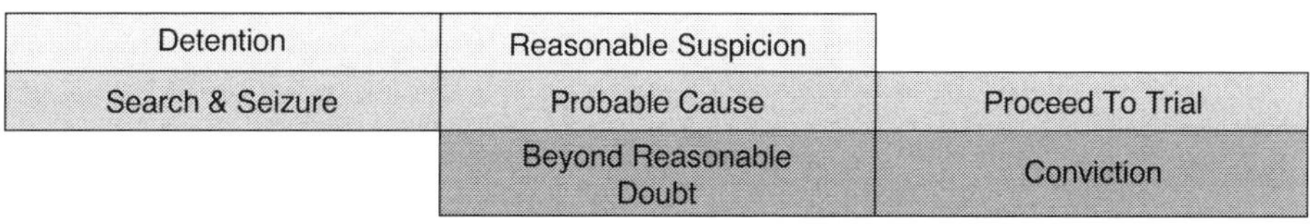

FIGURE 2.1 Levels of Fourth Amendment Due Process in Criminal Cases.

Procedural and Substantive Due Process

Due process should mean that laws are equally applied and legal processes are fundamentally fair. The U.S. Constitution, state constitutions, and other laws and regulations require due process. Due process applies to trials, administrative hearings, and governmental processes that constitute state action – it does not apply to private action. Different due process requirements may be applicable in various situations. Federal constitutional due process concerns arise when the federal government acts in such a way that denies a person of a life, liberty, or property interest.

PROCEDURAL DUE PROCESS involves questions of whether the process was followed and whether the process was fair. Impartiality of the jury and whether the defendant was given adequate notice are procedural issues. As a generality, in criminal cases and administrative hearings, due process requirements would include:

- Notice of the charges against you
- Knowledge of the rules by which you are judged
- Opportunity to be heard and present evidence
- Representation by counsel
- Ability to cross-examine adverse witnesses
- Fair process
- Adjudication by an impartial judge, jury, or tribunal
- Creation of a record of the hearing or trial
- Ability to appeal an unfair judgment

Due process is at the core of the presumption of innocence. Blackstone's Ratio, "It is better that ten guilty persons escape than that one innocent suffer" (Lord Blackstone, Commentaries on the Laws of England, 1769), and Franklin's Ratio, "It is better a hundred guilty persons should escape than that one innocent person should suffer," are arguments that trials should be fair. Also, the requirements of reasonable suspicion for investigation and detention and probable cause for searches, seizures, arrests, indictments, and convictions based on a beyond-a-reasonable doubt standard are all manifestations of due process in criminal trials.

SUBSTANTIVE DUE PROCESS is the notion that due process protects not only fair legal procedures but also fundamental civil rights. The Fifth and Fourteenth Amendments prohibit the federal and state governments from depriving citizens of "life, liberty, or property, without due process of law."

Civil substantive due process claims are brought under the Civil Rights Act, 42 U.S.C. §1983, for deprivations of rights, privileges, or immunities secured by the Constitution and laws. Criminal civil rights claims under 18 U.S.C. §242 add an element of willfulness. In *Zinermon v. Burch* (1990), a case involving the wrongful commitment of a patient in a mental institution, the Supreme Court held that §1983 supports three types of claims under the Due Process Clause of the Fourteenth Amendment:

1. violations of the right to procedural fairness [procedural due process],
2. violations of the rights found in the Bill of Rights that have been selectively incorporated under the Fourteenth Amendment, and
3. violations of the "substantive component [of due process] that bars certain arbitrary, wrongful government actions."

Critics of substantive due process claim that the term is an oxymoron and that courts should not "legislate from the bench" – that any unenumerated right should be established through the political process in legislation.

For a relatively short time, during the *Lochner* era of 1897–1937 [named for *Lochner v. New York* (1905) where the Court struck down a New York statute that prescribed maximum working hours for bakers], the court entertained a laissez-faire notion of freedom to contract and struck down various economic regulations as unconstitutional – the so-called "economic due process" rights.

The Court, referring to the Fourteenth Amendment substantive due process and equal protection, invalidated governmental actions that infringed upon certain fundamental rights:

- right of parents to educate their children – *Pierce v. Society of Sisters* (1925)
- right to contraception – *Griswold v. Connecticut* (1965)
- right to marry a person of a different race (miscegenation) – *Loving v. Virginia* (1967)
- right to same-sex marriage – *Obergefell v. Hodges* (2015)

In *Bowers v. Hardwick* (1986), the Court considered a law prohibiting sodomy and declared that the Constitution protects citizens only from government acts that violate "personal immunities" that are "fundamental," defined as "implicit in the concept of ordered liberty" (*Palko v. Connecticut*, 1937), or are "deeply rooted in the Nation's history and tradition" (*Griswold v. Connecticut*, 1965). In *Dobbs v. Jackson Women's Health Organization* (2022), the Court held that a right to an abortion is neither in a scheme of ordered liberty nor deeply rooted in the nation's history and thus not among unenumerated rights in the constitution. In that case,

Justice Thomas called on the Court to reconsider all its rulings based on substantive due process. See the discussion of civil rights violations in Chapter 4.

ACTUAL INNOCENCE – criminal jurisprudence has developed and evolved over centuries and has focused on trial fairness. Until recently, a defendant could not appeal his or her conviction based upon a showing of actual innocence (*plain error*) because appeals were based solely upon a denial of due process. In other words, "innocence" is a factual question for the factfinder to determine, but appeals are based on legal errors. Of course, claims of innocence are frequent and are met with skepticism.

Forensic science, which can now prove someone is innocent even after their conviction in court, is a relatively new development to which our jurisprudence is still responding. In particular, postconviction DNA testing became a more powerful and accepted technology for proving innocence. Furthermore, jurists became more aware of wrongful convictions.

Without a legal procedural error, defendants were left with Constitutional claims. In *Herrera v. Collins* (1993), the U.S. Supreme Court held that claims of *actual innocence* based upon newly discovered evidence are matters of fact and not a sufficient basis for an appeal – that some procedural defect must accompany *habeas* reviews (efforts to appeal a state ruling to federal court). In *District Attorney's Office for the Third Judicial District v. Osborne* (2009), the U.S. Supreme Court held that convicted persons do not have a constitutional due process right to DNA testing based on claims of actual innocence.

Furthermore, *statutes of limitations* limit the time defendants must bring postconviction relief, regardless of their innocence. Although this may be unfair to someone wrongfully imprisoned, it has been justified by the need for finality of judgment and the overall impact that holding otherwise would have on the judicial system.

Recently, all states and the federal government have enacted postconviction relief legislation allowing access to DNA testing and its introduction into court as new evidence. The laws vary greatly and may apply to more than DNA testing (see Reference Material: 50 State Postconviction Relief Survey). The *Innocence Protection Act of 2001* provides federal prisoners postconviction access to DNA testing under certain circumstances. These laws typically have a high bar for relief, requiring the defendant to show that the *new evidence* would prove his or her actual innocence over the original verdict. Unlike the original trial, the convicted person is not presumed innocent.

Interestingly, England has dealt with postconviction relief differently. Although they have no specific actual innocence laws, defendants there may contest the finding of a crime by showing, even years later, that the defendant did not commit or could not have committed the crime.

BOX 2.8 *HERRERA V. COLLINS* (1993) – CLAIM OF ACTUAL INNOCENCE

Officer David Rucker's body was found in his patrol car by a passerby along a highway in south Texas. Officer Enrique Carrisalez observed a vehicle speeding away from the scene of the murder on the same road. After Officer Carrisalez pulled the car over, the driver exchanged words and then shot Carrisalez in the chest, who died nine days later. Leonel Torres Herrera was arrested a few days later and was charged with the capital murder of Officers Rucker and Carrisalez. Before he died, Carrisalez identified Herrera from a photograph shown to him in the hospital. Carrisalez's partner also identified Herrera. The license plate of the car was traced to Herrera's girlfriend. Herrera's social security card had been found at the scene. Blood on the vehicle and Herrera's clothes was type A, the same as Officer Rucker's blood type. A handwritten letter was found on Herrera that "strongly implied" that he had killed Rucker. Herrera was convicted of killing Carrisalez and sentenced to death in 1982; later that year, he pleaded guilty to the murder of Rucker. An appeal and a habeas motion each failed.

Herrera filed a second *writ of habeas corpus* ten years after his conviction, claiming that new evidence demonstrated that he was "actually innocent" of both murders. He presented affidavits that Raul Herrera, his brother who had recently been murdered, had made statements that he had committed the murders. Herrera further claimed that executing an innocent person would constitute cruel and unusual punishment.

Chief Justice Rehnquist, writing for the majority, held that a claim of actual innocence based upon newly discovered evidence is not grounds for federal *habeas* relief. He wrote, "few rulings would be more disruptive of our federal system than to provide for federal *habeas* review of freestanding claims of actual innocence." He added:

> Were petitioner to satisfy the dissent's 'probable innocence' standard...the District Court would presumably be required to grant a conditioner order of relief, which would in effect require the State to retry petitioner 10 years after his first trial, not because of any constitutional violation which had occurred at the first trial, but simply because of a belief that in light of petitioner's new-found evidence, a jury might find him not guilty at a second trial.

The Court also held that the Texas courts' refusal to consider Herrera's newly discovered evidence did not violate his due process rights. In her concurrence, Justice O'Connor wrote, "the execution of a legally and factually innocent person would be a constitutionally intolerable event," but that Herrera was not innocent.

The dissent of Justice Blackmun, joined by two others, stated that "nothing could be more contrary to contemporary standards of decency or more shocking to the conscience than to execute a person who is actually innocent." He wrote, "We are really being asked to decide whether the Constitution forbids the execution of a person who has been validly convicted and sentenced, but who, nonetheless, can prove his actual innocence with newly discovered evidence." He noted, "the State of Texas' astonishing protestation to the contrary." Blackmun argued that the majority missed the point; the question was not whether a new trial would be more reliable than the first, but rather it was whether considering the new evidence, the State should be allowed to execute Herrera – that this standard of probable innocence for death-sentence relief is higher than reasonable doubt. Blackmun would have remanded the case to determine the merits of Herrera's claim of actual innocence.

Justice Scalia, in his concurring opinion, responded to this dissent:

> If the system that has been in place for 200 years (and remains widely approved) 'shocks' the dissenters' consciences… perhaps they should doubt the calibration of their consciences, or, better still, the usefulness of 'conscience shocking' as a legal test.

Note: Herrera's last words before his execution, four months after the Court's ruling, were, "I am innocent, innocent, innocent…I am an innocent man, and something very wrong is taking place tonight."

BOX 2.9 *DISTRICT ATTORNEY'S OFFICE V. OSBORNE* (2009) – CLAIM OF ACTUAL INNOCENCE

William Osborne was imprisoned for kidnapping and sexual assault. He and his friend, Jackson, both military service members, drove into Anchorage, where they picked up a prostitute. After driving to a secluded place, Osborne, using a blue condom, raped the prostitute at gunpoint and then beat her up, shot her in the head, and left her for dead in the snow. However, the gunshot had only grazed her head, and she pretended to be dead but survived. Jackson confessed to the crime, but Osborne did not. Abundant evidence was introduced to prove this case, including the eyewitness testimony of Jackson and the prostitute, as well as test results on the DNA from the blue condom performed by the FBI.

The DNA testing was an early form of DNA testing known as DQ-alpha testing. The DQ-alpha testing resulted in an inclusion of Osborne and an exclusion of Jackson but was a match for approximately 15% of the U.S. African-American population. RFLP DNA testing became available and was significantly more powerfully discriminating, but Osborne's defense attorney did not request it because she feared that the results might further incriminate her client.

Osborne appealed to the Alaska Superior Court. He argued that his trial lawyer had been ineffective for not pursuing the more discriminating RFLP DNA testing, and he sought such postconviction relief under §12.72.010(4) (2008) of the state law. He further stated that he had a state or federal due process right to the new DNA testing that had not been available at the time of his trial. The Superior Court denied his requests, but the Court of Appeals found that his attorney had made a tactical decision. The court remanded the case because the appellant might have a valid due process claim under the Alaska constitution. Upon remand, the Alaska Superior Court held that Osborne failed to satisfy the test for whether he had a right under the Alaska state constitution to retest the DNA.

Meanwhile, while his remanded case was still pending on the state level, Osborne also filed a claim under 42 U.S.C. §1983 civil rights action in the Federal District Court, claiming that his due process rights had been denied and requesting, at his own expense, the yet newer DNA STR analysis, which had not been previously available. The District Court dismissed his §1983 action, stating that he must bring this claim under a *writ of habeas corpus*. The Ninth Circuit Court of Appeals disagreed and remanded the case back to the District Court, which ruled in Osborne's favor this time. The Ninth Circuit Court of Appeals affirmed and held that Osborne had a limited constitutional due process right. The District Attorney's Office appealed, and the Supreme Court granted certiorari and heard the case 16 years after the crime.

In a 5–4 decision, the U.S. Supreme Court reversed, holding that "assuming that Osborne's claims can be pursued using §1983, he has no constitutional right to obtain postconviction access to the state's evidence for DNA testing." The Court found that Alaska provides for discovery in postconviction proceedings, including for DNA testing, which satisfies due process, but that he had not tried to use the State process. Thus, no substantive due process rights were infringed. The majority emphasized that 46 states already had laws at that time that allowed some access to DNA evidence, although prisoners often find it challenging to meet the conditions required by state statutes. Chief Justice Roberts wrote, "To suddenly constitutionalize this area would short-circuit what looks to be a prompt and considered legislative response."

The dissent filed by four justices asserted that Osborne had made full use of available state procedures but had been repeatedly rebuffed. In a separate dissent, Justice Souter stated that the application of the state process amounted to procedural unfairness in violation of his due process rights.

Summary

The U.S. Constitution guarantees *due process of law* to its citizens, but what this means has evolved. Eventually, it came to be defined by the Bill of Rights (the first ten Amendments of the U.S. Constitution) through selective incorporation. Although initially meant to protect citizens from the federal government, it became important as a protection of citizens from state governments.

Chief Justice Earl Warren, from 1953 to 1969, led a *defendant's rights revolution* that mirrored the *civil rights movement* of the 1960s. It established the constitutional regulation of criminal cases through the invocation of procedural due process.

Terms

Bill of Rights – the first ten Amendments to the U.S. Constitution.

Civil War (Reconstruction) Amendments – the Thirteenth, Fourteenth, and Fifteenth Amendments of the U.S. Constitution.

Due Process – the right to a fair legal process and respect for individual rights.

Cases

Barron v. City of Baltimore, 32 U.S. (7 Pet.) 243 (1833)
Bowers v. Hardwick, 478 U.S. 186 (1986)
Brown v. Board of Education, 347 U.S. 483 (1954)
Brown v. Mississippi, 297 U.S. 278 (1936)
District Attorney's Office for the Third Judicial District v. Osborne, 557 U.S. 52 (2009)
Dobbs v. Jackson Women's Health Organization, 597 U.S. 215 (2022)
Gideon v. Wainwright, 372 U.S. 335 (1963)
Gitlow v. New York, 268 U.S. 652 (1925)
Griswold v. Connecticut, 381 U.S. 479 (1965)
Herrera v. Collins, 506 U.S. 390 (1993)
Loving v. Virginia, 388 US 1 (1967)
Mapp v. Ohio, 367 U.S. 643 (1961)
Obergefell v. Hodges, 576 U.S. 644 (2015)
Palko v. Connecticut, 302 U.S. 319 (1937)
Pierce v. Society of Sisters, 268 U.S. 510 (1925)
Powell v. Alabama, 287 U.S. 45 (1932)
Slaughter-House Cases, 83 U.S. (16 Wall) 36 (1872)
Strickland v. Washington, 466 U.S. 668 (1984)
Wolf v. Colorado, 338 U.S. 25 (1949)
Zinermon v. Burch, 494 U.S. 113 (1990)

Statutes

Civil Action for Deprivation of Rights, 42 U.S.C. §1983 (1979)
Deprivation of Rights under Color of Law, 18 U.S.C. §242 (1996)
Post-Conviction DNA Testing, 18 U.S.C. §3600–3600A (2016)

Reference Material

Supreme Court of Ohio, 50 State Postconviction Relief Survey, https://www.supremecourt.ohio.gov/docs/Boards/CIPR/Report.pdf

Thought Questions

1. Why did the Founding Fathers draft the Bill of Rights to apply only to the federal government?
2. Why did the U.S. Supreme Court take so long to apply the Bill of Rights to the states?
3. Why didn't the state processes provide fundamental fairness in their state legal processes?
4. Why was the doctrine of selective incorporation used by the U.S. Supreme Court?
5. How should courts balance individual and collective societal interests?
6. Why are the courts the protectors of individual rights?

Further Reading

Chapman NS, McConnell MW, Due Process as Separation of Powers, *Yale Law Journal* 121(7):1672–1807, 2012.

Chemerinsky E, Procedural Due Process Claims, *Touro Law Review* 16:871–893, 2001.

Corwin ES, The Doctrine of Due Process of Law before the Civil War, *Harvard Law Review* 24(6):460–479, 1911.

Foner E, *The Second Founding: How the Civil War and Reconstruction Remade the Constitution*, W. W. Norton & Co., New York, 2019.

Hall KL, Finkelman P, Ely JW, *American Legal History: Cases and Materials*, 5th ed, Oxford Univ Press, Oxford, 2017.

Howard AED, *Magna Carter: Text and Commentary*, revised ed, Univ Press of Virginia, Charlottesville, 1998.

Hudson J, *The Formation of the English Common Law*, Routledge, Abington, 2018.

Stein P, *Roman Law in European History*, Cambridge University Press, Cambridge, 2020.

Strauss P, *Due Process*, Legal Information Institute, Cornell University, Ithaca, NY, 2013.

Chapter **3**

Judicial Apparatus

Learning Objectives

After reading this chapter, students are expected to be able to:

- recognize legal citations
- describe jurisdiction
- discuss federal jurisdiction
- explain the terms "case or controversy," "ripeness," and "standing."
- describe jury and bench trials
- define "the record"
- discuss bases for direct and collateral appeals
- describe *habeas corpus* proceedings.

Introduction

Over 100 million court cases are filed in the United States annually, with over 90% filed in state courts. Of these, over half of the cases are traffic violations. Only about 1% of the trials result in appeals. Approximately one-quarter of the cases are criminal cases. About 94% of state-level felony convictions and 97% of federal convictions result from plea agreements. Approximately 95% of civil lawsuits are dropped or settled before trial. The system would not be able to handle the caseload if it were not for civil settlements and plea agreements.

DOI: 10.4324/9780429272455-3

Historical Background

Following the Norman Conquest in 1066, William the Conqueror, Duke of Normandy, became King of England. The Norman kings of the Angevin dynasty (the House of Plantagenet) spoke Old French and they commonly appointed justices of the King's Court of Norman descent. Accordingly, French became the language of early English jurisprudence. There was no written Norman code of law, and the Old English legal system was largely unfamiliar to the new rulers. Since the Norman kings frequently spent time in France, English royal courts had some autonomy in shaping their jurisprudence. They retained elements of Anglo-Saxon law, such as the office of the sheriff, while incorporating aspects of Norman feudal law, particularly in matters of property and contract. Henry II, the first Angevin king, significantly expanded and centralized royal courts in the late 12th century. His legal reforms laid the foundation for English common law, establishing a more standardized judicial system.

While Latin remained the primary language for formal legal documents until 1731, French began to be used for legal records in the late 12th century. Under Edward I in the mid-13th century, ordinances and statutes were increasingly written in French. Many legal terms, such as *court*, *judge*, and *jury*, have French origins, reflecting the lasting influence of Norman rule on English law. English did not become the official language of the courts until the late 15th century under Henry VII, and written laws gradually transitioned to English in the 16th century.

Case Names

In our Anglo-American adversarial system, the cases are named or "styled" by the opposing parties, e.g., *Smith v. Jones*. The full names of all parties will be on the pleadings, but the names are truncated for other reasons for practical purposes. In criminal cases, the prosecution will be the governmental jurisdiction: U.S., State, Commonwealth, or People, e.g., *People v. Smith*. On appeal, the appellant's name is first. In *Habeas corpus* proceedings, the name of the prison custodian is used. In some unusual cases, "In re" will be used, meaning "in the matter of ___," e.g., *In re* Smith. The case may also be known by its docket number.

Reporter Services

Legal reporters (court reporters, law reporters) print judicial decisions certified to be published in reference book series for given court systems. Formal publication by a court reporter enables citation to the case and serves as a precedent for future cases. Only a small percentage of decisions

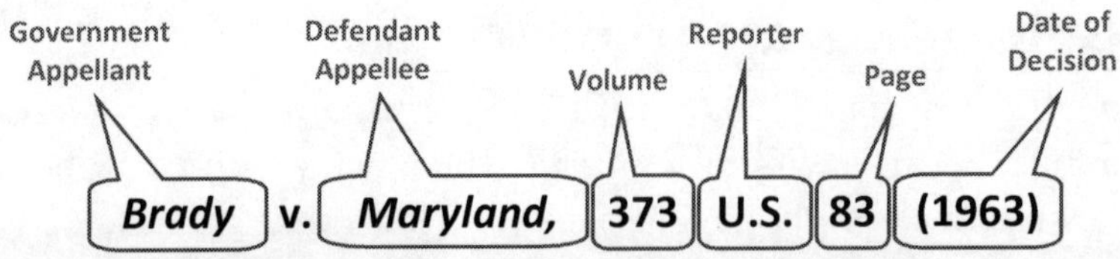

FIGURE 3.1 Legal Citation.

are published. All supreme court cases, but less than half of intermediate appellate opinions, and virtually no state trial cases are published. Intermediate appellate judges decide whether their cases are to be published or not. Federal cases are more likely to be published and may include federal district (trial) court cases. Reporters publish some cases as "unofficial" decisions that are not to be cited as precedent. Cases found on the internet are not considered judicially published.

In addition to the style of the case, citations will include an abbreviation for the reporter series and often the court, along with the year. For instance, *Miranda v. Arizona*, 384 U.S. 436, 86 S.Ct. 1602, 16 L.Ed. 2d 694 (1966) is a citation for a case styled *Miranda v. Arizona*, which is a case decided by the U.S. Supreme Court – the case was published in one reporter in volume 384, page 436, another in volume 86, page 1602, and another in volume 16, page 694. The three reporters of U.S. Supreme Court opinions are: (1) United States Reports (U.S.), which is the official reporter; (2) Supreme Court Reporter (S.Ct.), published by West Publishing Company; and (3) United States Supreme Court Reports, Lawyers' Edition (L.Ed., L. Ed.2d), published by Lexis. *Frye v. United States*, 293 F. 1013 (D.C. Cir. 1923) was decided by the D.C. Circuit Court and can be found on page 1013 of volume 293 in the Federal Reporter, which is abbreviated "F." "F.3d" is an abbreviation for Federal Reporter, third series and "F.Supp." would be the Federal Supplement. *U.S. v. Jameel*, 999 F.Supp.2d 848 (E.D. Va. 2014) refers to a 2014 case in the Eastern District of Virginia Federal Court published in the second series of the Federal Supplement. *Murray v. Commonwealth*, 762 S.E.2d 573 (Va. 2014) is a Virginia Supreme Court case published in Southeastern Reports, second series, an unofficial regional reporter for state cases. The official state reporter citation is 288 Va. 117 (2014).

Because our Anglo-American jurisprudence is based on legal precedent, it is essential to search for prior cases. Legal reporting began with Henry de Bracton's *On the Laws and Customs of England* in the 1230s; after that, the Year Books began the annual printing of cases from 1268 onward. This reporting helped establish English precedent and the Common Law. Legal research is taught as an essential skill in law schools. Published cases are usually found on the state's judicial website (e.g., https://www.courts.state.va.us/). LexisNexis and Westlaw are the two primary private online legal research services in the United States, and Casetext is a recent market entrant. *Shepardizing* is an important method of research, named after a publication (now a service) called Shepard's Citations that lists all cases that cite the case you are researching.

Court Structure

The United States has two parallel judicial systems: federal and state. Article III of the U.S. Constitution invests judicial power in the federal court system, which Congress has established in various Judicial Acts. State courts are established through state constitutions and laws.

Within each system, there are trial and appellate courts as well as special courts. In civil cases, the Attorney General might represent the state government, and a county or city attorney might represent the local government. A State or Commonwealth's Attorney, a District Attorney, or other prosecutor may represent the government in criminal cases. A United States Attorney (USA) or Assistant United States Attorney (AUSA) of the U.S. Department of Justice prosecute brings suit, defends, or argues cases in federal or state courts on behalf of the U.S. federal government. There are many more state courts than federal courts, and federal courts are more limited in what cases they can adjudicate.

Most jurisdictions, including the federal system, have trial courts, intermediate appellate courts, and a court of last resort, usually called the "Supreme Court." Ironically, in New York, the Court of Appeals is the court of last resort, and the Supreme Court is a state-wide trial court with jurisdiction in criminal and civil matters.

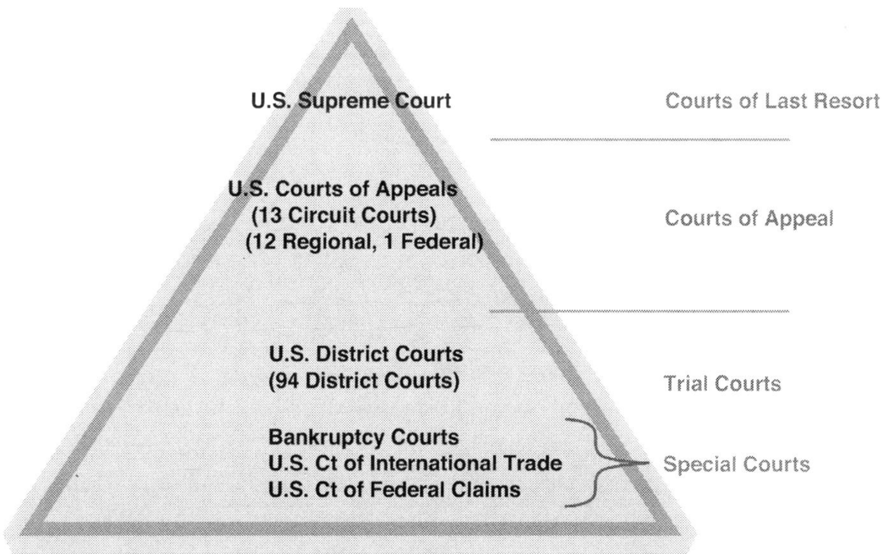

FIGURE 3.2 Federal Court System.

In the federal system, the lowest court of record is the District Court. The intermediate appellate court is the Court of Appeals, with three-judge panels, and the court of last resort is the U.S. Supreme Court, with nine Justices. The federal judiciary consists of 1 U.S. Supreme Court, 13 U.S. Courts of Appeals (12 regional circuit courts and 1 federal circuit court), and 94 U.S. District Courts (each district with a Bankruptcy court and Magistrate Judges who assist District Court Judges). Congress has also established a number of federal courts that have specialized jurisdiction, including the Court of Appeals for the Armed Forces, the Court of Federal Claims, the Court of International Trade, the Court of Appeals for Veterans Claims, and the Tax Court.

Judges and Magistrates

Individual District Court judges preside over federal court trial proceedings. Federal appellate courts generally sit as three-judge panels but sometimes sit *en banc*, when all the appellate court judges within a circuit sit together. The President of the United States nominates federal judges, and the Senate confirms them. They hold lifetime appointments, although they may be removed through congressional impeachment proceedings for misbehavior. Judges of the Supreme Court are called Justices. State judges may be elected or appointed and usually have a limited term.

Magistrate Judges in the federal system are judges appointed by the district court to assist District Judges in handling arraignments, motions, preliminary hearings, warrant issuance, and discovery in civil cases. They also handle misdemeanor trials and, with the consent of the parties, trials of civil cases. They also try federal misdemeanor and traffic cases in federal jurisdictions. Many state jurisdictions have magistrates, often considered successors of English *Justices of the Peace*.

Jurisdiction

Jurisdiction is the court's power to hear a case as authorized in its statutory creation. The court must have jurisdiction over the *person* (*in personam*) and the *subject matter* (*in rem*) to hear the case.

A court residing within a state, district, or locality may exercise personal jurisdiction over a person who resides, maintains connections, commits a crime, or is served notice of legal proceedings in the area served. Courts may also exercise jurisdiction over persons who consent to be subject to it. Typically, a court will exert personal jurisdiction over the defendant when the defendant has been served within the court's jurisdiction and voluntarily appears in court.

Unlike state courts, federal courts have the authority to exercise personal jurisdiction over any person within the United States (the long arm of the law) who has committed a crime within its judicial district. In civil cases, federal courts have a more limited reach of subpoenas and service of complaints.

State courts may have *general* or *limited* subject matter jurisdiction, but all federal courts are courts of limited jurisdiction. State courts with general jurisdiction, variously called superior courts, courts of common pleas, circuit courts, or district courts, have unlimited subject matter jurisdiction and are competent to hear civil and criminal cases. Conversely, other courts have limited subject matter jurisdiction and are competent to hear only criminal or civil cases. They may be further limited by the magnitude of the crime or damages sought in a suit. States have *special courts*, such as juvenile, divorce, and drug, have very limited jurisdiction. Courts of Magistrates and Justices of the Peace are lower courts that handle preliminary and minor criminal matters. State court systems will hear criminal cases, personal injury cases, probate (wills and estates), family law (marriages, divorces, adoptions), etc.

In situations where laws from multiple jurisdictions contradict each other, courts utilize a "choice of law" analysis to identify which jurisdiction's law should be applied.

Court jurisdiction is also divided between *original jurisdiction* and *appellate jurisdiction*. A lawsuit or prosecution is first heard in the trial court, which has original jurisdiction, but then to an appellate court.

Plaintiffs in civil lawsuits face limitations on their ability to sue. They must plead an actual *case or controversy*; it cannot be a theoretical case. The case must be *ripe* and sufficiently developed to proceed; the case cannot be a future wrong. Nor can the case be *stale* – it must not be so old that the wrong has been effectively accepted; statutes of limitations and repose may limit the time a legal claim can be brought. Furthermore, the plaintiffs must have *standing* to bring a claim to the court; they cannot sue as bystanders or as stand-ins but must be directly aggrieved. They must be an appropriate party for the court's jurisdiction and fit the personal and subject matter of the court's jurisdiction. When plaintiffs have a choice of multiple courts within a jurisdiction or among jurisdictions in which they may sue, they can choose a particular *venue* or *forum* that they believe would be most convenient or most favorable to their cause. However, the U.S. Supreme Court has recently substantially curtailed much forum shopping, when first, the Court held that corporations are only subject to general jurisdiction in the state of their incorporation (*Daimler AG v. Bauman*, 2014) and then subsequently limited personal jurisdiction to the states where defendants reside (*Bristol-Myers Squibb Co. v. Superior Court of San Francisco County*, 2017)).

BOX 3.1 *MAYFIELD, III V. DALTON* (1997) – CASE OR CONTROVERSY

Marine Lance Corporal Mayfield and Lance Corporal Vlacovsky sued the Secretary of the Navy and 25 others (including Weedn) over the constitutionality of the military's DNA identification program. They had been reprimanded for disobeying an order to give blood samples. They argued that the compulsory taking of specimens without proper safeguards to maintain the donor's privacy violated the Fourth Amendment prohibition against unreasonable searches and seizures. They feared that information obtained from the repository samples regarding the donors' propensities for hereditary diseases and genetic disorders might be used to discriminate against applicants for jobs, insurance, or benefit programs. The petition referred to past federal abuses, such as the Central Intelligence Agency's use of LSD, a psychoactive drug, on unsuspected citizens and the Tuskegee study of Black men with untreated syphilis. The District Court held that taking specimens without the service members' consent did not constitute an unreasonable seizure violating the Fourth Amendment, and the potential, nefarious uses were too speculative to be justiciable. The Court of Appeals held that the case had been rendered moot by the honorable separation of Mayfield and Vlacovsky from the military, vacated the District Court's judgment, and remanded the case with instructions to dismiss the case as moot.

Federal Jurisdiction

Federal courts have limited jurisdiction, hearing only cases as authorized by the Constitution and federal laws. They primarily hear cases involving either a *federal question* (involving federal laws) or *diversity* (across jurisdictions).

Federal question jurisdiction is a type of subject matter jurisdiction that gives U.S. federal courts the power to hear cases arising under the laws, treaties, or Constitution of the United States but not claims arising under state law. A federal question involves the U.S. Constitution, federal statute, federal regulation, or international treaty.

However, diversity jurisdiction is a type of subject matter jurisdiction available for civil state-law claims where every plaintiff is from a different state than every defendant (complete diversity) and the amount in controversy exceeds $75,000. A claim based upon diversity arises from a dispute between states or between a state and citizens of another state, lawsuits involving citizens of different states, and against foreign states and citizens.

The geopolitical territory covered by the U.S. Supreme Court is the entire United States, its territories, and possessions, but it has no authority over the internal affairs of other countries. Federal District Courts are located in each state, and there may be more than one district court in a state. Federal Courts of Appeals are regional and encompass several states. State, city, and county courts have jurisdiction within their respective boundaries.

Federal courts will hear cases of constitutionality, treaties, ambassadors, disputes between states, admiralty law, bankruptcy, habeas corpus, etc. Most crimes are violations of state law, not federal law, and thus would be prosecuted in the state court system. Title 18 of the Federal Criminal Code contains numerous federal crimes, such as:

- Financial fraud
- Bank robbery
- Counterfeiting
- Kidnapping
- Threatening the president or other federal officials or buildings
- Committing a crime on federal property
- Committing a crime using interstate commerce
- Conspiring to commit a federal crime
- Using a firearm to commit a crime
- Manufacturing and distributing controlled substances
- Domestic and international terrorism

Some offenses may violate both federal and state laws. For example, robbery of a convenience store would be a state crime, but because the store engages in interstate commerce, it is also a federal crime. When there is concurrent jurisdiction between the state and the federal government, such as the Iwo Jima memorial in Arlington, Virginia, either government has the authority to prosecute a crime occurring on those monument grounds, and an agreement of the state and federal prosecutors will determine the venue.

Federal agencies with authority to investigate federal offenses include the Federal Bureau of Investigation (FBI), Drug Enforcement Agency (DEA), Bureau of Alcohol, Tobacco, Firearms and Explosives (ATF), Immigration and Customs Enforcement (ICE), Customs and Border Protection (CBP), U.S. Secret Service (USSS), the Internal Revenue Service (IRS), Postal Inspection Service (PIS), U.S. Fish and Wildlife Service (FWS), and various Inspectors General offices, among others.

Judicial Process

Most civil and criminal cases are resolved through negotiation before they go to trial. The resulting civil settlement or plea may include waiving the right to appeal. Judges may be involved in the negotiations in civil trials, but in criminal cases, judges only have the discretion to accept a plea agreement.

When the case proceeds to trial, significant pretrial activity will involve motions and discovery. During the trial, the jury is the "trier of fact," and the judge is the "trier of law." The jury *weighs* the facts in the evidence provided to them to arrive at a *verdict* in the case and any other matters of fact asked of them by the judge. The judge rules, as a matter of law, on the objections and motions of the lawyers. A criminal defendant may waive his or her right to a jury (often requiring the consent of the prosecution and judge) and elect to allow the judge to decide the case, in which case he or she is both the trier of fact and the trier of law. These trials without juries are called *bench trials* because a judge from the bench decides them. In a criminal trial, the *ultimate question* of fact is the question of guilt or innocence embodied in the verdict. In criminal trials, a guilty verdict will be followed by sentencing. In civil trials, a verdict will result in dismissal or the granting of damages or other relief to the plaintiff.

Appeals

The criminal defendant and civil parties to the trial may appeal the judgment to an appellate court. An appeal is a party litigant's formal request to change an official decision. The prosecution cannot appeal a "not guilty" verdict because of the Fifth Amendment prohibition against *double jeopardy.* Generally, appeals are made after a final judgment is rendered; however, an *interlocutory appeal* is occasionally made during a trial to settle a specific issue. Importantly, in federal court, if the District Court suppresses evidence or a defendant's confession, the federal prosecutor may take an interlocutory appeal of that issue. If the prosecutor could not do that, and the defendant is acquitted, the government would never be able to appeal the trial court's suppression ruling.

Courts are reluctant to re-examine or reopen cases already decided, prefer *finality of judgment*, and abhor continuous litigation and appeals. Actual innocence cases are an exception to those judicial disinclinations.

From the trial court, defendants may have a direct *appeal of right* to the lowest appellate court. Common Law jurisprudence did not adopt an affirmative right of appeal until the 19th century. A federal right to appeal did not exist in the United States until 1889 in capital cases and two years later in other criminal cases. Some states still do not formally recognize the right to a criminal appeal – in those states, courts may, at their discretion, allow an appeal for good cause shown.

After an appeal of right, further appeals are *discretionary appeals*, in which higher appellate courts decide whether to hear a further appeal from the lower appellate court. A petition to appeal to the U.S. Supreme Court requires filing a petition for *writ of certiorari* ("*cert*"). Some state court systems use the same terminology, but other terms are used elsewhere: *writ of review, leave to appeal*, or *certification for appeal.*

The *appellant* (*movant, petitioner*) is the party who files the appeal, and the *appellee* (*respondent*) is the party against whom an appeal is filed. Multiple appeals may result in the appellant and appellee switching roles as the case proceeds up the appellate ladder.

A *direct appeal* is based upon errors of law, misrepresentation of facts, or withholding of facts, resulting in a fundamentally unfair trial and denial of due process of law. To succeed on appeal, the error cannot merely be *harmless* but must instead be found to be *prejudicial*, and such an error would more likely than not have changed the outcome of the trial. An error not *preserved* for review by a timely objection may still be considered if the aggrieved party can show that it is a plain error that is material to the case.

An appellate court uses *standards of review* to assess the lower court's decisions. A determination that a previous decision was invalid because it was *arbitrary and capricious* is a willful and unreasonable action by a jury or administrative agency without consideration or regard for the facts and circumstances. Determining that a finding of a material fact made by a jury or administrative agency is not supported by *substantial evidence* means the record shows no support for a material fact. Determining that the judge's ruling on a question of fact is *clearly erroneous* means that the appellate tribunal has a definite and firm conviction that the lower court made a mistake. Under a *de novo* (*plenary, legal, independent*) review, the appellate court will review a question of law or mixed law and fact as if for the first time and without considering the ruling below. (A new trial in which all issues are reviewed as if for the first time is called a trial *de novo* and often occurs in appeals of misdemeanors from a court not of record to a general trial court.) A determination of *abuse of discretion* means the appellate court disagrees with the lower court judge's discretionary ruling on a question of law. The appellate court will normally defer to the lower court's judgment unless it is a *plain error* rather than a *harmless error*.

A *collateral attack* on a final judgment can only occur once all appeals have been exhausted. It is not based upon the merits of the case but on some other basis. Collateral attacks will require an independent but narrow inquiry into the validity of the process, such as an infringement of constitutional rights or a jurisdictional violation not adjudicated on direct appeal. Claims of actual innocence or ineffective assistance of counsel presented through *habeas corpus* proceedings are examples of collateral appeals. A *writ of coram nobis* is a common law motion, rarely used, to bring to the court's attention material issues of law outside the record and unknown to the court at trial. It is intended to correct a final judgment by the same court to address a fundamental error, such as ineffective counsel, prosecutorial misconduct, or a deprivation of the right to counsel. Unlike a writ of habeas corpus, the defendant does not need to be in custody.

To succeed on a writ of habeas corpus based upon *ineffective assistance of counsel*, the petitioner must meet the *Strickland v. Washington* (1984) test by showing (1) that the trial counsel's performance fell below an objective standard of reasonableness and (2) that the deficient performance resulted in prejudice to the outcome of the case – that there is a reasonable probability that it would have been different. This isn't easy to prove. Often, the failure that forms the basis for the ineffectiveness of the counsel claim can be justified as a strategic decision by the counsel, which defeats the incompetence allegation. Mere incompetence may be insufficient to show ineffective assistance of counsel. Appeals have been lost where the defense attorney fell asleep during the prosecutor's cross-examination of the defendant, the defense attorney was heavily intoxicated throughout the trial, and the defense attorney was delusional.

The parties' lawyers will file legal briefs to explain their legal arguments. A *Brandeis brief* (in honor of the former Justice Louis Brandeis) is the term for a robust, fact-filled brief. When a non-party litigant may want to express their opinion to the appellate court, it may grant permission for the *amicus curiae* (singular) or *amici curiae* (plural), meaning the friend(s) of the court, to file an *amicus* brief to give their advice and opinion as helpful to the court in ruling on the case.

The court will also have the *trial record* for review. The trial record includes the transcript of all proceedings in the case, pleadings, and, in some instances, paper exhibits and photographs. Appeals are usually questions of law or the sufficiency of evidence and are limited only to issues raised by the appellant at trial or in postconviction motions based on the trial court's record. No additional new evidence or hearing of witnesses for the court to consider will be allowed. Therefore, the record must be preserved. When the appellate court entertains a question of fact or a legal ruling, it will review the entire case record.

Sometimes, oral arguments are presented in the appellate court, where each side is given a short time, usually about 15 minutes, to present their arguments and a more limited time for rebuttal by the appellant. During their presentations, the judges on the panel will usually interrupt to ask questions challenging the litigants' legal and factual theories.

Appeals in intermediate appellate courts (not supreme courts) are heard by a panel of three judges without a jury, while *En Banc* hearings are before the entire judicial bench. Such appellate courts may:

- *Affirm* the judgment of the lower court.
- *Reverse and remand* the decision for further proceedings by lower courts.

- *Dismiss* the case [the court may dismiss *with prejudice*, meaning that their word is final, and the judgment is not appealable].
- *Reverse in part and Affirm in part* the decision below.
- Issue a *Writ of Mandamus* that orders a government official to properly fulfill their official duties or correct an abuse of discretion.

The opinion of the court may be:

- *Majority* opinion – the opinion of the court based upon a majority of the judges
- *Concurring* opinion – a separate opinion that agrees with the holding of the majority
- *Plurality* opinion – *where* several written opinions have no majority agreement, the opinion joined by the greatest number of judges is called the plurality opinion
- *Dissent* – a separate opinion that disagrees with some or part of the majority's holding
- *En Banc* opinion – an opinion by the entire bench that hears the case, not just a panel
- *Per curiam opinion* – an opinion by the court without attribution to the judges

In a tie vote, which can only occur when an even number of en banc judges or Supreme Court Justices hear a case, the lower court ruling will stand, which accounts for the fact that panels and Supreme Courts have odd numbers of judges. If a judge recuses themselves, that action may cause an even number of judges on a Supreme Court case. However, in panels of intermediate appellate courts, there are always other judges on the court to add to the panel to make it an odd number.

The court may decide whether to publish its opinion. Published appellate court holdings have precedential value, are citable, and comprise the caselaw – accordingly, appeals function as a process for both error correction and clarifying and interpreting the law.

The U.S. Supreme Court

The Court typically will agree to hear a case only when it involves an unusually important legal principle or when lower federal courts disagree on a point of law. A *writ of certiorari* is granted an average of 80 times per year – approximately 1% of the *cert* applications. If the Supreme Court denies *cert*, then the decision of the Court of Appeals stands. In a few exceptional circumstances, the Supreme Court is required by law to hear an appeal.

In the legal literature, the U.S. Supreme Court is referred to as "the Court," whereas a lesser court is referred to as "the court" – without the "c" being capitalized.

BOX 3.2 THE U.S. SUPREME COURT BUILDING

The Supreme Court moved into its current neoclassical home in 1935. The building faces the U.S. Capitol. Marble figures are seated on either side of the main steps. The male figure on the right is the "Guardian" or "Authority of Law." The female figure on the left is the "Contemplation of Justice." "Equal Justice under Law" is inscribed above the entablature supported by 16 marble columns of the main entrance. The sculpture on the gable represents "Liberty Enthroned" guarded by "Order and Authority."

FIGURE 3.3 The U.S. Supreme Court Building.

BOX 3.3 OYEZ! OYEZ! OYEZ!

At the beginning of each session, the court's clerk or a bailiff announces:

> The Honorable, the Chief Justice and the Associate Justices of the Supreme Court of the United States. Oyez! Oyez! Oyez! All persons having business before the Honorable Supreme Court of the United States are admonished to draw near and give their attention, for the Court is now sitting. God save the United States and this Honorable Court.
>
> ["Oyez" is Latin for "listen"]

Habeas Corpus

The federal *writ of habeas corpus* is a proceeding for unlawful detention or imprisonment guaranteed by the Suspension Clause of the U.S. Constitution:

> The privilege of the *writ of habeas corpus* shall not be suspended, unless when in cases of rebellion or invasion the public safety may require it.
>
> *[Art. 1, Sec. 9]*

Federal habeas proceedings are collateral attacks by criminal defendants, either federal or state defendants, who file the petition in federal court. Both federal and state prisoners must exhaust all direct appeals or their state remedies before filing a federal petition for a writ of *habeas corpus*. They are civil, not criminal, *ex parte* actions against whomever is holding the defendant. For example, a *habeas* writ may be sought where it is alleged that the state court lacked jurisdiction over the defendant, or the law broken was unconstitutional.

In the wake of the bombing of the Alfred P. Murrah building in Oklahoma City by Timothy McVeigh, Congress passed the Antiterrorism and Effective Death Penalty Act of 1996 (AEDPA) (28 U.S.C. §2254) that substantially curtailed the availability of the writ. The AEDPA restricted the grounds on which *habeas* claims may be brought to convictions contrary to "clearly established federal law" or to an "unreasonable determination of the facts in light of the evidence." The AEDPA also held that *habeas* petitions must be filed within one year of the loss of a direct appeal or within one year of discovering new evidence through the exercise of due diligence, and it banned the filing of more than one petition. In *McQuiggin v. Perkins* (2013), the Supreme Court held that a prisoner who alleges actual innocence may file a petition outside of the statute of limitations and allow a court to consider the merits of the petitioner's claim of a showing that, more likely than not, no reasonable juror would have convicted him in the light of the new evidence.

Judicial Activism versus Judicial Restraint

The *political question doctrine* holds that courts should deem an issue nonjusticiable and refuse jurisdiction because the court is the wrong forum to decide the question when the issue is fundamentally political rather than legal (*Baker v. Carr,* 1962). Legislative bodies are large groups composed of elected representatives whose job is to legislate, whereas courts have single or small panels of judges who are often appointed to their positions. Thus, courts will usually defer to legislative bodies because it seems proper. It is a judicial sin for judges to substitute their own will for that of the legislature, although it is not always clear when a judge has committed this sin. A judge imposing his or her policy view into an interpretation is sometimes referred to as *Lochnerizing* (referring to the 1905 case of *Lochner v. New York*).

Judges may have expertise in law, but they rarely have expertise in science or technical matters and in many other matters that come before them. Judges do not necessarily have greater expertise than others to make decisions. Judge Antonin Scalia famously wrote in *Cruzan v. Director, Missouri Department of Health* (1990):

> The point at which life becomes 'worthless,' and the point at which the means necessary to preserve it become 'extraordinary' or 'inappropriate,' are neither set forth in the Constitution nor known to the nine Justices of this Court any better than they are known to nine people picked at random from the Kansas City telephone directory.

However, the Bill of Rights enumerates rights that are supposed to be beyond the control of legislation or executive action, and the courts must scrutinize legislation to guard against encroachments.

Judicial activism by activist courts (e.g., the Warren court) is often considered "legislating from the bench" rather than merely interpreting the law. Familiar examples of such activism are *Gideon v. Wainwright* (1963), which required appointments of counsel for indigents accused of felonies, and *Miranda v. Arizona* (1966), which set out the warnings to be given to suspects before questioning.

Judicial restraint is a policy preference that limits the exercise of their own power and only hesitatingly strikes down laws. However, judicial review and interpretation of the law are important functions of the courts. The courts often protect individuals and minorities from the people's will established through legislative bodies and government officials. The majority does not need the same protection because they can secure what they want through the political process. Judicial restraint is most often exhibited by judges who strictly construe the Constitution, also called originalists, and refrain from legislating from the bench. When Justice Amy Coney Barrett took the oath of office on October 26, 2020, she made the following remarks:

> The confirmation process has made ever clearer to me one of the fundamental differences between the federal judiciary and the United States Senate. And perhaps the most acute is the role of policy preferences. It is the job of a senator to pursue her policy preferences. In fact, it would be a dereliction of duty for her to put policy goals aside. By contrast, it is the job of a judge to resist her policy preferences. It would be a dereliction of duty for her to give into them. Federal judges don't stand for election. Thus, they have no basis for claiming that their preferences reflect those of the people. This separation of duty from political preference is what makes the judiciary distinct among the three branches of government.

The *counter-majoritarian difficulty* is that courts have no way of enforcing their decisions except through the political branches of government. The courts can make unpopular decisions, but not too often. When the U.S. Supreme Court ruled in *Brown v. Board of Education* (1954) that the *separate but equal* doctrine was unconstitutional, some believed that the Court got ahead of society, while others thought it was a necessary precondition to desegregation.

In response to the Supreme Court's 1832 ruling that the seizures of land in Georgia violated treaties, President Andrew Jackson responded, famously but probably apocryphally, "John Marshall has made his decision; now let him enforce it."

BOX 3.4 *GIDEON V. WAINWRIGHT* (1963) – JUDICIAL ACTIVISM, RIGHT TO COUNSEL

Clarence Earl Wainwright had an eighth-grade education and was a petty thief from the age of 18, living in and out of jail. He was accused of burglary when a pool hall in Panama City, Florida, was burglarized. The break-in occurred sometime between midnight and morning. A door was broken, a cigarette machine was smashed, $5 in change from the cash register, a few bottles of beer and soda, and an alleged $50 from the jukebox were stolen. Henry Cook reported seeing Gideon in the poolroom at around 5:30 that morning, leaving with a wine bottle and money in his pockets. Based on this accusation, Gideon was arrested and charged with breaking and entering with the intent to commit a misdemeanor, a felony under Florida law.

Gideon appeared in court without an attorney, asking the judge to appoint counsel for him because he could not afford an attorney. The judge denied Gideon's request because Florida law permitted the appointment of counsel only for poor defendants charged with capital offenses. Gideon attempted to represent himself, and despite his best efforts, the jury found him guilty and sentenced him to five years in prison.

He wrote in pencil on prison stationery from prison, an appeal *in forma pauperis* to the U.S. Supreme Court. The unanimous Court held that states must provide legal counsel to indigent defendants charged with a felony as a matter of right. The Court decision specifically cited its previous ruling in *Powell v. Alabama* and discussed a firm set of "procedural guarantees" based on the Constitution.

Gideon received a new trial with the appointment of defense counsel at the government's expense – the lawyer made all the difference. The defense attorney picked apart the testimony of eyewitness Henry Cook and suggested that he likely had been a lookout for the group who broke into the pool hall. The cab driver who had picked Gideon up stated that Gideon had no wine, beer, or soda, despite Cook's testimony that he had watched Gideon walk from the pool hall to the phone and then wait for a cab. This testimony wholly discredited Cook, and the jury acquitted Gideon after one hour of deliberation.

Note: approximately 2,000 individuals were freed in Florida alone because of the Gideon decision. Since the decision, public defenders have become commonplace.

BOX 3.5 *WOOLEY V. MAYNARD* (1977) – JUDICIAL ACTIVISM, RIGHT TO FREE SPEECH

As required by statute, the New Hampshire state motto, "Live Free or Die," was embossed on car license plates. Another New Hampshire statute made it a misdemeanor to "knowingly [obscure]... the figures or letters on any number plate" and was interpreted by the State Supreme Court to include the state motto. George Maynard and his wife, Jehovah's Witnesses, found the motto to be repugnant to their moral, religious, and political beliefs – that giving up their life for the state, even if it meant living in bondage, is contrary to their convictions, life is more precious than freedom. Accordingly, they covered the motto on their license plates with a piece of black tape but left the rest of the information exposed. A police officer issued a $25 citation for covering the motto, and another officer later issued a second citation. Maynard spent 15 days in jail when he refused to pay. The federal District Court found for the Maynards and ordered the state not to arrest or prosecute them for the offense. The Governor then appealed to the U.S. Supreme Court. In a 6–3 decision, the Court held that New Hampshire could not constitutionally require citizens to display the state motto on their vehicle license plates. The Court found that the statute effectively required individuals to "use their private property as a 'mobile billboard' for the State's ideological message." The State's interests in requiring the motto did not outweigh the First Amendment's free speech principles.

Comment: this seems much ado for a piece of tape on a license plate and a $25 fine, but the First Amendment issues were paramount to the court. Here, six justices imposed their will over the state legislature, executive, and judicial branches.

Summary

Most cases filed with courts do not go to trial, and few that go to trial are appealed. A case is known by its name (style) and legal citation.

Plaintiffs and prosecutors bring their cases in federal, state, or local courts with jurisdiction to hear the case. The courts have a hierarchical structure presided over by magistrates, judges, and justices. They may hear a case when the court has personal and subject matter jurisdiction. In civil cases, the plaintiff must have standing, and the case must be ripe. Cases may be brought to federal courts if they involve a federal question or diversity.

Generally, there is a right of first appeal, but after that, the appeals are at the courts' discretion. Intermediate appeals are heard by a panel of judges and are based on the trial record; no new evidence can be introduced. Judges should typically interpret and apply the law and not make new laws.

Terms

Amicus Brief – a brief of a non-party as a friend of the court.
Appeal of Right – an appeal that a court must hear.
Bench Trial – a trial conducted without a jury.
Concurring Opinion – an independent opinion that supports the majority holding.
Court of Last Resort – the highest appellate court available to a party.
Dissenting Opinion – an opinion contrary to the majority or plurality holding.
Federal Diversity – a basis of federal jurisdiction based upon citizenship from different states or international citizenship.
Habeas Corpus – a collateral federal or state proceeding alleging wrongful detention or imprisonment.
Jurisdiction – the power of a court to hear a case.
Personal Jurisdiction – the court's power to hear the parties' case.
Plurality Opinion – an opinion in a case without a majority opinion that received the most support.
Prejudicial – evidence that would unfairly sway a jury's opinion and would likely result in a verdict that it would not have rendered without the evidence.
Remand – to order back to the lower court for further proceedings or a new trial.
Subject Matter Jurisdiction – the court's power to hear the case's subject matter.
Trier of Fact – the jury in a jury trial; the judge in a bench trial.

Cases

Baker v. Carr, 369 U.S. 186 (1962)
Bristol-Myers Squibb Co. v. Superior Court, San Francisco County, 582 U.S. 255 (2017)
Brown v. Board of Education, 347 U.S. 483 (1954)
Cruzan v. Director, Missouri Department of Health, 497 U.S. 261 (1990)
Daimler AG v. Bauman, 571 U.S. 117 (2014)
Gideon v. Wainwright, 372 U.S. 335 (1963)
Lochner v. New York, 198 U.S. 45 (1905)
Mayfield III v. Dalton, 109 F.3d 1423 (9th Cir. 1997)
McQuiggin v. Perkins, 569 U.S. 383 (2013)
Miranda v. Arizona, 384 U.S. 436 (1966)
Strickland v. Washington, 466 U.S. 668 (1984)
Wooley v. Maynard, 430 U.S. 705 (1977)

Statutes

Antiterrorism and Effective Death Penalty Act (AEDPA), 28 U.S.C. §2254 (1996)

Thought Questions

1. Why was actual innocence not a basis for appeal in the Common Law?
2. What does preserving the record during a trial mean, and why is it essential?
3. Was the Court in *Gideon v. Wainwright* legislating or defending the rights of citizens?

Further Reading

Baker JH, *An Introduction to English Legal History*, 4th ed, Oxford Univ Press, Oxford, 2011.

Langbein JH, *The Origins of Adversary Criminal Trial*, Oxford Univ Press, Oxford, 2010.

Langbein JH, Lerner RL, Smith BP, *History of the Common Law: The Development of Anglo-American Legal Institutions*, Aspen Publishers, New York, 2009.

Maitland FW, Montague FC, *A Sketch of English Legal History*, The Lawbook Exchange, Ltd, Clark, NJ, 2010.

Chapter 4
Civil Law

Learning Objectives

After reading this chapter, students are expected to be able to:

- define civil law
- describe the similarities and differences between civil and criminal law
- list possible civil remedies
- describe intentional torts
- explain the four elements of negligence
- discuss contract law.

Introduction

Here, we will use the term *civil law* to refer to the branch of law in Anglo-American jurisprudence involving civil lawsuits rather than criminal prosecutions and not the system of *Civil Law* jurisprudence practiced in continental Europe derived from Roman law.

Significant areas of civil law include torts, contracts, property law, commercial law, family law, administrative law, intellectual property law, and wills and probate. We will only focus here on tort law and contract law.

DOI: 10.4324/9780429272455-4

BOX 4.1 INVOLVEMENT OF FORENSIC SCIENTISTS IN CIVIL LITIGATION

Although many forensic scientists will not be involved in civil litigation, virtually any forensic scientist could be engaged if hired by a civil litigant. Forensic engineers will spend most of their time in civil litigation. Forensic psychologists will frequently testify to testamentary capacity or competency to contract. Forensic document examiners will commonly testify to fraudulent signatures. Forensic pathologists may testify in medical malpractice and wrongful death cases, often on issues of survivability of injuries and pain and suffering.

When forensic scientists participate in civil cases as expert witnesses, they often find that the challenge and level of scrutiny are significantly higher than in criminal cases. Plaintiffs and defendants are usually corporate entities willing to pay large sums of money for legal research and teams of experts.

Historical Background

Danelaw (*Dena lagu* in Old English) is the area of ancient England under the Anglo-Saxon rule in which Danish laws applied. The Old Norse term is *lag*, for "things laid down or fixed," which evolved into the Old English *lagu* and then into Middle English as *lawe*. In 12th-century England, before recognizable juries were established, free landowners were bound to attend local open-air judicial proceedings; these freemen owed "suit" to it; they were its suitors. During the 18th and 19th centuries, lawyers brought "actions" at law and "suits" in equity (discussed below). However, the merger of Common Law and equity in the English Judicature Acts of 1873 and 1875 led to the combination term "lawsuit"; the terms "claims" and "claimants" are now more common in England. In the United States, the 1938 Federal Rules of Civil Procedure also merged actions at law and suits in equity into "civil actions." A particular count or cause of action in a lawsuit is called a "claim."

Civil versus Criminal Law

While criminal law involves *the State* prosecuting those who break the laws, civil law concerns the rights and duties of individual citizens; in other words, it involves compensation for personal injuries and civil wrongs and resolving disputes between citizens. Ordinary citizens bring lawsuits against other citizens in civil lawsuits. Any citizen can bring a suit in a court of competent jurisdiction. Of course, civil actions are not limited to citizens; corporations, businesses, institutions, and government entities can also sue and be sued. Plaintiffs and their attorneys face defendants and their attorneys in civil court.

Civil wrongs are breaches of duty or wrongful acts that infringe the legal rights or otherwise harm the complaining party, such as a tort, a breach of contract, or a breach of trust. Civil lawsuits seek enforcement of contracts and quasi-contracts, compensation for damages, punitive awards, and judicial orders to do or not to do things. Examples of civil proceedings include divorce proceedings, probate of wills, breach of contract, tort litigation, and other *causes of action*.

There is an overlap between civil and criminal law. A person who has intentionally killed another can be charged in criminal court with homicide and can also be sued civilly for wrongful death. Civil contempt may result in jail time. A public nuisance is both a tort and a crime. The burden of proof is higher in criminal prosecutions (i.e., beyond a reasonable doubt) than in civil actions (i.e., preponderance of the evidence).

Civil Remedies

A legal maxim declares: "For every wrong, there is a remedy," meaning that those who suffered from bodily injury, harm to their property, damage to their reputation or dignity, or any other harm may go to court for redress. This embodies the notion of *equity*–fairness and justice. Before the late 19th century, plaintiffs would go to Courts of Equity (Chancery Courts) for remedies other than money awards or where there was no remedy at law, i.e., *restitution* or *unjust enrichment*. Aggrieved plaintiffs would have to come to court *with clean hands*, meaning they did not provoke or contribute to the injury. Today, courts of law and equity have merged, and judges have the power to award a full range of remedies:

- *COMPENSATORY DAMAGES* are monetary awards to compensate for the defendant's injury or loss through an economic value on the harm done. This award theoretically makes the person whole – it returns the person to the condition that existed before the injury. In breach of contract, the monetary awards are *expectation damages*, determined as the expected "benefit of the bargain."
- *SPECIAL DAMAGES* are for other non-compensatory but actual out-of-pocket expenses arising from the injury.
- *GENERAL DAMAGES* are for non-economic losses (e.g., pain and suffering, mental anguish, grief).
- *COURT COSTS and ATTORNEYS' FEES* may be ordered paid by the losing party to the winning party in certain circumstances, such as class action suits, civil rights violations, and copyright disputes.
- *PUNITIVE* or *EXEMPLARY DAMAGES* are sometimes awarded as punishment when the actions have been egregious, intentional, malicious, fraudulent, grossly negligent, or reckless.

- *NOMINAL DAMAGES* are token awards, often $1, made as a symbolic gesture in recognition that the plaintiff prevailed but did not sustain actual injury.
- *DECLATORY JUDGMENTS* are binding pronouncements of the court defining the legal relationship between the parties and their rights in the matter.
- *SPECIFIC PERFORMANCE* is a court order requiring a party to perform a specific act.
- *TEMPORARY INJUNCTIONS and TEMPORARY RESTRAINING ORDERS* are directives to cease an ongoing activity or prohibit the performance of a specific act that would cause immediate and irreparable harm until the court has a chance to hear the case and decide what it should do.
- *PERMANENT INJUNCTIONS* are court orders prohibiting a party from doing something.

Plaintiffs often pursue the parties with *deep pockets* – usually the institutions where people work rather than the people themselves. Financially insolvent defendants are *judgment-proof* because they have no money to pay out any monetary award. Multiple defendants are generally *jointly and severally liable* for the monetary award, meaning that all or part of the total award may be collected from any and each of the individual defendants. The *collateral source rule* prohibits the introduction of evidence of payment to the plaintiff from another source for the same injury, such as insurance. Many states have altered or partially abrogated this rule by statute to avoid windfall profits to plaintiffs and seeming unfairness to defendants. The *economic loss rule* provides that a party suffering only financial harm may recover damages based only upon a contractual claim and not on a tort theory. However, this rule has not been consistently applied.

Generally, plaintiffs will prevail in approximately half of the civil lawsuits litigated. Punitive damages are awarded in 5%–10% of the cases.

Vicarious Liability

Vicarious liability means that someone other than the tortfeasor may be held liable in court for the tortfeasor's actions. Through the doctrine of *respondeat superior* ("let the master answer"), employers may be held responsible for their employee's negligent or wrongful acts because they are acting under their supervision and control.

However, the employer is not liable for the negligence of its *independent contractors*, who work not as employees but under contract and without direct supervisory control. Vicarious liability may also arise from a "principal" and "agent" relationship. Similarly, parents may be held liable for injuries caused by their children.

Civil rights claims under §1983 of the Civil Rights Act can be brought against local governments, government officials, and their supervisors of *deliberate indifference* for a pattern of negligent hiring, negligent entrustment, failure to properly supervise or equip an employee, failure to discipline, or failure to train (*Monell v. Dept. of* Social Services, 1978; *City of Canton v. Harris*, 1989; *Samuels v. LeFevre*, 1998).

Statutes of Limitations and Statutes of Repose

Statutes of limitations define the time for plaintiffs to file a lawsuit. The period varies by state and type of claim from one to ten years, but most typically two or three years. The period generally commences at the time of injury or when the plaintiff discovers or should have discovered the injury. The statutory period may be extended (tolled) for special circumstances, for instance, waiting for the minor plaintiff (incapable of bringing suit) to reach the age of majority or for fraudulent concealment of the misdeed. Although often confused with statutes of limitations, *statutes of repose* are triggered by some event other than injury, exist to immunize defendants from long-term liability, and cannot be tolled. Statutes of repose commonly apply to probate, construction liability, and commercial product liability.

Torts

Torts, also known as *personal injury suits*, constitute a broad area of law. A tort (French for wrong, Latin for twisted or crooked) is a private civil wrong for wrongful act or omission that gives rise to a legal cause of action by an injured party, the plaintiff, against the alleged wrongdoer or tortfeasor, the defendant. Generally, the plaintiff sues the defendant for injury or harm caused by the defendant's careless (negligent) or intentional actions. In addition to physical injuries, lawsuits may allege emotional, economic, or reputational injuries and violations of privacy, property, or constitutional rights.

Modern torts are heavily affected by insurance and insurance law, as many, if not most, cases are settled through claims adjustment rather than by trial and are defended by insurance lawyers with insurance policies that limit possible payment.

Personal injury suits have proliferated and resulted in haphazard awards, with a few plaintiffs winning huge judgments and others nothing – seemingly akin to a lottery. Some would-be plaintiffs cannot even play due to the lack of a solvent defendant to sue. Furthermore, much of the monetary awards will go to the lawyers through litigation costs and contingency fees. This situation has resulted in a pushback beginning in the mid-20th century from legislatures that have sought tort reform, limiting the actions and awards that the courts can give out – although sometimes these laws have been struck down by courts on state constitutional grounds. Some states have replaced the tort system with no-fault programs for workers and motor vehicle drivers.

Tort law can be categorized as intentional torts, negligence, and strict liability. Tort law is governed by both statutory and caselaw. Most civil litigation is accomplished in state and local courts applying state law. The Federal Tort Claims Act of 1946 (28 U.S.C. §1346(b)) ("FTCA") governs suits against the federal government and its employees.

Tort Historical Background

In Anglo-Saxon law, wrongs were righted by compensatory payments to the person wronged or their clan. There was no clear distinction between crimes and other wrongs. When compensation was not possible, the wrongdoer was imprisoned or otherwise put to the mercy of the King. After the Norman Conquest, payments were made only to the courts or the King, which became a source of revenue. Eventually, the ability of victims to seek redress for their grievances came to be seen as an essential right of Englishmen. In the United States, several state constitutions expressly provided for redress for torts. However, tort law was not well developed until U.S. Supreme Court Justice Oliver Wendell Holmes, Jr., expounded on the topic in the 1880s and recognized that from the earliest English law, the basis of tort liability was a failure to exercise due care. Later, the American Law Institute's Restatement of Torts, first published in 1933 and now in its third edition, has been highly influential on tort law.

Intentional Torts

Intentional torts generally arise from willful injury against a person or property, but the technical definition is somewhat broader – non-accidental acts or omissions by a tortfeasor who knew or should have known would cause harm. The injured plaintiff must prove that the defendant committed an overt act or failure to act with the intent to cause harm and that the act or omission injured the plaintiff. The intent requirement is satisfied when the defendant intends to injure one individual but injure another through transferred intent. Causation can be satisfied if the defendant was a substantial factor in causing the harm.

Intentional torts can be subcategorized as *torts against the person* (e.g., assault, battery, false imprisonment, intentional infliction of emotional distress), *property torts* (e.g., trespass, nuisance, conversion), *dignitary torts* (e.g., defamation, invasion of privacy, breach of confidence, publicity/personality rights), and *economic/business torts* (e.g., fraud, tortious interference of contract, conspiracy, restraint of trade). Examples of intentional torts include:

- *ASSAULT* – an intentional attempt or credible threat to inflict injury on another person, which creates a reasonable apprehension of bodily harm or offensive contact in the victim.
- *BATTERY* – an unconsented offensive contact with a person. It differs from assault in that it requires actual contact. Harm or intent to harm is not required.
- *DEFAMATION* – intentional telling of harmful untruths about another – either published in print, through the media (libel), or orally (slander).
- *FALSE IMPRISONMENT* – intentional confinement of someone without legal authority, such as an unlawful arrest or detention of someone. It is a legal protection of freedom of movement.
- *FRAUD* – wrongful deception intended to result in financial or personal gain.
- *INTENTIONAL INFLICTION OF EMOTIONAL DISTRESS* – intentional conduct that results in extreme emotional distress.
- *WRONGFUL DEATH* – a claim by a spouse or close relative of the victim for their death and the resulting emotional distress, loss of consortium, and loss of support; the civil equivalent of a homicide case.

The *eggshell skull* doctrine holds that an individual is liable for all the consequences of their actions even if the victim suffers unusual damage due to a pre-existing vulnerability or medical condition. Thus, an assailant would be liable for the death of a person with an eggshell skull who is struck in the head only lightly and with no intent to kill. The wrongdoer takes the victim in the condition they find him and is responsible for all the consequences, whether they were foreseeable or not.

BOX 4.2 O.J. SIMPSON CASES

State of California v. Orenthal James Simpson: in 1994, O.J. Simpson's ex-wife, Nicole Brown Simpson, and her friend, Ronald Goldman, were stabbed to death outside her condominium in Los Angeles. O.J. Simpson was charged with first-degree murder with two counts of special circumstances. The penalty for first-degree murder in California is death, life without the possibility of parole, or a prison term of 25 years to life. The prosecution consisted of Los Angeles County Deputy District Attorneys, and the defense consisted of a "dream team" of defense attorneys. The trial began in January 1995, lasted eight months, and involved 150 witnesses. The prosecution had to prove guilt beyond a reasonable doubt. A jury found Simpson not guilty.

Rufo et al., v. Orenthal James Simpson: the victim's families sued for wrongful death. Law firms represented the parties; none of the lawyers involved in the criminal case was involved in the civil case. The civil trial, which began in October 1996, lasted four months and involved 120 witnesses. The plaintiffs had to prove their case by a preponderance of the evidence. A jury held Simpson responsible for the deaths, and the families were awarded \$8.5 million compensatory and \$25 million punitive damages.

COMMON DEFENSES TO INTENTIONAL TORTS: a successful defense may absolve the defendant from full or partial liability for damages. Many of these defenses depend upon the plaintiff's conduct. When the plaintiff does not come with "clean hands," affirmative defenses that the defendant must prove by a preponderance of the evidence may include:

- *ASSUMPTION OF RISK* – the plaintiff may have explicitly or implicitly consented to a risky activity or otherwise assumed the risk of injury by willingly putting himself in a position where harm might result. In other words, he knew or should have known the activity was risky and did it anyway. The plaintiff's assumption of risk is a complete bar to recovery (*volenti non fit injuria* – to a willing person, no injury is done). This is still the law in some states.
- *CONTRIBUTORY NEGLIGENCE* – the plaintiff was partially at fault. The defendant must show that the plaintiff engaged in unreasonable actions that contributed in some way to the injury. Since the full harm would not have happened without the plaintiff's conduct, it acts as a complete bar to recovery. This is the law in a few states.
- *COMPARATIVE NEGLIGENCE* – most states have some form of comparative negligence, in which the plaintiff's conduct is compared to the defendant's. In pure comparative negligence, the damage award is reduced by the percentage fault of the plaintiff. In the 50% modification, the plaintiff is barred if the plaintiff's negligence exceeds the defendant's. In the 49% rule, recovery is barred unless the plaintiff's negligence is less than the defendant's. In the slight-gross rule, recovery is barred if the plaintiff's negligence is more than slight.

Under the *last clear chance* doctrine, plaintiffs may overcome comparative and contributory negligence defenses if they can show that the defendant had the last clear opportunity to avoid the accident.

Negligence

Negligence involves harm or injury resulting from an unreasonably careless or unsafe act or omission by a tortfeasor, who is legally responsible and *liable* for that harm. The plaintiff files a civil complaint alleging harm from the failure to render reasonable care to the defendant, who is another person, business, corporation, or government agency. A grocery store may be held liable for the slip and fall of a customer on a wet floor. Medical and legal malpractice suits are professional negligence suits involving substandard care. The four elements that a plaintiff must prove to prevail in a negligence claim are:

1. *DUTY OWED:* the plaintiff must establish that a duty is owed to the plaintiff by the defendant. A relationship between the parties may give rise to a duty. A physician-patient relationship, an attorney-client relationship, or a shopkeeper-customer relationship may give rise to a duty. Through some relationships, one person owes another a duty of reasonable care.
2. *BREACH OF DUTY:* the plaintiff must prove that the defendant violated or breached the duty by failing to render the proper *standard of care* owed to the plaintiff – the care that a reasonably prudent person would exercise in like circumstances. The standard of care may be breached either by acts of commission or omission. Experts may testify to the usual and customary practices in the field as the standard of care. However, courts may recognize the practices of a substantial minority or a particular school of thought. Statutes and professional practice guidelines may define the standard of care. Specialists are held to a higher standard than general practitioners – to the standard of other specialists under similar circumstances.
3. *CAUSATION:* the plaintiff must prove a causal connection between the breach of the duty and the injury sustained by the plaintiff. Legal causation is not the same as immediate causation or scientific causation. Instead, it refers to causation for which liability will attach and requires both that it was a *cause in fact* (factual causation) and that it was the *proximate* cause (proximate causation). Factual causation exists if the event would not have occurred *but for* the act or omission of the tortfeasor. Factual causation is a question of fact often proved through expert testimony. Causation for cancer may be difficult to ascertain from a scientific standpoint, e.g., did asbestos exposure cause this cancer? However, it may be so obvious that negligence can be assumed under the doctrine of *res ipsa loquitur* ("the thing itself speaks"), e.g., a sponge left in a patient after abdominal surgery. Proximate causation ("legal causation") exists if the causal linkage is not so indirect or distant that the result may not create liability – usually based on whether

the result is reasonably *foreseeable*. Proximate causation is a question of law for the judge to decide.

4. *DAMAGES:* the plaintiff must prove a demonstrable injury for which the court may award damages. The injury may be physical, psychological, or financial.

BOX 4.3 *PALSGRAF V. LONG ISLAND RAILROAD CO.* (1928) – CAUSATION, FORESEEABILITY

Helen Palsgraf was purchasing a train ticket to the beach when two men ran to catch a train. One of the men tripped and nearly fell. While two railroad employees assisted him in boarding the train, a package containing fireworks he was holding fell on the tracks and exploded at some distance from Palsgraf. The explosion caused a large coin-operated set of scales to fall at the other end of the platform, which struck and injured Palsgraf. She successfully sued the railroad company for alleged negligence of its employees, but the defendant appealed the case to the New York Court of Appeals. Benjamin Cardozo, later a U.S. Supreme Court Justice, writing for the split Court, held that the railroad owed no duty of care to Palsgraf. Any negligence of the railroad employees assisting the man with a package was not a proximate cause of Palsgraf's injury because her injury could not reasonably be foreseen by their actions.

Strict Liability

Strict liability supports a personal injury lawsuit without a showing of intention or negligence. The concept was introduced in 1965 in the *Restatement of Torts, Second*, an influential treatise issued by the American Law Institute (ALI), which summarized and updated the general principles of Common Law tort law in the United States. It was applied to injuries from defective consumer products and abnormally dangerous activities in the landmark case of *Greenman v. Yuba Power Products*, Inc. (1963). Product liability is an area of tort law in which product manufacturers, distributors, and sellers are held responsible for the injuries caused by their products when they are found to be unreasonably unsafe due to a defective design, a manufacturing defect, or a failure to warn. Strict product liability strongly incentivizes manufacturers and merchants to sell safe products and makes it easier for consumers to recover from any injuries they suffer. The product must not have been altered, and the user, when injured, was making foreseeable use of the product. Ultra-hazardous activities are so dangerous that the person engaged in such an activity can be held strictly liable for injuries caused to another person, regardless of whether reasonable precautions were taken to prevent others from injury. Keeping dangerous animals is such an ultra-hazardous activity.

BOX 4.4 *GREENMAN V. YUBA POWER PRODUCTS, INC.* (1963) – STRICT PRODUCT LIABILITY

Greenman's wife bought him a Shopsmith, a combination power tool used as a saw, drill, and wood lathe for Christmas. Two years later, he bought an attachment to use the Shopsmith as a lathe. Greenman suffered severe injuries when a piece of wood suddenly flew out and struck him on the forehead while properly using the Shopsmith. Ten months later, he sued the manufacturer for claiming breaches of warranties, and the case was eventually appealed to the Supreme Court of California. An expert testified in the trial court that inadequate set screws were used and that there were other means to prevent the accident. The court held that no showing of negligence was necessary, but the manufacturer was strictly liable for product defects that caused consumer injuries. The court found that a defect in the design and manufacture of the machine rendered the Shopsmith unsafe for use. Greenman was unaware of the danger and used the machine as intended. The purpose of imposing strict liability on the manufacturer is to ensure that the manufacturers bear the costs of injuries resulting from defective products rather than the injured persons powerless to protect themselves. A manufacturer implicitly represents to the public that a product is safe when it places the product on the market.

Contracts

Contract law involves agreements or promises between parties, whether written or oral, which are enforceable by courts of law. Parol agreements are oral or written agreements not under seal, judicially recognized, or formally recorded by the county – a simple contract. Parties can be individuals, groups, corporations, associations, agencies, etc.

The four elements of a contract are (1) offer, (2) acceptance, (3) consideration, and (4) performance. A contract is formed with an offer and an acceptance, and it is completed with consideration and performance. These contractual agreements become legally binding and enforceable by law when both parties voluntarily agree (mutual assent) – a "meeting of the minds" of the specifics of the agreement – and the parties are found to be adults of sound mind (competency/capacity) and the contract is not against the law, unconscionable, or fraudulent (legality).

Generally, the contract is a transaction involving a reciprocal exchange of obligations. Consideration is the payment or promise to pay or the benefit or detriment that the promisor receives, which reasonably and fairly induces the promisee to make the promise/contract. Typically, it is a promise to give something for a promise to pay.

Contract law varies from state to state, although commercial transactions have been harmonized by adopting the Uniform Commercial Code (UCC), published by the Uniform Law Commission (ULC). The *Restatement of Contracts, second*, published by the ALI, is also a persuasive authority. A court may enforce the contract through specific performance (forcing a party to uphold its side of the bargain) or through monetary damages for breach of contract. However, the contract may declare that disputes will be resolved through arbitration rather than the courts.

Contract Historical Background

Contract law has ancient origins, and aspects of current contract law can be traced back to Roman law. In medieval England, a claim for payment of a contractual debt in the Common Pleas would require some "express quid pro quo" and would entail a *wager of law*, in which each side and their witnesses would attend court and swear oaths but would risk perjury if they lost. If the claimant could meet the 40-shilling threshold and allege some breach of the King's peace, he could bring the case to the Court of the King's Bench, where "assumpsit" actions (for obligations being assumed) were based simply on proof of the original agreement. The Common Law of contract developed around the action of *assumpsit* from the close of the 14th century and evolved over the subsequent centuries. In the 1500s, litigation sharply increased. Over the late 17th and 18th centuries, international commercial trade increasingly affected English contract law. It came to be dominated by the *Lex Mercatoria*, the laws of the merchants, based upon principles of commercial certainty, good faith, fair dealing, and the enforceability of seriously intended promises. In the late eighteenth and early 19th centuries, contractual theory transformed from an emphasis on the equitable justice or fairness of the exchange as the court saw it to an emphasis on the promissory agreement bargained by the parties.

Formation

A contract is formed when two or more parties agree to reciprocal promises, typically after a negotiation. The agreement must involve a *meeting of the minds* between the parties, in which both must understand the agreement and that understanding is the same. Mutual assent is found when the agreement has been ratified, usually through a process of *offer* and *acceptance*. The offeror may offer the offeree terms or options, which may be revoked at any time before a valid acceptance. The offeree may ratify the agreement through an expression of acceptance. The proffer by the offeree of different terms is a counteroffer. However, despite no offer and acceptance, a contract can be implied in fact.

Consideration

Consideration is something of value given by a *promissor* to a *promisee* in exchange for something of value given by a promisee to a promissor – a reciprocity of inducement to enter the bargain. Things of value can be money, acts, forbearances, or promises to pay or do something, but they cannot be done in the past or for love or altruism. Consideration must be sufficient, but courts do not weigh the adequacy of consideration as private parties will determine the value of things for themselves.

Formality

Contracts are not always necessarily formal documents written in legalese. Agreements may be made verbally or written on a napkin without a signature. However, the law requires that certain documents, such as real estate transactions, be reduced to a formal written document signed and dated.

- *STATUTE OF FRAUDS* – legislation that requires certain types of contracts to be formally reduced to writing to prevent fraud. The statute is a misnomer because it is not itself about fraud. Typically, contracts that need to be in writing and signed include real estate and guarantees that last over a year and cost more than $500.
- *PAROL EVIDENCE RULE* – a Common Law evidentiary rule that excludes the admission of *parol evidence* – previous negotiations to explain, modify, or supplement the written contract. Thus, under this rule, courts will look only to the text within the four corners of the document unless the contract incorporates another document by reference. The rule has been controversial among legal scholars. Today, most states no longer use the parol evidence rule and will instead allow testimony that bears on the contract.
- *PRIVITY OF CONTRACT* – a Common Law principle that allows parties to a contract to sue each other but prevents a third person from suing under it. As a rule, a contract cannot confer rights or impose obligations arising under it on any person except the parties. However, the requirement of privity has been somewhat relaxed under modern laws. Implied warranty and strict liability allow a third-party beneficiary or other foreseeable user to sue the seller of a defective product.
- *IMPLIED CONTRACT* – courts may infer a contract or contractual terms and conditions from the actions of the parties involved despite the absence of a written or verbal agreement – a *contract implied in fact*. An express contract is formed by the written or verbal words of the agreement, but an implied contract comes into existence as the result of actions – in keeping with the adage: "Actions speak louder

than words." *Quasi-contracts* or *contracts implied in law* are found where the equity of the situation demands a remedy (restitution, unjust enrichment). The reasonable fair market value of goods or services rendered, *quantum meruit*, is the usual measure of the damages for quasi-contracts, except where the plaintiff deserves restitution for relying on the defendant's promises.

Unconscionable Contracts

Unconscionable contracts are so one-sided and unfair to one party that they are unenforceable under the law. One party has no real, meaningful choice because of the unequal bargaining power of the other party. Standard form contracts with boilerplate in fine print, where one can only take it or leave it, are often found to be unenforceable *contracts of adhesion* (*leonine contracts*). Contracts are also unconscionable where there is a finding of undue influence, duress, or unfair surprise under situations involving pressure, lack of information, or misleading information. Releases, waivers, exculpatory clauses, and limiting warranties, which purport to release or limit liability for injuries and damages, are routinely struck down by courts. If the court finds a contract to be unconscionable, the court will declare the contract to be void and will award no damages or specific performance but instead will release the parties from their contractual obligations.

Commercial Contracts

Contracts made in a commercial context are regulated. Every state has enacted the UCC to provide uniform and seamless continuity of trade and commerce across borders. Certain areas of commerce, such as real estate and food, are highly regulated by federal and state laws.

- *UNIFORM COMMERCIAL CODE (UCC)* – the ULC was formed in 1892 to create uniform commercial laws to be enacted by each state. Federal legislation had yet to play a significant role. The ULC sought to harmonize the laws of sales and other commercial transactions across the United States. Several uniform acts that dealt with specific aspects of commerce in the early 1900s were promulgated. In 1940, the ULC began drafting a comprehensive code for all commercial transactions of the complex American economy, and in 1942, the ALI joined the effort. The UCC was first published in 1952 and was adopted, with some variation, in all 50 states and most territories over the subsequent two decades. Statutory interpretation by different states has contributed to variation, but by and large, commerce flows freely across state boundaries, with businesses generally not having to worry about various commercial laws in different jurisdictions.

Consumer Contracts

Consumer contracts are made between a merchant seller and a consumer, where the merchant is the final seller of a finished product, and the consumer is the user. In addition to the UCC, the Consumer Protection Act and the Federal Trade Commission (FTC) regulate such sales to prevent fraud and abuse, protect consumers, and ensure fair trade, competition, and accurate information in the marketplace. In general, written consumer contracts must be readable and understandable, often in specified font size and with itemized prices. However, no written agreement is required when goods have been received and accepted, payment has been made and accepted, or goods are specially manufactured for the consumer. Although parties are generally free to agree upon any contract terms as they deem appropriate, consumer laws often prohibit terms or provisions that are unfair to the consumer or may potentially be abused by the seller. Consumer laws prohibit *price gouging*, where a merchant might take advantage of market conditions to charge unconscionably excessive prices. Consumer laws might also prohibit or restrict the use of *acceleration clauses* requiring the purchaser to pay the remaining installment payments in the event of a default.

Most states have a Department of Consumer Affairs devoted to regulating certain industries to protect consumers who use goods and services from those industries. Many states have adopted the Uniform Deceptive Trade Practices Act, prohibiting unfair or fraudulent business practices and untrue or misleading advertising. State and federal laws also protect consumers from improper debt collection.

- *FEDERAL TRADE COMMISSION ACT (FTC Act)* – was enacted in 1914 to create the FTC, which enforces antitrust statutes and promotes consumer protection by prohibiting deceptive trade practices. The FTC's Bureau of Consumer Protection investigates consumer complaints of violating consumer protection statutes and deceptive trade practices.
- *CONSUMER PRODUCT SAFETY ACT (CPSA)* – was enacted in 1972 to establish the Consumer Product Safety Commission (CPSC) to develop safety standards, pursue recalls, or ban products that present unreasonable or substantial risks of injury or death to consumers. The CPSA excludes from jurisdiction those products that expressly lie in another federal agency's jurisdiction, i.e., food, drugs, medical devices, firearms, and motor vehicles.
- *FAIR DEBT COLLECTION PRACTICES ACT (FDCPA)* – was enacted in 1977 to protect personal, family, and household debts, but not business debts or individual debts incurred for business purposes, from third-party debt collectors using mail or other means of interstate commerce to directly or indirectly attempt to collect a debt.

The FDCPA provides a 30-day period during which the consumer may dispute the validity of the debt and request verification. Despite consumer protections, the principle of caveat emptor (buyer beware) is still important.

Rescission

Contracts are meant to bind parties to an agreement, and courts will generally look to uphold them, but there are times when contracts are canceled (*rescinded*). Many contracts contain cancellation periods and contingency-based *escape clauses.* Courts may cancel a contract if they find the agreement was based on fraudulent or mistaken information or that the deal was made under duress or undue influence. Contracts involving agreements for illegal activities will be void. Regulations govern the rescission of contracts in many instances.

Federal and state consumer protection laws allow consumers to cancel certain contracts or sales of goods without giving a reason. The FTC gives consumers a three-day *cooling-off period* to cancel certain sales for a full refund if the sale occurs somewhere other than the seller's usual place of business (door-to-door, trade shows, etc.), except for sales made by telephone, mail, or the internet. Other federal laws provide cooling-off periods for borrowers refinancing a mortgage or taking out a home equity loan.

Violations of Civil Rights

Civil (and criminal) lawsuits can be brought for violations of constitutional laws. Federal civil rights laws are discussed here, but most states have similar laws.

- *SECTION §1983 CIVIL RIGHTS* – in 1866, Congress passed the Civil Rights Act, the "Ku Klux Klan Act," making it a crime to violate the guaranteed rights of citizens (18 U.S.C §242), which they intended to be used against the Ku Klux Klan. In 1871, Congress added civil remedies (42 U.S.C. §1983). During this time, the "Radical Republicans" also passed the three Civil War amendments and a habeas corpus statute that gave prisoners incarcerated in state prisons the ability to challenge their incarcerations in federal court. §1983 reads:

  > Every person who, under color of any statute … subjects, or causes to be subjected, any citizen of the United States or other person within the jurisdiction thereof to the deprivation of any rights, privileges, or immunities secured by the Constitution and laws,

> shall be liable to the party injured in an action at law, suit in equity, or other proper proceeding for redress, ...

In the 1961 case of *Monroe v. Pape*, the Court held that §1983 provides a civil remedy for constitutional violations by state or local governmental officials in carrying out their official responsibilities – "under color of law." It is a procedural conduit for civil lawsuits against individuals, not agencies or institutions, for violations of constitutional rights or federal law, not state law or city ordinances. The right infringed must be clearly established. Tortious actions, not mere negligence, are liable under §1983. State statutes of limitations apply, generally three years.

[42 U.S.C. §1985 is the civil conspiracy version where two or more government agents conspire to deprive the defendant(s) of his/her (their) civil rights.]

[18 U.S.C. §242 is the analogous criminal provision for willfully violating federal civil rights, but it requires proof beyond a reasonable doubt and the defendant's specific intent to do something the law forbids.]

- *BIVENS CLAIMS* – in *Bivens v. Six Unknown Named Agents* (1961), the Court created a cause of action, independent of the FTCA, for an individual whose Fourth Amendment protection against unreasonable search and seizures. *Bivens* claims were extended to inadequate prison care (*Carlson v. Green*, 1980) and federal employment sex discrimination (*Davis v. Passman*, 1979) but are unlikely to be applied to new contexts dissimilar to the excessive force facts in *Bivens* (*Egbert v. Boule*, 2022).
- *CIVIL RIGHTS OF INSTITUTIONALIZED PERSONS ACT (CRIPA)* – the 1980 CRIPA protects persons in institutions, such as nursing homes, correctional facilities, and mental health facilities, from unconstitutional conditions.
- *AMERICANS WITH DISABILITIES ACT (ADA)* – the 1990 ADA prohibits discrimination based on disability in public places and requires employers to make reasonable accommodations for disabilities.
- *VIOLENT CRIME CONTROL AND LAW ENFORCEMENT ACT* (VCCLEA) – this 1994 Crime Bill, passed partly based on the Rodney King incident, grants the Department of Justice (DOJ) broad investigative powers and prosecutorial authority for cases of alleged use of excessive force. The DOJ uses this power to investigate, prosecute, and enter consent decrees with local police agencies that manifest a pattern or practice of police abuse.

Governmental Immunity

Sovereign immunity: *sovereign immunity*, recognized in Roman law and English Common Law, is a bar to lawsuits rooted in the medieval notion that "the King can do no wrong" that applies to American state and federal governments that have not given their consent to be sued. Consent would typically take the form of a statute and not simply because an official or an attorney representing the state decided to litigate the merits of a suit.

The 11th Amendment of the U.S. Constitution: the *Eleventh Amendment* is a constitutional embodiment of state sovereign immunity, promulgated after a citizen of South Carolina sued Georgia for unpaid debts from the American Revolutionary War. It withdraws jurisdiction from lawsuits against states by citizens of other states or foreign citizens and federal lawsuits in state courts unless the state consents. In *Hans v. Louisiana* (1890), immunity was extended to states for lawsuits by their own citizens. The Eleventh Amendment grants immunity to states but not state or local agencies unless they are acting as an arm of the state (*Lake County Estates v. Tahoe Regional Planning Agency*, 1979). In *Ex parte Young* (1908), the Court held that the Eleventh Amendment does not preclude suit against a state official unless such is the equivalent of a suit against the state; in that case, the Court ruled that federal courts may enjoin state officials from violating federal law. In *Fitzpatrick v. Bitzer* (1976), the Court stated, "the Eleventh Amendment and the principle of state sovereignty which it embodies ... are necessarily limited, by the enforcement provisions of §5 of the Fourteenth Amendment," but congressional intent to subject states to suit must be clearly stated. In *Alden v. Maine* (1999), the Court held that, although the Fair Labor Standards Act of 1938 purports to authorize private actions against States in their own courts, Congress lacks power under Article I to abrogate the States' sovereign immunity in federal court.

The 1946 Federal Tort Claims Act and the 1887 Tucker Act: *the Federal Tort Claims Act* (FTCA) is a partial waiver of sovereign immunity for tortious acts of federal employees, and the *Tucker Act*, is a waiver of immunity for breaches of federal government contracts and federal payments. The FTCA makes the federal government a self-insurer, paying for the negligent or wrongful acts or omissions of its employees acting within the scope of their official duties. The federal government becomes the defendant, replacing the employee, and bears the liability for its employee's actions. Discretionary acts of federal employees are specifically shielded as an exception to the FTCA. The FTCA has a two-year statute of limitations for filing a tort claim. The Feres doctrine is a specific exemption from the FTCA that bars military service members injured while on active duty from successfully suing the federal government. However, the *National Defense Authorization Act for Fiscal Year 2020* (NDAA) created a limited exception for medical malpractice. Most states have similar tort claims acts that waive sovereign and Eleventh Amendment immunity. The *Tucker Act* was passed in 1887 to grant jurisdiction to the Federal Claims Court (and District Courts for cases involving ≤$10,000) and waive sovereign immunity for monetary damages for contractual claims and non-contractual claims for money owed to the claimant by the federal government.

Absolute immunity: *absolute immunity* applies to cases where a challenge would impact government operations. Generally, the higher the official's level, the higher the immunity. Absolute immunity applies to judges, legislators, prosecutors, and members of parole boards when acting in their judicial capacity. The immunity applies to damages and not equitable relief; e.g., judges may be sued for injunctive or declaratory relief. The rationale given is that public officials have a duty to the public to make complex decisions, and it would be unfair to hold them to perfection; the threat of liability would discourage decision-making, discourage individuals from seeking office, and defending lawsuits would drain their time, energy, and money rather than allowing them to do their job.

Qualified immunity: *qualified immunity* bars recovery of damages against government workers for performing their discretionary duties within their scope of employment, in good faith, and not willfully illegally. Discretionary acts, as opposed to ministerial acts, require deliberation or judgment. Such workers should not have to look over their shoulders, worrying that someone will sue them for their decisions. It protects those "who make reasonable but mistaken judgments about open legal questions" (*Ashcroft v. al-Kidd, 2011*) and protects "all but the plainly incompetent or those who knowingly violate the law" (*Malley v. Briggs*, 1986). As government workers, forensic scientists are usually shielded by qualified immunity for acts done in the ordinary course of their duties.

Qualified immunity is constitutional immunity from civil rights claims under §1983, and *Bivens* claims. In *Harlow v. Fitzgerald* (1982), the Court declared that qualified immunity protects government officials "from liability for civil damages insofar as their conduct does not violate clearly established statutory or constitutional rights of which a reasonable person would have known." In other words, a police officer will be shielded from liability where the law is unclear, and she acted in good faith, defined by policies, procedures, training, and experiences as adjudged by the totality of the circumstances. In *Saucier v. Katz* (2001), the Court recognized two distinct queries: whether the official violated the plaintiff's constitutional rights and whether those rights were "clearly established" at the time of the incident. In *Pearson v. Callahan* (2009), the Court indicated that these were questions for lower courts to make. To find the law to be "clearly established," the courts must look to prior cases of a similar fact pattern. However, this requirement is a practical barrier that often shields egregious police behavior, and accordingly, qualified immunity has become highly criticized.

The 1976 Foreign Sovereign Immunities Act: *the Foreign Sovereign Immunities Act* grants foreign governments immunity from lawsuits except about certain actions relating to commercial activity in the United States and the 1978 Diplomatic Relations Act grants immunity to diplomats in compliance with 1961 Vienna Convention on Diplomatic Relations (effective in 1972).

Presidential Immunity: *presidential immunity* was recognized in *Trump v. U.S.* (2024). As head of the executive branch of the U.S. federal government, presidents have absolute immunity for acts within their core constitutional authority, presumptive immunity in other official acts, and no immunity for unofficial acts.

BOX 4.5 *ALMECIGA V. CENTER FOR INVESTIGATIVE REPORTING, INC.* (2015)

Forensic Science in Civil Court

Erica Almeciga sued the *Center for Investigative Reporting, Inc. (CIR. Inc.)* for breach of contract. She alleged that her life was threatened by the Los Zetas gang when she appeared in the 2013 YouTube documentary, *I was a Hitman for Miguel Treviño*. She claimed that CIR, Inc. did not have her consent to publish her interview, but CIR, Inc. produced the release form with her signature. Almeciga then claimed that CIR, Inc. had forged her signature and brought in a handwriting expert to testify that it was not her signature, based upon exemplars of Almeciga's handwriting produced for the litigation. The defendants found other exemplars of hers that did not look like the signatures produced for the court and on which her expert had based her opinion. A *Daubert* hearing [discussed later] was held on the admissibility of testimony from the handwriting expert. New York Federal Judge Jed Rakoff ruled the testimony inadmissible because such expertise was unreliable. He wrote:

> It is hardly surprising that Carlson's expert report reads more like a series of subjective observations than a scientific analysis. ... For decades, the forensic document examiner community has essentially said to courts, 'Trust us.' And many courts have. But that does not make what the examiners do science.

Judge Rakoff declared that Almeciga had perpetrated fraud on the court when she denied the signature, generated altered signature exemplars, and fabricated allegations. He then dismissed the lawsuit.

Summary

Plaintiffs bring civil lawsuits against other parties for wrongdoing and sometimes to prevent injury. Most civil actions are for torts (personal injury) or breach of contract. The remedy for most civil actions is financial compensation for damages, but specific performance, injunctions, and restraining orders are judicial orders compelling someone to do or not do something. Someone can be held liable for the acts of another (*vicarious liability*) when a special relationship exists, such as an employer-employee relationship. Civil actions must be brought within a specific time set by a statute of limitations unless the statute is tolled in the case for some reason.

Torts are brought based on intentional acts, negligence, or strict liability. Negligence cases involve a duty owed, a breach of the duty, a causal connection, and damages. Strict liability involves injury from a commercial product without a need to show any intention or negligence.

Contracts involve an offer, acceptance, consideration, and performance. Contracts may be oral, in writing, and sometimes implied. An action for breach of contract may be brought for a failure to pay or to perform. Consumers have statutory protections.

The government has special defenses against lawsuits brought against it and its employees and agents; in particular, qualified immunity grants police broad protection except for excessive force.

Terms

Contracts – legally recognized agreements involving reciprocal promises.

Damages – injuries for which a defendant is liable.

Intentional Torts – non-accidental harm caused by a tortfeasor.

Joint and Several Liability – liability of any and all tortfeasors for tortious conduct.

Negligence – accidental harm caused by a tortfeasor.

Qualified Immunity – bars suits against government officials acting in their official capacity in good faith.

Remedies – judicially ordered relief, e.g., restitution, specific performance, injunction.

Rescission – cancellation of a contract.

Respondeat Superior – the doctrine of vicarious liability of the supervisor for the employee.

Sovereign Immunity – traditional immunity for government actions.

Statute of Limitations – statutorily defined period within which someone can be sued or prosecuted for a crime.

Strict Liability – legal imposition of responsibility without regard to fault.

Tortfeasor – a person, group, or entity that commits a tort, a wrongdoer.

Torts – personal injury suits.
Unconscionable Contracts – contracts that are so unfair as to be unenforceable.
Vicarious Liability – imputed liability from the actions of others.

Cases

Alden v. Maine, 527 U.S. 706 (1999)
Almeciga v. Center for Investigative Reporting, Inc., 121 F. Supp. 3d 379 (S.D.N.Y. 2015)
Ashcroft v. al-Kidd, 563 U.S. 731 (2011)
Bivens v. Six Unknown Federal Agents, 403 U.S. 388 (1971)
Carlson v. Green, 446 U.S. 14 (1980)
City of Canton v. Harris, 489 U.S. 378 (1989)
Davis v. Passman, 442 U.S. 228 (1979)
Egbert v. Boule, 596 U.S. 482 (2022)
Ex parte Young, 209 U.S. 123 (1908)
Fitzpatrick v. Bitzer, 427 U.S. 445 (1976)
Greenman v. Yuba Power Products, Inc., 377 P.2d 897 (1963)
Hans v. Louisiana, 134 U.S. 1 (1890)
Harlow v. Fitzgerald, 457 U.S. 800 (1982)
Lake County Estates v. Tahoe Regional Planning Agency, 440 U.S. 391 (1979)
Malley v. Briggs, 475 U.S. 335 (1986)
Monell v. Dept. of Social Services, 436 U.S. 658 (1978)
Monroe v. Pape, 365 U.S. 167 (1961)
Palsgraf v. Long Island Railroad Co., 162 N.E. 99 (1928)
Pearson v. Callahan, 555 U.S. 223 (2009)
Samuels v. LeFevre, 885 F. Supp. 32 (N.D.N.Y, 1998)
Saucier v. Katz, 533 U.S. 194 (2001)
Trump v. United States, 603 U.S. ___ (2024)

Statutes

Americans with Disabilities Act (ADA), 42 U.S.C. §12101, et seq. (1990)
Civil Action for Deprivation of Rights, 42 U.S.C. §1983 (1979)
Civil Rights of Institutionalized Persons Act (CRIPA), 42 U.S.C. §**§1997–1997j** (1980)
Consumer Product Safety Act (CPSA), 15 U.S.C. §§2051–2089 (1972)
Deprivation of Rights under Color of Law, 18 U.S.C. §242 (1996)
Diplomatic Relations Act, 22 U.S.C. §254 (1978)
Fair Debt Collection Practices Act (FDCPA), 15 U.S.C. §§1692–1692p (1977)
Federal Tort Claims Act (FTCA), 28 U.S.C. **§1346(b) and** §§2671–2680 (1946)
Federal Trade Commission Act (FTC Act), 15 U.S.C. §§41–58 (1914)

Foreign Sovereign Immunities Act (FSIA), 28 U.S.C. §§1330, 1332, 1391(f), 1441(d), and 1602–1611 (1976)
Tucker Act, 28 U.S.C. §§1346(a) and 1491 (1887)
Violent Crime Control and Law Enforcement Act, Police Pattern or Practice, 34 U.S.C. §12601 (1994)

Thought Questions

1. Should wrongful death lawsuits be allowed after criminal prosecutions for homicide?
2. How does the concept of fault fit into intentional torts, negligence, and strict liability?
3. How are forensic scientists involved as experts in civil lawsuits?

Further Reading

Abraham KS, *The Forms and Functions of Tort Law*, Foundation Press, St. Paul, MN, 2017.
Chirelstein MA, *Concepts and Case Analysis in the Law of Contracts*, 7th ed, Foundation Press, St. Paul, MN, 2013.
Ross DL, *Civil Liability in Criminal Justice*, 8th ed, Routledge, New York, 2023.

Chapter 5

Crimes and Defenses

Learning Objectives

After reading this chapter, students are expected to be able to:

- list the categories of crime
- explain inchoate crimes
- explain the elements of crimes
- define general and specific intent
- recognize the categories of homicide
- discuss rape and sex offenses
- describe property crimes
- list the affirmative defenses.

Introduction

Crimes are forbidden conduct or absence of required conduct punishable by the state. Criminal justice is based upon the fair administration of the rules of our ordered society embodied in criminal codes and enforced by law enforcement, the judicial system, and the correctional system.

 DOI: 10.4324/9780429272455-5

Historical Background

Originally, an aggrieved individual or group would seek redress in court. Over time, private vengeance gave way to state prosecutions by the state in the name of the victim, and criminal law separated from civil tort law.

Crimes were defined in Anglo-American law in the Common Law. Over the centuries, Common Law criminal law evolved into robust legal jurisprudence, that remains highly influential.

A *criminal code* or *penal code* (from the French Penal Code of 1791) is an aggregation of disparate criminal laws of a particular jurisdiction. The codification process enables the imposition of a comprehensive, systematic, consistent, and rational approach. Criminal codes are thought to be more accessible to laypersons. However, critics argue they are too rigid and inflexible in particular cases and should change over time. Generally, codification of law is the rule in Civil Law jurisdictions but uncommon in Common Law jurisdictions. England has not adopted a criminal code.

In the United States, a reform effort to codify criminal law swept the country in the late 19th and early 20th centuries. California passed the first penal code in the United States in 1872. All crimes are now defined by statute. The 1962 American Law Institute's (ALI's) Model Penal Code (MPC) is not itself a law but guidance to reform criminal law into a more organized and coherent system, which was highly influential to the development of modern penal codes. Title 18 of the United States Code (U.S.C.) is the criminal code for the U.S. federal government. In *U.S. v. Hudson and Goodwin* (1812), the U.S. Supreme Court held that Common Law offenses could not be enforced in federal courts. However, states vary in their consideration of Common Law crimes, with some having abolished them while others have chosen to continue to recognize the crimes or the elements of the crimes.

The promulgation of criminal laws in all jurisdictions of the United States means that legislators, rather than judges, now make criminal law in the United States. This shift has resulted in broader and more severe criminal laws. Judicial review of such laws may result in them being struck down if found to be void for vagueness, *ex post facto* (laws passed after the fact), a bill of attainder (law passed to punish someone), against public policy, containing cruel and unusual punishment, or in violation of the constitutional rights of due process, equal protection, or the right of privacy.

Criminal Law Philosophy

Conduct or behavior, not thoughts, beliefs, or status, is criminalized. Conduct is criminalized because the act is:

- *MALUM IN SE* – evil in itself; moral turpitude, e.g., lying, stealing, cheating, or

- *MALUM PROHIBITUM* – evil only because it is prohibited by law; wrong because we say so.

  Scholars have determined that the purposes of criminal punishment are:

  1. DETERRENCE of the perpetrator and others from committing future crimes,
  2. INCAPACITATION of the perpetrator by taking away their liberty to continue to commit other crimes,
  3. RETRIBUTION for the crime by victims, their families, and society generally, and
  4. REHABILITATION of the perpetrator such that they will not continue to perpetrate crimes.

Immanuel Kant espouses a retributive view when he declares that a criminal should be punished if the perpetrator were the last person on earth as a matter of his categorical imperative. Meanwhile, Jeremy Bentham and John Stuart Mill, espousing a utilitarian view, would say that such punishment would not serve societal purposes. Should taxpayer dollars be expended to prosecute you for jaywalking when no cars were on the road?

The primary purpose of the U.S. criminal justice system is deterrence. Victim rights advocacy has increasingly emphasized retributive justice. Sentences have become harsher, and today, the United States has the largest incarcerated population of 2.2 million in state and federal prisons, a 500% increase over the past 40 years. Authorities had largely given up on attempting to rehabilitate convicts in the 1970s, despite the continued use of the term *correctional facilities*, but there is a renewed interest in rehabilitation. Norway has a rehabilitation program that has cut its recidivism rate from 70% to 30% and is the basis for the California model in the United States. The 2007 Second Chance and the 2018 First Step Acts have reduced sentences and funded programs to facilitate inmate re-entry into society.

Restorative justice emphasizes repairing the harm done to victims by allowing victims to participate in the process and offering offenders an opportunity to redeem themselves. Restorative justice programs complement traditional methods, such as retributive justice.

Classification and Criminal Statistics

Traditionally, crimes were categorized by level of punishment:

- CAPITAL OFFENSE – homicide, treason, and others punishable by death or life imprisonment without the possibility of parole.

- FELONY – a major crime potentially punishable by imprisonment for one year or more.
- MISDEMEANOR – a minor crime potentially punishable by jail or prison time of less than one year.
- INFRACTION – petty offenses punishable by fines but no jail time.

Punishment should be proportional to the crime and the criminal's culpability and heinousness. However, this categorization is jurisdiction-dependent, and modern penal codes vary somewhat.

Crimes are often categorized as:

- CRIMES AGAINST PERSONS – offenses whose victims are always individuals, e.g., murder, rape, robbery, and assault.
- CRIMES AGAINST PROPERTY – offenses that aim to obtain money, property, or other benefits. e.g., theft, bribery, and burglary.
- CRIMES AGAINST SOCIETY – offenses against certain types of activities that are prohibited by society, e.g., animal cruelty, drug violations, gambling, and prostitution.

This simplistic categorization is useful. However, there is much overlap among the categories. For instance, robbery is both a property crime and a crime against persons. Crimes against persons are often called violent crimes, and crimes against society are often called victimless crimes.

Statistical categorizations tend to be simpler and partial. Data is aggregated across jurisdictions that have differing definitions and requirements for conviction. Many crimes are not prosecuted or fully prosecuted, so crime statistics will vary if tallied by police reports, arrests, or convictions. Further, some crimes, such as sexual assaults, are multiple times higher when based on population surveys rather than law enforcement reporting because so many such crimes go unreported. Multiple crimes occurring in a single incident also complicates the statistics.

The FBI's Crime Data Explorer (CDE) is based upon the law enforcement community's voluntary reporting and publishes annual estimates of major crimes:

TABLE 5.1 Crime Rates, 2022

Violent Crimes	1.2M	Property Crimes	6.5M
Homicide	21,156	Burglary	899,293
Rape	133,294	Larceny-theft	4,672,363
Robbery	220,450	Motor vehicle theft	942,173
Aggravated assault	893,908		

Elements of a Crime

The *elements of a crime* are the facts that must each be proved with evidence beyond a reasonable doubt to convict a defendant of a crime. The *actus reus* is the unlawful act, omission, or possession of the crime, and the *mens rea* is the criminal intent of the crime. The act and intent must occur simultaneously (concurrence) for a crime to have been committed. Causation of harm is an element in some crimes, particularly homicides.

Actus Reus: the *actus reus* is the forbidden conduct or wrongful act of the crime. Behavior can be criminalized, but not mere thoughts or status. Justice Stewart wrote in *Robinson v. California* (1962), in holding that it is unconstitutional to impose punishment for having a disease, that even "one day in prison for the 'crime' of having a common cold" would be cruel and unusual, but in *Powell v. Texas* (1968) criminalizing public drunkenness did not violate the Eighth Amendment's cruel and unusual prohibition. A person with epilepsy cannot be held criminally liable for injuries that result from a seizure because there is no willful act. The act committed must be voluntary. The act can be mere verbalized speech. The act can be an omission where there is a legal duty to act (i.e., child neglect). A legal duty can arise by statute, contract, voluntary assumption, or relationship (i.e., parent). Actual or constructive possession where it is conscious possession (i.e., drugs, stolen property) is sufficient to be a culpable act. The act may be imputed to the defendant through the actions of others based upon the legal doctrine of vicarious liability (i.e., aiding and abetting, conspiracy).

Mens Rea: *mens rea* is also known as *evil intent*, *guilty mind*, *vicious will*, or *moral culpability*. When people act, the law presumes that they are acting rationally, but clearly, people do not always behave or act rationally. People sometimes act emotionally, impulsively, stupidly, or impaired by drugs, mental illness, or mental incapacity. Sometimes, people seem to act irrationally when they act on incomplete or incorrect information or otherwise do not know better. Some psychologists have even declared that humans are predictably irrational due to hidden forces that shape our decisions. This notion that an actor must have a criminal intent is at the heart of the Common Law requirement of *mens rea*. Regardless, there is a tension between unfairness in criminally punishing the individual versus allowing criminal behavior to go unpunished and sending the wrong message to others in society. This is particularly evident in discussions of the insanity defense.

The ALI MPC has been particularly influential on the development of *mens rea* when it introduced its notion of the modes of culpability based on mental state:

- PURPOSEFULLY – the actor intends (has the "conscious object") the prohibited conduct and the harm caused.
- KNOWINGLY – the actor knows that his conduct is prohibited and will likely cause harm.

- RECKLESSLY – the actor performs prohibited conduct in conscious disregard of a "substantial and unjustifiable risk" of harm.
- NEGLIGENTLY – the actor performs conduct unaware of a "substantial and unjustifiable risk" of harm but should have been aware because a "reasonable person" would recognize the risk of harm.
- STRICT LIABILITY – the actor performs conduct that violates the law, and his mental state is irrelevant.

The intent required of *mens rea* may be a *general intent* or, additionally, a *specific intent.*

General Intent: general intent is the intent to commit the forbidden act. A general intent to commit the act is generally presumed when a law does not specify an intent. A defense of a mistake of fact to rebut a general intent must be an honest and reasonable belief.

Specific Intent: specific intent is the intent to produce a particular harmful result. For example, a general intent might be found when a person pulls a trigger, but specific intent might be found when that person intended to kill someone – it is much easier to prove the former than the latter. The act's performance often presumes a general intent. Specific intent crimes include theft, bribery, forgery, arson, and robbery. A defense of a mistake of fact to rebut a specific intent need only be an honest belief – it need not be reasonable. Mental incompetence or intoxication may be a defense to specific intent.

BOX 5.1 INTENT

Alex takes a coat from the coat rack of a hotel:

- Theft, if Alex had the intent to take and keep the coat that he knew was not his
- Mistake of fact/claim of right if Alex thought it was his coat
- Mistake of fact/claim of right if Alex thought the coat was abandoned
- Unauthorized use if Alex did not intend to deprive the owner of it permanently

Exceptions to a *mens rea* requirement:

- VICARIOUS LIABILITY: the actions and intentions of others are imputed to another, even where there is no intention by the defendant to commit a criminal act. In general, vicarious liability does not apply in criminal law due to the mens rea element. However, accomplices (accessories, conspirators, principals in the second degree, those aiding and abetting) who act in concert with others to perpetrate a crime are held to be equally responsible for the crime and the consequences of the crime, even if they had no intention of causing the harm. Thus, all train robbers acting together are responsible for blowing up a bridge, even though only one did. "Accessories after the fact," persons who knowingly comfort or assist criminal perpetrators, could also be convicted of the crime at Common Law but are now generally charged with a lesser crime than the principal.

- STRICT LIABILITY: statutory crimes are defined as behavior proscribed by statute without regard to intent (although general intent may be inferred), often for regulatory or public welfare purposes, e.g., traffic violations, statutory rape, open container laws.
- ENTERPRISE LIABILITY: corporations are not allowed to argue they did not have a culpable intent and are not responsible for their agents.

Causation: proof that the criminal act caused the harm is the element known as *causation*. Causation is not an element of most crimes, but it applies to criminal homicides, mainly because, unlike other crimes that prohibit conduct, homicide is a prohibition of a result. Legal causation is not the same as scientific causation. Legal causation involves both *cause in-fact*, the "but for" test, and a legal nexus, the proximate cause, the foreseeability test.

BOX 5.2 *ROBERTSON V. COMMONWEALTH* (KY 2002) – HOMICIDE CAUSATION

Officer Kane attempted to arrest Robertson for possession of marijuana. Robertson broke free and fled onto a bridge spanning the Ohio River. Officer Partin drove his vehicle onto the bridge and exited to pursue Robertson, who jumped over a concrete barrier onto a pedestrian walkway. Partin attempted to follow him but fell into the space between the barrier and the walkway to his death. The conviction for Manslaughter was affirmed.

BOX 5.3 *BURRAGE V. UNITED STATES* (2014) – HOMICIDE CAUSATION

Banka died of a combined heroin, oxycodone, and benzodiazepine overdose. Charges were brought against the heroin dealer using the statutory enhanced penalty for the death "resulting from" heroin. The forensic toxicologist and the forensic pathologist stated the death was due to a mixed drug intoxication with all the drugs contributing, but they could not say if Banka would have lived without the heroin. The Court held that the facts did not satisfy the "but for" test, and thus, the heroin was not an independently sufficient cause of the victim's death.

Corpus Delicti: *corpus delicti* is the "body of the crime," which refers to the material substance of a crime that constitutes the foundation of that crime. It is the evidence needed as corroborating evidence that the crime occurred. It could be the remains of a house in the case of arson. In criminal homicide cases, it constitutes more than just the body of the victim. Thus, at least theoretically, even if the accused confesses to a murder without the body or other evidence of the death of the person, the confession is not sufficient for a conviction.

Lesser Included Offenses: a *lesser included offense* is a crime for which all elements are also found in a more serious crime. For example, robbery requires all the same elements as larceny but also force or intimidation to accomplish the taking; therefore, larceny is a lesser included offense in the offense of robbery. Other examples include assault as a lesser included offense of sexual assault, drug possession as a lesser included offense of drug possession with intent to distribute, and manslaughter as a lesser included offense of murder. However, an offense will not be a lesser included offense if it carries a maximum penalty greater than that of the charged offense.

Under the *merger doctrine*, lesser offenses are generally included in the greater offense. Therefore, a person who commits a robbery cannot be convicted of both the robbery and the theft that was part of it because there is only one element between the offenses that differs, i.e., the threat or infliction of harm. Solicitation to commit a crime and attempt to commit a crime, although not strictly speaking lesser included offenses, merge into the completed crime, but the crime of conspiracy is independent and does not merge into the completed crime.

In jury trials, the court is permitted to instruct jurors that they can find the defendant guilty of the most serious crime charged or of a lesser included offense. A lesser included offense instruction will only be given if the evidence supports the lesser offense. In capital murder cases, where a convicted defendant may face capital punishment, the U.S. Supreme Court in *Beck v. Alabama* (1980), has ruled that courts must instruct juries that they may find the defendant guilty of a lesser included non-capital offense such as felony murder when the evidence would support such a verdict.

Inchoate Crimes

Inchoate crimes are uncompleted, anticipatory, or incipient crimes. They are lesser crimes completed by taking a punishable step toward committing another crime, the target offense. The inchoate offenses are:

- ATTEMPT – the target crime failed to be completed, but the last step before the target offense was taken, and the defendant had the specific intent to complete it.

- SOLICITATION – an offer of money to someone with the specific intent of inducing that person to commit a crime; the crime does not have to be completed.
- CONSPIRACY – the agreement of two or more persons with intent to commit an illegal act and one does an overt act in furtherance of the conspiracy (a step in accomplishing the crime); the target crime does not have to be completed.

Attempt and solicitation will merge with the target crime when prosecuted, but conspiracy can be charged separately. As a constitutional matter of double jeopardy, the U.S. Supreme Court in *Brown v. Ohio* (1977) applied the *Blockburger test* (*Blockburger v. U.S.* (1932)), that a defendant may be convicted of two offenses arising out of the same criminal incident if each crime contains an element not found in the other. However, a defendant may not be convicted of a lesser included offense and the greater offense.

Homicide

Homicide: *homicide* is a general term for the killing of one person by another – it may or may not be a crime.

- CRIMINAL HOMICIDE: a willful (non-negligent) and unlawful (non-justified) killing of one human being by another, also called murder.
- JUSTIFIABLE HOMICIDE: lawful killing in self-defense or the defense of others, of an enemy during war by a combatant, or as a judicial execution.
- EXCUSABLE HOMICIDE: an accidental killing without criminal intent or criminal negligence.
- FELONY MURDER: statutes may hold a person who, while committing certain felonies, unintentionally causes the death of a person is guilty of murder. Such felonies might include burglary, arson, robbery, kidnapping, rape, or escape.

Homicide is prosecuted and punished according to the depravity and moral culpability involved, but there is substantial variation in the definition and classification of homicides from the original Common Law and from state to state; see:

- https://www.findlaw.com/criminal.html

The following schema is prototypical of modern penal codes.

Murder: *murder* is the unlawful killing of another human being without justification or excuse but with high moral culpability – particularly with *malice*. Malice is not merely anger or ill-will but a legal notion of evil or cold-blooded murder.

- FIRST-DEGREE MURDER: murder committed with actual or imputed *malice aforethought* or premeditation:
  - the willful killing of another human with premeditation. Premeditation is not necessarily planned, but a rational decision to kill (need only take seconds), or
  - felony murders during rape, arson, robbery, kidnapping, burglary, and others specified by statute. The killing may be unintentional or accidental. The malice is inferred from the underlying felony.
- SECOND-DEGREE MURDER: murder committed without premeditation:
  - with malice or disregard for serious bodily harm from a depraved heart or abandoned and malignant heart; or
  - felony murders during felonies not listed for first degree. The killing may be unintentional or accidental. The depraved heart may be inferred from the underlying felony.

The usual sentence for murder in the first degree is life imprisonment or death. A typical sentence for murder in the second degree is 20 years in prison.

Manslaughter: *manslaughter* is the unlawful killing of another human being without malice or a depraved heart. Manslaughter embodies the notion of a hot-blooded killing.

- VOLUNTARY MANSLAUGHTER: a willful killing committed without malice or committed in the *heat of passion*, without a cooling-off period, after a provocation that would cause a reasonable person extreme emotional disturbance – to the point of losing control. It is not murder because it is not committed with the malice of a depraved heart. Voluntary manslaughter can be a defense to second-degree murder:
  - e.g., a parent's negligence results in a child's death
  - e.g., spousal adultery *in flagrante delicto*
  - e.g., occurring during mutual combat (i.e., barroom fight)
- INVOLUNTARY MANSLAUGHTER: an unintentional (accidental) killing occurring through criminal negligence or a seriously reckless act or omission to act when there is a duty to act. Criminal negligence requires gross negligence, which is more than required for a civil negligence finding and involves an unreasonable risk or disregard of human life. Many states require an awareness of the threat to others by the defendant, while other states require that a reasonable person would know the danger involved (objective standard). The act need not be unlawful, just grossly negligent:
  - e.g., occurring while under the influence of drugs or alcohol

    - e.g., from failure by the responsible attendant to notice a patient's oxygen tank is empty
    - e.g., a parent's negligent act results in a child's death
- MISDEMEANOR MANSLAUGHTER (Constructive Manslaughter, Unlawful Act Manslaughter): an unintentional killing that occurs during the commission of a misdemeanor or low-level felony that does not trigger the felony murder rule. Malicious intent inherent in the crime is constructively applied to the consequences of the crime.
- VEHICULAR MANSLAUGHTER: the unintentional killing of a person, specifically from the reckless use of a motor vehicle. Intentional use of the vehicle as a deadly weapon would not be involuntary manslaughter. It particularly applies to deaths resulting from driving while intoxicated.

A typical sentence for voluntary manslaughter is ten to 20 years imprisonment.

A typical sentence for involuntary manslaughter is one to ten years imprisonment.

A typical sentence for misdemeanor manslaughter is less than one year imprisonment.

BOX 5.4 HOMICIDE EXAMPLES

1	A man stalks another man and waits outside a bar, then shoots him.	First-degree murder (premeditated)
2	A man in a bar shoots another man after being insulted by him.	Second-degree murder (depraved heart)
3	A man gets into a fight with another man, and they both draw guns, and one man is shot dead.	Voluntary manslaughter (mutual combat)
4	A man comes home to find his wife in bed with another man and shoots him in the heat of the moment.	Voluntary manslaughter (spousal rage)
5	The bartender shoots the gun into the air to stop a barroom brawl, the bullet goes through the ceiling and strikes an occupant on the second floor and kills him.	Involuntary manslaughter (accidental killing)
6	The bank is being robbed. An old lady in the waiting room is told to get down on the floor. She has a heart attack and dies.	First-degree felony murder (committed during a robbery)
7	A beautiful, flirtatious wife tells her husband that the bartender raped her. The husband goes to the car, gets his gun, and then walks into the bar and shoots the bartender [Anatomy of a Murder, 1959].	First-degree murder (premeditated) or Voluntary Manslaughter (heat of passion)

Sexual Offenses

Sexual Assault: *sexual assault* is variously defined, but the National Institute of Justice (NIJ) suggests it be defined as any nonconsensual sexual act proscribed by federal, tribal, or state law, including when the victim lacks the capacity to consent, including rape or attempted rape; groping, fondling, or unwanted sexual touching; sexual indecency with a child; sexual harassment; sexual extortion; and sodomy.

Rape: there is considerable variance in the definition of rape from state to state; see: https://apps.rainn.org/policy/. The two primary elements of most state laws include penetration and lack of consent. The 2012 revised UCR definition of *rape* declares: penetration, no matter how slight, of the vagina or anus with any body part or object, or oral penetration by a sex organ of another person, without the consent of the victim. The Common Law definition of rape, now known as *forcible rape* or *legacy rape*, is the carnal knowledge of a female forcibly and against her will. This legacy definition requires force and is female-specific. Under current statutes, males may also be victims of rape. Some states have abandoned the term *rape* in favor of other terms, such as *sexual assault*, *sexual intercourse without consent*, and *criminal sexual conduct*.

- STATUTORY RAPE: nonforcible sexual activity with a person who has not yet reached the age of consent.
- DATE RAPE: forced sexual intercourse or sodomy that occurs within a social situation outside of marriage where lack of consent may be due to mental impairment (i.e., drug-facilitated).

Assault

Assault and Battery: in early English Common Law, *battery* was an unconsented touching, and *assault* was the attempt or threat to inflict injury. Today, assault and battery are used together or interchangeably, or battery is merged into assault.

Simple Assault: *simple assault* is an unlawful physical attack or an attempted or threatened attack involving (1) intentionally or recklessly causing bodily injury, (2) threatening imminent bodily injury, and the victim is under the apprehension of imminent harm, or (3) offensive or provocative physical contact.

Aggravated Assault: *aggravated assault* is an unlawful attack by one person upon another to inflict severe or aggravated bodily injury with an additional aggravating factor: (1) intent to cause or does cause serious bodily injury or manifesting extreme indifference to human life, (2) during an attempt to commit rape or other serious crime, or (3) using a dangerous weapon.

Intimidation: *intimidation* is the unlawful placing of another person in reasonable fear of bodily harm using threatening words and/or other conduct but without displaying a weapon or subjecting the victim to an actual physical attack.

Mayhem: *mayhem* is the intentional infliction of permanent injury from an unlawful physical attack that may disable or disfigure someone.

Property Crimes

Larceny/Theft: *larceny* or *theft* is the unlawful appropriation of property with the intent of permanently depriving the owner of the property. The *actus reus* is the trespassory taking of something of value, and the carrying away (*asportation*) or the act of taking "constructive possession" is where the thief exercises control over the object. The mens rea requires the specific intent to steal the property – to permanently deprive the owner. The intent may be presumed in the actions of the thief. Theft can be accomplished through wrongful taking, trick, embezzlement, false pretenses, acquiring lost property, issuing a bad check, false promise, or extortion. Theft may be subsumed in another crime when accompanied by force, threat or fraud.

Robbery: *robbery* is the taking or attempting to take anything of value from the care, custody, or control of a person or persons by force or threat of force or violence, putting the victim in fear. It is a violent crime, both a property crime and a crime against the person.

Burglary (Breaking and Entering): *burglary* is the unlawful entry into a structure with intent to commit theft, rape, or other felony. The Common Law definition, breaking and entering a dwelling at night with an intent to steal, is far narrower than current versions – the entry does not have to be forcible, the structure does not have to be a house, and it does not have to be committed at night. The *actus reus* is the trespass (entry with or without breaking); the *mens rea* is the intent to commit theft, rape, or other felony (not the intent to enter). The trespass with intent is sufficient; the completion of the robbery, rape, or other felony is not necessary, but if committed, may be charged in addition to the burglary.

Arson: *arson* is any willful or malicious burning of a dwelling house, public building, motor vehicle or aircraft, or personal property of another.

Federal Crimes

The U.S. Constitution reserves the "police power" to make all necessary laws on health, welfare, and morals to the states through the Tenth Amendment. The founding fathers thought that law enforcement would be the responsibility of states. States handle well over 90% of crimes. However, Congress has created federal crimes and federal investigative agencies; the various federal agencies have promulgated rules requiring enforcement. There are now approximately 5,000 federal crimes; most have been enacted since FDR's New Deal in the 1930s. Examples of federal offenses include financial fraud, bank robbery, counterfeiting, kidnapping, threatening the president or other federal officials or buildings, committing a crime on federal property, committing a crime using interstate commerce, engaging in a conspiracy to commit a crime, using a firearm to commit a crime, and manufacturing and distributing controlled substances.

Hobbs Act (1946): the *Hobbs Act* makes it a crime to interfere with interstate commerce using violence, extortion, or bribery. The Hobbs Act allowed federal crackdowns on loansharking, union embezzlement, drugs, and obscenity, among other schemes.

Racketeer Influenced and Corrupt Organizations Act (RICO) (1970): *RICO* provides for criminal and civil actions for acts performed as part of ongoing criminal organization activities. It makes it a crime for an individual to belong to, profit from, or operate an organization that engages in a pattern of racketeering and has committed two specified crimes within the last ten years. Racketeering activity means any act or threat of certain violent activity or other specified illegal acts. The Act specifies 35 crimes that are underlying racketeering acts. RICO statutes provide enhanced penalties and forfeiture and permit prosecutors to seek a pretrial order to allow the seizure of assets and prevent the transfer of assets of potentially forfeitable property. RICO statutes hold the leaders responsible for the crimes they have ordered or assisted others to commit. The statute was initially passed to prosecute the Mafia, but because it was written broadly, it has been widely used in other contexts. States have also passed RICO laws.

Continuing Criminal Enterprise Act (CCE) (1970): this sister legislation of RICO, the *Kingpin Statute,* makes it a crime for a person to belong to an organization of five or more persons to commit or conspire to commit a continuing series of felony drug violations and who obtains substantial income or resources from the enterprise. Unlike the broad RICO acts, it is specific to major narcotics organizations.

Computer Fraud and Abuse Act (CFAA) (1984): the CFAA establishes computer crimes and extends civil tort law to intangible property. Before this legislation, computer crimes were prosecuted as mail and wire fraud, but this was often an inadequate basis for prosecution. The Act prohibits accessing a computer without authorization or beyond the scope of an authorization (trespass) with the intent of obtaining information for financial gain, damage (including viruses and worms), or threatening to damage the computer, espionage, fraud, trafficking in passwords, or identity theft. Although, in theory, the legislation is limited in jurisdiction to government and other "protected computers," in practice, any ordinary computer has come under the jurisdiction of the law, including cell phones due to the interstate nature of most Internet communication. Pirating software may violate copyright laws, trafficking in counterfeit goods laws, and/or the Digital Millennium Act.

Stored Communications Act (SCA) (1986): the Electronic Communications Privacy Act of 1986 (ECPA) amended the original 1968 wiretap statute. Title II of the ECPA, the SCA, establishes certain privacy rights to stored electronic communications and transactional records held by Internet service providers (ISPs), by limiting access by government and non-government entities to these records. It was enacted due to concerns that the Fourth Amendment did not sufficiently protect them. For "wire or electronic communications," the government must obtain a search warrant if it has been in storage for 180 days or less but may use a subpoena if held longer. The Act needs to be updated.

Other Crimes

Of course, there are a myriad of state and federal crimes that are beyond what has been described here, some of which are listed here:

Unlawful Restraint
Trafficking of Persons
Sexual Offenses
Abuse or Neglect
Criminal Mischief
Vandalism
Fraud and Other Deceptive Practices
Forgery
Credit Card Abuse
Money Laundering
Computer Crimes
Hate Crimes
Terrorism
Impersonation
Invasion of Privacy
Bigamy
Bribery
Perjury and Falsification
Obstruction; Escape
Abuse of Office
Disorderly Conduct
Public Indecency
Possession
Barratry
Violation of a Court Order
Etc., …

Defenses

There are six basic criminal defense strategies:

1. No crime occurred.
2. The wrong person is charged (i.e. mistaken identity).
3. The defendant is charged with the wrong crime (often in drug cases).
4. The action of the defendant was legally justified (affirmative defenses).
5. The defendant is not culpable of the crime (i.e. insanity).
6. Jury nullification (the jury does not enforce the crime despite the defendant's guilt).

A successful defense may result in either a reduced charge (partial defense) or an acquittal (complete defense). Direct attacks consist of:

- NEGATIVE DEFENSE – denial of the factual allegation of the prosecution or establishment of reasonable doubt, e.g., lack of intent. A defense of innocence might be based on an alibi, mistaken identity, or a frame-up. The defense has the burden of producing sufficient evidence to raise the issue, but no more.
- AFFIRMATIVE DEFENSE – admits the act but alleges factual allegations that defeat or mitigate the legal consequences of the defendant's otherwise unlawful conduct, e.g., self-defense, insanity, entrapment, renunciation, necessity. The defense has the burden of proving the affirmative defense by a preponderance of evidence.

Statutes of Limitations: laws provide time limits, known as *statutes of limitations*, for the prosecution of crimes and for civil actions, but they vary between states. More serious crimes will be given more extended periods than minor crimes. Heinous crimes, such as murder, kidnapping, sexual assault of a minor, arson, and misappropriation of public funds, may have no statute of limitations. The federal government has a general five-year statute of limitations (18 U.S.C. §3282), although specific crimes are exempted from the restriction, i.e., capital crimes, terrorism, certain sex offenses, white-collar crimes, tax crimes, major fraud. If the suspect is indicted or charged with the crime within the statute of limitations, the defendant may be tried whenever he or she is found. The statutory period may be *tolled* (suspended) for various reasons, e.g., the statutory period will be tolled where the accused flees the state or is in hiding, will only resume once the criminal reenters the state, or is no longer in hiding; DNA testing may also toll the statute.

Self-Defense: the law permits people to defend themselves, others, and property. The ALI MPC permits deadly force to protect oneself against death, serious bodily injury, kidnapping, or rape. In most states, the defendant must have an honest and reasonable belief that he/she is facing an unlawful threat of imminent death or serious bodily injury by an aggressor without provocation, and the force used was reasonable under the circumstances (proportional, not excessive).

- RETREAT LAWS, the minority rule – generally in states in the Northeast and Midwest. *Retreat laws* require a person to retreat before using force, especially deadly force, if possible, to do so in safety.
- THE CASTLE DOCTRINE, the majority rule – the *Castle Doctrine* is an exception to the duty to retreat when the threat occurs in the home ["A man's home is his castle"].
- STAND-YOUR-GROUND LAWS (True Man Laws), an extension of the majority rule – generally in Southern and Western states, retreat is unnecessary; an expansion of the Castle Doctrine from the home to any place you have a right to be.

Police officers have a special duty not to retreat from danger, but they cannot use deadly force to stop fleeing felons unless they present a significant risk of death or serious bodily injury to themselves or others. Local police policies and procedures govern police use of force.

Battered Wife Problem: where a wife who is repeatedly beaten, incapable of defending herself, and fearful for her life shoots her husband in his sleep, the usual legal mechanisms for mitigation of homicide do not apply. Self-defense does not apply because the threat is not imminent. Heat of passion does not apply. She is guilty of first-degree murder unless the state law has an extreme emotional disturbance or special battered wife syndrome law.

Insanity defense: most states and the federal government recognize an *insanity defense*. The insanity defense is an affirmative defense that excuses the defendant for the crime but is also a negative defense to negate the element of criminal intent. Defendants are presumed sane, and the defense must assert and prove their insanity. In federal court, the defendant must prove the defense of insanity by clear and convincing evidence. Defendants found to be insane are acquitted of the crime but then are generally automatically committed to a mental health treatment facility for an indefinite time.

The insanity defense is controversial because it excuses even the most evil and abhorrent conduct. Four states (Idaho, Kansas, Montana, and Utah) have abolished the insanity defense and declared that a mental condition may not be a defense to any charge of criminal conduct.

Insanity is a legal term, not a medical term, and its definition has varied over time and jurisdiction:

- THE M'NAGHTEN RULE (*Right-from-Wrong Test*) (*Regina. v. M'Naghten*, England, 1843) – because of disease of the mind, the defendant: (1) did not know the nature and quality of the act committed or (2) did not know that the act was wrong.

- THE IRRESISTIBLE IMPULSE TEST – the defendant's state of mind was such that he could not control the actions leading to the crime, even though he may have known the act was wrong.
- THE DURHAM RULE (*Product Rule*) (*Durham v. U.S.*, 1954) – an accused is not criminally responsible if the unlawful act was the product of mental disease or mental defect.
- THE SUBSTANTIAL CAPACITY TEST (The ALI MPC §4.01(1), 1962) – a person is not responsible for criminal conduct if, at the time of such conduct as a result of mental disease or defect, he lacks substantial capacity either to appreciate the criminality of his conduct or to conform his conduct to the requirements of law.
- GUILTY BUT MENTALLY ILL (GBMI) (from legislative reforms in 1982) – where the defendant is guilty, mentally ill, and lacked the substantial capacity either to appreciate the wrongness of his conduct or to conform his conduct to the requirements of law. The defendant is not acquitted but punished and treated for mental health while in prison. GBMI requires the defendant to prove the mental illness at the time of the crime by a preponderance of the evidence.
- DIMINISHED CAPACITY (Partial Responsibility) (*People v. Wells*, 1949) – mental illness, although not sufficient to prove insanity, is enough to show a lack of capacity for the requisite intent at the time of the crime, thus reducing the crime to a lower offense. In some states, it may be used only at sentencing.

The Common Law M'Naghten right-from-wrong rule is the most common form of defense. This insanity test is solely based upon the defendant's cognition or awareness. Defendants generally assert that they did not know their action was wrong. Some states will define "wrong" as *legally wrong*, meaning against the law, while others will define it as *legally and morally wrong*, meaning that the defendant did not understand that the conduct was socially wrong. The irresistible impulse rule is a stricter test because it adds a volitional element, that the defendant could not control his or her conduct, to the cognitive element of the M'Naghten rule. The subsequent Durham rule was found difficult to apply, and it was overruled in 1972 in *U.S. v. Brawner* (1972) in favor of the ALI formulation; only New Hampshire still uses a similar rule. The substantial capacity test was built on the Durham rule and combined the cognitive test of the M'Naghten Rule and the volitional test of the irresistible impulse rule. Many states adopted the substantial capacity test, but after the 1982 John Hinckley trial, in which Hinckley successfully claimed insanity for shooting President Reagan, many states and the federal government switched back to the M'Naghten rule. The Diminished Capacity claim is found in the United States Sentencing Guidelines but also fell from favor after the reduction of Dan White's first-degree murder charge of Harvey Milk to voluntary manslaughter when the defense argued that his eating Twinkies caused a chemical imbalance in his brain. The Insanity Defense Reform Act of 1984 requires defendants in federal cases to prove by "clear and convincing evidence" that they were unable to appreciate the wrongfulness of their actions due to a severe mental disease or defect. Nonetheless, many states do recognize temporary insanity in addition to permanent insanity.

In *Kahler v. Kansas* (2020), Kahler, who had killed four family members, challenged the Kansas version of an insanity defense. Kansas had adopted a "cognitive incapacity" test for the insanity defense, which examines whether a defendant was able to understand what he was doing when he committed a crime. A defendant may raise mental illness only to show that he lacked the culpable mental state required as an element of the offense charged or to argue for a lesser punishment. It specifically did not recognize a moral-incapacity defense, which asks whether the defendant could not distinguish right from wrong. The Court held that due process does not require Kansas to adopt an insanity test that turns on a defendant's ability to recognize that his crime was morally wrong.

An insanity defense is not the same as a finding that a defendant is *not mentally competent to stand trial*. The former refers to the time of the crime, and the latter to the time of the trial. Where the defendant is found not mentally competent to stand trial, the trial will be delayed until the defendant regains his/her competence to stand trial.

Other Defenses: affirmative defenses that have not been described above include:

Mistake of fact	Infancy	Entrapment
Factual impossibility	Consent	Excuse
Duress, necessity	Justification	Laches
Against public interest	Consent	Act of god

BOX 5.5 *REGINA V. DUDLEY AND STEPHENS*

On July 5, 1884, the 52' yacht, the Mignonette, was wrecked at sea during a gale while rounding the Cape of Good Hope. The crew, consisting of three men and a 17-year-old boy, abandoned the boat minutes before it sank. They were 700 miles from land with little prospect of rescue. They ran out of food after the second day. Other than a sea turtle, they could not drink or eat for the next 18 days. The boy fell into a coma, and two of the men decided to kill the boy and eat him. Four days later, another ship rescued the three men. When they arrived in England, two of the men were tried for murder and convicted. The defense of necessity was raised. Lord Coleridge found them guilty, refusing to recognize the defense of necessity for the willful homicide. The defendants eventually served a six-month sentence.

Summary

Crimes are defined variously in the penal codes of the federal government and the states. Although state laws govern most crimes, federal crimes have grown quickly. There are approximately five times more property crimes than violent crimes.

Actus reus (guilty act) and *mens rea* (guilty intent) are elements of a crime. The ALI MPC uses purposefully, knowingly, recklessly, and negligently to categorize *mens rea*. Crimes can be general (intended an act) or specific (intended a result) intent crimes; theft and murder are examples of specific intent crimes. Causation is an element of criminal homicide. Lesser offenses can be included in crime, e.g., theft is included in robbery. *Inchoate crimes* are uncompleted, anticipatory, or incipient crimes, which include attempt, solicitation, and conspiracy.

First- and second-degree murder is usually distinguished by the element of premeditation. Manslaughter is generally considered to be a criminal homicide without malice or a depraved heart. Voluntary manslaughter is committed with *heat of passion*, e.g., ballroom brawls resulting in death, or the killing of a spousal paramour caught *in flagrante delicto*. Involuntary manslaughter involves a criminally liable accidental killing.

Common Law *rape* is the carnal knowledge of a female forcibly and against her will. The UCR definition of *rape* is penetration, no matter how slight, of the vagina or anus with any body part or object or oral penetration by a sex organ of another person without the consent of the victim. *Sexual assault* is variously defined but has generally replaced rape as a crime charged.

Simple assault is an unlawful physical attack or an attempted or threatened attack, and *aggravated assault* is an unlawful attack by one person upon another to inflict severe or aggravated bodily injury. *Larceny* (theft) is the taking of property with the intent of permanently depriving the owner of it. *Robbery* is theft by force or threat of force. Common Law *burglary* is the breaking and entering a dwelling at night with the intent to steal property. The modern crime of *breaking and entering* is the unlawful entry into a structure with intent to commit theft, rape, or other felony.

Most defenses are *negative defenses*, intending to inject doubt into the prosecutor's case, but *affirmative defenses* admit the crime but require proving by a preponderance of evidence that the conduct should not be penalized.

Terms

Actus Reus – criminal conduct.

Castle Doctrine – laws that permit using force to defend oneself within a home without retreat.

Felony – traditionally a crime punishable by a year or more in prison.

General Intent – the intent to commit the crime.

Inchoate Crime – incomplete, incipient, or anticipated crime.
Mens Rea – a culpable mental state.
Misdemeanor – traditionally a crime punishable by less than a year in prison.
Penal Codes – comprehensive and ordered statutes defining crimes in a jurisdiction.
Specific Intent – the intent to cause a specific harm.
Stand-Your-Ground Law – laws that permit the use of force to defend oneself or others without having to retreat in places where one has a lawful right to be.
Statute of Limitations – statutorily defined period within which someone can be sued or prosecuted for a crime.
Vicarious Liability – imputed liability from the actions of another.

Cases

Beck v. Alabama, 447 U.S. 625 (1980)
Blockburger v. United States, 284 U.S. 299 (1932)
Brown v. Ohio, 432 U.S. 161 (1977)
Burrage v. United States, 571 U.S. 204 (2014)
Durham v. United States, 214 F.2d 862 (D.C. Cir. 1954)
Kahler v. Kansas, 589 U.S. 271 (2020)
People v. Wells, 202 P.2d 53 (Cal. Sup. Ct. 1949)
Powell v. Texas, 392 U.S. 514 (1968)
Regina v. Dudley and Stephens, 15 Cox C.C. 624, 117 Eng. Rep. 101 (Q.B. 1844)
Regina v. M'Naghten, 8 ER 718, Rep 229, England (1843)
Robertson v. Commonwealth, 82 S.W.3d 832 (Ky. 2002)
Robinson v. California, 370 U.S. 660 (1962)
United States v. Brawner, 471 F.2d 969 (D.C. Cir. 1972)
United States v. Hudson and Goodwin, 11 U.S. (7 Cranch) 32 (1812)

Statutes

Computer Fraud and Abuse Act (CFAA), 18 U.S.C. §1030 (1984)
Continuing Criminal Enterprise Act (CCE), 21 U.S.C. §848 (1970)
Counterfeit Goods Trafficking, 18 U.S.C. §2318 (1962), §2320 (1984)
Crimes, 18 U.S.C. §§1–2725
Criminal Infringement of a Copyright, 17 U.S.C. §506(a) (1976) & 18 U.S.C §2319 (1982)
Criminal Procedure, 18 U.S.C. §§3001–3772
Digital Millennium Copyright Act, 17 U.S.C. §§1201–1205 (1998)
Electronic Communications Privacy Act (ECPA), 18 U.S.C. §§2510–2523 (1986)

First Step Act of 2018, Pub. L. No. 115–391
Hobbs Act, 18 U.S.C. §1951 (1946)
Insanity Defense, 18 U.S.C. §17 (1984)
Offenses Not Capital, 18 U.S.C. §3282 (1948) [general five-year statute of limitations for federal crimes]
Racketeer Influenced and Corrupt Organizations Act (RICO), 18 U.S.C. §§1961–1968 (1970)
Second Chance Act of 2007, Pub. L. No. 110–199
Stored Communications Act (SCA), 18 U.S.C §§2701–2713 (1986)

Thought Questions

1. Why have all states promulgated penal codes?
2. Why is there no statute of limitations for homicide, but there is for most crimes?
3. Which definition of insanity mirrors today's philosophy on crime?

Further Reading

Dressler J, *Understanding Criminal Law*, 8th ed, Carolina Academic Press, Durham, NC, 2018.
Duff RA, Green SP, *Philosophical Foundations of Criminal Law*, Oxford Univ Press, Oxford, 2013.
Langbein JH, The Origins of Public Prosecution at Common Law, *American Journal of Legal History* 17(4):313–335, 1973, https://doi.org/10.2307/845098.
Titus Reid S, *Criminal Law: The Essentials*, 3rd ed, Oxford Univ Press, Oxford, 2016.

Chapter 6

Criminal Procedure

Learning Objectives

After reading this chapter, students are expected to be able to:

- list the sequence of criminal procedures
- describe the steps necessary for formal charging of a defendant
- describe the differences between a grand jury and a preliminary hearing
- discuss the role of diversion programs
- describe the rights of a defendant
- explain Constituional control of criminal procedure

Introduction

Only about half of all people arrested for a felony crime will eventually be convicted of the crime. In a 1986 study by Boland and Sones, of every 100 adults arrested for a felony crime, 52 will not be convicted. Of those not convicted, 6 will be referred to diversion programs or other courts for prosecution, 23 will have their cases rejected for prosecution at screening, 22 will be dismissed in court, and 1 will be acquitted at trial. Of the 48 convicted, 45 will plead guilty, and 3 will be found guilty at trial.

Some compassion, flexibility for circumstances, and allowance for exceptional cases depend upon discretion in applying criminal justice procedures.

 DOI: 10.4324/9780429272455-6

Police have some discretion to enforce specific laws, investigate crimes, search for people and places, and detain and arrest people. Prosecutors have some discretion to file charges, seek indictments, drop cases, reduce charges, and enter plea agreements. Judges have some discretion to set bail and conditions for release, accept pleas, determine delinquency, dismiss charges, impose sentences, and revoke probation. Prison officials have some discretion in making facility assignments, awarding privileges, and punishing for disciplinary actions. Probation and parole authorities have some discretion in determining the date and conditions of parole and revoke parole. In the federal system, parole has been abolished. Juries who disagree with the law may ignore the law and not convict guilty defendants called jury nullification.

In 1968, Herbert Packer described the criminal procedure as two competing values. A *Criminal Control Model* focuses on an efficient system to control crime, resulting in swift and severe punishment of offenders. The probable innocent are weeded out early, and the remaining probable guilty are pushed swiftly through the system to be found guilty and moved into corrections facilities. This model emphasizes the utilitarian notion of the greatest good for society and views the legal system as an impediment and obstruction to efficient crime control. A *Due Process Model* focuses on a just and fair system. This model presumes the defendant's innocence and rejects the premise that screening the probable innocent by police and prosecutors is reliable. Both factual guilt and legal guilt must be proven in a procedurally correct manner. This model emphasizes the individual rights of the accused.

Historical Background

In medieval England, with no formal police forces, law enforcement was a communal duty. Crime control relied on citizens to raise a *hue and cry* when they witnessed a crime or discovered a dead body. Able-bodied men who heard the call would form a *posse comitatus* and pursue and capture the criminal. Victimized private individuals prosecuted crimes. Jurors conducted their own investigations. By the 12th century, prosecutions, especially for serious offenses like homicide, which were considered violations of the King's peace, began gradually shifting from private individuals to the Crown through mechanisms such as itinerant justices and assize courts. Over time, legal authority became more centralized, and public prosecutions superseded private prosecutions.

The American colonies were early adopters of public prosecution, recognizing crime as a matter of public concern. Connecticut became the first colony to adopt a system of government prosecution in 1704. Public prosecution was well established by the time of the U.S. Constitution's ratification, though law enforcement remained decentralized, rudimentary, and generally reactive. Sheriffs were the most important law enforcement officials and were responsible for investigating complaints, making arrests, and collecting taxes. Night watchmen were established in larger cities and towns to keep watch for fires, ensure doors were locked, and ensure people behaved. Slave patrols were used in the South to monitor and control enslaved peoples and later to enforce Black Codes.

By the 19th century, rapid industrialization and urbanization in England exposed the need for new public safety measures. In 1829, Sir Robert Peel established London's Metropolitan Police, the first modern police force. Inspired by this model, American cities established their first municipal police forces – Boston in 1838, New York City in 1845, and Philadelphia in 1855. These forces replaced the old night watch system with full-time, salaried officers dedicated to crime prevention and public safety. Private detectives emerged in the 1840s and 1850s; the Pinkerton National Detective Agency was founded in 1850. Police detective units began forming in the mid to late 19th century. August Vollmer (1876–1955), often considered the father of modern law enforcement, pioneered many police reforms, including establishing the first U.S. crime labs at Berkeley and then Los Angeles in 1923. Crime labs became more common and more sophisticated in the mid-20th century, revolutionizing criminal investigations. The evolution and professionalization of police forces have continued to the present.

Criminal Procedure Mechanics

The usual state criminal conviction process begins with filing a police complaint, investigating, building a probable cause case against the accused, and issuing a warrant, after which the defendant is arrested and booked. The defendant is then informed of the charges against him/her, bail is set, a preliminary hearing is held, a plea is entered, a trial is held if the defendant pleads not guilty, and the defendant is sentenced and imprisoned if found guilty.

An accused formally enters the criminal justice system when first taken into custody, arrested, and booked. Once charged, the defendant will be detained or released on bail or on their own recognizance but remain in the criminal justice system. The defendant may exit out of the system when cleared by investigation and released without prosecution or when charges have been dropped, adjudication disposed of the case, or the defendant is found not guilty. The accused may also be diverted from the criminal justice system, hoping for an alternative disposition but with a possible return as a defendant.

For the federal government, most criminal procedure is set out in Title 18 of the U.S.C.

BOX 6.1 CRIMINAL PROCEDURES

1. Investigation
2. (Grand Jury)
3. Charging
4. Arrest and Booking
5. Presentment
6. Arraignment
7. (Preliminary Hearing)
8. Pretrial Conference
9. Pretrial Proceedings
10. Trial
11. Sentencing
12. Postconviction Remedies

Investigation

Unless police apprehend and arrest a person committing a crime, the criminal justice system's first effort is to investigate a tip, report a crime, or file a formal complaint by law enforcement. Where the crime goes unreported, it will not be investigated and prosecuted. Police conduct investigations in municipalities, county sheriffs, state troopers in state agencies, and federal special agents in national law enforcement agencies. The investigation will determine if a crime has been committed, produce evidence, name any known suspect or suspects, and generate a police report. A suspect may be cleared at this stage.

Pretrial Screening and Charging

A prosecutor will decide to press charges against an accused suspect, drop the charges, or make a placement in a diversion program. If charges are pressed, a prosecutor will draw up a charging document (a complaint, information, or indictment) containing the formal accusation. This charging document initiates criminal procedures, and a court will usually issue an arrest warrant or a summons. The accused suspect becomes a defendant.

Grand Jury

In federal and some state cases, a *grand jury* will precede formal felony charges and arrest to ensure probable cause to proceed against the accused suspect, although a judge may issue an arrest warrant before indictment if urgent circumstances require it. Grand juries are mandated in federal cases by the Fifth Amendment to the U.S. Constitution:

> No person shall be held to answer for a capital or otherwise infamous crime, unless on a presentment or indictment of a Grand Jury, except in cases arising in the land or naval forces, or in the Militia when in actual service in time of War or public danger.

This clause of the Bill of Rights has yet to be incorporated within the due process clause of the Fourteenth Amendment and thus does not apply to the states. More than half of the states do not require a grand jury to commence a criminal prosecution and instead employ a preliminary hearing or probable cause hearing to prosecute unless the crime is one of a selected set of felonies.

Grand jury proceedings are held to decide whether there is probable cause to press formal charges and indict the accused. Grand juries were more important in the early period of the United States when any citizen (e.g., law enforcement officers, lawyers hired by victims, neighbors) could prosecute cases; the grand jury would screen out incompetent or malicious prosecutions. Official public prosecutors displaced private prosecutions in the late 19th century.

Grand juries are closed proceedings conducted in secret without defense counsel present. The grand jury is composed of a large group, often from 15 to 24 jurors depending on a specific jurisdiction, who may hear several cases for over six months to two years. Decisions may be made with a 2/3 or 3/4 super majority vote. Grand juries have powers to initiate investigations, call witnesses, and compel their attendance. Typically, however, they receive the prosecutor's evidence and accede to the recommendation when probable cause exists.

If the grand jury returns a true bill, an indictment (the charging document from a grand jury) and a *writ of capias* or summons will be issued to arrest the defendant. If the grand jury fails to indict, the accused may never know that he/she was ever under investigation.

Preliminary (probable cause) hearings are generally considered alternatives to grand juries. Both hearings determine probable cause to bind the defendant over to further proceedings (trial). However, the prosecutor meets with the grand jury in secret. In contrast, preliminary hearings are open and include the defendant and his/her counsel, requiring the defendant to be first formally charged. Witnesses in the preliminary hearing may be cross-examined by the defendant or his/her attorney.

Arrest

A person falls under police custody when apprehended and arrested, is detained pursuant to an arrest warrant, or if a person turns themself in.

The probable cause to arrest, particularly under exigent circumstances, is a relatively lax standard and must be developed before arrest. If the arrest occurs without a judicial warrant, the defendant must be taken before a judicial officer for a judicial determination of probable cause. Defendants accused of minor crimes may merely be summoned to court without arrest.

The U.S. Supreme Court held in *Escobedo v. Illinois* (1963) that an accused is entitled to request a defense counsel before interrogation while in custody and then in *Miranda v. Arizona* (1966) that the accused must be given warnings that include the right to counsel, the right to an appointed counsel if the defendant cannot afford one, and the right to remain silent. Miranda warnings must be given when the accused is in the custody of the police and they want to question them; it does not matter whether the interrogation occurs in jail, at the scene of the crime, or on a sidewalk, if the subject is deprived of their freedom in any significant way, whether formally arrested or not.

The arrestee will be given Miranda warnings, questioned, booked, and held in jail awaiting further proceedings.

BOX 6.2 MIRANDA WARNINGS

You have the right to remain silent. Anything you say can be used against you in court. You have the right to talk to a lawyer for advice before we ask you any questions. You have the right to have a lawyer with you during questioning. If you cannot afford a lawyer, one will be appointed for you before questioning. If you decide to answer questions now without a lawyer present, you have the right to stop answering at any time.

Booking

In minor offenses, a defendant may be summoned directly to court without an arrest or booking. Otherwise, an arrestee will be taken to the police booking station to be *booked*, a police clerical procedure that includes records entry, photography, fingerprinting, and DNA sampling. A search for outstanding arrest warrants will be conducted.

Bail

Bail is the release from court or police custody on the condition that the accused will show up in court and not flee or fail to appear. Typically, this pretrial detainment is jail. This system requires that the accused post a bail bond, a deposit of money, or some form of property that will be forfeited to the government if the accused fails to show it. Furthermore, failure to attend court will cause the accused to be charged with the crime, and an arrest warrant will be issued. Private bail bond agents may post the money on behalf of the accused for an upfront fee.

The 8th Amendment states, "Excessive bail shall not be required," thus establishing bail as a constitutionally protected right. What an "excessive bail" is a matter of discretion by the magistrate. Many states have a bail schedule that sets the amount for a crime. The magistrate may also deny bail if the accused poses a "flight risk."

It is widely recognized that bail impacts the economically disadvantaged more harshly than others. Bail reform efforts to eliminate cash bail entirely or tailor bail to the accused have met with some success.

Presentment (Initial Appearance)

In the initial judicial appearance or *presentment*, the accused is brought before a magistrate to be informed of the charges against them. The magistrate should first confirm that the person presented is the person named in the indictment. The charges may be set forth in a complaint with an affidavit summarizing the evidence or in an indictment returned by a grand jury. The magistrate will ensure that the defendant understands the claims of the government.

The magistrate will also inform the defendant of his or her constitutional rights, including the right to counsel.

If a defendant cannot afford an attorney, an attorney will be appointed to represent the defendant. The defendant must convince the magistrate of the inability under penalty of perjury and be declared *in forma pauperis* (IFP). The defendant may always retain a lawyer of his or her choice even after the magistrate appoints an attorney.

The U.S. Supreme Court has held that the Fourth Amendment speedy trial clause requires an arrestee to appear before a magistrate within 48 hours of a warrantless arrest, but most states require that the person be presented within 24 hours.

Generally, if the charge is a misdemeanor or the indictment or information has been filed, the defendant may be arraigned at the initial appearance. Otherwise, the arraignment will be held later, often before the trial judge.

Arraignment

During *arraignment*, the accused will be formally addressed by name, read the charges, including the date, time, and place of occurrence, the range of punishment for the charge, and asked how they will plead. This occurs in a *plea colloquy*, a conversation between the judge and the defendant, who has been sworn under oath.

Possible pleas generally include guilty and not guilty. A plea of *nolo contendere* (plea of no contest), in which the conviction is accepted but no factual admission of guilt, allows payment of a fine or imposition of sentence and termination of further proceedings. Peremptory pleas are made for particular circumstances preventing a trial, such as double jeopardy or pardon. An Alford plea allows a defendant to plea agreement and maintain innocence yet enter a guilty plea to avoid a severe punishment where the prosecution is likely to succeed at trial.

A guilty plea must be made intelligently, knowingly, and voluntarily; the court must advise the defendant of, among other things, (1) the nature of the charge, (2) the potential penalties that might result from the plea, including any mandatory minimum sentence, and (3) the defendant's rights to not plead guilty, and to request a jury trial. The court must ask the defendant if he understands these points, and the court must receive a voluntary affirmative response to each. The defendant must also admit to all the elements of the crime.

Diversion

Pretrial diversion is a voluntary process that removes the offender from the traditional criminal justice process for rehabilitation and avoiding a criminal record. As determined by the statutory scheme, the defendant may be diverted into a rehabilitation program between arrest and sentencing. The offender is placed into a civil control proceeding. Diversion programs may apply to substance abusers, the mentally ill, veterans, domestic abusers, or other special populations, depending upon the statutory scheme of the jurisdiction.

Preliminary Hearing (Probable Cause Hearing)

Most states require a *preliminary hearing* (*probable cause hearing*) without a grand jury. It is sometimes thought of as the trial before the trial. Some states require preliminary hearings only in serious crimes and felonies, sometimes upon the defendant's request. The hearing is held to determine whether there is sufficient credible evidence – probable cause – to justify proceeding with trial. The preliminary hearing is a public hearing in front of a magistrate. The defendant has the right to counsel, to question witnesses, and to present evidence at such hearings. In most jurisdictions, if the judge and prosecutor agree, the defendant may waive or voluntarily relinquish the preliminary hearing to avoid revealing their strategy. Since the burden of proof is much less than at a trial, the prosecutor will not want to call all potential witnesses to testify, perhaps only a police officer. Hearsay is often admissible in preliminary hearings. If the magistrate finds probable cause that the defendant committed the crime, then the defendant is bound over for further proceedings; otherwise, the charge will be dismissed. If dismissed, the defendant may be charged again for the same crime. Double jeopardy does not attach at that stage. If probable cause is found, the defendant may be held over for action of the grand jury, or in some states, an official accusation against the defendant is formally written in a charging document from the prosecutor or magistrate.

Pretrial Conference

In some states, cases that have not already been disposed of are scheduled for a pretrial conference between the prosecution, the defense, and a judge to determine whether the case will proceed to trial or be resolved with a plea and whether discovery has been completed. Judges may not participate in plea negotiations.

More than 90% of criminal cases are resolved with a plea agreement rather than a trial. Plea agreements allow defendants to avoid the cost of defending themselves, the risk of harsher punishment, and trial publicity; the prosecution saves the time and expense of trial; the court is spared of the burden of the trial; and victims are spared the impact of the trial. Courts would not be able to handle the caseload if all cases proceeded to trial. Defendants in pretrial detention may get out of jail immediately following the judge's acceptance of a plea, depending on the agreement.

Plea discussions usually involve prosecutors offering defendants a lesser charge, dropping some charges when there are multiple charges, or recommending a more lenient or specific sentence. A two or three offense-level reduction in the sentencing guidelines may be offered where the defendant accepts responsibility. A prosecutor may also offer a diversion program, such as providing expungement if the defendant undergoes rehabilitation or makes restitution for the crime and successfully completes probation. Generally, the court must approve a plea agreement as being in the interest of justice.

Plea agreements are essentially a private process, but this is changing due to the victims' rights movement. In some states, victims have successfully advocated for the right to have input into the agreement process and to make the details of plea agreements public before they are announced in court.

Other Pretrial Proceedings

Other actions may occur before trial, in addition to the pretrial conference. The attorneys may file motions regarding discovery, and admission or suppression of evidence at trial. Pretrial hearings may be held on Constitutional issues (confessions, searches, identification, etc.). Preliminary issues and ground rules for trial should be resolved before trial.

Trial

A case rarely proceeds to trial for adjudication, but when it does, it is tried by a petit jury (as contrasted with the larger grand jury) for determination of guilt and sometimes sentencing or a judge without a jury (bench trial). Twelve jurors are typically required in federal and state criminal courts, but some states require as few as six. The jurors are chosen randomly from the citizenry of the court within its jurisdiction. They are then screened by a *voir dire* process in which both the prosecution and defense may remove a limited number of potential jurors through peremptory challenge (without cause) and others for cause. However, race-based peremptory challenges are prohibited (*Batson v. Kentucky*, 1986). The jury and the judge in bench trials are the triers of fact and weigh the probative value of facts admitted into evidence. The judge makes rulings on issues of law. The prosecution has the burden of proof to prove their case beyond a reasonable doubt. After the presentation of the evidence by the prosecution and defense and their summations, and after any jury instructions by the judge, the trial jury must deliberate in private, come to a unanimous decision, and return a verdict on the guilt or innocence of each charge. If a unanimous decision is not reached, the jury is hung, and a prosecutor may seek to retry the case.

Interlocutory appeals are appeals of temporary non-final orders or rulings made during trials to resolve a legal issue in dispute (*Cohen v. Beneficial Industrial Loan Corp.*, 1949; *Hallock v. Bonner*, 2d Cir. 2004). Although rare, they have been used extensively in the Trump trials.

Post-Trial Motions

After the verdict, if found guilty, the defendant may make post-trial motions for a new trial based on improper procedure or a motion *non obstante veridicto* (*n.o.v.*), asking the judge to find the defendant not guilty despite the jury finding based on the sufficiency of the evidence.

Sentencing

Sentencing will proceed after postconviction motions are adjudicated and after receipt of a presentence report or possibly after a separate sentencing hearing. In capital cases, and in some states where juries recommend the sentence, a separate penalty phase before the jury is required. This is called a bifurcated trial. Judges most often impose the sentence recommended by the jury. Nevertheless, the court's probation department will prepare a report for the judge summarizing the mitigating and aggravating factors in the commission of the crime and the defendant's personal and criminal background. The judge will consider the information in the pre-sentence report, additional evidence offered by the parties, comments by the victim, and other relevant information. In cases where a jury does not recommend a sentence, or in bench trials or plea cases, sentences are generally at the judge's discretion. The statutory sentencing range and sentencing guidelines limit this discretion. The judge may consider alternatives, such as fines, incarceration in jail or prison, probation, community service, restitution to any victims for financial harm, or some combination.

Postconviction Remedies

Postconviction remedies include appeal or collateral attack via a *writ of habeas corpus*, which generally is a remedy for illegal detention. The defendant may appeal the case to a higher court, but the prosecutor cannot do so after an acquittal. Appeals are presented to panels of judges without juries. Appellate courts do not retry cases, although they may remand cases back to the trial court to be retried. In some states, writs of actual innocence allow the appellate court to hear new evidence supporting actual innocence. Published appellate opinions, i.e., those officially printed in a reporter service, are the basis of judicial precedent.

BOX 6.3 TYPICAL CRIMINAL PROCEDURE

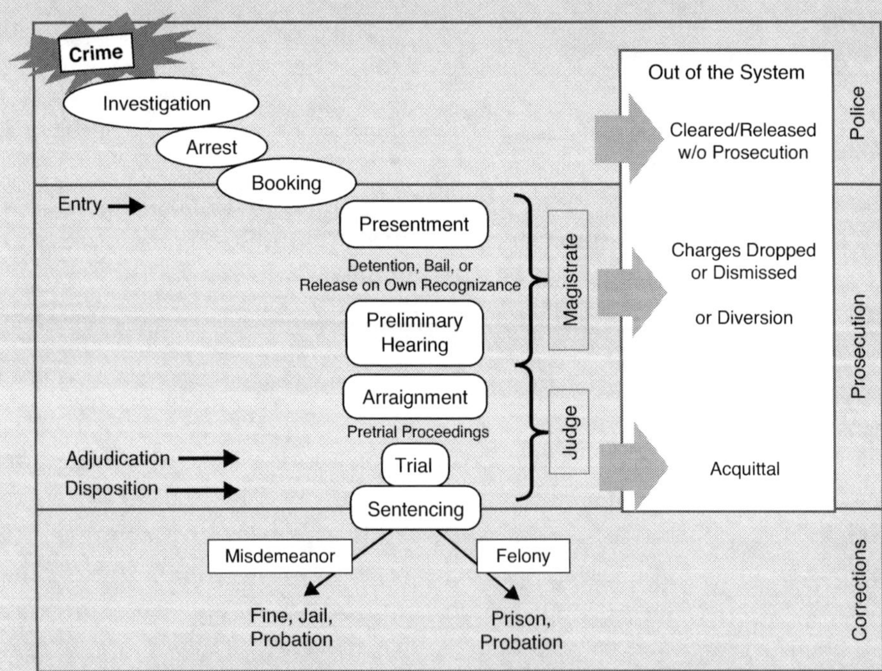

FIGURE 6.1 Criminal Procedures

Criminal Procedure Constitutional Control

Criminal procedure is governed by the U.S. Constitution, as well as federal and state law. Much of the criminal procedure has been developed over the last 75 years since the Supreme Court began to apply the Bill of Rights to the states to ensure that the accused is afforded due process. Fundamentally, *probable cause* is the standard to proceed for arrests, charging, preliminary hearings, and grand juries, but *beyond a reasonable doubt* is the standard for conviction at trial. Criminal procedure continues to evolve as police adopt new tactics and technologies, society changes, and the courts struggle to maintain a proper balance.

A state's police power is limited by (1) the Constitution, (2) the necessity of a legitimate public purpose, and (3) the reasonable exercise of that power (*President Riverboat Casino, Inc. v. Missouri Gaming Commission*, 2000).

The Constitution, as originally ratified by the states, contained few provisions regarding crimes.

- Treason is defined and requires at least two witnesses to the same overt act or by a confession in open court.
- The right to a jury trial in criminal cases is established and will be held in the state where the crime is committed.
- Bills of attainder, special (state or federal) legislation passed to punish a person or group statutorily, are prohibited.
- *Ex post facto* laws (state or federal) passed after the fact to punish a person or group retroactively are prohibited.
- Habeas corpus proceedings to release someone from unlawful detention are established as a right.

The Bill of Rights contains four amendments (IV, V, VI, VIII) that involve criminal procedure.

- The Fourth Amendment protects citizens from unreasonable search and seizure and establishes probable cause as a fundamental notion. It was written in response to general warrants and other writs that the British used to allow their agents to search anyone or any place at any time. Three chapters of this book are devoted to this.
- The Fifth Amendment establishes the rights of the accused and prosecuted. Notably, it mentions for the first time the concept of due process of law; it provides that citizens are not subject to criminal prosecution without due process. It requires indictment by a grand jury, although this provision is limited to federal crimes. It prohibits retrial for the same set of facts (double jeopardy). It establishes the right against compulsory self-incrimination (the right to remain silent).

- The Sixth Amendment assures the right to a speedy trial by a jury of one's peers, to be informed of the crimes with which one is charged, and to confront one's accusers. The amendment also provides the accused with the right to compel testimony from witnesses and the right to legal representation.
- The Eighth Amendment prohibits excessive bail, excessive fines, and cruel and unusual punishments.

BOX 6.4 CONSTITUTIONAL PROVISIONS APPLICABLE TO CRIMINAL LAW

Art. I, Sec. 9	Right to habeas corpus
	Prohibition of bills attainder
	Prohibition of *ex post facto laws*
Art. III, Sec. 2	Right to jury trial in criminal cases
Art. III, Sec. 3	Treason
Amendment IV	No unreasonable search and seizure
	Warrant requirement
Amendment V	Right to grand jury
	No double jeopardy
	Privilege against self-incrimination
	No taking of private property without just compensation
Amendment VI	Right to speedy trial
	Right to a jury trial where the crime occurred
	Notice of accusations
	Right to confront witnesses
	Right to subpoena
	Right to the assistance of counsel
Amendment VIII	No excessive bail
	No excessive fines
	No cruel and unusual punishments

Exclusionary Rule

The *exclusionary rule*, a judicially created rule in which evidence obtained outside constitutional limits is excluded from prosecution, is the primary tool of the courts to enforce compliance with constitutional constraints on law enforcement. It has become a bulwark of American criminal jurisprudence. Violations of search and seizure rules in England and Canada do not result in evidence being excluded. Possible remedies for police excesses include:

- Civil actions – civil actions were the only mechanism for enforcement when the Bill of Rights was adopted.
- Criminal actions – the police have been given broad statutory powers with exemptions that protect them, making criminal actions highly unlikely, except in excessive use-of-force cases.
- Administrative actions – police and civilian boards may discipline or fire police officers to guard against police excesses.
- Legislative actions – politicians do not want to be seen as soft on crime. The Bill of Rights is the primary protection from government encroachment on our civil rights. Legislatures may pass laws that restrict the power of the police.
- Exclusionary Rule – despite its drawbacks, the exclusionary rule has become the primary tool to enforce unconstitutional behavior. It is the only tool that courts have available. It is designed to dissuade police from future unconstitutional actions.

The *exclusionary rule* is a legal principle that holds that evidence collected or analyzed in violation of the defendant's constitutional rights is generally inadmissible for criminal prosecution. Although it is most often applied in Fourth Amendment contexts, it can also apply to the Fifth and Sixth Amendments and other constitutional violations.

The U.S. Supreme Court first applied an exclusionary rule in 1914 in *Weeks v. U.S.* In that case, the Court unanimously held that evidence illegally obtained by federal officers could not be used in federal criminal prosecutions. In 1949, in *Wolf v. Colorado*, the Court held that the Fourth Amendment was incorporated and applied to the states through the due process clause of the Fourteenth Amendment but was unwilling to include the *Weeks rule* regarding the exclusion of the evidence. Then, in 1961, in *Mapp v. Ohio*, the Court extended the exclusionary rule to the states as the need for it became apparent. Thus, the rule has only been applied to the states over the last half-century.

The exclusionary rule is a prophylactic rule formulated by the judiciary as a deterrent rather than an independent constitutional right. The exclusionary rule is not a perfect remedy. It results in suppression of the evidence, and only criminals ever directly benefit. The Court has acknowledged that the rule extracts a "high social cost of letting persons obviously guilty go unpunished for their crimes" (*Nix v. Williams*, 1984). The public often sees it as the bad person "getting off on a technicality." However, it has proven to be a powerful motivator for modifying police behavior. Moreover, it is the only tool the courts have.

Fruit of the Poisonous Tree: the fruit of the poisonous tree doctrine is a legal doctrine that extends the exclusionary rule to evidence that was indirectly derived – if the "tree" is tainted, so is its "fruit." Specifically, if evidence that falls within the scope of the exclusionary rule leads law enforcement to other evidence that they would not otherwise have been located, then the exclusionary rule applies to the newly discovered evidence. If the primary evidence was illegally obtained but held admissible under good faith or some other exception, its derivatives (or "fruit") may also be admissible. *Silverthorne Lumber Co. v. U.S.* (1920) established the "fruit of the poisonous tree" doctrine, but the term was not coined until Justice Frankfurter used it in *Nardone v. U.S.* (1939).

Exceptions to the Exclusionary Rule

The exclusionary rule is not in the Constitution; it is a judge-made rule and, as such, is not a right. Courts have carved out exceptions to the exclusionary rule where the costs of exclusion outweigh its deterrent or remedial benefits (*Illinois v. Krull*, 1987). The Court in *Herring v. U.S.* (2009), noted:

> To trigger the exclusionary rule, police conduct must be sufficiently deliberate that exclusion can meaningfully deter it, and sufficiently culpable that such deterrence is worth the price paid by the justice system. As laid out in our cases, the exclusionary rule serves to deter deliberate, reckless, or systemic negligence. The error in this case [warrant had been rescinded without the officer knowing] does not rise to that level.

- *GOOD FAITH* – the evidence is not excluded if officers reasonably rely on information they act on in good faith (*U.S. v. Leon*, 1984). The erroneous information need not be police errors (*Herring v. U.S.*, 2009; *Arizona v. Evans*, 1995). If a magistrate signs a warrant, the officers may act on it in good faith, even if it is later declared invalid (*Massachusetts v. Sheppard*, 1984).
- *INDEPENDENT SOURCE* – when the government violates the Fourth Amendment by conducting an illegal search, the independent source doctrine allows admission of evidence that is later discovered by means wholly independent of any constitutional violation (*Murray v. U.S., 1988*). For example, evidence initially discovered during an illegal entry of a dwelling may be admissible in evidence as an exception to the exclusionary rule if a later search is conducted under a valid warrant based solely on information that was obtained before the illegal police activity and that does not include what was seen during the illegal entry or seizure.
- *INEVITABLE DISCOVERY* – this doctrine allows admission of evidence discovered in an unlawful search or seizure where it

would have been found anyway through an independent line of investigation already pursued when the unlawful search or seizure occurred. (*Nix v. Williams*, 1984).

- *ATTENUATION* – where the relationship between the evidence challenged and the unconstitutional conduct is too remote and attenuated, the evidence may be admissible. The Supreme Court has noted three factors to consider when determining attenuation: (1) temporal proximity, (2) the presence of intervening circumstances, and (3) the purpose and flagrancy of the official misconduct. (*Utah v. Strieff*, 2016). The evidence of admission may be admissible despite its initial illegality if the initial taint has been purged by a later admission or similar event (*Wong Sun v. U.S.*, 1963).

It should also be noted that illegally obtained evidence or confessions do not prevent the government from introducing the illegally gathered evidence to attack the credibility of the defendant who testifies at trial during cross-examination to prevent perjury (*U.S. v. Havens*, 1980). Illegally obtained evidence may also be used in grand jury proceedings and proceedings other than those related to criminal matters.

BOX 6.5 *UTAH V. STRIEFF* (2016) – ATTENUATION DOCTRINE

Police surveilled a house and stopped Strieff without reasonable suspicion as he drove away from his home. During the unlawful stop, the police discovered that Strieff had an outstanding traffic warrant, for which the officer arrested him. A search incident to the arrest revealed drugs and paraphernalia. Justice Thomas found the evidence admissible because the arrest warrant "attenuated the connection between the unlawful stop and the evidence seized from Strieff incident to arrest."

Summary

After a police investigation, a grand jury indictment, or the arrest of a suspect apprehended during the commission of a crime, formal charges are brought against the suspect, who is now the defendant. The defendant will be summoned to court or arrested, given Miranda warnings, interrogated, and booked. The defendant will be held in jail or released on *bail* or *his or her own recognizance* to await further proceedings. The defendant will be brought before a magistrate within 24–48 hours at an initial appearance to be presented with the charges against him or her and advised of his or her rights. At an *arraignment*, the defendant will be advised of his or her rights and, during a plea colloquy, asked how they will plead. The defendant may be offered a civil *diversionary program* to avoid criminal liability. In state courts and without a grand jury, a *preliminary hearing* may be held, unless waived, to ensure there is probable cause to proceed to trial or not. Pretrial proceedings, including a pretrial hearing, may be held before trial. Then, a trial will be conducted, and the defendant will be sentenced if found guilty. Post-conviction remedies may follow, including an appeal or *writ of habeas corpus.*

Criminal procedure is governed by the U.S. Constitution's text, particularly the Fourth, Fifth, Sixth, and Eighth Amendments. The *exclusionary rule* maintains that evidence obtained from an illegal search and seizure may be excluded from the evidence used at trial, and the *fruit of the poisonous tree* doctrine holds that further evidence derived from such search and seizure may also be excluded. Exceptions to the exclusionary rule include good faith, independent source, inevitable discovery, and attenuation rules.

Terms

Arraignment – a hearing before the trial judge to obtain the defendant's plea of guilty or not guilty.

Attenuation – lessening of impact; gradual loss; where the connection between the evidence challenged and the illegal activity is so remote as to allow it to be admissible.

Bail – money or property posted to guarantee a later appearance in court.

Burden of Proof – the task required of a party to prove a claim.

Complaint – a formal request for police intervention by a citizen.

Diversion Program – a program that takes a defendant out of the system in an attempt for rehabilitation.

Exclusionary Rule – the prohibition of illegally obtained evidence in a criminal trial.

Grand Jury – secret hearing by a panel of citizens to determine probable cause to charge the defendant or to investigate criminal activity.

Indictment – a charging document issued by a grand jury.

Plea Colloquy – the exchange between the judge and the defendant, in which the defendant pleads guilty or not guilty.

Preliminary Hearing – a public hearing by a magistrate to determine probable cause to proceed.

Probable Cause – more than a mere reasonable suspicion but less than by a preponderance, substantial chance of criminal activity; the standard required for arresting someone, for issuing a warrant, and for bringing someone to trial; it is based upon the totality of the circumstances.

Writ of Capias – an arrest warrant issued by a court upon the return of an indictment.

Cases

Arizona v. Evans, 514 U.S. 1 (1995)
Batson v. Kentucky, 476 U.S. 79 (1986)
Cohen v. Beneficial Industrial Loan Corp., 337 U.S. 541 (1949)
Escobedo v. Illinois, 378 U.S. 478 (1964)
Hallock v. Bonner, 387 F.3d 147 (2d Cir. 2004)
Herring v. United States, 555 U.S. 135 (2009)
Illinois v. Krull, 480 U.S. 340 (1987)
Mapp v. Ohio, 367 U.S. 643 (1961)
Massachusetts v. Sheppard, 468 U.S. 981 (1984)
Miranda v. Arizona, 384 U.S. 436 (1966)
Murray v. United States, 487 U.S. 533 (1988)
Nardone v. United States, 308 U.S. 338 (1939)
Nix v. Williams, 467 U.S. 431 (1984)
President Riverboat Casino, Inc. v. Missouri Gaming Commission, 13 S.W.3d 635 (MO, 2000)
Silverthorne Lumber Co. v. United States, 251 U.S. 385 (1920)
United States v. Havens, 446 U.S. 620 (1980)
United States v. Leon, 468 U.S. 897 (1984)
Utah v. Strieff, 579 U.S. 232 (2016)
Weeks v. United States, 232 U.S. 383 (1914)
Wolf v. Colorado, 338 U.S. 25 (1949)
Wong Sun v. United States, 371 U.S. 471 (1963)

Statutes and Other Authorities

Criminal Procedure, 18 U.S.C. §§3001–3772

Thought Questions

1. What is the purpose of diversion programs?
2. Why would a state prefer a grand jury to a preliminary hearing or *vice versa*?
3. Should the courts recognize other exceptions to the exclusionary rule?

Further Reading

Boland B, Sones R, Prosecution of Felony Arrests, 1981, NIJ, NCJ 101380, 1985, https://www.ncjrs.gov/app/abstractdb/AbstractDBDetails.aspx?id=101380
Kesselring KJ, *Making Murder Public: Homicide in Early Modern England*, 1480–1680, Oxford University Press, Oxford, 2019.
Packer HL, *The Limits of Criminal Sanction*, Stanford Univ Press, Redwood City, CA, 1968.
Worral JL, *Criminal Procedure*, 3rd ed (Justice Series), Pearson, New York, 2017.

Chapter 7

Search and Seizure I

Reasonableness

Learning Objectives

After reading this chapter, students are expected to be able to:

- explain the purpose of the Fourth Amendment
- discuss the meaning of a search within the context of the Fourth Amendment
- detail the scope of the Fourth Amendment
- list items and objects that may be seized
- illustrate by example constitutional and unconstitutional searches

Introduction

The Fourth Amendment, the cornerstone of police power regulation in the United States, was born in a society where the government could intrude into private lives without restraint. However, it was crafted with reasonableness as the vital principle, ensuring that government intrusion is balanced and justified. The Fourth Amendment's *Reasonableness Clause* states:

> The right of the people to be secure in their persons, houses, papers, and effects, against unreasonable searches and seizures, shall not be violated,…

Early on, the Court noted that "the test of reasonableness cannot be stated in rigid and absolute terms," *Harris v. U.S.* (1947).

DOI: 10.4324/9780429272455-7

Historical Background

James Madison penned the Bill of Rights, comprising the first ten amendments to the Constitution. These amendments, which expressly restricted governmental power, responded to requests from several states for enhanced constitutional protection of individual liberties.

The Fourth Amendment was crafted as a direct response to the despised writs of assistance and general warrants that the colonists endured. These warrants, issued by the British Crown, granted the bearer the authority to search or seize anyone or anything, wherever they wished, during the King's reign, solely based on a vague claim of disloyalty by anyone with a grievance. General warrants had been used for centuries to suppress political and religious dissent. They were extensively used in colonial and revolutionary America to raid colonial homes for seditious papers or other evidence of disloyalty. Colonists saw them as tools of tyranny.

Boston lawyer James Otis Jr. challenged the British colonial government in Paxton's case (1761) when writs of assistance (a type of general warrant) were to be re-issued after the death of King George II.

State after state went on to outlaw general warrants in their constitutions before the Fourth Amendment prohibited it in the federal Constitution. President John Adams thought the dreaded general warrants were the spark that lit the revolutionary fires.

Madison drew language from the Massachusetts constitution of 1780, which originated in James Otis' 1761 court argument against general warrants; he rejected the narrower version of the 1776 Virginia constitution (*Harris v. U.S.*, 1947).

The federal government was limited and weak when then-Representative James Madison wrote the Bill of Rights. It was an age before the industrial revolution, before police departments, before surveillance technologies, gasoline, electricity, cellphones, and the internet. Enslaved Black people and women did not yet vote.

Fourth Amendment

When James Madison drafted the Bill of Rights, he intended it to be a set of rights the new central government could not abridge. Among these rights, he wanted to include the prohibition of general warrants and the right to be left alone. Madison would have thought that the Bill of Rights enforcement would be through civil lawsuits brought by private citizens. There were no police then, but Madison thought government officials might want to conduct searches to find incriminating evidence. Madison would have conceived the searches as trespassing on your land, invading your home, and seizing your private property. Thus, notions of privacy and the right to be left alone were intertwined with governmental searches and seizures.

James Madison drafted the prohibition of general warrants and the right to be left alone into the Fourth Amendment:

> The right of the people to be secure in their persons, houses, papers, and effects, against unreasonable searches and seizures, shall not be violated, and No Warrants shall issue, but upon probable cause, supported by Oath or affirmation, and particularly describing the place to be searched, and the persons or things to be seized.

This text consists of two clauses:

1. *Reasonableness Clause* that prohibits unreasonable searches and seizures, and
2. *Warrant Clause* that eliminates the hated general warrant.

Since the Bill of Rights was meant to be a check on the central government, the founding fathers saw it as applying to the new federal government, not state governments. This was confirmed in the 1791 Supreme Court case of *Barron v. Baltimore* (1833).

Scope of the Fourth Amendment

Who is protected? The Fourth Amendment begins with "The right of the people…" The *people* are not just *citizens.* It should be remembered that at the time of the drafting, enslaved Black people and women were disenfranchised and could not vote. The preamble of the Constitution describes the Government of the people, by the people, and for the people. "People" would seem to apply to everyone. In *U.S. v. Verdugo-Urquidez* (1990), the Supreme Court declared that "people" includes aliens within the United States who have developed a substantial connection with this country.

Protection from whom? Although the Fourth Amendment does not explicitly state from whom the protections apply, it applies to government actors and not private actors. The Bill of Rights protects citizens against unwarranted *state action* (government action), not private action. Private employers, corporations, and associations can often lawfully do what the government cannot do. Government actors include government employees and other agents working on behalf of the government. Although there was no law enforcement as we know it today at the time of the drafting, it speaks directly to law enforcement. Specifically, when originally written, the Fourth Amendment applied only to federal government actors. This limitation persisted for nearly two centuries, and very few cases referred to it. The Fourth Amendment search and seizure requirements were first applied to the states through the Fourteenth Amendment *Due Process* clause in *Mapp v. Ohio* (1961) and have since become a controlling factor to law enforcement at all levels.

What is protected? The Fourth Amendment does not cover all property but specifies "…to be secure in their persons, houses, papers, and effects…." When Madison drafted these words, he seemed to be thinking about seizures on private property and that a search warrant would be required to authorize the trespass necessary to conduct the seizure. Particularly, the reference to houses has suggested to many the notion embodied in the epithet: "a man's home is his castle" – that the home is a place of special status, where people have an expectation of privacy and being left alone (*U.S. v. Chadwick*, 1977).

Today, we understand that the Fourth Amendment protects both property and liberty rights. Liberty rights, including privacy, are not explicitly mentioned in the text but are inferred. In an early case, *Boyd v. U.S.* (1886), the U.S. Supreme Court discussed a zone of privacy created by the Fourth and Fifth Amendments. Later, the Court in *Griswold v. Connecticut* (1965) specifically found a constitutional right to privacy in the "penumbras" and "emanations" of the constellation of other constitutional protections.

The notion of personal privacy "…to be secure…," together with property interests in "persons, houses, papers, and effects," create a constitutionally protected zone of privacy and property. This zone protects your personal liberty, private matters, and property, not public ones. Your private matters are notional and require privacy protection, and your property interests are tangible and require trespassory protection; public matters are not secret, and public property does not invoke trespass. When Louis Brandeis and his law partner Samuel Warren published "The Right to Privacy" in the Harvard Law Review in 1890, they termed this the "right to be let alone."

BOX 7.1 *BOYD V. UNITED STATES* (1886) – ZONE OF PRIVACY

Thirty-five cases of plate glass produced by the Union Plate Glass Company of Liverpool, England, and delivered to E.A. Boyd & Sons were seized at the Port of New York for not paying import duties. The government prosecutors moved the judge to order Boyd & Sons to produce their invoice. Boyd complied but claimed the order was a form of self-incrimination. This action resulted in the forfeiture of goods. Technically, neither the Fourth nor Fifth Amendments applied since there was no search and the case was not criminal. Nonetheless, the Supreme Court held that the Fourth and Fifth Amendments, taken together, protect a zone of privacy. The court order to produce the document was ruled to be the equivalent of an unconstitutional search. Citizens cannot be compelled to produce what the government cannot search for and seize. Justice Bradley wrote:

> The principles… affect the very essence of constitutional liberty and security… they apply to all invasions on the part of the government and its employees of

> the sanctity of a man's home and the privacies of life. It is not the breaking of his doors and the rummaging of his drawers that constitutes the essence of the offence, but it is the invasion of his indefeasible right of personal security, personal liberty, and private property, where that right has never been forfeited by his conviction of some public offence,...

The holding has since not been expressly overruled but has been limited or negated by subsequent Court rulings in later times with the proliferation of police departments, new technologies, and extensive regulations. Particularly, nontestimonial evidence, contraband, instrumentalities of a crime, and fruits of a crime may now be searched for and seized under proper circumstances (*Fisher v. U.S., 1976*). Nonetheless, the case was an early landmark that articulated an important legal privacy perspective.

Much of the early Fourth Amendment case law focused on whether the government obtained information by physically intruding on a constitutionally protected area. Hence, in *Olmstead v. U.S.* (1928), the Court permitted wiretapping because it did not involve a trespass. As technology changed, the ability of the government to gather sensitive information changed. In *Katz v. U.S.* (1967), the Court developed a new Fourth Amendment framework based upon an individual's reasonable expectation of privacy.

BOX 7.2 *KATZ V. UNITED STATES* (1967) – REASONABLE EXPECTATION OF PRIVACY

Charles Katz used a public pay phone booth near his hotel room to transmit illegal gambling wagers. The FBI recorded his conversations with a microphone taped to the outside of the phone booth over a period of six days. The government argued this was not a search because there was no physical intrusion into the phone booth. Justice Potter Stewart held that electronic eavesdropping was an unreasonable search, "The Fourth Amendment protects people, not places." The court explicitly overruled *Olmstead v. U.S.* (1928), which had upheld the federal wiretap of public telephone lines outside the home and offices of the defendant to listen into private conversations for months over the claims of the defendant that it was a violation of his Fourth and Fifth Amendment rights.

In his concurrence in Katz, Justice Harlan declared:

> ...there is a twofold requirement, first, that a person has exhibited an actual (subjective) expectation of privacy and, second, that the expectation be one that society is prepared to recognize as 'reasonable.' ...The critical fact, in this case, is that '[o]ne who occupies it, [a telephone booth] shuts the door behind him and pays the toll that permits him to place a call is surely entitled to assume' that his conversation is not being intercepted.

Protected from What? The Fourth Amendment declares, "...unreasonable searches and seizures shall not be violated..." Thus, people are protected only from *unreasonable* searches and seizures. Searches and seizures are separate and independent elements, both protected by the Fourth Amendment – there can be a search and no seizure or a seizure and no search.

A search within the meaning of the Fourth Amendment that triggers constitutional protections involves *looking*. A search may be an exploration or examination by the government of an individual's house, premises, or person to discover evidence for criminal prosecution. A search may be found when a person's reasonable expectation of privacy is invaded due to state action. A search may be found when the state trespasses on a person's property. A court will not find a "search" if it is looking outside a constitutionally protected zone. A search for a body in a city park is not a search for Fourth Amendment purposes.

A seizure within the meaning of the Fourth Amendment that triggers constitutional protections involves a *taking*. A seizure may directly interfere with an individual's possessory interest by state action. A seizure may be found where the government exercises dominion or control over a person or thing because of an apparent violation of law. Items subject to police seizures fall into three general categories:

1. *Evidence* of a crime, such as clothing containing blood or a mask worn by a robber
2. *Contraband*, such as drugs, counterfeit money
3. *Fruits of a crime*, such as stolen goods

The fundamental determinant of whether a search and seizure pass constitutional muster is whether the search and seizure were reasonable. A warrant that authorizes the search and seizure, conducted within the warrant's scope, will be presumed reasonable. Warrants are issued based on probable cause. Well-recognized exceptions to the warrant requirement permit a finding of reasonableness, such as plain view, consent, hot pursuit, exigency, and incident to an arrest. With some reluctance, the exceptions have been broadened. Probable cause and reasonableness findings may allow courts to find searches and seizures constitutionally permissible. A court may look at the exigency of the circumstances, the degree of suspicion, and the intrusiveness and scope of the search considering all the circumstances.

The government cannot conduct unreasonable searches and seizures within the constitutionally protected zone. It will generally require a warrant based on probable cause. Outside the protected zone, the government has much more leeway in conducting criminal investigations. It can do what it wants, when it wants, for as long as it wants, assuming that the activity is not otherwise prohibited by law.

What Is a Search?

The real question is not what a search is, but what is an unreasonably intrusive search by government agents that the Fourth Amendment constitutionally protects? When the U.S. Supreme Court speaks of a search, they are not talking about any hunt, looking, or investigation, but a hunt, looking, or investigation within a constitutionally protected zone of an expectation of privacy. Thus, a search of a public place is not a search at all for purposes of the Fourth Amendment. There is a privacy and trespassory component to the protected zone, which includes your person, home, and, to some extent, your car and any other place where you have a reasonable expectation of privacy. In *Byrd v. U.S.* (2018), for example, the Court held that someone in otherwise lawful possession and control of a rental car has a reasonable expectation of privacy even if the rental agreement does not list him as an authorized driver.

- CURTILAGE – the curtilage is the zone of habitation that extends beyond the physical home. It is the land immediately surrounding a house, including any closely associated sheds, barns, garages, and similar structures. It excludes any associated open fields and any associated structures with other residents living in them. The curtilage delineates the boundary within which a homeowner can reasonably expect privacy. The curtilage harbors the intimate activities associated with the sanctity of a man's home and the privacies of life (*Oliver v. U.S.*, 1984). It is part of the home for many legal purposes,

FIGURE 7.1 Protected Zone.

FIGURE 7.2 Curtilage.

including searches and self-defense laws. The curtilage is part of the home for Fourth Amendment purposes (*Florida v. Jardines*, 2013). In *U.S. v. Dunn* (1987), the court defined the curtilage as that which "harbors the intimate activity associated with the… privacies of life" and found four factors to be considered when deciding if a location is included within the curtilage: (1) whether the location is in proximity to the home? (2) Whether the location is within an enclosure around the house? (3) What is the nature and uses to which the location is put? (4) Were steps taken by the residents to protect the location from observation by people passing by?

BOX 7.3 *COLLINS V. VIRGINIA* (2018) – CURTILAGE

The police learned that a motorcycle in the possession of Ryan Collins was likely stolen. Photographs on Collins' Facebook profile showed a motorcycle parked in the driveway of a house. An officer drove to the house without a search warrant and removed the tarp covering the motorcycle, revealing the stolen motorcycle's license plate and vehicle identification numbers. The officer then waited in his car for Collins and arrested him when he returned. Collins moved to suppress the evidence arguing that Officer Rhodes violated the Fourth Amendment when he trespassed on the house's curtilage to search. The automobile exception does not permit the warrantless entry of a home or its curtilage to search for a vehicle therein.

- *PUBLIC INVITATION* – a front walkway and a doorbell or knocker are typically treated as an invitation, or license, to the public to approach the home's front door to deliver mail, sell goods, etc. This invitation extends to the police, who may "knock and talk" to gather evidence without a warrant.

BOX 7.4 *FLORIDA V. JARDINES* (2013) – DOG SNIFF

After receiving an anonymous tip that a particular house was being used for illegally growing marijuana, police brought a drug-sniffing police dog to the front door. The dog alerted at the door to the scent of contraband. A search warrant was issued, leading to the homeowner's arrest. Justice John Roberts held that the police were "invited" to the front porch and the door of the residence, but that the use of a trained detection dog to sniff for narcotics at the front door for odors from within the residence was a "search," and beyond the scope of the invitation. Therefore, without consent, the dog sniff of the premises requires both probable cause and a search warrant, despite three previous cases in which the Court held that a dog sniff was not a search when deployed against (1) luggage at an airport, (2) against vehicles in a drug interdiction checkpoint, and (3) against vehicles during routine traffic stops. In this case, however, the officer was within the house's curtilage and not as an invited guest into the home.

- *OPEN-FIELDS DOCTRINE* – the legal doctrine holds that a search outside the *curtilage* (the zone of habitation) of a homeowners' property is not constitutionally protected and does not require a warrant. Open fields do not provide the setting for activities that the Fourth Amendment intended to shelter from government intrusion or surveillance. The open-fields doctrine applies to any unoccupied or underdeveloped area outside the curtilage. The area need not be "open" or a "field." The government's intrusion upon an open field is not a search in a constitutional sense, although it may be a trespass at common law.

BOX 7.5 *OLIVER V. UNITED STATES* (1984) – OPEN-FIELDS DOCTRINE

Ray Oliver was convicted after police officers, without a warrant, drove their car onto Oliver's property past his house and walked past a no-trespassing sign about a mile before finding his marijuana plants. The U.S. Supreme Court declared that there is no reasonable expectation of privacy in an open field where hikers or airplanes may see things. Thus, there was no search for Fourth Amendment purposes.

- *PERSONAL COMMUNICATIONS* – private conversations are personal and thus afford a reasonable expectation of privacy from interception by third parties. Where information is disclosed to another or made public through disclosure to third parties, it is no longer private and thus not protected; in other words, divulging information to another person or third parties extinguishes your reasonable expectation of privacy concerning that conversation or information.

BOX 7.6 *UNITED STATES V. WHITE* (1971) – THIRD-PARTY DISCLOSURE

James White was convicted of narcotics charges after talking to a friend, who, with knowledge and without a warrant, had been fitted with a concealed microphone and radio transmitter (a wire). The Court held that the electronic surveillance was not a search because White lost any reasonable expectation of privacy when he confided in a friend who might disclose the secret to the police; in other words, the information was no longer private. The recorded conversation merely documented what the informant would report.

Justice Harlan dissented, declaring that:

> the uncontrolled consensual surveillance in an electronic age is a tolerable technique of law enforcement given the values and goals of our political system. … [this tolerance should be balanced against] the likely extent of its impact on the individual's sense of security. … the Orwellian Big Brother, … third-party electronic monitoring, subject only to the self-restraint of law enforcement officials, has no place in our society, … and at the least warrants should be necessary.

- *SURVEILLANCE AS A SEARCH* – prolonged surveillance, whether in person, electronic, or video, can constitute a search within the meaning of the Fourth Amendment, but the court must consider it intrusive.

BOX 7.7 *UNITED STATES V. HOUSTON* (2016) – POLE CAMERA SURVEILLANCE

Police mounted a pole camera on a utility pole on public property next to a residence. From 200 yards away, the camera had an open view of the farmhouse but could not peer into the residence. The camera was used without a warrant for ten weeks, and then they obtained a warrant. Rocky Joe Houston was convicted of firearms possession. The sixth Circuit held that ten weeks' worth of video of what happened on a suspect's property using a video camera on a public utility pole is not a "search" under the Fourth Amendment. The Court distinguished Justice Alito's concern in *United States v. Jones* that long-term monitoring (four weeks in that case) would "secretly monitor and catalogue every single movement" of the defendant. Instead, the pole camera was stationary and only recorded the defendant's activities outdoors on the farm and not away from the farm.

BOX 7.8 *UNITED STATES V. JONES* (2012) – GPS TRACKER

In 2004, the FBI and the Washington, DC police began investigating Jones and Maynard for narcotics violations. Law enforcement officers surreptitiously placed a Global Positioning System (GPS) transponder on Jones's Jeep to monitor the vehicle's movements. It was tracked 24 hours a day for four weeks. They had obtained a warrant, but it was invalid because it was issued by another jurisdiction and had expired. The defense moved to suppress the GPS data. The government argued that courts had previously held GPS trackers were merely technological aids for recording vehicle movements in plain view because they could assign police to monitor the cars' movements on public roads. The motion was denied, and Jones was eventually convicted of possession with intent to distribute cocaine and sentenced to life in prison.

The U.S. Supreme Court unanimously held that placing a GPS on a vehicle to monitor its movements is an unconstitutional search, but the court split 5–4 on the rationale and the breadth of the decision.

Justice Antonin Scalia, for the majority, gave a trespassory rationale. He cited cases back to 1886 to argue that a physical intrusion, or trespass, into a constitutionally protected area – to find something or to obtain information – was the historical basis for determining whether a "search" had occurred under the meaning of the Fourth Amendment. He acknowledged that most search and seizure case law had shifted away from that approach founded on property rights and toward an approach based on a person's "expectation of privacy." However, a trespassory test had not been abandoned, which guaranteed the minimum level of protection under the Fourth Amendment when adopted.

A trespassory test does not exclude expectation of privacy test as well. He found that the Fourth Amendment protects effects, and a car is undoubtedly an effect. The transponder occupied space on a protected effect, and the device placement amounted to physical trespass. He concluded that physical trespass plus information gathering is a *per se* search but added, "It may be that achieving the same result through electronic means, without an accompanying trespass, is an unconstitutional invasion of privacy, but the present case does not require us to answer that question." This ruling is narrow and did not address a warrant requirement or other reasonableness exceptions because the government advanced none in the case.

In a concurring opinion, Justice Samuel Alito and three others reached the same result based upon a reasonable expectation of privacy rather than trespass. Alito argued that the majority's reliance on trespass was "neither necessary nor sufficient to establish a constitutional violation." The four-justice minority opined that the continuous monitoring of every movement of an individual's car for 28 days violated a "reasonable expectation of privacy." They pointed to *United States v. Knotts* (1983) and thought that the prolonged surveillance in this case is a violation of the expectation of privacy that a short period would not be. In *Knotts*, a short-distance signal beeper in the defendant's car was tracked for less than a day during a single trip. The *Knotts* Court held that a person traveling on public roads has no expectation of privacy in his movements because the vehicle's starting point, direction, stops, or destination could be seen by anyone else on the road.

Justice Sonia Sotomayor wrote a separate concurring opinion. She agreed with Alito's reasoning on prolonged surveillance, but thought even a short-term GPS surveillance is unconstitutional because GPS surveillance can precisely record an individual's every movement and hence can reveal completely private destinations, like "trips to the psychiatrist, the plastic surgeon, the abortion clinic, the AIDS treatment center, the strip club, the criminal defense attorney, the by-the-hour motel, the union meeting, the mosque, synagogue or church, the gay bar and on and on." Sotomayor wrote:

> People disclose the phone numbers that they dial or text to their cellular providers; the URLs that they visit and the e-mail addresses with which they correspond to their Internet service providers, and the books, groceries, and medications they purchase to online retailers... I would not assume that all information voluntarily disclosed to some member of the public for a limited purpose is, for that reason alone, disentitled to Fourth Amendment protection.

- *ELECTRONIC COMMUNICATIONS* – private conversations through the internet are shared with internet service providers (ISPs), who also maintain stored information on where messages come from and go to and at what time. In the early days of telegraphs and original dial telephones, *pen registers* (aka dialed number recorder (DNR)) collected the phone numbers of outgoing calls, and *trap and trace devices* collected phone numbers of incoming calls, neither of which devices recorded the content of the communication. The terms "pen register" and "trap and trace" have been expanded and applied to devices and software that perform the same function for modern internet metadata. Similarly, GPS tracker information conveys location data but no content.

BOX 7.9 *SMITH V. MARYLAND* (1979) – USE OF PEN REGISTERS

At police request, the telephone company installed a pen register at its central offices to record the numbers dialed from the telephone of Smith's home. Smith's motion to suppress "all fruits derived from" the pen register was denied, and he was convicted. The U.S. Supreme Court held that the installation and use of the pen register was not a "search" within the meaning of the Fourth Amendment. Hence, no warrant was required because there was no invasion of a constitutionally protected area (the telephone company's property) or an infringement of a legitimate expectation of privacy. Justice Blackmun found that there was no expectation of privacy:

> All telephone users realize that they must 'convey' phone numbers to the telephone company, since it is through telephone company switching equipment that their calls are completed. All subscribers realize, moreover, that the phone company has facilities for making permanent records of the numbers they dial, for they see a list of their long-distance (toll) calls on their monthly bills. In fact, pen registers and similar devices are routinely used by telephone companies for the 'purposes of checking billing operations, detecting fraud, and preventing violations of law.'

Stored Communications. In 1986, Congress acknowledged that traditional Fourth Amendment protections were lacking and enacted the Electronic Communications Privacy Act (ECPA) as an update on the Federal Wiretap Act of 1968, which had addressed protections on telephone landline privacies. The provisions include the Pen Register Act, which requires law enforcement to obtain a court order, and the Stored Communications Act (SCA), which creates Fourth Amendment-like privacy protection for email and other digital communications stored on the internet. The SCA limits the ability of the government to compel an ISP to release content information and metadata (such as logs and "envelope" information from email) without a search warrant; additionally, it restricts commercial ISPs from disclosing content information to nongovernment entities.

BOX 7.10 *RILEY V. CALIFORNIA* (2014) – CELLPHONES

In this case, the U.S. Supreme Court unanimously held that the warrantless search and seizure of digital cellphone contents, even if seized incident to an arrest, is unreasonable and, therefore, unconstitutional. The Court chose to review two cases in a consolidated opinion, one involving flip phones and the other involving a modern smartphone, which holds more information about the user.

In the first case, David Leon Riley was pulled over for expired registration tags. During the stop, the police officer also found that Riley was driving with a suspended driver's license. According to police policy, the car was inventory searched in preparation for impounding the vehicle, which led to the discovery of two handguns under the hood of the vehicle. Riley was placed under arrest, and his cellphone was seized and searched, which revealed photographs and video that were subsequently used as evidence to connect him to the Lincoln Park gang and convict him of gangland murder.

In the second case, Brima Wurie was arrested after police observed him participate in an apparent drug sale. At the police station, the officers seized two cellphones from Wurie's person, including the "flip phone" at issue. Shortly after arriving at the station, the phone began receiving multiple calls from a source identified as "my house." The police traced that number to Wurie's apartment. They obtained a search warrant and found drugs, drug paraphernalia, a firearm, ammunition, and cash in the apartment. A motion to suppress was denied at trial but reversed and granted on appeal of his conviction, declaring that cellphones are distinct from other physical possessions that may be searched incident to arrest without a warrant because of the amount of personal data on cellphones and the minimal impact of the requirement on law enforcement.

Chief Justice John Roberts, writing for the Court, noted that existing Fourth Amendment frameworks—like the third-party doctrine—may be "ill suited to the digital age."

The Court held the warrantless cellphone search fails the test established in *Chimel*:

> Digital data stored on a cell phone cannot be used as a weapon to harm an arresting officer or effectuate the arrestee's escape. Law enforcement officers remain free to examine the physical aspects of a phone to ensure that it will not be used as a weapon--say, to determine whether a razor blade is hidden between the phone and its case. Once an officer has secured a phone and eliminated any potential physical threats, however, data on the phone can endanger no one.

Justice Roberts declared that cellphones differ both quantitatively and qualitatively from other objects in a person's pocket:

> Modern cell phones are not just another technological convenience. With all they contain and all they may reveal, they hold for many Americans 'the privacies of life.' The fact that technology now allows an individual to carry such information in his hand does not make the information any less worthy of the protection for which the Founders fought.

Justice Samuel Alito wrote an opinion, concurring in part:

> we should not mechanically apply the rule used in the predigital era to the search of a cell phone. Many cell phones now in use are capable of storing and accessing a quantity of information, some highly personal, that no person would ever have had on his person in hard-copy form.

Alito further suggested that Congress or state legislatures may need to consider new laws that draw "reasonable distinctions based on categories of information or perhaps other variables." Otherwise, "...it would be very unfortunate if privacy protection in the 21st century were left primarily to the federal courts using the blunt instrument of the Fourth Amendment."

Note: the rationale in *Riley* applies not only to searches incident to arrest but also to warrantless searches based on the automobile exception. Justice Roberts did not discount the possibility that the exigent circumstances exception might apply in a particular case.

BOX 7.11 *CARPENTER V. UNITED STATES* (2018) – CELLPHONE TRACKING

A group of thieves from Detroit conducted a string of armed robberies over four months in Michigan and Ohio. The robbers told the customers and staff to give up their cellphones. Police captured four robbers, one of whom confessed and turned over his cellphone. A magistrate, per the SCA, granted the FBI's request for a court order for "transactional records" from various wireless carriers for 16 different phone numbers, for

> all subscriber information, toll records and call detail records including listed and unlisted numbers dialed or otherwise transmitted to and from target telephones... as well as cell site information for the target telephones at call origination and at call termination for incoming and outgoing calls.

The FBI also obtained a court order for disclosure of the information. They obtained a search warrant based upon the SCA that authorizes searches based on "reasonable grounds" rather than "probable cause." The FBI tracked Carpenter's cell site location information (CSLI) for 127 days and determined that Carpenter was within a two-mile radius of four robberies. Using this information, Carpenter was convicted and sentenced to 116 years in federal prison.

In a 5–4 split, the Court held that the third-party doctrine applied to telephone communications in *Smith v. Maryland* (1979) could not be applied to cellphone technology and ruled that the government must obtain a warrant to access historical cellphone records.

Chief Justice John Roberts, writing for the majority, noted that cellphones can be seen as a "feature of human anatomy" as individuals "compulsively carry cell phones with them all the time" and "give the Government near perfect surveillance."

He argued that technology:

> has afforded law enforcement a powerful new tool to carry out its important responsibilities. At the same time, this tool risks Government encroachment of the sort the Framers, 'after consulting the lessons of history,' drafted the Fourth Amendment to prevent.

and adds:

> Seismic shifts in digital technology made possible the tracking of not only Carpenter's location but also everyone else's, not for a short period but for years and years. Sprint Corporation and its competitors are not your typical witnesses. Unlike the nosy neighbor who keeps an eye on comings and goings, they are ever alert, and their memory is nearly infallible. There is a world of difference between the limited types of personal information addressed in *Smith* and *Miller* and the exhaustive chronicle of location information casually collected by wireless carriers today.

Justice Roberts noted that the "detailed, encyclopedic, and effortlessly compiled" data used in tracking a person by cell towers was qualitatively like that of using a GPS tracking device, as determined by *Jones*. Roberts stressed that the decision is a very narrow ruling; it does not affect other parts of the third-party doctrine, such as banking records, nor does it prevent collection of cell tower data without a warrant in emergencies or for national security issues.

Justice Anthony Kennedy, joined by three others, dissented and cautioned against tying the hands of law enforcement:

> This case involves new technology, but the Court's stark departure from relevant Fourth Amendment precedents and principles is, in my submission, unnecessary and incorrect, requiring this respectful dissent. The new rule the Court seems to formulate puts needed, reasonable, accepted, lawful, and congressionally authorized criminal investigations at serious risk in serious cases, often when law enforcement seeks to prevent the threat of violent crimes. And it places undue restrictions on the lawful and necessary enforcement powers exercised not only by the Federal Government, but also by law enforcement in every State and locality throughout the Nation. Adherence to this Court's longstanding precedents and analytic framework would have been the proper and prudent way to resolve this case.

Justice Alito wrote in his dissent:

> I share the Court's concern about the effect of new technology on personal privacy, but I fear that today's decision will do far more harm than good. The Court's reasoning fractures two fundamental pillars of Fourth Amendment law, and in doing so, it guarantees a blizzard of litigation while threatening many legitimate and valuable investigative practices upon which law enforcement has rightfully come to rely.

In his dissent, Justice Gorsuch argued for a strict trespassory approach. He declared that cellphone location records are the property of cellphone owners and that the Fourth Amendment does not allow law enforcement agencies to search a person's property without a warrant. He also stated his belief that *Katz* was wrongly decided and that the Fourth Amendment does not provide any right to a "reasonable expectation of privacy."

Note: On remand, when the defense argued that the cellphone tracking data should have been subject to the exclusionary rule, the Court found the FBI acted in good faith and thus still allowed that evidence to be used against Carpenter. Carpenter was sentenced to 116 years in prison.

Carpenter is seen as drawing "a line between short-term tracking of public movements, similar to what law enforcement could do prior to the digital age, and prolonged tracking that can reveal intimate details through habits and patterns."

Cellphone Dragnets. Since 2016, law enforcement has increasingly sought "geofence" warrants requesting location data for users within a particular vicinity of a crime during a particular time span from Google and other service providers – somewhat similar to investigation of video cameras that may have captured a crime. It has sometimes been dubbed a cellphone dragnet. Google collects the Location History of over 500 million users every two minutes. About one-third of Google users have enabled "Location History," that allows personalized map information, location of a lost cellphone, and traffic updates. The data is stored in Google's "Sensorvault." Google has established a three-step process that requires a narrowing of the search prior to providing account-identifying information (i.e., name and email address). The Fourth Circuit Court in *U.S. v. Chatrie* (4th Cir., 2025) upheld a search when conducted by an objectively reasonable warrant based upon a finding of good faith by the officer.

BOX 7.12 *UNITED STATES V. CHATRIE* (2023) – CELLPHONE DRAGNET

The initial investigation of an armed robbery of a bank was unfruitful. A detective noted on a security video recording that the suspect was carrying a cellphone and obtained a geofence warrant for all anonymized Location History data from 30 minutes before the robbery to 30 minutes after the robbery within 150-meter radius of the bank (the geofence). This first step yielded 209 location data points from 19 accounts. The detective then requested information from one hour before the robbery to one hour after the robbery that was unbounded by the geofence from nine accounts. This second step yielded 680 data points from these nine accounts. In a third step, the detective requested the subscriber information for three accounts, one of which belonged to the suspect. After his conviction, Chatrie appealed the denial of his motion to suppress the location data, claiming that the geofence warrant violated his Fourth Amendment rights, that the fruits of the warrant should be suppressed because the search invaded his reasonable expectation of privacy and that the warrant was invalid for lack of probable cause and particularity. The District Court found the search to be constitutional based on the good faith exception and the Fourth Circuit Court of Appeals affirmed on an initial appeal and again in an *en banc* rehearing resulting in a *per curiam* decision with seven concurring opinions and one dissent. The Chief Judge noted,

> One camp insists that disallowing geofence warrants would contravene our precedent, hamstring law enforcement in investigating crimes, and chill innovation at any private company that handles a large database of users. The other camp is just as adamant that granting blanket approval to these warrants would contravene our precedent and compromise the privacy interests of cell phone users.

As of December 13, 2023, Google stopped responding to subpoenas for reverse-location searches of individuals within the vicinity of a crime of a given timeframe ("geofence warrants"), which had increased dramatically since 2018 because they no longer store "Location History" data in Google Maps in a way that allows the company to access it.

Locked Cellphones. The massive amount of content on cellphones is often crucial to criminal investigations but also has significant privacy implications; thus, access to this content has become a consequential legal battlefield. In particular, the law is unsettled concerning the compulsion to give a biometric key to unlock a cellphone. In *United States v. Kirschner* (2010), the court held that divulging a passcode amounts to testimony and is subject to the Fifth Amendment's protection against self-incrimination; the court held the government could not compel the production of the passcode. *In the Matter of the Search of a Residence in Oakland, California* (2016), a federal magistrate held that biometric features, such as a fingerprint, as the functional equivalent of a passcode, are *testimonial* and that compulsion to submit biometric features is an abuse of power and violates the Fifth Amendment right against self-incrimination. However, in *In the Matter of the Search of a White Google Pixel 3XL Cellphone in a Black Incipio Case* (2019), the court held that fingerprints or facial features were physical characteristics not subject to Fourth Amendment protection and not *testimonial* or subject to Fifth Amendment protection and thus permitted compulsion to produce such biometric data. In *State v. Andrews* (2020), the court held that the production of a passcode is testimonial and subject to the Fifth Amendment's protection against self-incrimination but allowed compulsion based upon applying the *foregone conclusion* exception to the Fifth Amendment protection. Numerous other courts are grappling with this issue, and the lack of a clear consensus suggests that the U.S. Supreme Court will eventually have to resolve the issue.

Cell-site Simulators. Law enforcement has used mobile cellphone tower simulator technology ("Stingray," "Hailstorm," "TriggerFish"), generically known as international mobile subscriber identity (IMSI)-catchers, to geolocate cellphones in real time. IMSI catchers are substantially different than previous phone-tracking technology, as they are not only capable of revealing phones' location, but they also record phone numbers and the content of voice and text communication. Furthermore, IMSI technology has the potential to edit data, divert calls and text messages, or spoof the identity of a caller. IMSI catchers will also intercept or block 911 calls that pose a safety risk. The official position of the Department of Justice (DOJ) was that IMSI-catchers do not require a search warrant because they are a pen register, which, based upon *Smith v. Maryland*. The Cell-Site Simulator Warrant Act of 2021 permits the use of IMSI catchers, but only upon probable cause and the issuance of a search warrant.

Summary

The Fourth Amendment's reasonableness clause was written in reaction to the general warrants issued by the English government. Generally, it protects "people" from unreasonable government intrusions into their privacy – their private thoughts and their private places. Specifically, it protects people from unreasonable searches and seizures by government actors to ensure their security in their "persons, houses, papers, and effects." The Fourth Amendment covers arrests and the taking of evidence, contraband, and fruits of a crime.

The protected zone includes the person and their home and, to some extent, the vehicles they are driving or parked at home – places where you have a reasonable expectation of privacy. Outside the protected zone, the police can search for anything, anywhere, and anytime. More specifically, the protected zone includes the home's *curtilage* – the habitation zone; it does not include open fields or anywhere outside the curtilage. A GPS tracker placed on a car is a search for Fourth Amendment purposes and requires a search warrant. Intrusive surveillance is considered a Fourth Amendment search and requires a search warrant.

If private information is disclosed to a third party, it is no longer considered private for Fourth Amendment purposes, and thus, a microphone placed on an informant does not require a search warrant. Similarly, telephone and internet communications involve third-party disclosure and are not constitutionally protected, but Congress has passed legislation to provide some protection. However, a cellphone search requires a search warrant because police have time to obtain a warrant and because of the amount of private information in the cellphone. The law regarding searches of electronic communications continues to evolve.

Terms

Curtilage – the zone of habitation beyond the dwelling that includes a reasonable expectation of privacy.

Exclusionary Rule – the prohibition of illegally obtained evidence in a criminal trial.

Exigency – an urgent need.

Open Fields – a legal euphemism for the private land that extends beyond the curtilage.

Reasonable – sound judgment, appropriate or fair; in a judicial sense, it is the objective notion of what an ordinary person of sound judgment would do or think if in the same circumstance.

Reasonable Expectation of Privacy – an expectation of privacy deemed reasonable in public norms.

Search – to look for something; in a constitutional sense, it is looking for something within the zone of Fourth Amendment protection.

Third-party disclosure – revealing information to others not party to the original communication.

Cases

Barron v. City of Baltimore, 32 U.S. (7 Pet.) 243 (1833)
Boyd v. United States, 116 U.S. 616 (1886)
Byrd v. United States, 584 U.S. 395 (2018)
Carpenter v. United States, 585 U.S. 296, (2018)
Chimel v. California, 395 U.S. 752 (1969)
Collins v. Virginia, 584 U.S. 586 (2018)
Fisher v. United States, 425 U.S. 391 (1976)
Florida v. Jardines, 569 U.S. 1 (2013)
Griswold v. Connecticut, 381 U.S. 479 (1965)
Harris v. United States, 331 U.S. 145 (1947)
In the Matter of a Search of a Residence in Oakland, California, 354 F. Supp. 3d 1010 (N.D. Cal. 2019)
In the Matter of the Search of a White Google Pixel 3XL Cellphone in a Black Incipio Case, 398 F. Supp. 3d 785 (D. Idaho 2019)
Katz v. United States, 389 U.S. 347 (1967)
Mapp v. Ohio, 367 U.S. 643 (1961)
Oliver v. United States, 466 U.S. 170 (1984)
Olmstead v. United States, 277 U.S. 438 (1928)
Riley v. California, 573 U.S. 373 (2014)
Smith v. Maryland, 442 U.S. 735 (1979)
State v. Andrews, 234 A.3d 1254 (N.J. 2020)
United States v. Chadwick, 433 U.S. 1 (1977)

United States v. Chatrie, __ F. 4th __, No. 22-4489 (4th Cir. Rehearing En Banc, 2025)
United States v. Dunn, 480 U.S. 294 (1987)
United States v. Houston, 813 F.3d 282 (6th Cir. 2016)
United States v. Jones, 565 U.S. 400 (2012)
United States v. Kirschner, 823 F.Supp.2d 665 (E.D. Mich. 2010)
United States v. Knotts, 460 U.S. 276 (1983)
United States v. Verdugo-Urquidez, 494 U.S. 259 (1990)
United States v. White, 401 U.S. 745 (1971)

Statutes

Cell-Site Simulators, 18 U.S.C. §3119 (2023)
Electronic Communications Privacy Act (ECPA), 18 U.S.C. §§2510–2523 (1986)
Federal Wiretap Act, 18 U.S.C. §2511 (1968)
Pen Register Act, 18 U.S.C. §§3121–3127 (1986)
Stored Communications Act (SCA), 18 U.S.C. §§2701–2712 (1986)

Thought Questions

1. Why did Justice Harlan dissent in the *U.S. v. White* case?
2. What are the Big Brother privacy concerns in the *U.S. v. Houston* pole camera case?
3. What is the significance of the recent holding by a lower federal court that biometric data is testimonial when used to compel the opening of a locked cellphone?
4. Is there really such a notion as Reasonable Expectation of Privacy anymore?

Further Reading

Bandiero A, *Search & Seizure Survival Guide: A Field Guide for Law Enforcement*, 2018 ed, Blue to Gold, LLC, CreateSpace Independent Publishing Platform, Scotts Valley, CA, 2019.

Dressler J, Michaels AC, Simmons R, *Understanding Criminal Procedure, Volume One: Investigation*, 7th ed, Carolina Academic Press, Durham, NC, 2017.

Gizzi MC, Curtis RC, *The Fourth Amendment in Flux: The Roberts Court, Crime Control, and Digital Privacy*, Univ Press of Kansas, Lawrence, KS, 2016.

Gray D, *The Fourth Amendment in an Age of Surveillance*, Cambridge Univ Press, Cambridge, 2017.

Kanovitz JR, Ingram JL, Devine CJ, *Constitutional Law for Criminal Justice*, 15th ed, Routledge, New York, 2019.

Chapter 8

Search and Seizure II

Warrant Searches

Learning Objectives

After reading this chapter, students are expected to be able to:

- discuss the significance of arrest warrants and search warrants
- list the targets of warrants
- list the elements of a valid warrant
- explain the requirement for particularity in describing places, persons, and things
- discuss the finding of probable cause (PC) to support a warrant
- explain how confidential and anonymous sources are used to support a warrant affidavit
- discuss the execution of warrants.

Introduction

Searches and seizures without a warrant are *per se* unreasonable unless they fall into one of the well-recognized exceptions. Warrants meet the threshold reasonableness test because warrants are based upon PC, meet constitutional

DOI: 10.4324/9780429272455-8

requirements, and are issued by neutral and detached magistrates. The Fourth Amendment's *Warrant Clause* states:

> no Warrants shall issue, but upon probable cause, supported by Oath or affirmation, and particularly describing the place to be searched and the persons or things to be seized.

This clause seems disconnected from the Reasonableness Clause that precedes it, which protects against unreasonable searches and seizures. The Fourth Amendment does not say that all searches and seizures require a warrant but seems to imply it, and the Supreme Court has held that warrantless searches are, per se, unreasonable (unless falling into one of the exceptions).

During American Revolutionary times, governmental searches were based on warrants, and warrantless searches and seizures were virtually non-existent. When Madison penned the Fourth Amendment, he intended to eliminate *general warrants* used by England against the colonists, which allowed general searches at any time and multiple times on the allegation of disloyalty by an anonymous source. As Madison intended, warrants issued by the U.S. federal government are to be based on PC, limited in scope, and reasonable in application.

Judicial Approval

The PC upon which warrants are based is determined not by an accuser or law enforcement officer but by a judge or magistrate, whose job is to scrutinize the request for a warrant. Thus, a neutral referee is a limitation on governmental power that underpins all warrants. Justice Robert Jackson, in *Johnson v. U.S.* (1948), declared:

> The point of the Fourth Amendment, which is often not grasped by zealous officers, is not that it denies law enforcement the support of the usual inferences reasonable men draw from evidence. Its protection consists in requiring that those inferences be drawn by a neutral and detached magistrate, instead of being judged by the officer in the often competitive enterprise of ferreting out crime.

The magistrate must sign the warrant before it is executed; it cannot be signed afterward to validate it or be authorized before it is written.

Judicial approval may come from a judge of a court of record but is most often a lower-level judicial officer, i.e., a magistrate or justice of the peace. A warrant is valid only if issued by a neutral and detached magistrate, not a state attorney general who led the investigation and later prosecuted the case (*Coolidge v. New Hampshire*, 1971).

Some jurisdictions authorize telephonic search warrant applications. See, for example, Federal Rule of Criminal Procedure 41(d)(3): "In accordance with Rule 4.1, a magistrate judge may issue a warrant based on information communicated by telephone or other reliable electronic means."

Magistrates approve approximately 95% of all warrant requests submitted. This should not come as a surprise since the police (the affiant) must submit sworn affidavits, and they have a good idea of what is needed for the approval. Magistrates are allowed to assume that what is submitted is true. Nonetheless, the system forces the police to write a justification that is in itself useful. Magistrates sometimes do not approve a warrant if it is overly broad, lacks sufficient particularity, or fails to establish PC. The affiant may rectify the deficiencies and return to the magistrate for approval.

Targets of Search Warrants

Warrants may be issued to recover the following:

1. persons to be arrested
2. evidence of a crime
3. contraband, i.e., unlawful drugs, guns, etc.
4. fruits of the crime.

Arrest warrants are for seizures of persons; search warrants are for searches and seizures of property.

In the past, instrumentalities used as a weapon or means in a crime or intended for use to commit a crime were distinguished from "mere evidence" that was not the fruit of a crime and were not a basis of search warrants. This distinction between instrumentalities and mere evidence was done away with in *Warden v. Hayden* (1967), where the seizure of clothing worn by a bank robber was upheld, even though it was not an instrumentality or the fruit of the crime. The federal code was amended to allow the search for and seizure of any evidence, and many states have broadened the warrant authority of their statutes; however, some states still limit the things to be seized.

Elements of Valid Search Warrants

A valid search warrant has four essential elements:

1. PC
2. supporting oath or affirmation
3. particularized description of the place to be searched and the person or things to be seized
4. signature of the magistrate.

To obtain a warrant, the applying officer, the *affiant,* must submit an application and a sworn affidavit to a neutral and detached magistrate. The place to be searched and the persons or things to be seized must be described with particularity. There must be sufficient detail of the facts and information for a magistrate to make an independent determination of PC that the items to be searched for are in the place to be searched and are evidence of the commission of a crime and, of course, the appropriateness of a search warrant. The affiant must sign the affidavit, attesting under penalty of perjury that the facts are true and accurate. An oath is a verbal sacred vow to tell the truth based on a religious conviction. An affirmation is a solemn declaration allowed to those who conscientiously object to taking an oath. It has precisely the same legally binding effect as an oath but is taken to avoid the religious implications of a religious oath. They are sworn documents. The court often seals the affidavits to protect the investigation and cooperating individuals.

The magistrate's PC determination is a conclusion of law. Only the facts in the affidavit may be considered – not any additional verbal comments made to the magistrate or other documents unless incorporated into the affidavit. The facts presented in the affidavit must establish the fair probability that contraband or evidence of a crime will be found in a particular place. The affidavit must show a nexus between the suspected criminal activity and the place to be searched. A court may not reach PC simply by piling hunch upon hunch (*U.S. v. Roach*, 2009).

Probable Cause

Probable Cause (PC) is law enforcement's most important and most often used phrase. The U.S. Supreme Court has several times addressed the definition of PC, which is more than a mere reasonable suspicion but less than by a preponderance and far less than for conviction:

> the facts and circumstances within their (the officers') knowledge and of which they had reasonable, trustworthy information (are) sufficient in themselves to warrant a man of reasonable caution in the belief that an offense has been or is being committed.
>
> Brinegar v. U.S. *(1949)*

> probable cause requires only a probability or substantial chance of criminal activity, not an actual showing of such activity.
>
> Illinois v. Gates *(1983)*

> The term 'probable cause' means less than evidence which would justify condemnation. It imports a seizure made under circumstances which warrant suspicion. Finely tuned standards such as beyond a reasonable doubt or by the preponderance of the evidence, useful in formal trials, have no place in the magistrate's decision.
>
> New York v. P.J. Video, Inc. *(1986)*

Magistrates will look for some factual basis, some information, that is not too shaky to support the contention that a crime has been or will be committed. The facts must be provided sufficiently in the officer's affidavit for the magistrate to conclude independently that PC exists; facts known to the officer but not in the affidavit cannot be used to justify the warrant. A direct link between the crime and the evidence is unnecessary (*U.S. v. Ray*, 2007). The findings from a successful search cannot alone justify the issuance of the warrant in the first place.

Confidential and Anonymous Informants

Usually, an officer relies on ordinary witnesses or their observations as the factual basis for the warrant, but sometimes, the information comes from confidential or anonymous sources, which are inherently suspect. When information is based on confidential informants, the affiant must swear that an informant who provided the proffered information exists and must provide corroboration of the informant's allegations. Early on, the U.S. Supreme Court in *Draper v. U.S.* (1959) held that information from an informant that is corroborated may be used for PC for an arrest, even if it is hearsay and not normally admissible in a criminal trial. An informant's tip alone may not justify exigent circumstances (*U.S. v. Bates,* 1997).

Confidential informants are often criminals who have talked in exchange for leniency or money. Some confidential informants are serving sentences for crimes they have committed. Sometimes, they are low-level drug dealers who are arrested and then given a deal to identify their suppliers – flipping little fish to catch big fish. Beyond the questionable credibility and motivation of such informants, they are inherently suspect because they cannot be cross-examined to test the quality of the information before a warrant is issued. Furthermore, defendants cannot be convicted on uncorroborated testimony of an accomplice; thus, police need additional evidence to secure a conviction.

Totality of the Circumstances: the finding of PC based on confidential informants has been directly addressed by the U.S. Supreme Court. In *Aguilar v. Texas* (1964), the Court held that

> the magistrate must be informed of some of the underlying circumstances relied on by the person providing the information and some of the underlying circumstances from which the affiant concluded that the informant, whose identity was not disclosed, was creditable or his information reliable.

Another requirement was added in *Spinelli v. U.S.* (1969), the Court went further by requiring that a magistrate must be informed of the "underlying circumstances from which the informant had concluded" that a crime had been committed. The *Aguilar-Spinelli* two-pronged test is as follows: (1) is the informant reliable? and (2) do we know the basis of the informant's knowledge? The Supreme Court overruled the "overly rigid" *Aguilar-Spinelli* test in *Illinois v. Gates* (1983) in favor of a more flexible, fluid, and common sense all things considered test, the *totality of the circumstances* test, for determining PC.

BOX 8.1 *ILLINOIS V. GATES* (1983): CONFIDENTIAL/ ANONYMOUS INFORMANTS

The police in Bloomingdale, Illinois, received an anonymous letter that stated:

> This letter is to inform you that you have a couple in your town who strictly make their living on selling drugs. They are Sue and Lance Gates; they live on Greenway, off Bloomingdale Rd. in the condominiums. Most of their buys are done in Florida. Sue, his wife, drives their car to Florida, where she leaves it to be loaded up with drugs, then Lance flies down and drives it back. Sue flies back after she drops the car off in Florida. May 3 she is driving down there again and Lance will be flying down in a few days to drive it back. At the time Lance drives the car back, he has the trunk loaded with over $100,000.00 in drugs. Presently, they have over $100,000.00 worth of drugs in their basement. They brag about the fact they never have to work and make their entire living on pushers. I guarantee if you watch them carefully, you will make a big catch. They are friends with some big drugs (sic) dealers, who visit their house often.

Investigation revealed that an "L. Gates" had purchased an airline ticket from Chicago to West Palm Beach, that Gates had made the trip to Florida, that Gates had met a woman at a Holiday Inn room registered to Susan Gates, and that the couple had gotten into a car together driving toward the Chicago area in a car with license plates registered to Gates. During their return trip, a warrant was issued. Upon the Gates's arrival home, the police recovered over 350 lb. of marijuana from a search of their car and additional marijuana and weapons from a search of their residence.

After the trial conviction, the state appellate courts found the searches unlawful because the affidavit did not provide sufficient evidence to establish PC based on the Spinelli-Aguilar test. The prosecution appealed to the Supreme Court, asking whether a magistrate may issue a search warrant on "the basis of partially corroborated anonymous informant's tip?"

The Court abandoned the Spinelli-Aguilar test for PC and upheld the conviction. Chief Justice Rehnquist wrote that PC should be found from the totality of the circumstances:

> Probable cause is a fluid concept—turning on the assessment of probabilities in particular factual contexts—not readily, nor even usefully reduced, to a

> neat set of legal rules ... The task of the issuing magistrate is simply to make a practical, common-sense decision whether, given all the circumstances set forth in the affidavit before him, ... there is a fair probability that contraband or evidence of a crime will be found in a particular place. ... [Footnote 13] Probable cause requires only a probability or substantial chance of criminal activity, not an actual showing of such activity.

The *totality of the circumstances test* has struck many commentators as giving magistrates too much flexibility in finding the informant's reliability. In practice, it is tough to appeal lower courts' rulings. Several states (AL, HI, MA, NY, VT, WA) have rejected the *Gates* rationale and retained the stricter two-pronged *Aguilar-Spinelli* test.

The totality of the circumstances test was also applied to review the establishment of a reasonable suspicion sufficient to make an investigative stop without a warrant in *U.S. v. Sokolow*, 1989; also see *U.S. v. Arvisu*, 2002.

Particularity

Warrants must be reasonable in scope. The place to be searched and the things to be seized must be described with *particularity* – reasonable specificity; overly broad or open-ended searches are not allowed. In *Groh v. Ramirez* (2004), the Court held that a warrant that did not provide sufficient particularity describing the person or things to be seized is invalid even where sufficient details are in the warrant application because officers serve only the warrant, not the affidavit. The warrant must be complete on its face so that any officer can properly execute it.

The place to be searched is generally a private premises, a residence or a building. The description of the place to be searched must be definite and enable officers to identify it to the exclusion of all other premises. A warrant for an apartment building without specifying the apartment is invalid.

Some circumstances call for a specific description of an item, i.e., a.45 ACP Ruger pistol. However, in most cases, the place to search is often known before the details of what will be found there; thus, the description may need to be more general. The warrant may need to be somewhat speculative as to the evidence that might be found. The warrant may specify a category of contraband rather than the specific contraband to be seized, and the use of catch-all phrases, such as "or any other evidence of the commission of the crime alleged in the warrant," may be permissible. The Court in *U.S. v. Hubbell* (2000) held that the Fifth Amendment privilege against self-incrimination protects a witness from being compelled to disclose the existence of incriminating documents that the Government cannot describe with reasonable particularity.

Searches of places of third parties, those not suspected of criminal activity, are permissible where PC exists to believe that evidence of someone's guilt or other items subject to seizure will be found (*Zurcher v. Stanford Daily*, 1978). Although an arrest warrant alone will suffice for officers to enter a defendant's own home to arrest her (*Payton v. New York*, 1981), an arrest warrant does not authorize entry into another person's residence without a search warrant where the suspect may be found (*Steagald v. U.S.*, 1981).

A warrant authorizes the seizure of only the things described. However, officers may seize things not based upon the warrant but because they are in plain view, discovered inadvertently, and it is apparent that it is evidence.

In some cases, officers might recognize that the items sought might be secreted on a person at the place searched. In such cases, the warrant should describe the persons to be searched, if known. In *Ybarra v. Illinois* (1979), the court held that a warrant describing a premises only and not specifying the person to be searched is insufficient; however, adding "and any persons on the premises at the time of service" will cure this concern in many states.

In *Michigan v. Summers* (1981), the Court ruled that detention and search of persons at the scene is allowed despite an absence of PC to arrest them, there is no particularized suspicion of involvement in criminal activity, and no posing any threat to the officer's safety. Furthermore, the Court held that persons in the immediate vicinity of the premises could be detained, although detentions must be limited to the immediate vicinity of the premises searched (*Bailey v. U.S.*, 2013). In a subsequent case, the Court allowed the handcuffing of detainees for the search duration (*Muehler v. Mena*, 2005).

Staleness

Probable cause cannot be based on information so old that it is no longer probable that the items sought will still be found in the place to be searched (*U.S. v. Mathis*, 2004; *U.S. v. Roach*, 2009; *U.S. v. Hython*, 2006). The nature of the thing to be seized and the criminal activity factor into the determination of staleness. Ongoing and continuous activity or a longstanding pattern of repeated activity may overcome staleness concerns.

Anticipatory Warrants

Anticipatory search warrants may be issued contingent upon a future triggering event, such as delivering a package to a premises. When law enforcement anticipates that evidence or other things of interest may be at a certain place at some point in the future but are not currently, an anticipatory warrant may be issued. "[T]he fact that the contraband is not presently located at the place described in the warrant is immaterial, so long as there is probable cause to believe that it will be there when the search warrant is executed" (*U.S. v. Grubbs*, 2006).

Sneak and Peak Warrants

Section 213 of the 2001 Uniting and Strengthening America by Providing Appropriate Tools Required to Intercept and Obstruct Terrorism Act of 2001 (USA PATRIOT Act) amended 18 U.S.C. §3103a, to allow delayed notice, otherwise known as *Sneak and Peek* (aka covert or surreptitious entry) warrants. Such warrants allow officers to enter the premises without the owner's or occupant's permission or knowledge and clandestinely search the premises but not seize any tangible property. The secret entry usually involves a stealthy breaking and entering. A 30-day, sometimes more, delay in the notice of the search avoids flight, destruction of evidence, or placing a witness in peril. Notice permits an individual to challenge the legality of the search. Sneak and peak warrants have been used primarily in drug cases. Covert entry has been held constitutionally permissible in *Dalia v. U.S.* (1979) and *U.S. v. Freitas* (1986).

Defective Warrants

Warrants are presumed valid as they have been vetted through the magistrate, and the law enforcement officer requesting the warrant has sworn to the truthfulness of the facts upon which it was issued. Warrants are reviewed using the information contained within the four corners of the document unless the affidavit and other exhibits have been incorporated by reference. An insufficient affidavit cannot be made sufficient by oral testimony.

Defendants who have standing may contest the lawfulness of a search warrant on many grounds, including a lack of PC to believe that the things to be searched for are in the place to be searched, that the objects to be searched for are evidence of a crime, that the affidavit did not consist of particularity as to place or things, or that the informants gave sufficient information to allow a magistrate to make a credibility determination. The warrant may also be attacked for false or misleading statements made knowingly or with a reckless disregard for the truth by the affiant (*Lee v. State*, Wyo. 2000). The failure of an officer to disclose in his warrant request that the suspect had not been living in the house for seven months resulted in a considerable monetary judgment against the city (*Bravo v. City of Santa Maria*, 2016).

Where some information proves incorrect, the law enforcement officer's good faith in relying on the warrant will often save the evidence from exclusion (*U.S. v. Leon*, 1984). The good faith exception extends to clerical errors and other defects where exclusion would have little deterrent effect (*Herring v. U.S.*, 2009).

The U.S. Supreme Court has set a high bar for challenging warrants in *Franks v. Delaware* (1978) concerning allegations of false statements by the affiant. The defendant must challenge the factual accuracy of the affidavit by a showing of evidence in a motion *in limine* (*Franks Hearing*) that:

1. a false statement was made knowingly (perjury) or in reckless disregard of the truth, and
2. the false statement is necessary to find PC.
    - *FRANKS HEARING*: a Franks hearing is the mechanism for a defendant to challenge the facts in a warrant. The defendant must prove by clear and convincing evidence that the officer committed perjury or something close to it. Specifically, the defendant must make a substantial preliminary showing that a false statement was made knowingly and intentionally, or with reckless disregard for the truth, by the affiant in the warrant affidavit, where the allegedly false statement is necessary to find PC.

Execution Requirements

Warrants must be reasonable in execution. Each warrant is good for only one search (*one warrant, one search* rule). Federal law, local law, and ordinances define the mechanics of the execution of warrants.

Currently, in most states, warrants are issued to a class of officers, but if the warrant is directed to a given officer, only that officer may execute it. The officer executing the warrant must read the affidavit for sufficiency and not assume that a signed warrant is valid (*People v. Randolph*, Colo. 2000).

States may prescribe the period within which a warrant may be executed, but if not, it must be executed within a reasonable period. Regardless, the warrant must be executed while there is still PC to believe the items are still on the premises. Search warrants must be executed during daylight, typically from 6:00 a.m. to 9:00 p.m., unless a "night-time warrant" is issued (*Welsh v. Wisconsin*, 1984).

Generally, the officer must "knock and announce" his identity. In *Wilson v. Arkansas* (1995), the U.S. Supreme Court held that the common law knock-and-announce principle is part of the Fourth Amendment reasonableness inquiry. This rule reduces violent confrontations, protects privacy, and allows occupants time to voluntarily admit the officers. In *Hudson v. Michigan* (2006), the court recognized three exceptions to the knock-and-announce rule: when there is a reasonable suspicion of (1) a threat of physical violence to the officers, (2) when there is a risk of destruction of evidence, and (3) when knocking and announcing would be futile. Knock-and-announce cases usually occur during the execution of a search warrant. The Court held that violation of the knock-and-announce rule does not require excluding the seized evidence. Also, exigency may provide a basis for immediate entry without a warrant (*Brigham City v. Stuart*, 2006). Only 15 to 20 seconds without a response in a drug raid may be sufficient time to wait before entry by police after knocking and announcing their presence (*U.S. v. Banks*, 2003).

"No-knock warrants" may be issued. In *U.S. v. Ramirez* (1998), the court held that with such a no-knock warrant, the police are only required to have a reasonable suspicion that knocking and announcing would be dangerous or futile or inhibit the effective investigation of the crime. The court noted that property may be destroyed while executing the warrant. The reasonableness of an unannounced, no-knock entry must be decided by lower courts on a case-by-case basis (*Richards v. Wisconsin,* 1997; *Clark v. City of San Antonio*, 2012). As a result of the 2020 Breonna Taylor case in Louisville, Kentucky, in which she was shot and killed by police during an alleged no-knock warrant execution, some states have now banned no-knock warrants.

An officer is justified in using the force necessary to execute the warrant. The physical force needed to open the door to enter the premises cannot be used unless the crime involved is a felony and there is some reason to believe exigent circumstances exist to require it. The property damage must not be excessive or unnecessary. Officers may not use deadly force or force that may cause serious bodily harm except to protect themselves. The amount of force justified to carry out the court instructions to perform the search will generally depend upon the circumstances. If the occupants refuse to open the door after police knock and announce themselves, or if there are no occupants on the premises at the time of the warrant, police may use necessary means to gain entry. The federal code (18 U.S.C. §3109) allows breaking into outer and inner doors after giving notice and being refused entry, but some states have more restrictive laws. If nobody appears present and there is no exigency, it is usually advisable to delay entry until the legal occupant can admit the officers. A battering ram used without specific knowledge of danger or exigency was deemed an unreasonable search (*State v. Thompson*, La. 1997).

Plaintiffs successfully sued when damages to the home were not reasonable in executing the warrant (*Thomas v. Bauman*, 2020).

Officers should respect occupants and show basic courtesy toward them; for instance, they should generally allow the occupants to get dressed. The safety of the officers is paramount, and precautions should be taken if one or more occupants are to be arrested at the time of the search.

The search may last as long and be as thorough as reasonably necessary to execute the warrant fully.

In general, the officer must have the search warrant in hand during execution and should be given to the occupant or left in the place searched. The affidavit on which the warrant is based is not given to the occupant or left at the scene.

Return of the Warrant

The warrant must be returned to the court with the inventory of items found and seized. Some statutes prescribe when the return must be accomplished, but in other states, the return should be accomplished without unnecessary delay. In *City of West Corvina v. Perkins* (1999), the Court ruled that due process does not require officers to leave instructions on how property may be returned to their owners.

Good Faith

Errant police searches and seizures pursuant to an invalid warrant or improper execution may be excused if performed and executed in a good faith effort. Courts recognize that mistakes can be made unintentionally and that there is a high cost to society for allowing perpetrators to go free. Good faith has been a shield against nullification based on technicality or inadvertent mistakes.

BOX 8.2 *MARYLAND V. GARRISON* (1987) – GOOD FAITH

Baltimore police officers obtained and executed a warrant to search the person of McWebb and "the premises known as 2036 Park Avenue third floor apartment" for controlled substances and related paraphernalia. The officers unexpectedly saw McWebb enter the building and go through two locked doors to the third floor. The police had a reasonable belief that there was only one apartment on the third floor, but in fact, there were two, one belonging to McWebb and the other to Garrison. They searched and seized contraband from Garrison's apartment without realizing their mistake. The search ended when they realized their mistake. Despite having no warrant to search Garrison's apartment, Garrison was convicted of possession. That the warrant was overly broad and did not particularly describe McWebb's apartment apart from that of Garrison's was not a fatal flaw, rendering the warrant invalid because it was thought to be sufficient at the time of execution. Thus, the execution of the warrant was proper and did not violate the Fourth Amendment.

> ...the officers properly responded to the command contained in a valid warrant even if the warrant is interpreted as authorizing a search limited to McWebb's apartment rather than the entire third floor. Before the officers discovered the factual mistake, they perceived McWebb's apartment and the third-floor premises as the same; therefore, their execution of the warrant reasonably included the entire third floor. Under either interpretation of the warrant, the officer's conduct was consistent with a reasonable effort to ascertain and identify the place intended to be searched within the meaning of the Fourth Amendment.

Example 1. Federal Search Warrant Application

"Application for a Search Warrant" (n.d.). Retrieved February 12, 2025. US Department of Justice. https://nsarchive.gwu.edu/sites/default/files/documents/5513699/United-States-v-Levashov-Application-for-a.pdf

AO 106 (Rev. 04/10) Application for a Search Warrant

UNITED STATES DISTRICT COURT
for the
District of Alaska

In the Matter of the Search of
(Briefly describe the property to be searched or identify the person by name and address)
In re Application for a Warrant Under Rule 41 of the Federal Rules of Criminal Procedure to Disrupt the Kelihos Botnet

Case No. 3:18-mj-00324-DMS

APPLICATION FOR A SEARCH WARRANT

I, a federal law enforcement officer or an attorney for the government, request a search warrant and state under penalty of perjury that I have reason to believe that on the following person or property *(identify the person or describe the property to be searched and give its location)*:

See Attachment A, incorporated here by reference.

located in the ______ District of Alaska, there is now concealed *(identify the person or describe the property to be seized)*:

See Attachment B, incorporated here by reference.

The basis for the search under Fed. R. Crim. P. 41(c) is *(check one or more)*:

- ☑ evidence of a crime;
- ☐ contraband, fruits of crime, or other items illegally possessed;
- ☐ property designed for use, intended for use, or used in committing a crime;
- ☐ a person to be arrested or a person who is unlawfully restrained.

The search is related to a violation of:

Code Section	*Offense Description*
18 USC §§ 1030, 1343, and 2511.	Fraud and related activity in connection with computers, wire fraud, and illegal wiretapping.

The application is based on these facts:

See attached Affidavit in Support of Search Warrant.

☑ Continued on the attached sheet.

☐ Delayed notice of ____ days (give exact ending date if more than 30 days: ________) is requested under 18 U.S.C. § 3103a, the basis of which is set forth on the attached sheet.

Applicant's signature

Elliott Peterson, Special Agent, FBI
Printed name and title

Sworn to before me and signed in my presence.

/S/ DEBORAH M. SMITH
CHIEF U.S. MAGISTRATE JUDGE
SIGNATURE REDACTED
Judge's signature

Date: 3/30/18

City and state: Anchorage, Alaska

Hon. Deborah M. Smith, United States Magistrate Judge
Printed name and title

FIGURE 8.1 Example 1. Federal Search Warrant Application

Supporting Affidavit

"Application for a Search Warrant" (May 3, 2018). Retrieved February 12, 2025. US Department of Justice. https://nsarchive.gwu.edu/sites/default/files/documents/5513699/United-States-v-Levashov-Application-for-a.pdf

IN THE UNITED STATES DISTRICT COURT
FOR THE DISTRICT OF ALASKA

IN RE APPLICATION FOR A WARRANT UNDER RULE 41 OF THE FEDERAL RULES OF CRIMINAL PROCEDURE TO DISRUPT THE KELIHOS BOTNET	Case No. 3:18-mj-00324-DMS

AFFIDAVIT IN SUPPORT OF AN APPLICATION UNDER RULE 41 FOR A SEARCH WARRANT

I, Elliott Peterson, being first duly sworn, hereby depose and state as follows:

INTRODUCTION AND AGENT BACKGROUND

1. I am a Special Agent with the Federal Bureau of Investigation in Anchorage, Alaska. I currently investigate criminal and national security computer intrusions in the Anchorage Field Office as a member of the Counter Intelligence / Cyber Squad. I have investigated cyber and computer intrusion matters for over five years and I specialize in the investigation of complex botnets, including Peer to Peer botnets, as well as botnets facilitating account takeover fraud and Distributed Denial Of Service attacks (DDOS).

2. I make this affidavit in support of an application for a warrant under Federal Rule of Criminal Procedure 41 to authorize an online operation to disrupt the Kelihos botnet currently under the control of Peter Yuryevich LEVASHOV, a criminal hacker. The operation, which is particularly described in Attachment A and Attachment B, involves the distribution of updated peer lists, job messages and/or IP filter lists, further described in Attachment B, to the TARGET

MAY 3 0 2018

FIGURE 8.2 Supporting Affidavit

Example 2. Federal Search Warrant Application

"Affidavit in Support of an Application under Rule 41 for a Search Warrant" (May 3, 2018). Retrieved February 12, 2025. US Department of Justice. https://archives.fbi.gov/archives/about-us/history/famous-cases/anthrax-amerithrax/08-431Application.pdf

AO106(Rev 5/85) Affidavit for Search Warrant

UNITED STATES DISTRICT COURT
FOR THE DISTRICT OF COLUMBIA

In the Matter of the Search of

2002 Saturn SL1, blue, 4 door sedan, bearing VIN # [redacted], registered to Bruce Edwards Ivins, at [redacted], Frederick, MD

FILED
JUL 11 2008
NANCY MAYER WHITTINGTON, CLERK
U.S. DISTRICT COURT

APPLICATION AND AFFIDAVIT FOR SEARCH WARRANT

CASE NUMBER: 08-431

I Charles B. Wickersham being duly sworn depose and say:

I am a(n) Postal Inspector with the U.S. Postal Inspection Service (Official Title) and have reason to believe that ☐ on the person of or ☒ on the property or premises known as (name, description and or location)

2002 Saturn SL1, blue, 4 door sedan, bearing VIN # [redacted], registered to Bruce Edwards Ivins, at [redacted], Frederick, MD

in the District of Maryland, there is now concealed a certain person or property, namely
firearms and other weapons, ballistics vests or other protective gear, and any writings identifying a plan to kill witnesses or names of intended victims, or any other relevant documents, notes and records in various formats, including computer files and other electronic media, as more fully described in Attachment A.

which is (state one or more bases for search and seizure set forth under Rule 41(b) of the Federal Rules of Criminal Procedure)
evidence relevant to the commission of an act of terrorism, to include the use of a weapon of mass destruction (anthrax) and the murder and attempt to murder officers and employees of the United States, and to threaten witnesses involved in, and obstruct the investigation of, such act of domestic terrorism.
in violation of Title 18 United States Code, Section(s) 2332a and 1114 and 1512(a)(2). The facts to support a finding of Probable Cause are as follows:

SEE ATTACHED AFFIDAVIT HEREIN INCORPORATED BY REFERENCE AS IF FULLY RESTATED HEREIN

Continued on the attached sheet and made a part hereof. ☒ YES ☐ NO

Rachel Carlson Lieber, AUSA
U.S. Attorney's Office, Washington, DC
(202) 353-8055

Signature of Affiant
Charles B. Wickersham, Postal Inspector
United States Postal Inspection Service

United States District Court
For the District of Columbia
A TRUE COPY
NANCY MAYER WHITTINGTON, C
Deputy Clerk

Sworn to before me, and subscribed in my presence

07/11/08
Date

at Washington, D.C. (pursuant to the domestic terrorism search warrant provisions of Rule 41(b)(3))

Deborah A. Robinson
United States Magistrate Judge
Name and Title of Judicial Officer

Signature of Judicial Officer

1

FIGURE 8.3 Example 2. Federal Search Warrant Application

Supporting Affidavit

"Affidavit in Support of a Search Warrant" (October 31, 2007). Retrieved February 12, 2025. US Department of Justice. https://www.justice.gov/archive/amerithrax/docs/08-430-m-01app.pdf

AFFIDAVIT IN SUPPORT OF SEARCH WARRANT

I, Charles B. Wickersham, being duly sworn, depose and say:

I have been a Postal Inspector of the United States Postal Inspection Service (USPIS) for approximately twenty months. I am authorized to investigate crimes involving violations of Title 18 U.S.C. Sections 2332(a), 1114, and 1512(a)(2).

This affidavit is respectfully submitted in support of an application for warrants to search the following premises and vehicles, pursuant to the domestic terrorism search warrant provision found at Rule 41(b)(3) of the Federal Rules of Criminal Procedure, in that it involves threats to witnesses in, and obstruction of, a domestic terrorism investigation, pending in the District of Columbia.

(1) [redacted] Frederick, Maryland, a single family residence. The residence has white painted wood siding, with a white front door that is located on the right side of the front of the home. The front door has an exterior storm door. Left of the front door are two windows cased with red shutters. A black railing leads up several stairs to the front door where the numbers [redacted] are indicated in black above the door. The search will include a large white shed with peeling paint, that is located on the rear of the property, along with the backyard. Bruce Edwards Ivins purchased the house [redacted] Investigation has disclosed the property has been his principle residence since September, 2001.

(2) Automobile #1: a vehicle with Maryland registration [redacted], expiration [redacted], and Vehicle Identification Number 1G8ZH52882Z112568. The vehicle is described as a 2002 Saturn SL1, blue, 4 door sedan, and is registered to Bruce Edwards Ivins, [redacted], Frederick, MD. Bruce Edwards Ivins purchased the vehicle [redacted] and has been the sole owner, and is the primary user.

(3) Automobile #2: search a vehicle with Maryland registration [redacted], expiration [redacted] and Vehicle Identification Number [redacted]. The vehicle is described as a 1993 Honda Civic, blue, 4 door sedan, and is registered to Bruce Edwards Ivins, [redacted] Frederick, MD. Bruce Edwards Ivins purchased the vehicle 12/02/1999 and has been the sole owner. The vehicle is primarily used by Ivins's wife, [redacted] and is driven on occasion by Bruce Edwards Ivins.

(4) Automobile #3: A warrant to search a vehicle with Maryland registration [redacted] expiration [redacted], and Vehicle Identification Number [redacted] The vehicle is described as a 1996 Dodge van, red, and is registered to [redacted] [redacted], Frederick, MD. [redacted] purchased the vehicle [redacted] and the vehicle is driven on occasion by Bruce Edwards Ivins.

FIGURE 8.4 Supporting Affidavit

Example 3. Federal Search Warrant

"Search Warrant" (n.d.). Retrieved February 12, 2025. United States District Court, Eastern District of Louisiana. https://www.assetsearchblog.com/wp-content/uploads/sites/197/migrated/Jeffersonsearchwarrant.pdf

United States District Court

EASTERN DISTRICT OF LOUISIANA

In the Matter of the Search of
(Name, address or brief description of person or property to be searched)

1922 Marengo Street
New Orleans, Louisiana 70155

SEARCH WARRANT

CASE NUMBER:

TO: Federal Bureau Of Investigations and any Authorized Officer of the United States

Affidavit(s) having been made before me by S/A Edward S. Cooper (Affiant) who has reason to believe that ☐ on the person of or ☒ on the premises known as (name, description and/or location)
1922 Marengo Street
New Orleans, Louisiana 70155
SEE SCHEDULE A

he Eastern District of Louisiana there is now
ealed a certain person or property, namely (describe the person or property)
SCHEDULE B

I am satisfied that affidavit(s) and any recorded testimony establish probable cause to believe that the person or property so described is now concealed on the person or premises above-described and establish grounds for the issuance of this warrant.

YOU ARE HEREBY COMMANDED to search on or before ______________ (Date)
(not to exceed 10 days) the person or place named above for the person or property specified, serving this warrant and making the search (in the daytime – 6:00 A.M. to 10:00 P.M.) (at any time in the day or night as I find reasonable cause has been established) and if the person or property be found there to seize same, leaving a copy of this warrant and receipt for the person or property taken, and prepare a written inventory of the person or property seized and promptly return this warrant to W. Eugene Davis, U.S Circuit Court (U. S. Judge or Magistrate) as required by law.

July 25, 2005 - 11 am at Lafayette, LA
Date and Time Issued — City and State

W. Eugene Davis, U.S. Circuit Court Judge — W Eugene Davis
Name and Title of Judicial Officer — Signature of Judicial Office

FIGURE 8.5 Example 3. Federal Search Warrant

Example 4. State Search Warrant Application

"Search Warrant" (n.d.). Retrieved February 12, 2025. Franklin County Municipal Court. https://shadowanyone.com/searchwarrant/

FISA Warrants

The Foreign Intelligence Surveillance Act (FISA) was passed in 1978 in response to President Richard Nixon's use of federal resources to spy on domestic political and activist groups. The act provides judicial and congressional oversight of the government's covert surveillance of foreign activities and U.S. persons in the United States while maintaining secrecy to protect

No. __________

FRANKLIN COUNTY

MUNICIPAL COURT

Columbus, Ohio

STATE OF OHIO

VS.

Dr Apartment F3 Reynoldsburg, Ohio 43068
A three story apartment building with cream colored siding, brown front door, with wooden chair by front door, and the numbers " " on first floor midsection of building, and "F3" in black letters on brown apartment door on third floor.

Reynoldsburg, Ohio
Franklin County
and the curtilage thereof

blue towel, gray handled knife, condom, condom wrappers, blood, tissue, bodily fluid, and other biological samples that contain DNA, trace evidence, to include hairs, fibers, clothing, mattress, bedding, sheets, linens, and other items related to the sexual assault at Dr Apartment number F3 Reynoldsburg, Ohio 43068, that are unknown at this time.

Filed 27 day of MARCH, 2008

Clerk, Franklin County Municipal Court, Columbus, Ohio

By ______________ Deputy

Order on Affidavit of

Detective

Reynoldsburg Division of Police

FIGURE 8.6 Example 4. State Search Warrant Application

national security. It has been expanded to include lone wolves that act with little connection to a foreign government and other terrorists. FISA permits electronic surveillance by Presidential order without a court order for up to a year. Alternatively, federal law enforcement and intelligence agencies can submit requests for surveillance warrants to the Foreign Intelligence Surveillance Court (FISC).

BOX 8.3 *KLAYMAN V. OBAMA* (2013) – GOVERNMENT SURVEILLANCE

Edward Snowden, a former Central Intelligence Agency (CIA) employee, and Booz Allen Hamilton subcontractor leaked top-secret global surveillance information from the National Security Agency (NSA) and its international partners to Wikileaks, which was then published by The Washington Post and The Guardian in 2013.

Shortly after the disclosure, Larry Klayman, founder of Freedom Watch, and Charles and Mary Strange, parents of an NSA cryptologist and support person for Navy Seal Team VI, who was killed in Afghanistan, filed two lawsuits. Plaintiffs alleged that the government is conducting a "secret and illegal government scheme to intercept vast quantities of domestic telephonic communications" and challenging the constitutionality of this bulk data program.

In Klayman I, the plaintiffs filed suit against Verizon Communications, the President, the Attorney General, the NSA Director, the Department of Justice (DOJ), and the NSA, claiming the bulk collection of phone record metadata violates the First, Fourth, and Fifth Amendments and Section 215 of the U.S. Patriot Act.

In Klayman II (*Obama v. Klayman*, 2015), the plaintiffs added Facebook, Yahoo!, Google, Microsoft, YouTube, AOL, PalTalk, Skype, Sprint, AT&T, and Apple to the list of defendants claiming the bulk collection of phone record metadata violates the First, Fourth, and Fifth Amendments and Section 2702 of Stored Communications Act.

U.S. Federal Judge Richard J. Leon ruled that bulk collection of American telephone metadata likely violated the Fourth Amendment and wrote:

> I cannot imagine a more 'indiscriminate' and 'arbitrary' invasion than this systematic and high-tech collection and retention of personal data on virtually every single citizen for purposes of querying and analyzing it without prior judicial approval... Surely, such a program infringes on 'that degree of privacy' that the founders enshrined in the Fourth Amendment.

Judge Leon described the technology used as "almost Orwellian." He also had "serious doubts about the efficacy" of the program. He noted the government could not cite "a single instance in which analysis of the NSA's bulk metadata collection actually stopped an imminent attack, or otherwise aided the government in achieving any objective that was time sensitive." He distinguished the 1979 case, *Smith v. Maryland*, which had allowed the collection of phone numbers. He described the collections of telephone records in *Smith* as a short-term forward-looking capture, but the bulk metadata collections of the NSA as a long-term historical retrospective analysis. Judge Leon expressed his opinion that the Fourth Amendment needs to adapt to the digital age. The Court issued a preliminary injunction barring the government from collecting the telephone records of the plaintiffs but stayed its order pending appeal.

In 2015, the D.C. Circuit Court of Appeals held that the plaintiffs did not have the necessary standing for the preliminary injunction and remanded the case to the District Court. Eventually, after additional litigation, Judge Leon dismissed the suit against the government in 2017 because the plaintiffs lacked standing to sue, and in 2019, the D.C. Circuit affirmed the dismissal.

Note: Edward Snowden issued a statement in response to the initial ruling declaring,

> I acted on my belief that the NSA's mass surveillance programs would not withstand a constitutional challenge... Today, a secret program authorized by a secret court was, when exposed to the light of day, found to violate Americans' rights. It is the first of many.

Snowden is still a fugitive living in Russia. In October 2020, Snowden was granted permanent residency in Russia. His lawyer said that granting an unlimited residence permit became possible after changes in the migration legislation of the Russian Federation in 2019.

Administrative Warrants

Administrative warrants are issued by administrative agencies or officials, not by judges. Administrative warrants are used to enforce administrative regulations and laws; while judicial warrants are generally used in criminal investigations and prosecutions. Administrative warrants do not follow the same constitutional requirements under the Fourth Amendment as do judicial warrants. They are limited and do not authorize forcible entry into private spaces without consent. They do not have to be made public. Examples of administrative searches include nursing home inspections, food inspections, OSHA inspections, border inspections, workplace drug testing, and immigrations and customs enforcement (ICE) arrests of non-citizens. Such searches are conducted many thousand times daily – far exceeding the number of criminal investigations. Administrative warrants are governed by 49 U.S.C. §32707 in the federal government.

Until 1967, the Fourth Amendment was thought to apply only to criminal searches and seizures (*Frank v. Maryland*, 1959). In 1967, in

Camara v. Municipal Court, involving the nonconsensual search of a private residence, and its companion case, *See v. City of Seattle*, involving the nonconsensual search of a commercial building, the Court ruled that house and building inspections require warrants. The warrant requirement was reaffirmed and extended to OSHA inspections in *Marshall v. Barlow's, Inc.* (1978). The Court explained that warrants were required for civil and criminal searches "to safeguard the privacy and security of individuals against arbitrary invasions by government officials."

The *Camara* and *See* decisions held that PC is the applicable standard for issuing warrants, but the PC standard for administrative warrants is flexible and less stringent than for issuing a criminal warrant. In *Marshall v. Barlow's, Inc.* (1978), the Court explained that administrative inspection warrants should be based upon a general regulatory plan derived from a neutral source containing specific neutral criteria, with limits at the discretion of the inspector or investigator. In other words, a reasonable inspection program with specific criteria and protections substitutes for PC. Courts balance the administrative scheme, weighing the governmental purpose, need, practicality, and intrusiveness of the inspection against the individual's privacy interest as the test of the reasonableness of the government scheme. Regardless, this calculus is generally favorable to the government.

If evidence of a crime is revealed during an administrative search, then it may be seized and used for prosecution (*Michigan v. Tyler*, 1978).

Summary

The Fourth Amendment does not explicitly state when a warrant is necessary, but the wording implies that it should typically be the basis for government searches and seizures. A search and seizure pursuant to a warrant is *per se* reasonable. A magistrate must independently determine whether an application is sufficiently specific, and that PC exists to issue a warrant. Arrest warrants are issued for people, and search warrants are issued for evidence, contraband, and fruits of a crime.

A valid search warrant has four elements: (1) PC, (2) supporting oath or affirmation, (3) particular description of the place to be searched and the person or things to be seized, and (4) signature of the magistrate. The particularity of the place requires more specificity than the things to be seized. The *totality of the circumstances* determines PC. Good faith may cure a defective warrant. A Franks hearing may be held to determine if an officer perjured himself or herself in their affidavit.

Search warrants are then executed and returned to the magistrate with an inventory of items found and seized. Search warrants are valid for a limited time. They are typically executed only during daylight at home after knocking and announcing their presence with a copy of the warrant in hand. Special warrants may be issued that permit non-routine execution practices.

FISA and administrative warrants have different procedures.

Terms

Affiant – the officer who requests the warrant in an affidavit.

Affirmation – a formal, solemn declaration affirming the truth, made without reference to God, to which the penalty of perjury applies; this serves as a non-religious equivalent of an oath.

Execution – the service of a warrant.

Foreign Intelligence Surveillance Court (FISC) – hears requests for surveillance warrants of foreign agents, lone wolves, and terrorists.

Franks Hearing – a motion *in limine* filed by the defendant to challenge a warrant issued because the affiant knowingly made false or misleading statements.

Oath – an oath is a formal vow invoking a divine witness to speak the truth, to which the penalty of perjury applies.

Particularity – reasonable specificity in the description of places, items, and persons as the basis for issuance of a warrant.

Probable Cause – more than a mere reasonable suspicion but less than by a preponderance, substantial chance of criminal activity; the standard required for arresting someone, for issuing a warrant, and for bringing someone to trial; it is based upon the totality of the circumstances.

Cases

Aguilar v. Texas, 378 U.S. 108 (1964)
Bailey v. United States, 568 U.S. 186 (2013)
Bravo v. City of Santa Maria, Nos. 14–55557, 14–55687 (9th Cir. 2016)
Brigham City v. Stuart, 547 U.S. 398 (2006)
Brinegar v. United States, 338 U.S. 160 (1949)
Camara v. Municipal Court, 387 U.S. 523 (1967)
City of West Covina v. Perkins, 525 U.S. 234 (1999)
Clark v. City of San Antonio, 714 F. App'x 446 (5th Cir. 2018)
Coolidge v. New Hampshire, 403 U.S. 443 (1971)
Dalia v. United States, 441 U.S. 238 (1979)
Draper v. United States, 358 U.S. 307 (1959)
Frank v. Maryland, 359 U.S. 360 (1959)
Franks v. Delaware, 438 U.S. 154 (1978)
Groh v. Ramirez, 540 U.S. 551 (2004)
Herring v. United States, 555 U.S. 135 (2009)

Hudson v. Michigan, 547 U.S. 586 (2006)
Illinois v. Gates, 462 U.S. 213 (1983)
Johnson v. United States, 333 U.S. 10 (1948)
Klayman v. Obama, 957 F.Supp.2d 1 (D.D.C. 2013) [Klayman I]
Lee v. State, 2 P.3d 517 (Wyo. 2000)
Marshall v. Barlow's, Inc., 436 U.S. 307 (1978)
Maryland v. Garrison, 480 U.S. 79 (1987)
Michigan v. Summers, 452 U.S. 692 (1981)
Michigan v. Tyler, 436 U.S. 499 (1978)
Muehler v. Mena, 544 U.S. 93 (2005)
New York v. P.J. Video, Inc., 475 U.S. 868 (1986)
Obama v. Klayman, 800 F.3d 559 (D.C.Cir.2015) [Klayman II]
Payton v. New York, 445 U.S. 573 (1980)
People v. Randolph, 4 P.3d 477 (Colo. 2000)
Richards v. Wisconsin, 520 U.S. 385 (1997)
See v. City of Seattle, 387 U.S. 541 (1967)
Spinelli v. United States, 393 U.S. 410 (1969)
State v. Thompson, 693 So.2d 282 (La. 1997)
Steagald v. United States, 451 U.S. 204 (1981)
Thomas v. Bauman, 835 F. App'x 5 (6th Cir. 2020)
United States v. Arvisu, 534 U.S. 266 (2002)
United States v. Banks, 540 U.S. 31 (2003)
United States v. Bates, 522 U.S. 23 (1997)
United States v. Freitas, 800 F.2d 1451 (9th Cir. 1986)
United States v. Grubbs, 547 U.S. 90 (2006)
United States v. Hubbell, 530 U.S. 27 (2000)
United States v. Hython, 443 F.3d 480 (6th Cir. 2006)
United States v. Leon, 468 U.S. 897 (1984)
United States v. Mathis, 357 F.3d 1200 (10th Cir.2004)
United States v. Ramirez, 523 U.S. 65 (1998)
United States v. Ray, No. 06–4747 (4th Cir. 2007)
United States v. Roach, 582 F.3d 1192 (10th Cir. 2009)
United States v. Sokolow, 490 U.S. 1 (1989)
Warden v. Hayden, 387 U.S. 294 (1967)
Welsh v. Wisconsin, 466 U.S. 740 (1984)
Wilson v. Arkansas, 514 U.S. 927 (1995)
Ybarra v. Illinois, 444 U.S. 85 (1979)
Zurcher v. Stanford Daily, 436 U.S. 547 (1978)

Statutes

Additional Grounds for Issuing Warrant, 18 U.S.C. §3103a (2001)
Administrative Warrants, 49 U.S.C. §32707

Breaking Doors or Windows for Entry or Exit, 18 U.S.C. §3109 (1995)
Federal Intelligence Surveillance Act (FISA), 50 U.S.C. §§1801–1885c (1978)
Uniting and Strengthening America by Providing Appropriate Tools Required *to Intercept and Obstruct Terrorism Act of 2001* (USA PATRIOT Act), Pub. L. No. 107–56
Warrant, 18 U.S.C. §3103

Thought Questions

1. Why don't we eliminate the requirement if warrants are generally rubber-stamped?
2. Why is particularity a more significant requirement for places searched than for things seized?
3. Why should a warrant be declared valid if there was incorrect information in the affidavit, even though the affiant did not know it and acted in good faith on the evidence she presented?

Further Reading

Edens A, Flores-Gonzales VD, Peterson EH, *350 Search Warrants, Court Orders, and Affidavits* (The Detective's Guide), Police Publishing, Terra Haute, IN, 2019.

Chapter **9**

Search and Seizure III

Warrantless Searches

Learning Objectives

After reading this chapter, students are expected to be able to:

- list and describe well-recognized exceptions to the warrant requirement
- describe reasonable articulable suspicion and its role in investigations
- explain exigency
- describe when dogs can and cannot be used for searches
- explain the exclusionary rule and its application.

Introduction

The Fourth Amendment eliminates general warrants and prohibits unreasonable searches and seizures in a text consisting of two clauses – a *Reasonableness Clause* and a *Warrant Clause*. Again, the Fourth Amendment reads:

> The right of the people to be secure in their persons, houses, papers, and effects, against unreasonable searches and seizures, shall not be violated, and No Warrants shall issue, but upon probable cause, supported by Oath or affirmation, and particularly describing the place to be searched, and the persons or things to be seized.

DOI: 10.4324/9780429272455-9

The Reasonableness Clause requires that all searches and seizures be reasonable. The Warrant Clause requires probable cause for all warrants, but how they tie together is unclear – either the Warrant Clause modifies the Reasonableness Clause requiring a warrant for all searches and seizures (conjunctive interpretation) or is independent of it and does not require warrants universally (disjunctive interpretation). Until the 1960s, courts applied a conjunctive approach, but increasingly, courts have held a search or seizure to be reasonable despite the absence of a warrant. Furthermore, the amendment does not define any terms, particularly *unreasonable*, *search*, *seizure*, *warrant*, or *probable cause*. Specifically, the Fourth Amendment does not explicitly grant any exceptions to the warrant requirement for governmental searches and seizures. Nonetheless, all courts now acknowledge exceptions to the warrant requirement. States cannot add exceptions that the U.S. Supreme Court has not recognized. Most searches and arrests are conducted without a warrant.

Well-Recognized Exceptions

"It was recognized by the framers of the Constitution that there were reasonable searches for which no warrant was required" (*U.S. v. Rabinowitz*, 1950). In *City of Ontario v. Quon* (2010), the U.S. Supreme Court quoted *Katz v. U.S.* (1967), stating that although warrantless searches "are *per se* unreasonable …there are a few specifically established and well-delineated exceptions …"

Courts have traditionally held that these well-recognized exceptions include:

- Plain View
- Consent Searches
- Stop and Frisk
- Searches Incident to Arrest
- Automobile Exception
- Exigency/Emergency
- Hot Pursuit
- Special Needs

Except for the exigency exception, the U.S. Supreme Court has sought to establish categorical rules that provide clear guidance to law enforcement rather than a case-by-case evaluation that would provide less clear guidance.

Plain View

Police may search and seize property without a warrant that is in *open view* of the public in public spaces, such as streets, parks, commercial spaces open to the public, apartment lobbies, and hallways (*Payton v. New York*, 1980). The *plain view* doctrine is an exception to the warrant requirement when police intrude into private spaces. When an item is in plain sight, there is no expectation of privacy and, thus, no search. Since a search is not involved, it functions as a warrantless seizure of an item. To hold otherwise would "lead to an absurd result and at times perhaps even defeat the ends of justice" (*Minnesota v. Dickerson*, 1993).

The plain view exception holds when the view is from a lawful vantage point, the police have a lawful right to access the object itself, and the incriminating nature of the object (i.e., contraband or evidence) is immediately apparent to the police – that they have probable cause to seize the object. The view of the object need not be inadvertent (*Horton v. California* (1990).

"Plain view" is a constitutional term of art. Police officers may observe spaces from the air in an airplane or helicopter despite fences blocking public view because they have a legitimate right to be there, and the police might observe what they do (*California v. Ciraolo*, 1986; *Florida v. Riley*, 1986). Officers may enhance their observations with binoculars or a flashlight (*Texas v. Brown*, 1983), but not using a thermal imager, which was not generally available to the public then (*Kyllo v. U.S.*, 2001). The doctrine has since been extended to plain feel, smell, and hearing. Dogs may be used to enhance their sense of smell. However, smell alone was insufficient to enter a residence in *State v. Timberlake* (1990).

An officer who sees contraband through a house window cannot enter the house to seize it because to do so without a warrant would be trespassing, and the search would be illegal. In *Washington v. Chrisman* (1990), the Court held that when an officer accompanied a student to his room to check his identification card, the officer's view of contraband from a doorway justified entry and seizure.

Officers must have probable cause (*Texas v. Brown,* 1983), not merely a reasonable suspicion (*Arizona v. Hicks*, 1987), to believe that items in plain view are contraband, evidence, or fruits of a crime to seize them. Without further search, the items must be "immediately apparent" as evidence, contraband, or the fruit of a crime. In *Arizona v. Hicks* (1987), officers entered an apartment under exigent circumstances and noticed a record player, which they suspected might have been stolen. They turned the record player over to check the serial number against a list of stolen items and their serial numbers. The Court held that the serial number was not in plain view and that picking up and turning over the record player was an unauthorized additional search; accordingly, the evidence of the stolen property was excluded. In *Minnesota v. Dickerson* (1993), an officer felt a lump in a suspect's pocket during the pat down of the suspect and, after squeezing it, believed it to be crack cocaine. The Court held that the squeeze was an unauthorized additional search because there was no probable cause to believe it was contraband before the squeeze. However, "immediately apparent" does not mean absolute certainty. For instance, an officer may seize bloody clothing but will not know the source of the blood until after DNA testing is conducted.

The plain view doctrine is applicable during computer searches when an officer discovers pornography while searching for other evidence (*U.S. v. Wong*, 2004; *U.S. v. Carey*, 1999).

BOX 9.1 *CALIFORNIA V. CIRAOLO* (1986) – AERIAL OBSERVATION

Dante Carlo Ciraolo grew marijuana plants in his backyard, shielded from view by two fences. An officer saw the plants from an airplane at 1,000 feet without a warrant. Chief Justice Burger concluded that the search was constitutionally permissible. Police riding in a double-decker bus could see over the fence, or the neighbor from her second-story window could see. The constitution does not require the police traveling in the public airways to obtain a warrant to observe what is visible to the naked eye.

BOX 9.2 *FLORIDA V. RILEY* (1989) – AERIAL OBSERVATION

Michael Riley was convicted when police in a helicopter flying 400 feet above the ground spotted marijuana growing in a greenhouse beside his mobile home, not visible from the ground due to a wall and trees. The Court declared that the Fourth Amendment did not prohibit the search because Riley had no reasonable expectation of privacy because it was viewable from passing air traffic.

BOX 9.3 *FLORIDA V. HARRIS* (2013) – DOG SNIFF

An officer stopped Harris in his truck for an expired tag. He noticed Harris was shaking, appeared agitated, and saw an open beer can. Harris refused to consent to search his truck. A dog was then used to sniff the air around the truck. After the dog was alerted, a search of the car revealed drugs. Harris moved to suppress the search for lack of probable cause. The Court held that the search and seizure were constitutional. Justice Elena Kagan stated that the dog's certification and continued training were adequate indications of the dog's reliability and thus sufficient to presume the dog's alert provides probable cause to search, using the "totality-of-the-circumstances" Gates test.

BOX 9.4 *KYLLO V. U.S.* (2001) – THERMAL IMAGERY

Police used thermal imagery to find marijuana plants growing in an attic. Justice Scalia held the search to be unconstitutional without a warrant when the device was not commonly available to the public. The Court reasoned that obtaining any information regarding the home's interior by sense-enhancing technology that could not otherwise have been obtained without physical "intrusion into a constitutionally protected area" constitutes a search, at least where the technology in question is not generally in public use. The dissent pointed out that this holding would be outdated when the technology became generally available.

Consent

Consent as an exception to the warrant requirement was first recognized in 1946 in *Zap v. U.S.* It is a waiver of the warrant requirement (*U.S. v. Matlock*, 1974). People have a right to refuse to give consent. Miranda warnings are not required for consent. Generally, courts will assume someone has not waived their rights, and the burden is on the prosecution to prove the waiver.

Consent is valid if (1) the consent is voluntary, (2) the person giving consent has actual or apparent authority, and (3) the search is confined to the scope of the consent.

The person requesting the search does not have to identify themselves as a law enforcement officer and can be an undercover agent or an informer (*Lee v. U.S.*, 1942; *Hoffa v. U.S.*, 1966). Undercover agents may misrepresent their identity when obtaining consent to enter (*Lewis v. United States*, 1966). The "consent-once-removed" doctrine applies when an undercover officer enters a house at the express invitation of someone with authority to consent, establishes probable cause to arrest or search, and then immediately summons other officers for assistance (*United States v. Bramble*, 9th Cir. 1996).

Consent must be given freely, knowingly, and without express or implied coercion or duress. Voluntariness of the consent is determined from the totality of the circumstances (*Schneckloth v. Bustamonte*, 1973; *Florida v. Bostick*, 1996). Officers cannot search based on consent when they claim they have a warrant that they do not have (*Bumper v. North Carolina*, 1968). An unduly long detention can invalidate consent (*Florida v. Royer*, 1983).

A person impaired by the influence of drugs or alcohol is not competent to give consent. A minor is generally considered incompetent to consent but may consent if it can be shown that the consent was given voluntarily, knowingly, and intelligently. A parent may consent for their child.

Consent may be given expressly in words, gesturing, or conduct, but mere acquiescence is not consent. In *Howe v. State* (1996), merely stepping away from the door was not clear consent. However, when an officer boarded a bus for a routine check for drugs and weapons, approached Drayton, and asked him if he minded being searched, Drayton's raising his arms was sufficient consent in *U.S. v. Drayton* (2002).

A person may waive their Fourth Amendment protections if they do not object to a search, and the police are not required to inform them of their right to decline the search (*Schneckloth v. Bustamonte*, 1972; *Ohio v. Robinette*, 1996). In *Turner v. State* (2000), consent was not found when the police followed the subject into the apartment without asking to be let in; the court stated, "We interpret failure to object to the police officer's thrusting himself into Shaibu's apartment as more likely suggesting submission to authority than implied or voluntary consent." However, the case for voluntary consent is stronger if the person is offered the right to refuse their consent. Several cities and states now require police to inform citizens of their right to refuse a search.

Consent can be withdrawn at any time, but police are not required to search in a way that allows the person to revoke the consent (*Schneckloth v. Bustamonte*, 1973; *U.S. v. Rich*, 5th Cir. 1993), but the consent must be clear and unambiguous (*U.S. v. Ross*, 8th Cir. 2001) and not merely expressing disapproval of the search (*U.S. v. Gray*, 8th Cir. 2004). Consent cannot be revoked after evidence has been found or after arrest. Exceptions to the ability to revoke consent: (1) airport passenger screening (*U.S. v. Herzbrun*, 1984); *U.S. v. Pulido-Baquerizo,* 1986) and (2) prison visitations (*U.S. v. Spriggs*, 1993). Mere refusal of consent to a search does not constitute reasonable suspicion or probable cause (*U.S. v. Fuentes*, 1997).

The authority to consent is based on an expectation of privacy. Tenants have this expectation of their living quarters, but the owner will not. Similarly, a hotel clerk cannot consent to search a hotel guest's room (*Stoner v. California*, 1964). Such authority can be shared (joint) among several people who occupy the space. Anyone with apparent authority can consent for common or shared spaces, living rooms, kitchens, etc., but not for an individual's (including a spouse's) private space, such as a private room, closet, desk, or purse.

An occupant can consent for other occupants despite their absence, but not over the express objection of an occupant who is physically present (*Georgia v. Randolph*, 2006). Where the police reasonably detain or arrest and remove the objecting occupant, then the consent of the remaining occupant is sufficient (*Fernandez v. California*, 2014).

Someone left with the custody of an article, such as a car, has the authority to consent to a search. Consent extends to searches of containers where the police believe that the scope of the consent extends to such searches (*Florida v. Jimeno*, 1991).

Apparent authority is found where there is good faith and reasonable understanding that consent has been given or implied, even if it is later discovered that the person did not have actual authority to give consent (*Illinois v. Rodriguez*, 1990).

Stop and Frisk (Terry Stop)

The U.S. Supreme Court, in the landmark case of *Terry v. Ohio* (1968), deliberately created the "stop and frisk" as a new tool for police to combat civil unrest and urban crime. The rule allows an officer to explore whether probable cause of illegal activity exists. Proponents note that it has proved to be very useful to police. Before *Terry*, brief detention of a person to ask questions would invoke the exclusionary rule. Critics see the *Terry* decision as an erosion of the probable cause requirement for police intrusions and a vehicle for racial profiling and implicit bias. Few *Terry* stops result in arrests, and even fewer result in the discovery of a weapon. Critics have suggested that they cause distrust of the police and cynicism of the legal system.

Police contact citizens in three ways: (1) consensual encounters, (2) investigative detentions (Terry stops), and (3) full-fledged arrests (*U.S. v. Seslar*, 1993). Like anyone else, a police officer may walk up to anyone and ask questions, and the person may ignore the officer and walk away. However, police are not required to advise the person that they are free to leave *U.S. v. Mendenhall* (1980). If the person engages in conversation, then it becomes a consensual encounter. Where the inquiry becomes an interrogation, and the person is not free to leave, it becomes a Terry stop. Terry stops are *detentions* and, for Fourth Amendment purposes, are seizures of persons. A Terry stop requires that the officer have a reasonable articulable suspicion. The detention must not encompass moving the person to the police station for questioning (*Hayes v. Florida*, 1985). If the questioning fails to comply or gives the officer probable cause, the encounter can quickly escalate to an arrest (*U.S. v. Brigham*, 2004).

Reasonable suspicion is a legal standard of proof that is less than probable cause but more than "an inchoate and unparticularized suspicion or 'hunch'" that permits brief stops and detentions but is insufficient for custodial arrests or full searches. It must be based on "specific and articulable facts" (*articulable suspicion*), taken together with "rational inferences from those facts," and the suspicion must be associated with the specific individual (*individualized suspicion*) (*State v. Patterson*, 2000). Reasonable suspicion is not based upon the officer's subjective thoughts but on whether reasonable persons in the same circumstances would believe that criminal activity is afoot. Reasonable suspicion is based on the totality of the circumstances on a case-by-case basis. It is recognized that reasonable suspicion is not infallible.

Reasonable articulable suspicion has been based upon recognition of the person from a wanted poster (*U.S. v. Hensley*, 1985), unprovoked flight from police (*Illinois v. Wardlow,* 2000), a revoked driver's license (*Kansas v. Glover,* 2020), secondhand hearsay from an informant (*Adams v. Williams,* 1972), or an anonymous tip corroborated by independent police investigation (*Alabama v. White,* 1990) but not if uncorroborated (*Florida v. J.L.,* 2000). Based on their experience, officers may find reasonable suspicion when the person is standing in the wrong place, is nervous, carrying certain objects, has furtive behavior, or engages in other, usually innocuous behavior.

An officer may ask a person to show their identification when stopped. In *Hiibel v. Sixth Judicial District Court of Nevada* (2004), the Court found the subsequent arrest of a person who refuses to identify himself as lawful where state law requires it.

Generally, the officer may detain the person for as long as it takes to confirm or dispel the suspicion as long as the investigation is diligently pursued (*U.S. v. Sharpe,* 1985; *County of Riverside v. McLaughlin,* 1991). Officers cannot detain someone for an unreasonable time or search that person further than a frisk without a warrant (*Florida v. Royer,* 1983). In *U.S. v. Montoya de Hernandez* (1985), the Court allowed a 16-hour detention at an airport where the detainee was suspected of swallowing cocaine-filled balloons. Arkansas has set a limit of 15 minutes, and Nevada has a limit of 60 minutes for detention.

After a Terry stop, an officer, for his own protection, may *pat down* (*frisk*) the outer clothing of the person and areas within the subject's control to search for a weapon, but only if the officer reasonably suspects that the person is armed or can reach a weapon. The frisk is not a full search, only a pat down. In *Minnesota v. Dickerson* (1993), the Court held that if during a frisk for a weapon, "plain feel" reveals an object that is "immediately apparent" to be contraband, then the officer may lawfully seize the object.

Traffic stops are essentially Terry stops. They are warrantless detentions controlled by the Fourth Amendment. A reasonable suspicion of wrongdoing is based upon the totality of the circumstances that may justify an investigatory vehicle stop (*U.S. v. Cortez,* 1981). Stopping an automobile and detaining the driver to check his driver's license and registration without an articulable suspicion is unreasonable under the Fourth Amendment (*Delaware v. Prouse,* 1979). In *Rodriguez v. U.S.* (2015), the Court declared that extending a traffic stop to conduct a dog sniff constitutes an unreasonable seizure because the authority for the seizure ends when tasks tied to the traffic infraction are, or reasonably should be, completed. However, roadblocks for safety checks for driving under the influence are constitutional (*Michigan Dept. of State Police v. Sitz,* 1990). Pretextual stops are stops for minor violations used as a pretext to conduct investigations. The Court in *Whren v. U.S.* (1996) deemed pretextual stops constitutional and held that neither an officer's intent nor motivation is relevant to the fourth amendment

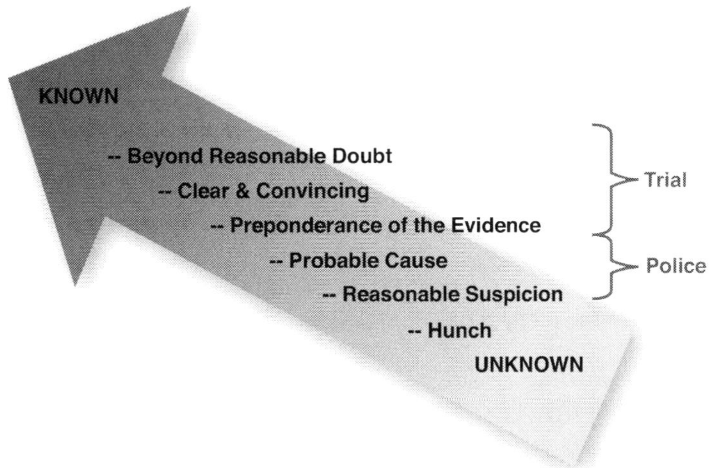

FIGURE 9.1 Spectrum of Certainty.

standard of "reasonableness." Many states have banned pretextual stops based on racial profiling or other set factors.

Once an officer returns the driver's identification, the officer need not inform the driver that they are free to go (*Ohio v. Robinette*, 1996). The Court held that officers may order drivers out of their cars (*Pennsylvania v. Mimms,* 1977) and frisk them if the officer reasonably suspects that they may be armed and dangerous (*Arizona v. Johnson*, 2009). Passengers may also be ordered out of the car (*Maryland v. Wilson*, 1997) and frisked (*Brendlin v. California*, 2007). The car itself may be subject to a protective sweep (*Michigan v. Long*, 1983).

Search Incident to Arrest

A full custodial arrest permits the contemporaneous warrantless search of the arrestee and the area within the arrestee's immediate control. Furthermore, it permits searches of closets and other spaces from which an attack might occur when an arrest occurs in a home and searches of car compartments when arresting a recent car occupant.

Under Common Law, a search incident to an arrest was permitted. The search incident to an arrest doctrine was first referenced by the U.S. Supreme Court in dictum in 1914 (*Weeks v. U.S.*) "A search or seizure without a warrant as an incident to a lawful arrest has always been considered a strictly limited right" (*Trupiano v. U.S.*, 1948).

Every state has a statute or code that authorizes law enforcement officers to make arrests. States vary in officers' ability to arrest for a misdemeanor. An arrest may even be for a minor crime, such as a misdemeanor seatbelt violation, punishable by only a fine (*Atwater v. City of Largo Vista,* 2001). Regardless, arrests are regulated by Fourth Amendment constitutional law, not state law (*Ker v. California*, 1963; *Virginia v. Moore*, 2008).

An arrest occurs when an officer exercises dominion or control (actual seizure) or where the person detained reasonably believes that he or she is not free to leave (constructive seizure). Handcuffs are unnecessary for an arrest (*Brower v. County of Inyo* (1989). Application of physical force to a person with the intent to restrain them, including shooting at a fleeing subject, constitutes a seizure (*Torres v. Madrid*, 2021). If there is a question of whether an arrest has occurred, courts will consider:

1. the seizure and detention of a person
2. the intention to arrest
3. the arrest authority of the officer
4. the reasonable belief of the person detained that they are not free to leave, free to decline the officer's requests, or otherwise terminate the encounter

An arrest must be based on probable cause to believe the individual has committed a crime, with or without a warrant. No further probable cause is required to conduct a search incident to the arrest; the probable cause for arrest authorizes the search. Arrest warrants give police authority to enter the defendant's house.

The rationale for the warrant exception for searches incident to an arrest is to protect the safety of the officers and prevent the destruction of evidence (*Chimel v. California*, 1969), except for extensive digital information in cellphones and evidence collected from the bodies of arrestees, where the Court balances the desire for an intrusive warrantless search against reasonableness, the privacy interest of the arrestee, and the opportunity to obtain a warrant (*Riley v. California*, 2014; *Winston v. Lee,* 1985; *Missouri v. McNeely,* 2013; *Birchfield v. North Dakota*, 2016).

The arrest must be lawful based upon probable cause rather than state law (*Virginia v. Moore,* 2008). However, the Court in *Herring v. U.S.* (2009) allowed evidence from an invalid warrant when the police relied on it in good faith. In some cases, fingerprints may be permissible despite an illegal arrest (*Davis v. Mississippi,* 1969; *Frisbie v. Collins,* 1952; *U.S. v. Guevara-Martinez,* 2001).

The arrest must also be made in good faith. It cannot be a mere ruse or pretext to search, particularly when a minor charge is later dropped (*State v. Sullivan*, 2000; *U.S. v. Pampinella*, 1955). Issuing a traffic citation to a driver is not an arrest; officers must have consent or probable cause to search the car incident to a traffic citation (*Knowles v. Iowa*, 1998).

The search must be contemporaneous to the arrest or immediately after that. A search made before an arrest may be considered a lawful search incidental to arrest where the fruits of the search were not necessary to support the probable cause for the arrest. Contemporaneous is not the same as simultaneous; the search is permissible if conducted during the same period as the arrest (*State v. Williams*, 1987). In general, once a person is arrested and in police custody, the arrestee can no longer attack the officer or destroy evidence that would justify a search incidental to an arrest. However, the Court carved out an exception to this rule in a vehicle search when it is reasonable to believe that evidence of the crime for which the occupant was arrested might be found in a vehicle (*Arizona v. Gant*, 2009). Also, clothing from an inmate may be searched despite a lengthy period since arrest (*U.S. v. Edwards*, 1974).

A full-body search of the person may be conducted in cases of a valid full-custody arrest without a search warrant, regardless of the arresting officer's fear (*U.S. v. Robinson*, 1973). Such searches include searching their clothing, even after the arrestee has been jailed (*U.S. v. Edwards*, 1974). However, a strip search is an extreme invasion of personal rights and strip searches are not generally permitted absent a reasonable suspicion that the arrestee is concealing weapons or other contraband based on the crime charged, the particular characteristics of the arrestee, and circumstances of the arrest (*Flores v. City of* Mount Vernon, 1999; *Nelson v. McMullen*, 2000; *Doe v. Calumet City*, 1994); although strip searches of inmates are permitted (*Florence v. Board of Chosen Freeholders of the County of Burlington*, 2012). In *Schmerber v. California* (1966), the Court recognized that existing caselaw seemed to suggest an unrestricted right to search a lawfully arrested person, but such decisions did not apply to "searches involving intrusions beyond the body's surface." Biologic and other evidence collected intrusively from the body are discussed in Chapters 10 and 11.

For decades, officers searched for evidence areas under an arrestee's control. In *Harris v. U.S.* (1947), where evidence of another crime was found during a warrantless exploratory search incident to an arrest, the Court held that police may search for any evidence regardless of what the arrest was for. The search in that case that was deemed constitutional involved a thorough five-hour exploratory search of multiple rooms in a house. Reversing prior law, the Court in *U.S. v. Rabinowitz* (1950) limited the search to areas within the arrestee's "immediate control." In *Chimel v. California* (1969), after noting that the search is conducted "in order to remove any weapons that the [arrestee] might seek to use in order to resist arrest or effect escape" and to prevent the "concealment or destruction of evidence," the Court defined "immediate control" as limited to the clothing and immediate area around the arrestee within his or her reach because a weapon or evidence may be grasped within that area. This *Chimel* rule refers to the reachable area, the arrestee's wingspan, or the lunge area.

BOX 9.5 *CHIMEL V. CALIFORNIA* (1969) – HOUSE SEARCH INCIDENT TO AN ARREST

Police officers, armed with an arrest warrant but not a search warrant, were admitted to the defendant's home by his wife. The defendant arrived home and was served with the warrant as he entered. Although he denied the officers' request to "look around," they searched the entire house "based on the lawful arrest." The Court assumed the arrest was proper and held that the officers could search the area "within the immediate control" of the person arrested to discover and remove weapons and to seize evidence to prevent its concealment or destruction, but the warrantless search of the house was not constitutionally justified as an incident to that arrest.

In *Trupiano v. U.S.* (1948), the Court invalidated a search and excluded the evidence when the officers had time to obtain a warrant. In *Mincey v. Arizona* (1978), the Court invalidated a four-day warrantless search conducted after an initial quick search that surpassed the scope of the search incident to a crime. In *Thompson v. Louisiana* (1984), the Court invalidated a two-hour warrantless search for the same reason.

In *Maryland v. Buie* (1990), the Court held that a *protective sweep* of the entire premises is constitutional if there is a reasonable belief based upon articulable facts that a threat exists of unseen third parties that pose a danger to those on the arrest scene. The protective sweep is a "cursory inspection," not an exploratory search, and does not extend to desk drawers or other concealed areas (*U.S. v. Melgar*, 1996). However, if police discover evidence of criminal activity in "plain view" while conducting a protective sweep, that evidence may be used against the defendant at trial.

Unless another warrant exception applies (exigency, automobile exception, inventory), movable opaque containers within reach of the arrestee cannot be opened and searched because the containers are within a person's reasonable expectation of privacy (*U.S. v. Chadwick*, 1977). It is presumed that the arrestee cannot grab a weapon or evidence from within the container. The police may secure the container from loss or destruction based on reasonable suspicion that it may contain contraband, evidence, or fruit of a crime. Still, the container cannot be opened and searched without a warrant because there will be time to obtain a warrant.

Searches incident to the arrest of vehicle drivers pose special considerations. An officer may order an occupant out of a car for a traffic stop (*Maryland v. Wilson*, 1997), but a traffic citation does not constitute an arrest and does not, by itself, justify a search (*Knowles v. Iowa*, 1998). In addition to the arrest of the driver, an officer may arrest passengers if there is probable cause for a crime and the passenger may have committed the crime

(*Maryland v. Pringle*, 2003); a passenger, like the driver, is seized for Fourth Amendment purposes and has standing to challenge the search (*Brendlin v. California*, 2007).

In *New York v. Belton* (1981), the Court applied the *Chimel* rule to the arrest of vehicular drivers, holding that the vehicle's passenger compartment is within reach of the arrested driver and can be searched for weapons or evidence. The Belton rule holds that police may make a contemporaneous search of the passenger's compartment and the contents of containers, including the glove box, whether opened or closed, but cannot search the vehicle's trunk. In further refinement, the Court held in *Thornton v. U.S.* (2004) that the police may search a vehicle incident to an arrest where the arrestee is a recent occupant and physically close enough to return to the vehicle. However, in *Arizona v. Gant* (2009), the Court held that after the arrestee is secured and can no longer reach the passenger's compartment, then a search of the car incident to the arrest would no longer be authorized unless officers have a belief that the vehicle contains evidence of the offense of the arrest.

Inventory searches occur when cars are impounded. Police may impound vehicles if the driver is arrested and no one else is available to drive them away, if it appears to be abandoned, in an unsafe location, or may constitute a public hazard. Officers may inventory the vehicle contents before or after towing. Closed containers and locked areas within the car may be opened pursuant to a departmental policy that involves sufficient regulation not based upon suspicion (*South Dakota v. Opperman*, 1976; *Illinois v. Lafayette*, 1983). No consent, probable cause, or reasonable suspicion is necessary for this administrative function. If contraband or weapons are found incidental to the inventory, they may be lawfully seized. Although some discretion is permitted, the Court envisions a standard, routine, mechanical process and not a pretext for the sole purpose of criminal investigation or ruse for general rummaging (*Colorado v. Bertine*, 1987; *Florida v. Wells*, 1990). The Supreme Court has not yet ruled on whether papers and documents found during an inventory search.

BOX 9.6 *CANIGLIA V. STROM* (2021) – COMMUNITY CARETAKING

Edward Caniglia's wife called the police for a welfare check, concerned that her husband owned firearms and may have committed suicide. Caniglia agreed to meet with the police. The police concluded that he was a danger to himself and others. Caniglia agreed to a mental health evaluation. During his observation in the hospital, the police searched his house and, with the assistance of his wife, found and confiscated his firearms and ammunition. After his release, he demanded the return of his property. When they were not immediately returned, he sued the city and its police department. The trial court ruled that Caniglia's due process rights were infringed because the police failed to return his property or instruct him to retrieve it after he was deemed safe but denied his other claims of conversion. The government appealed, and the appellate court affirmed the trial court's ruling, declaring that the police did not exceed the proper province of their community caretaking responsibilities and cited *Cady v. Dombroski* (2017), which allowed the warrantless search of an impounded car and had commented on the frequent noncriminal "community caretaking functions" of the police. The U.S. Supreme Court, in a unanimous decision, held that the search of the home and seizure of the firearms was unconstitutional and that the community caretaking exception applied to vehicles, not homes because what is reasonable for vehicles is different from what is reasonable for homes.

In concurring opinions, it was noted that allowance for warrantless searches might still be made under the exigency exception when there is no time to obtain a warrant, for red flag laws, for a suicidal person, or to check on a medical person. Justice Alito wrote, "...an important real-world problem. Today, more than ever, many people, including many elderly persons, live alone."

Automobile Exception

The automobile exception must be distinguished from vehicle searches incident to arrests and inventory searches. During the prohibition era, in *Carroll v. U.S.* (1925), where the car itself was the instrument for illegally transporting liquor, the U.S. Supreme Court held that a warrantless search of an automobile is valid if there is probable cause to believe it contains contraband. In that case, the police had no probable cause to search the car or occupants before they spotted the car traveling down the highway that they suspected of bootleg liquor. The police had to search the car before they could arrest the occupants. There was no opportunity for a search warrant.

The evolution of this doctrine has been tortuous and confusing as the rationale for it has transitioned from exigency to a lesser expectation of privacy (*Husty v. U.S.*, 1931; *Chambers v. Maroney*, 1970); *Coolidge v. New Hampshire*, 1971; *U.S. v. Chadwick*, 1977; *U.S. v. Ross*, 1982) but appears now to have simplified and settled (*California v. Acevedo*, 1991).

The automobile exception is its own exception to the warrant requirement, and an arrest need not be associated with it. In *Pennsylvania v. Labron* (1996), the Court declared, "If a car is readily mobile and probable cause exists to believe it contains contraband, the Fourth Amendment thus permits police to search the vehicle without more." There are three requirements for the automobile exception:

1. the vehicle must be not in a place regularly used for residential purposes,
2. readily mobile – appears operational, and
3. probable cause to believe that contraband or evidence of a crime will be in the vehicle.

The *automobile exception* applies to "mobile conveyances," which include cars, trucks, airplanes, boats, motor homes, etc. (*California v. Carney*, 1985).

In *U.S. v. Ross* (1982), the *Carroll doctrine* was interpreted to permit a police officer to search an entire motor vehicle, including the trunk, luggage, and packages found therein, which might reasonably contain the items for which they have probable cause to search. The Court in *California v. Acevedo* (1991) settled prior inconsistent rulings, holding that containers in the vehicle, including passengers' belongings (*Wyoming v. Houghton*, 1999), could be opened and searched pursuant to the automobile exception if the container can conceal the object of the search.

Exigency/Emergency

The *exigent circumstances exception* occurs when police have the necessary probable cause to obtain a warrant but not the time to do so. The circumstances make the delay in getting a warrant unreasonable, perhaps allowing the subject's escape or the destruction or removal of evidence. The *emergency aid exception* occurs when prompt action is necessary to justify the police entering the premises to assist individuals in distress or danger or to prevent serious property damage. Urgency is the basis for both concepts and why they are often conflated (*People v. Ramey,* 1976; *U.S. v. McConney*, 1984).

In *Johnson v. U.S.* (1948), the Court recognized that sometimes "exceptional circumstances in which, on balancing the need for effective law enforcement against the right of privacy, it may be contended that a magistrate's warrant may be dispensed with." Now, even warrantless entry into a private home can be justified by exigency (*Warden v. Hayden*, 1967; *Brigham City v. Stuart*, 2006). Exigency and public safety almost always trump individual privacy rights, but it must be a legitimate emergency; for example, emergency care overrode the need for Miranda warnings (*State v. Boretsky*, 2006).

The U.S. Supreme Court has recognized three main categories of exigency: (1) engaging in a hot pursuit of a fleeing suspect, (2) protecting a person or the public from an immediate danger, and (3) preventing the imminent destruction of evidence (*Brigham City v. Stuart*, 2006).

Exigency requires a case-by-case balance of governmental intrusion against privacy rights. The court in *U.S. v. Dawkins* (1994) declared that the prosecution must satisfy two criteria: (1) probable cause exists and (2) failure to obtain a warrant was justified by the circumstances. Thus, these cases present a mixed question of law and fact, involving the underlying facts and whether those facts satisfy the legal test of exigency. (*U.S. v. Anderson*, 1998). Courts have suggested factors helpful in making this assessment (*U.S. v. Dorman*, 1970; *U.S. v. Richard*, 1995). Sounds of likely destruction of evidence that might justify exigency include foot scurrying, running water, and toilet flushing (*U.S. v. Gomez*, 1980). Exigency determination is based on an objective, reasonable person's assessment of the situation, not the officer's subjective opinion (*Brigham City v. Stuart*, 2006; *People v. Smith*, 2020).

The exigent circumstances must not be police-created (*U.S. v. Segura*, 1981; *Kentucky v. King*, 2011). The search may not exceed the scope of the emergency or exigency (*Mincey v. Arizona*, 1978).

Any evidence observed in plain view may be seized and used as evidence (*Brigham City v. Stuart*, 2006). Police may temporarily detain a person without a warrant under exigent circumstances to preserve evidence (*Illinois v. McArthur*, 2001).

BOX 9.7 *MINCEY V. ARIZONA* (1978) – SCOPE OF EXIGENCY; NO HOMICIDE EXCEPTION

Undercover officers conducted a raid on an apartment occupied by Rufus Mincey. Shots were fired, one undercover officer was killed, and Mincey was wounded. Police officers rushed in to search for other possibly injured people and conducted a quick search of the premises but refrained from any further investigation. About ten minutes later, homicide detectives arrived and conducted a four-day search. Mincey claimed that the detectives should have obtained a search warrant. The Arizona Supreme Court concluded that the search was valid based on a newly found "murder scene" exception to the warrant requirement limited to determining the circumstances of death. The U.S. Supreme Court found that the four-day search conducted by the homicide officers was not justified under the emergency exception. The Court also rejected a murder scene exception to the warrant requirement.

> [T]he State points to the vital public interest in the prompt investigation of the extremely serious crime of murder. No one can doubt the importance of this goal. But the public interest in the investigation of other serious crimes is comparable. If the warrantless search of a homicide scene is reasonable, why not the warrantless search of the scene of a rape, a robbery, or a burglary?

BOX 9.8 *BRIGHAM CITY, UTAH V. STUART* (2006) – EXIGENCY

The police responded to a complaint about a loud party at 3 am. They saw minors drinking alcohol outside and approached the house. Through a window, they saw a fight involving a juvenile and four adults, one of whom spit blood when he was punched. The officers announced their presence and entered the home. The men were arrested for contributing to the delinquency of minors and other related offenses. In a unanimous decision, the Court held that police may make a warrantless entry into a home when they have an objectively reasonable basis to believe that an occupant is seriously injured or imminently threatened with such injury.

> 'The need to protect or preserve life or avoid serious injury is justification for what would be otherwise illegal absent an exigency or emergency'... The role of a peace officer includes preventing violence and restoring order, not simply rendering first aid to casualties; an officer is not like a boxing (or hockey) referee, poised to stop a bout only if it becomes too one-sided.

This is the first case that the Court allowed police entry into a home without a warrant, probable cause, or even reasonable suspicion.

In his concurrence, Justice Stevens wrote,

> This is an odd flyspeck of a case. The charges that have been pending against respondents for the past six years are minor offenses—intoxication, contributing to the delinquency of a minor, and disorderly conduct... the Court's unanimous opinion restating well-settled rules of federal law is so clearly persuasive that it is hard to imagine the outcome was ever in doubt.

Hot Pursuit

The *hot pursuit* (fresh pursuit) rule allows an officer to pursue a suspect fleeing onto private property without a warrant. It is an immediate pursuit, without significant interruption, of a person attempting to avoid arrest.

The U.S. Supreme Court recognized it first in *Warden v. Hayden* (1967). Although hot pursuit can be seen as a type of exigency, it was a recognized practice in Common Law and international law long before it was recognized in *Hayden*. It is a doctrine with its own specific elements. We treat it here as a separate exception to the warrant requirement.

At Common Law, the crime had to be a felony, but most states now allow hot pursuit after a misdemeanor. The person may have escaped arrest, or the officer attempted to arrest the person or had probable cause to believe the person was involved in a crime. The pursuit must start where the officer had a lawful right to be – in a public area or other space with no reasonable expectation of privacy. There must be a chase without time to get a warrant. The pursuit must be immediate and continuous, but the suspect is not required to be under personal observation the entire time. While the hot pursuit exception allows entry into a home without a warrant, it does not eliminate the requirement for police to knock and announce their presence (*Ingram v. City of Columbus*, 1999).

In *U.S. v. Santana* (1975), the Court held that the defendant could not escape from police by merely re-entering the private household from the doorway, where she had knowingly exposed herself to the public and had no expectation of privacy. The Court deemed the warrantless entry into the house lawful because it was in hot pursuit.

The police generally have hot pursuit authority anywhere within the state. Interstate hot pursuit compacts may allow the officer to pursue an offender across state lines. Adopting the Uniform Fresh Pursuit Act will allow the officer to enter their state in fresh pursuit to make an arrest. An officer must follow the state's rules where the arrest is made. In *Commonwealth v. Sadari* (2000), an arrest in Delaware was found unlawful when the Pennsylvania troopers did not bring the suspect to a Delaware Justice of the Peace.

Special Needs

The Special Needs doctrine defines an exception to the warrant and probable cause requirements when the primary purpose of the government search is to serve special needs other than law enforcement purposes, and it is reasonable to do so when balancing public and private interests.

Justice Blackmun first articulated the doctrine in his concurrence in *New Jersey v. T.L.O.* (1965), when he found a "special need" for public school officials to conduct suspicionless searches of student belongings without probable cause or a warrant. The Court formally adopted his formulation of the doctrine in *O'Connor v. Ortega* (1987).

Courts must determine the primary purpose of the special needs program and then perform a balancing assessment of (1) the nature of the privacy interest, (2) the character of the privacy interest, (3) the nature and immediacy of the government concerns, and the efficacy of the program for addressing them (*Vernonia School Dist. V. 47J v. Acton*, 1995; *Bd. of Educ. Of Indep. Sch. Dist. No. 92 of Pottawatomie Cty. v. Earls*, 2002).

Courts have found special needs in the following areas:

- *Public Schools* (New Jersey v. T.L.O., 1965; Vernonia School Dist. V. 47J v. Acton, 1995; Bd. of Educ. of Indep. Sch. Dist. No. 92 of Pottawatomie County. v. Earls, 2002)
- *Sobriety Checkpoints* (*Michigan Dept. of State Police v. Sitz*, 1990; but see *City of Indianapolis v. Edmond*, 2000)
- *Border Screens* (*United States v. Martinez-Fuerte*, 1976)
- *Airport Screens* (*People v. Materon*, 1985; *People v. Kuhn*, 33 N.Y.2d 203, (1973))

- *Government Employee Searches* (*O'Connor v. Ortega*, 1987)
- *Drug And Alcohol Testing Programs* (*National Treasury Employees Union v. Von Raab*, 1989; *Skinner v. Railway Labor Executives' Association*, 1989; but see *Chandler v. Miller*, 1987; *Ferguson v. City of* Charleston, 2001)
- *Probationer/Parolee Inspections* (*Griffin v. Wisconsin*, 1987; *Samson v. California*, 2006)

General Reasonableness

Despite the traditional articulation of well-established exceptions, courts have made new exceptions to the warrant requirement. Particularly, the exigency and special needs doctrines permit broad application. Thus, some legal scholars have argued that the Court's references to warrants and probable cause have become lip service, that warrantless searches are merely presumed unreasonable, and that *reasonableness* has become the true touchstone of what passes constitutional muster. These scholars have noted that the framers were concerned about the abuses of warrants, not warrantless searches. The Court has decided cases squarely on reasonableness grounds based on the totality of the circumstances without reference to an established exception in *Samson v. California* (2006), *Florence v. Board of Chosen Freeholders* (2012), and *Maryland v. King* (2013).

Administrative Searches

The general rule is that an administrative search of private premises requires a warrant (*Camara v. Municipal Court*, 1967; *See v. City of Seattle*, 1967), but as a practical matter, it is often difficult to know if a warrant is required for an administrative search. It often depends on the nature and purposes of the search and the nature and detail of the regulation. Inventory searches of impounded cars are administrative searches not requiring a warrant.

If the primary purpose of the search is to investigate a specific unlawful act with individualized suspicion, then a criminal search warrant may be necessary (*Michigan v. Tyler*, 1978; *Michigan v. Clifford*, 1984). The same warrant exceptions detailed above apply, including plain view (*Air Pollution Variance Board v. Western Alfalfa Corp.*, 1974), consent (*U.S. v. Thriftimart, Inc.*, 9th Cir., 1970), exigency (*Michigan v. Tyler*, 1978), and particularly special needs (*New Jersey v. T.L.O.*, 1965).

Sometimes, the primary purpose, whether civil or criminal, is blurred. In *New York v. Burger* (1987), the Court considered the random general search of junkyards for stolen car parts by police to be an administrative search under a new law regulating the automobile dismantling ("chop-shop") industry. The dissent considered the new law to be a mere pretext for allowing police to search for evidence of auto theft without the necessity of first obtaining a warrant. The New York Court of Appeals later ruled the law unconstitutional based on the New York state constitution (*People v. Keta*, 1992).

An exception for highly regulated industries (*Colonnade-Biswell* exception) is peculiar to administrative searches (*Colonnade Catering Corp. v. U.S.*, 1970; *U.S. v. Biswell*, 1972). Warrantless inspections, often unannounced, are allowed for licensed or highly regulated industries, where limited inspections are central to the regulatory scheme and regulations governing the procedures, times, and places. Owners have less expectation of privacy because they know they are subject to periodic inspections and have implicitly consented when engaging in the trade (*Donovan v. Dewey*, 1981). The administrative scheme must advance a substantial government interest, warrantless searches must advance that scheme, and the regulations must provide an adequate substitute for the warrant (*New York v. Burger*, 1987).

Summary

Most searches and seizures are conducted without warrants under a few well-established exceptions to the warrant requirement. These exceptions include plain view, consent searches, stop and frisk, searches incident to an arrest, automobile exception, hot pursuit, exigency/emergency, and special needs. A special highly regulated industry (*Colonnade-Biswell* exception) applies to administrative searches.

Terms

Exclusionary Rule – the prohibition of illegally obtained evidence in a criminal trial.

Exigent – an urgent need.

Frisk – a quick pat down of a person for weapons.

Fruit of the Poisonous Tree – secondary evidence that was obtained after police conduct that violated the defendant's rights.

Good Faith – well-intentioned police conduct used in the context of an honest mistake or reliance.

Individualized Suspicion – the notion that the suspicion is of a particular person.

Open View – visible from a constitutionally non-protected area.

Plain View – visible from a constitutionally protected area, where an officer has a legal right to be.

Protective Sweep – a quick search of a limited area for weapons and dangerous instrumentalities.

Reasonable Articulable Suspicion – a suspicion that is more than a hunch, but less than probable cause, that can be clearly stated; it is an objective standard that reasonable persons would also find suspicious given the same information.

Cases

Adams v. Williams, 407 U.S. 143 (1972)
Air Pollution Variance Board v. Western Alfalfa Corp., 416 U.S. 861 (1974)
Alabama v. White, 496 U.S. 325 (1990)
Arizona v. Gant, 556 U.S. 332 (2009)
Arizona v. Hicks, 480 U.S. 321 (1987)
Arizona v. Johnson, 555 U.S. 323 (2009)
Atwater v. City of Largo Vista, 532 U.S. 318 (2001)
Birchfield v. North Dakota, 579 U.S. 438 (2016)
Board of Educ. of Indep. Sch. Dist. No. 92 of Pottawatomie County. v. Earls, 536 U.S. 822 (2002)
Brendlin v. California, 551 U.S. 249 (2007)
Brigham City, Utah v. Stuart, 547 U.S. 398 (2006)
Brower v. County of Inyo, 489 U.S. 593(1989)
Bumper v. North Carolina, 391 U.S. 543 (1968)
Cady v. Dombrowski, 413 U.S. 433 (1973)
California v. Acevedo, 500 U.S. 565 (1991)
California v. Carney, 471 U.S. 386 (1985)
California v. Ciraolo, 476 U.S. 207 (1986)
Camara v. Municipal Court, 387 U.S. 523 (1967)
Caniglia v. Strom, 593 U.S. 194 (2021)
Carroll v. United States, 267 U.S. 132 (1925)
Chambers v. Maroney, 399 U.S. 42 (1970)
Chandler v. Miller, 520 U.S. 305 (1997)
Chimel v. California, 395 U.S. 752 (1969)
City of Indianapolis v. Edmond, 531 U.S. 32 (2000)
City of Ontario v. Quon, 560 U.S. 746 (2010)
Colonnade Catering Corp. v. United States, 397 U.S. 72 (1970)
Colorado v. Bertine, 479 U.S. 386 (1987)
Commonwealth v. Sadari, 752 A.2d 393 (Pa. 2000)
Coolidge v. New Hampshire, 403 U.S. 443 (1971)
County of Riverside v. McLaughlin, 500 U.S. 413 (1991)
Davis v. Mississippi, 394 U.S. 721 (1969)
Delaware v. Prouse, 440 U.S. 648 (1979)
Doe v. Calumet City, 641 N.E.2d 498 (IL 1994)
Donovan v. Dewey, 452 U.S. 594 (1981)
Ferguson v. City of Charleston, 532 U.S. 67 (2001)

Fernandez v. California, 571 U.S. 292 (2014)
Florence v. Board of Chosen Freeholders, 566 U.S. 318 (2012)
Flores v. City of Mount Vernon, 41 F. Supp. 2d 439 (S.D.N.Y. 1999)
Florida v. Bostick, 501 U.S. 429 (1996)
Florida v. Harris, 568 U.S. 237 (2013)
Florida v. J.L., 529 U.S. 266 (2000)
Florida v. Jimeno, 499 U.S. 934 (1991)
Florida v. Riley, 488 U.S. 445 (1989)
Florida v. Royer, 460 U.S. 491 (1983)
Florida v. Wells, 495 U.S. 1 (1990)
Frisbie v. Collins, 342 U.S. 519 (1952)
Georgia v. Randolph, 547 U.S. 103 (2006)
Griffin v. Wisconsin, 483 U.S. 868 (1987)
Harris v. United States, 331 U.S. 145 (1947)
Hayes v. Florida, 470 U.S. 811 (1985)
Herring v. United States, 555 U.S. 135 (2009)
Hiibel v. Sixth Judicial District Court of Nevada, 542 U.S. 177 (2004)
Hoffa v. United States, 385 U.S. 293 (1966)
Horton v. California, 496 U.S. 128 (1990)
Howe v. State, 916 P.2d 153 (Nev. 1996)
Husty v. United States, 282 U.S. 694 (1931)
Illinois v. Lafayette, 462 U.S. 640 (1983)
Illinois v. McArthur, 531 U.S. 326 (2001)
Illinois v. Rodriguez, 497 U.S. 177 (1990)
Illinois v. Wardlow, 528 U.S. 119 (2000)
Ingram v. City of Columbus, 185 F.3d 579 (6th Cir. 1999)
Johnson v. United States, 333 U.S. 10 (1948)
Kansas v. Glover, 589 U.S. 376 (2020)
Katz v. United States, 389 U.S. 347 (1967)
Kentucky v. King, 563 U.S. 452 (2011)
Ker v. California, 374 U.S. 23 (1963)
Knowles v. Iowa, 525 U.S. 113 (1998)
Kyllo v. United States, 533 U.S. 27 (2001)
Lee v. United States, 343 U.S. 747 (1942)
Lewis v. United States, 385 U.S. 206 (1966)
Maryland v. Buie, 494 U.S. 325 (1990)
Maryland v. King, 569 U.S. 435 (2013)
Maryland v. Pringle, 540 U.S. 366 (2003)
Maryland v. Wilson, 519 U.S. 408 (1997)
Michigan Dept. of State Police v. Sitz, 496 U.S. 444 (1990)
Michigan v. Clifford, 464 U.S. 287 (1984)
Michigan v. Long, 463 U.S. 1032 (1983)
Michigan v. Tyler, 436 U.S. 499 (1978)

Mincey v. Arizona, 437 U.S. 385 (1978)
Minnesota v. Dickerson, 508 U.S. 366 (1993)
Missouri v. McNeely, 569 U.S. 141 (2013)
National Treasury Employees Union v. Von Raab, 489 U.S. 656 (1989)
Nelson v. McMullen, 207 F.3d 1202 (10th Cir. 2000)
New Jersey v. T.L.O., 469 U.S. 325 (1987)
New York v. Belton, 453 U.S. 454 (1981)
New York v. Burger, 482 U.S. 691 (1987)
O'Connor v. Ortega, 480 U.S. 709 (1987)
Ohio v. Robinette, 519 U.S. 53 (1996)
Payton v. New York, 445 U.S. 573 (1980)
Pennsylvania v. Labron, 518 U.S. 938 (1996)
Pennsylvania v. Mimms, 434 U.S. 106 (1977)
People v. Keta, 593 N.E.2d 1328 (NY 1992)
People v. Kuhn, 306 N.E.2d 777 (NY 1973)
People v. Materon, 107 A.D.2d 408 (N.Y. App. Div. 1985)
People v. Ramey, 545 P.2d 1333 (Cal 1976)
People v. Smith, 46 Cal. App.5th 375 (2020)
Riley v. California, 573 U.S. 373 (2014)
Rodriguez v. United States, 575 U.S. 348 (2015)
Samson v. California, 547 U.S. 843 (2006)
Schmerber v. California, 384 U.S. 757 (1966)
Schneckloth v. Bustamonte, 412 U.S. 218 (1973)
See v. City of Seattle, 387 U.S. 541 (1967)
Skinner v. Railway Labor Executives' Association, 489 U.S. 602 (1989)
South Dakota v. Opperman, 428 U.S. 364 (1976)
State v. Boretsky, 894 A.2d 659 (N.J. 2006)
State v. Patterson, 758 So.2d 955 (La. 2000)
State v. Sullivan, 16 S.W.2d 551 (Ark. 2000)
State v. Timberlake, 726 N.W.2d 509 (Minn. Ct. App. 2007)
State v. Williams, 516 So.2d 1081 (Fl. Dist. Ct. 1987)
Stoner v. California, 376 U.S. 483 (1964)
Terry v. Ohio, 392 U.S. 1 (1968)
Texas v. Brown, 460 U.S. 730 (1983)
Thompson v. Louisiana, 469 U.S. 17 (1984)
Thornton v. United States, 541 U.S. 615 (2004)
Torres v. Madrid, 592 U.S. 306 (2021)
Trupiano v. United States, 334 U.S. 699 (1948)
Turner v. State, 754 A.2d 1074 (Md. Ct. Spec. App. 2000)
United States v. Anderson, 154 F.3d 1225 (10th Cir. 1998)
United States v. Biswell, 406 U.S. 311, (1972)
United States v. Bramble, 103 F. 3d 1475 (9th Cir. 1996)
United States v. Brigham, 382 F.3d 500 (2004)

United States v. Carey, 172 F.3d 1268 (10th Cir. 1999)
United States v. Chadwick, 433 U.S. 1 (1977)
United States v. Cortez, 449 U.S. 411 (1981)
United States v. Dawkins, 17 F.3d 399 (D.C. Cir.1994)
United States v. Dorman, 435 F.2d 385 (D.C. Cir. 1970)
United States v. Drayton, 536 U.S. 194 (2002)
United States v. Edwards, 415 U.S. 800 (1974)
United States v. Fuentes, 105 F.3d 487 (9th Cir. 1997)
United States v. Gomez, 633 F.2d 999 (2d Cir. 1980)
United States v. Gray, 369 F.3d 1024 (8th Cir. 2004)
United States v. Guevara-Martinez, 262 F.2d 751 (2001)
United States v. Hensley, 469 U.S. 221 (1985)
United States v. Herzbrun, 724 F.2d 773 (11th Cir. 1984)
United States v. Martinez-Fuerte, 428 U.S. 543 (1976)
United States v. Matlock, 415 U.S. 164 (1974)
United States v. McConney, 728 F.2d 1195 (9th Cir. 1984)
United States v. Melgar, 927 F. Supp. 939 (E.D. Va. 1996)
United States v. Mendenhall, 446 U.S. 544 (1980)
United States v. Montoya de Hernandez, 473 U.S. 531 (1985)
United States v. Pampinella, 131 F. Supp. 595 (N.D. Ill. 1955)
United States v. Pulido-Baquerizo, 800 F.2d 899 (9th Cir. 1986)
United States v. Rabinowitz, 339 U.S. 56 (1950)
United States v. Rich, 992 F.2d 502 (5th Cir. 1993)
United States v. Richard, 994 F.2d 244 (5th Cir. 1993)
United States v. Robinson, 414 U.S. 218 (1973)
United States v. Ross, 456 U.S. 798 (1982)
United States v. Ross, 263 F.3d 844 (8th Cir. 2001)
United States v. Santana, 427 U.S. 38 (1975)
United States v. Segura, 663 F.2d 411 (2d Cir. 1981)
United States v. Seslar, 996 F.2d 1058 (10th Cir. 1993)
United States v. Sharpe, 470 U.S. 675 (1985)
United States v. Spriggs, 827 F. Supp. 372 (E.D. Va. 1993)
United States v. Thriftimart, Inc., 429 F.2d 1006 (9th Cir. 1970)
United States v. Wong, 334 F.3d 831 (9th Cir. 2004)
Vernonia School District 47J v. Acton, 515 U.S. 646 (1995)
Virginia v. Moore, 553 U.S. 164 (2008)
Warden v. Hayden, 387 U.S. 294 (1967)
Washington v. Chrisman, 455 U.S. 1 (1982)
Weeks v. United States, 232 U.S. 383 (1914)
Whren v. United States, 517 U.S. 806 (1996)
Winston v. Lee, 470 U.S. 753 (1985)
Wyoming v. Houghton, 526 U.S. 295 (1999)
Zap v. United States, 328 U.S. 624 (1946)

Thought Questions

1. Why have the exceptions to the warrant requirement increased?
2. Why are administrative searches an exception to the warrant requirement?
3. Why are dog searches of cars allowed but not of front doors?
4. When might an officer rely on the person answering the door to consent to search the dwelling?

Further Reading

Bandiero A, *Search & Seizure Survival Guide: A Field Guide for Law Enforcement*, 2018 ed, Blue to Gold, LLC, CreateSpace Independent Publishing Platform, Scotts Valley, CA, 2019.

Dressler J, Michaels AC, Simmons R, *Understanding Criminal Procedure, Volume One: Investigation*, 7th ed, Carolina Academic Press, Durham, NC, 2017.

Gizzi MC, Curtis RC, *The Fourth Amendment in Flux: The Roberts Court, Crime Control, and Digital Privacy*, Univ Press of Kansas, Lawrence, KS, 2016.

Gray D, *The Fourth Amendment in an Age of Surveillance*, Cambridge Univ Press, Cambridge, 2017.

Kanovitz JR, Ingram JL, Devine CJ, *Constitutional Law for Criminal Justice*, 15th ed, Routledge, New York, 2019.

Chapter 10

Forensic Evidence I

Collection

Learning Objectives

After reading this chapter, students are expected to be able to:

- define when search warrants are needed for crime scene investigations
- articulate the distinction between personal property and evidence
- explain why a warrant is needed for a blood sample but not a breath sample
- discuss the constitutionality of compelling fingerprints, DNA, and handwriting specimens
- discuss workplace drug testing.

Introduction

Fourth and Fifth Amendment constitutional considerations regulate the collection of forensic evidence.

Searches of Places

The Fourth Amendment search and seizure requirements provide the primary regulation of the collection of forensic evidence. Federal and state laws, particularly penal codes, provide specificity and additional requirements, e.g., biological evidence laws (see Chapter 11).

DOI: 10.4324/9780429272455-10

Law enforcement: the constitutional law concern.ing evidence in criminal cases is essentially about searches and seizures of evidence. Fourth Amendment considerations apply directly to crime scene investigations. Most crime scene investigations are conducted without a warrant because the scenes are in a public venue or consent has been given for the search. However, a search warrant will be needed when the scene is on private property, and a search is objected to. Exigency will not apply to a crime scene that is under police control. There is no homicide exception to the warrant requirement (*Mincey v. Arizona,* 1978). Investigators risk the evidence being thrown out of court if they do not get a warrant when they should. The exclusionary rule and the fruit of the poisonous tree doctrine may prevent necessary evidence from being used in court. However, it is usually not the responsibility of crime scene investigators to obtain needed warrants – law enforcement officers will generally obtain the warrants on their behalf.

Items seized should be evidence, contraband, fruits of a crime, and instrumentalities. However, a distinction must be made between items of evidence and other items. The distinction is blurry; property can become evidence, and evidence can lose its evidentiary (probative) value. Once items have been seized by law enforcement, they can be categorized by how they will be disposed of:

- *Evidence* is retained for examination and use in court
- *Personal Property* that is not evidence must be returned
- *Contraband* are illegal possessions that will be retained as evidence or destroyed
- *Seized Goods* are forfeited fruits of crimes that will be returned to their rightful owners or sold at auction
- *Abandoned Property/Trash* will be destroyed or disposed of in some manner.

In *City of West Covina v. Perkins* (1999), the court held that the due process clause does not require the police to provide the owner of any seized property with information on state law or the procedures for returning the property.

Statutes have been passed to allow the seizure of the fruits of the crimes on the notion that persons should not profit from their illegal activities. The seized goods include stolen items and items purchased with money made from illicit activities. The sale of these items at asset forfeiture auctions has become an essential source of income for law enforcement agencies. In the recent case of *Timbs v. Indiana* (2019), the U.S. Supreme Court unanimously ruled that the Eighth Amendment's prohibition of excessive fines applies to the states through the due process clause of the Fourteenth Amendment. The Court, however, did not announce a test for what constitutes an excessive fine. In that case, a Land Rover was seized, four times the maximum fine for the drug violation and 30 times the actual fine. The trial court found the forfeiture to be an excessive fine and that the absence of the vehicle interfered with the defendant's reintegration into society. The ruling will affect many police departments that are dependent on asset forfeiture sales. Some legal commentators have argued that the case has implications for confiscating driver's licenses and jail time for those unable to pay bail for minor crimes.

A Tucker Act or Section 1983 civil rights action can be brought against the government in federal court for a legitimate claim of entitlement for deprivation of property without due process of law. If property is seized that is not evidence, then the owner may be able to sue for its return or just compensation.

After *California v. Greenwood* (1988), some evidence, particularly latent fingerprints and DNA, can often be collected and seized as abandoned.

BOX 10.1 *CALIFORNIA V. GREENWOOD* (1988) – NO SEARCH OF ABANDONED PROPERTY

Acting on information that Billy Greenwood was drug dealing, the police twice searched the opaque plastic garbage bags left in front of his house on the curb, outside the curtilage, for the trash collector – both times without a warrant. The police obtained warrants to search the home based on narcotics paraphernalia in the trash. The searches revealed the expected narcotics, and Greenwood was charged. The California trial and appellate courts found that the evidence should be suppressed because the searches of garbage constituted violations of the Fourth Amendment. The U.S. Supreme Court held that Greenwood had no reasonable expectation of privacy because it is common knowledge that garbage at the side of the street is readily accessible to animals, children, scavengers, snoops, and other public members. Moreover, Greenwood voluntarily placed his refuse at the curb to convey it to a third party, the trash collector, who might have sorted through it or permitted others, such as the police, to do so. The property had been abandoned, and accordingly, the seizure of the trash was not a search for Fourth Amendment purposes.

"Surreptitious DNA sampling" has become frequent among law enforcement tactics. DNA has been retrieved from items in a trash bag, cigarette butts, an expectorant on a sidewalk, an envelope licked shut, and a milk carton. The courts have ruled that these items were abandoned and, therefore, constitutionally seized and searched even if police used a ruse.

BOX 10.2 *RAYNOR V. STATE* (2011) – I

Glenn Raynor was convicted of multiple crimes, including a prior sexual offense, and was implicated in a rape, by a victim. The police did not have probable cause to arrest Raynor, but when invited by the police, Raynor agreed to come to the police station for an interview. Raynor appeared at the police station wearing a short-sleeved shirt for an interview. He sat in a chair for the interview, "rubbing his arms up and down the armrests of the chair." Officers requested a sample of his DNA, but he refused. After Raynor left the station, police swabbed the armrests and obtained a DNA sample. The DNA, obtained without his knowledge, was then used to convict him of the rape.

Raynor appealed his conviction to Maryland's intermediate court of appeals, arguing that the seizure of the DNA from the armrests was an unconstitutional search and seizure. The appellate court agreed with the trial court that the defendant had no reasonable expectation of privacy in the DNA he left behind on the chair. By the time Raynor's appeal reached Maryland's highest court in 2014, his counsel no longer disputed that the DNA from the armrests was lawfully obtained. (See Box 10.19.)

Medicolegal death investigation: medicolegal death investigators are in a different situation than police crime scene investigators at death scenes because their investigation is not necessarily for criminal prosecution. An example of a state death scene protocol reads:

> ...staff, having been requested and approved to respond to a death scene shall, on arrival, document and/or collect all items of evidence or property, including the body itself, within the scene and on the person of the decedent, which is deemed necessary in the determination of the cause and manner of death and/or to assist in the identification of the decedent. The scene and the evidence therein that is not deemed necessary in the determination of cause and manner of death and/or to assist in the identification is the responsibility of the local investigative authorities.

It may be that seizures by medicolegal authorities independent of law enforcement will not need warrants. Although there is little caselaw on this point, courts will likely find this practice constitutionally permissible because it was taken as property, not as evidence for use in criminal prosecution. This situation may be different in the case of known homicides.

BOX 10.3 *PEOPLE V. ROEHLER* (1985) – CORONER SEIZURE REQUIRES WARRANT

After performing autopsies of two boys, the Ventura County Coroner determined that they had accidentally drowned and released the bodies to an L.A. funeral home. The boys' deaths had occurred in the waters off Santa Barbara. The Santa Barbara Sheriff-Coroner received a call casting suspicion on their deaths. The Sheriff-Coroner obtained a search warrant, retrieved the bodies from the funeral home, and performed second autopsies revealing deaths by blunt force injury. The defendant, Roehler, was charged with the murders. As one line of defense, he alleged that the taking and autopsying of the bodies were illegal seizures and searches violating his Fourth Amendment rights and the evidence from such should be excluded.

The Appellate court declared a warrant for search in another county could be issued for a crime within its jurisdiction but agreed with the trial court that the warrant was constitutionally invalid because the informant's information was not corroborated and thus did not provide probable cause. The court also pointed out that, despite the no-property rule, the next-of-kin had a reasonable expectation of privacy interest in the dead bodies not to be violated by government intrusion.

The court ruled that the coroner's search and seizure was primarily an administrative search and seizure but was nonetheless state action subject to Fourth Amendment protection. The search and seizure may or may not lead to a criminal investigation – "not unlike the action of a police officer who temporarily detains a citizen on the street." The governmental intrusion required a warrant based upon probable cause but "a less rigorous administrative 'probable cause' standard" and cited *Camara v. Municipal Court*, *See v. Seattle*, and *Marshall v. Barlow's, Inc.* The defective warrant was sufficient to meet an administrative warrant's lesser probable cause requirement. This "probable cause" should be tailored to the government's interest, and the court found the "action was a reasonable exercise of governmental power under the United States Constitution; authorized by statute 'pursuant to an administrative plan containing specific neutral criteria,'" referring to the coroner statutes.

Non-evidentiary items are property to be returned to the next-of-kin or "friends" of the decedent if no next-of-kin exists. Evidence relevant to the medicolegal death investigation will be turned over to law enforcement or retained for examination, analysis, or use in court.

- *BODIES* – in homicide cases, bodies are considered evidence under the jurisdiction of the medicolegal death investigation authority. Dead bodies are not considered property – following the so-called "no-property rule" inherited from England (*Jones v. Ashburnham*, 1804). Bodies should be treated with dignity and respect as deceased human beings; nobody can be owned in life or in death. Thus, despite common understandings, the next-of-kin do not technically own the body of their loved one but have a sepulchral right (a custodial interest) to the custody and disposition of the body. Instead, most courts in the United States have found that bodies are *quasi-property* (*Crocker v. Pleasant*, 2001; *Wilson v. Wilson*, 2014). The quasi-property status allows for tortious actions, such as desecration or mutilation of a corpse (*State v. Highland*, 1912). When removed during surgery, the legal status of body parts is likely not property that can be owned (*Moore v. Board of Regents*, 1990). In *Brotherton v. Cleveland* (1991), a federal court found in favor of the plaintiff for corneal donations permitted by the coroner's office when the office staff did not ask permission from the next-of-kin but instead relied on the statutory implied consent. Organ and tissue donations generally require next-of-kin consent. Conversely, medicolegal autopsies are authorized by statute for public health and safety purposes and do not require next-of-kin consent. Accordingly, medical examiners and coroners have been allowed to retain brains, other whole organs, and tissues from autopsies without next-of-kin consent for criminal investigative purposes (*Albrecht v. Treon*, 2010; *Waeschle v. Dragovic*, 2009; *Shipley v. NYC*, 2015).

- *CLOTHES* – clothing is generally considered personal property and should be returned to families, even though it may no longer be usable. Of course, clothing may be seized as evidence in a criminal investigation where there is some reason to suspect it may have evidential value.
- *MEDICATIONS* – many medical examiners and coroner offices will merely photograph the prescription drug vials found in the home. Others will confiscate them for inventory to assist in the determination of cause and manner of death. The medications will be destroyed and not returned because they were prescribed only for the deceased patient. When a prosecutor prosecutes a drug dealer for distributing drugs that led to the death of his client, then the drugs may become evidence and will likely be admissible because they were initially seized for non-criminal purposes.

Searches of Persons

Searches of people are different from searches of places because people have rights in ways that property does not:

- Fourth Amendment – Right Against Unreasonable Searches and Seizures, including Right to Privacy
- Fifth Amendment – Right Against Self-Incrimination and due process
- Fourteenth Amendment – Due Process, including Right to Counsel.

Forensic evidence collection from the person may occur during detention without probable cause, incident to arrest (seizure of the person), or during booking (after arrest, responding to a summons, or voluntarily turning oneself in).

Generally, unless police have probable cause to believe a person is involved in criminal activity, they need permission to search the person or the person's property. The U.S. Supreme Court, in a plurality decision, ruled in *Florida v. Royer* (1983) that police may target and approach a person based on their behavior and can temporarily detain the person while they attempt to verify or dispel their suspicion of illegal activity. Still, they cannot detain the person longer than necessary or search their belongings without consent or a warrant.

In *Terry v. Ohio* (1968), the Court ruled that an officer may perform a pat down for a weapon if the officer has a reasonable suspicion that the person is armed and dangerous, but a frisk is not a search. In *Rodriguez v. U.S.* (2015), the Court held that the detention may not be longer than needed to handle the matter for which the stop was made; there was a traffic stop, and issuance of a ticket did not justify a further delay for a dog sniff search.

Individuals can refuse random police searches unless they are in custody, on probation, are wards of the state, immigrants, or at a border crossing or security checkpoint. Individuals must assert their right to refuse clearly and unequivocally. The U.S. Supreme Court ruled in *Florida v. Bostick* (1991) that if the police do not force a person to do something, the individual acts voluntarily, even if a reasonable person would feel intimidated and unable to say "no." Thus, if a person does what a police officer tells them to do before arrest, they have *voluntarily* complied with the *request*. If the police search the person who refuses anyway, then the refusal preserves the right to challenge the search later in court. Most courts have held that the refusal cannot be admitted as evidence of guilt nor as support for probable cause or reasonable suspicion, *Griffin v. California* (1965).

If a person is arrested and booked into jail, the jail staff will routinely examine and inventory the arrestee's personal property. If evidence is found on the property, it will be given to investigators. In *U.S. v. Edwards* (1974), the U.S. Supreme Court found that a warrant was not needed to search the clothing of a jailed subject locked in the property room.

Courts have held that there is no seizure of the person under a subpoena or summons; the judicial command to appear differs from seizures under arrest. Since there is no seizure of the person, a subpoena or summons does not carry the same stigma as an arrest. Moreover, there is no exigency involved, and therefore, a response to a subpoena or summons can be executed at a time of convenience. Furthermore, a court controls and supervises responses to subpoenas and summonses.

The Fourth Amendment also controls searches and seizures of the body. In general, taking specimens from the body requires probable cause and either (1) a search warrant or court order or (2) exigent circumstances (*Schmerber v. California,* 1962). Invasive bodily searches are generally not allowed (*Winston v. Lee*, 1985), e.g., bullets, blood, and urine collection, but non-invasive searches and capture of physical characteristics, such as images, fingerprints, voice exemplars, and handwriting exemplars are generally allowed (*U.S. v. Dionisio*, 1973; *U.S. v. Mara*, 1973). The Court in *Woolverton v. Multicounty Grand Jury* (1993) held probable cause was required for blood samples involving intrusions beneath the skin, but only reasonable individualized suspicion was needed for fingerprints.

BOX 10.4 *UNITED STATES V. EDWARDS* (1974) – PROPERTY IN POLICE CUSTODY

Edwards was lawfully arrested late at night for attempting to break into a Post Office through a wooden window. The next morning, he was given new clothes, and the clothes he had been wearing were seized and searched with probable cause for believing that his clothes might reveal incriminating paint chips. Paint chips subsequently found on the defendant's clothing matched paint chips from the windowsill. The Court held that the search and seizure did not violate the defendant's Fourth Amendment rights:

> [O]nce the accused is lawfully arrested and is in custody, the effects in his possession [his property] at the place of detention that were subject to search at the time and place of his arrest may lawfully be searched and seized without a warrant even though a substantial period of time has elapsed between the arrest and subsequent administrative processing, on the one hand, and the taking of the property for use as evidence, on the other. This is true where the clothes or effects are immediately seized upon arrival at the jail, held under the defendant's name in the 'property room' of the jail, and at a later time searched and taken for use at the subsequent criminal trial. The result is the same where the property is not physically taken from the defendant until sometime after his incarceration.

Nontestimonial Physical Characteristics: in the 1962 landmark decision in *Schmerber v. California* [see below under Alcohol Testing], the U.S. Supreme Court found taking blood for alcohol testing to be a reasonable search under the circumstances permissible under the Fourth Amendment. The Court also found that it did not violate the Fifth Amendment right against self-incrimination because the blood alcohol level was a physical characteristic and nontestimonial:

> It is clear that the protection of the privilege [against self-incrimination] reaches an accused's communications, whatever form they might take… On the other hand, both federal and state courts have held that it offers no protection against compulsion to submit to fingerprinting, photographing, or measurements, to write or speak for identification, to appear in court, to stand, or to make a particular gesture. The distinction which has emerged, often expressed in different ways, is that the privilege is a bar against compelling

'communications' or 'testimony,' but that compulsion which makes a suspect or accused the source of 'real or physical evidence' does not violate it.

Since *Schmerber*, the U.S. Supreme Court has repeatedly held that physical characteristics are not testimonial and can be compelled. The Supreme Court has held that handwriting (*U.S. v. Mara*, 1973) and voice exemplars (*U.S. v. Dionisio*, 1973) are physical characteristics that can be compelled over a defendant's objection. Both handwriting and voice are exposed to the public; thus, the person has no reasonable expectation of privacy in them, and obtaining exemplars are not searches within the Fourth Amendment protections. They are also not protected under the Fifth Amendment freedom from self-incrimination because they are non-testimonial and non-communicative in nature, and may be obtained by consent, grand jury subpoena, or court order.

Fingerprints are no different. In *Davis v. Mississippi* (1969), discussed below, the Court held that "Fingerprinting involves none of the probing into an individual's private life and thoughts that marks an interrogation or search." It held that taking fingerprints did not violate the Fourth Amendment when the seizure of the person is constitutional. At least two federal appellate decisions, *U.S. v. Hook* (2006) and *Williams v. Schario* (1996) concluded that the Fifth Amendment does not protect fingerprints, and dicta in *Doe v. U.S.* (1988) declared that fingerprints fall in the same category as blood, voice, and handwriting samples. In *Pennsylvania v. Muniz* (1990), a drunk driving case, the Court held that the videotaped slurred speech and failure of the horizontal nystagmus gaze test, "walk-and-turn" test, and "one-leg stand" test were nontestimonial physical characteristics, but Muniz's inability to state the date of his sixth birthday was testimonial and should have been excluded.

BOX 10.5 *UNITED STATES V. DIONISIO* (1973) – COMPULSION OF VOICE EXEMPLARS

A grand jury issued subpoenas that summoned 20 witnesses to give voice exemplars for comparison to intercepted voice recordings during a gambling investigation. Dionisio objected, and the trial court ordered him to comply. The Supreme Court held that the court order did not violate either the Fourth or Fifth Amendments. The compulsion to give a voice exemplar is not a search or seizure of the person. Voice is a physical characteristic that a person knowingly exposes to the public. The compulsion to exhibit physical characteristics is not protected. Neither is the voice exemplar testimonial nor communicative in nature; thus, it does not violate the right against self-incrimination.

BOX 10.6 *UNITED STATES V. MARA* (1973) – COMPULSION OF HANDWRITING EXEMPLARS

A grand jury issued a subpoena for the defendant to furnish a handwriting exemplar. The Court held, as it did in *Dionisio,* that a grand jury subpoena is not a seizure within the meaning of the Fourth Amendment, nor is its production a testimonial violation of the Fifth Amendment. The government was not obligated to make a preliminary showing of “reasonableness.” Handwriting is a physical characteristic that is constantly exposed to the public. There is no more expectation of privacy in a person’s script than in the tone of his voice.

The Court held in *Davis v. Mississippi* (1969) that the round-up and detention of a group of Black youths without warrants for the sole purpose of obtaining fingerprints to see whose fingerprint matched the latent prints from the rape victim’s house was an unconstitutional detention. The detentions were not based upon probable cause or individualized suspicion. The subsequent trial for rape was based on the fingerprint match from one of those individuals. The Court reversed the conviction because such fingerprint evidence derived from an unlawful detention was inadmissible. However, the Court noted that the collection of fingerprints during detentions did not necessarily violate the Fourth Amendment. As a result of this dictum, statutes were promulgated to provide for detention on less than probable cause for identification procedures using physical characteristics. In *Hayes v. Florida* (1985), the Court noted:

> We also do not abandon the suggestion … that, under circumscribed procedures, the Fourth Amendment might permit the judiciary to authorize the seizure of a person on less than probable cause and his removal to the police station for the purpose of fingerprinting.

Nonetheless, state courts are divided on whether, by a judicially authorized seizure, a person can be detained and fingerprinted based on reasonable suspicion only.

BOX 10.7 *DAVIS V. MISSISSIPPI* (1969) – FINGERPRINTING DURING DETENTION

The victim of a rape could not provide any description of her attacker other than his race and approximate age. The police conducted a dragnet operation, and several Black youths were taken to the police station without warrants or probable cause to arrest for questioning and fingerprinting. It was thought that one of them might have fingerprints that would match those found on the windows of the rape victim's home. Fingerprints obtained from Davis during his detention did match the prints from the scene. At trial, Davis objected to the admission of the fingerprint evidence as the product of unlawful detention, but he was convicted anyway. On appeal, the U.S. Supreme Court agreed with Davis and held that the detention violated his Fourth Amendment rights and that the fingerprint evidence was inadmissible. However, in dicta, the Court declared:

> It is arguable, however, that, because of the unique nature of the fingerprinting process, such detentions might, under narrowly defined circumstances, be found to comply with the Fourth Amendment even though there is no probable cause in the traditional sense. . . Detention for fingerprinting may constitute a much less serious intrusion upon personal security than other types of police searches and detentions. Fingerprinting involves none of the probing into an individual's private life and thoughts that marks an interrogation or search... [F]ingerprinting is an inherently more reliable and effective crime solving tool... Finally, because there is no danger of destruction fingerprints, the limited detention need not come unexpectedly or an (sic) an inconvenient time. For this same reason, the general requirement that the authorization of a judicial officer be obtained in advance of detention would seem not to admit of any exception in the fingerprinting context.

The U.S. Supreme Court has held that a person has no right to counsel when evidence is obtained for scientific analysis during the investigative phase before initiating adversary criminal judicial proceedings. Defense counsel has no function other than the futile advice not to give the sample. Later, the adversary process affords an adequate opportunity to challenge scientific evidence (*U.S. v. Wade*, 1967; *Lewis v. U.S.*, 1967). However, state law may guarantee a right to consult counsel in some jurisdictions (e.g., *Whisenhunt v. Alaska*, AK, 1987; *Friedman v. Commissioner of Public Safety*, MN, 1991; *Vermont v. Garvey*, VT, 1991). Furthermore, in *U.S. v. Patane* (2004), the Court held that physical evidence obtained from un-Mirandized voluntary statements made by a suspect, unlike the statements themselves, is later admissible in court.

Invasive Searches: bodily intrusions pit the individual's interests in privacy and security against society's interests in conducting the procedure to obtain the evidence.

In the 1952 decision in *Rochin v. California*, the U.S. Supreme Court found that the forced insertion of a tube to collect evidence in the stomach contents over the objection of the person was such egregious police behavior that it *shocked the conscience* of the Court and violated *decencies of civilized conduct* and notions of *fundamental fairness*. The Court held that the conduct was prohibited by the Fourteenth Amendment's due process of law applicable to the states as a matter of fundamental fairness. The

Court reversed the conviction and declared, "a conviction which rests upon evidence of incriminating objects obtained from the body of the accused by physical abuse is as invalid as a conviction which rests upon a verbal confession extracted from him by such abuse."

This case was decided before the Fourth Amendment exclusionary rule (*Mapp v. Ohio*, 1961) or the Fifth Amendment right against self-incrimination (*Malloy v. Hogan*, 1964) were applied to the states. After *Rochin*, courts in considering invasive bodily searches have not looked to whether the behavior was fundamentally unfair and shocked the conscience of the Court, but rather whether the searches were unreasonable under the Fourth and Fifth Amendments.

In *Winston v. Lee* (1985), police obtained a court order to remove a bullet from a robber. The Court held that such a surgical intrusion violates a person's right to be secure in his person, and the search would be unreasonable under the Fourth Amendment, even if likely to produce evidence of a crime. Some courts have distinguished major surgeries where life is endangered, and the bodily intrusions are unreasonable searches, from minor surgeries that may be permissible where the bullet is lodged just beneath the skin and life is not endangered. However, if the bullet has been embedded in the tissue for a prolonged time, such that the surface of the bullet has likely been corroded and not useful for comparison, then even minor surgery may be found to be impermissible.

Courts have considered various other bodily searches, but they attempt to balance exigency, need for the evidence, and intrusiveness in finding the search permissible, impermissible, or requiring a warrant. In general, intrusions beneath the skin's surface will be impermissible searches.

BOX 10.8 *ROCHIN V. CALIFORNIA* (1952) – FORCIBLE COLLECTION OF STOMACH CONTENTS

Based on some information that Rochin was selling narcotics, three deputy sheriffs entered his home through an open door and forced their way into the bedroom where he and his wife were in bed. When asked about two pill capsules on the nightstand, Rochin grabbed them and put them into his mouth. The officers jumped on him and struggled to extract the capsules. They took him to the hospital, where a tube was forcibly put down his throat to pump his stomach. An emetic was administered through the tube, causing him to vomit up the two capsules, which were tested and found to contain morphine. In a unanimous opinion by Justice Felix Frankfurter, the Court struck down the prior conviction, arguing that the means used to extract the evidence from Rochin "shocks the conscience" and violates the due process of law as guaranteed to all persons by the Fourteenth Amendment. Justices Douglas and Black argued that it also violated his Fifth Amendment right against self-incrimination.

BOX 10.9 *WINSTON V. LEE* (1985) – FORCIBLE SURGICAL REMOVAL OF BULLET

In a gunfight during an attempted robbery, both the shopkeeper and Rudolph Lee, the robber, were shot. Although Lee was able to run away from the store, police found him suffering from a chest wound a few blocks away, and he was taken to a hospital. The shopkeeper identified his assailant in the hospital. After that, the police obtained a court order for the surgical removal of the bullet. The Court held that compelled surgical intrusions implicate expectations of privacy and security of such magnitude to be "unreasonable" under the Fourth Amendment, even if likely to produce evidence of a crime.

> The reasonableness of surgical intrusions beneath the skin depends on a case-by-case approach, in which the individual's interests in privacy and security are weighed against society's interests in conducting the procedure. In a given case, the question of whether the community's need for evidence outweighs the substantial privacy interests at stake is a delicate one admitting of few categorical answers.

BOX 10.10 *UNITED STATES V. FOWLKES* (2014) – FORCIBLE RECTAL SEARCH

A wiretap implicated Mark Tyrell Fowlkes in drug dealing, and he was subsequently observed making drug deals. He was driving when police officers pulled over him and a passenger on the pretext of an expired registration. They were asked to get out of the car, and over Fowlkes' objection, the officers searched the vehicle. The officers saw marijuana in the side panel of the car and what they believed to be crack cocaine on the front seat. Fowlkes was transported to jail, where Sgt. Gibbs conducted a strip search witnessed by five officers. During the search, Fowlkes made some hand movements near his anus, which caused some of the officers to suspect he had something inside his rectum. After Fowlkes was handcuffed and tased, the officers observed an apparent plastic bag within Fowlkes's rectum. Wearing plastic gloves, Gibbs removed a plastic bag containing drugs from Fowlkes's rectum. Fowlkes was convicted of drug possession and drug distribution. The Ninth Circuit held that the seizure violated Fowlkes's Fourth Amendment rights and that the evidence should be suppressed. The forcible removal of drugs from an arrestee's body cavity, with attendant emotional and physical trauma, requires a warrant because he was under arrest and no exigent circumstances were present. Furthermore, Gibbs violated the jail's policy because he lacked the appropriate medical training to conduct a body search and failed to use sanitary conditions.

BOX 10.11 *CUPP V. MURPHY* (1973): FORCIBLE SEIZURE OF FINGERNAIL SCRAPINGS

Doris Murphy was strangled in her home. There were abrasions and lacerations on her throat. There was no sign of a break-in or robbery. Her ex-husband, Daniel Murphy, then living with his new wife, called the police to report the death. He voluntarily presented himself to the police for questioning. When a dark spot, possibly blood, was thought to be seen on his finger, the police asked to take scrapings of his fingernails, but he refused. Murphy began rubbing his hands and possibly used a key to scrape under his fingernails. Although he was not under arrest, fingernail scrapings were forcibly taken against his will without a warrant, which revealed skin, blood, and fabric from the victim. He was convicted of murder. The U.S. Supreme Court held that it is permissible for police to conduct a limited search of a defendant, albeit a brief but severe intrusion, when they believe the defendant is likely to destroy highly evanescent evidence.

Alcohol Testing of Drivers – although industrial production of automobiles began at the turn of the 20th century, Henry Ford began mass production in 1913. Already, the annual death toll from motor vehicle accidents in the United States was a few thousand fatalities per year. Drunk driving became a concern soon after that. The first roadside alcohol test was developed in 1938, and the first breathalyzer in 1954, but laboratory-based blood alcohol testing was still considered more reliable.

The first U.S. Supreme Court case was *Breithaupt v. Abram* in 1957 when the motor vehicle fatality rate had soared to nearly 40,000, many of which were alcohol-related. The court's decision came before the 1961 decision in *Mapp v. Ohio*, which found the blood draw to be permissible under state law despite its unreasonableness as a search for federal purposes.

The following case, *Schmerber v. California* in 1962 (after *Mapp v. Ohio*, 1961), found that blood drawn at the order of local officers without a warrant was a permissible search. The blood collection was a search and a seizure but did not violate the Fourth Amendment right against unreasonable searches and seizure because the warrantless search was exigent due to the natural destruction of the evidence through metabolism as well as due to other pressing needs of the case. The Court balanced the intrusiveness of the search with the needs of the criminal justice system. Nor did the blood collection violate the Fifth Amendment right against self-incrimination. The blood level was merely a physical characteristic and thus non-testimonial. Justice Brennan emphasized that the Court ruling was limited "only to the facts of the present record."

Because *Schmerber* was thought to have foreclosed the use of warrantless blood tests in most circumstances, some scholars argue that the Court's ruling was responsible for the proliferation of breathalyzers to test for alcohol and urine analysis to test for controlled substances in criminal investigations.

By the time the Court again addressed the topic, a half-century later, alcohol-testing technologies had vastly improved, particularly concerning breath testing. It was more accurate, reliable, easier to use, and had long been used. In addition, the rate of alcohol-related motor vehicle fatalities had fallen and did not seem as pressing. The decline in fatalities was multifactorial, including not only widespread driver alcohol testing but also seatbelt laws, more crashworthy vehicles, and the implementation of traffic cameras. In *Missouri v. McNeely* (2013), the Court held that metabolism alone did not constitute a *per se* exigency and distinguished *Schmerber* where metabolism was "combined with other pressing needs." In *Birchfield v. North Dakota* (2016), the Court held that blood and urine specimen collections are unreasonably intrusive, but breath testing was not. Most recently, in *Mitchell v. Wisconsin* (2019), the Court held that blood drawn without a warrant was permissible in cases where the person is hospitalized and unconscious. The Court seems to have attempted to guide officers using a practical compromise for when a warrant is and is not required.

Although these cases have dealt with alcohol, presumably, they provide some guidance for other licit and illicit drug use as well as principles that affect forensic evidence collection more broadly.

BOX 10.12 *BREITHAUPT V. ABRAM* (1957) – BLOOD ALCOHOL TESTING

Breithaupt, while driving his pickup truck, was involved in a collision that resulted in three deaths and serious injuries to himself. While Breithaupt was unconscious in the emergency room, a patrol officer requested that blood be taken for alcohol testing. He was subsequently convicted of involuntary manslaughter. The U.S. Supreme Court held that Breithaupt was not deprived of due process of law in violation of the Fourteenth Amendment because even if an unreasonable search under the Fourth Amendment, which had yet to be incorporated under the Fourteenth Amendment, New Mexico had rejected the exclusionary rule so that the violation would not aid him since it was a lawful state prosecution for a state crime. Taking a blood test by a skilled technician is not "conduct that shocks the conscience," nor is it such a method of obtaining evidence as offends a "sense of justice." The value of its deterrent effect far outweighs the bodily intrusion. Nor was taking the blood sample a coerced confession prohibited by the Fifth Amendment.

BOX 10.13 *SCHMERBER V. CALIFORNIA* (1962) – BLOOD ALCOHOL TESTING

Anoncenda Schmerber was involved in a motor vehicle accident. A police officer smelled liquor on his breath, and he was arrested for drunk driving and then taken to the emergency room for treatment of his injuries. The police officer directed that a blood sample be taken for alcohol testing. Over Schmerber's objection, the blood was taken. Testing revealed a high level of alcohol, and he was subsequently convicted. The U.S. Supreme Court found that the taking of the blood sample was a bodily intrusion, a search, and a seizure under the Fourth Amendment, but it was not an unreasonable seizure due to the exigent circumstances exception applied "on the facts of the present record." The officer "might reasonably have believed that he was confronted with an emergency, in which the delay necessary to obtain a warrant, under the circumstances, threatened the destruction of evidence." The Court also held that taking the blood sample did not violate his Fifth Amendment right against self-incrimination because the right applied only to testimonial evidence, not physical evidence.

BOX 10.14 *MISSOURI V. MCNEELY* (2013) – BLOOD ALCOHOL TESTING

Tyler McNeely was stopped for speeding and weaving, and he showed signs of intoxication. McNeely failed the field sobriety tests. After refusing to blow into a handheld breathalyzer, the officer drove McNeely to a medical center. McNeely refused a blood draw, even after being told his license would be revoked for one year for his refusal. The officer told the lab technician to draw a blood specimen anyway. A blood alcohol concentration of 0.154% resulted in his being charged with driving while intoxicated. The trial court suppressed the evidence, and the government appealed. The U.S. Supreme Court granted certiorari to resolve conflicting decisions on whether alcohol metabolism constitutes a *per se* exigency to justify an exception to the warrant requirement. In a divided decision, the U.S. Supreme Court ruled that the blood test in this case without a warrant was not a permissible search, that there is no categorical rule for exigency, and that exigency must be judged on a case-by-case basis using a totality of the circumstances analysis. This case was thought not to be a "now or never" situation. The Court held the mere fact of a drunk driving arrest and attendant natural metabolism of blood alcohol does not establish a *per se* exigency that would justify a blood draw over the subject's refusal without a warrant. The Court also noted the possibility of obtaining an expedited warrant. A warrantless blood draw would require exigency plus special facts and, according to a concurrence, would require a case-by-case analysis that provides no clear and practical guidance for law enforcement.

BOX 10.15 *BIRCHFIELD V. NORTH DAKOTA* (2016) – BREATH AND BLOOD ALCOHOL TESTS

This case is a consolidation of three cases involving refusal for breath alcohol testing, the refusal for blood alcohol testing, and an implied consent blood draw. The Court tried to resolve the uncertainty created under *McNeely* by addressing how the Fourth Amendment applies to both blood draws and breath tests, considering the implied consent statutes that states had enacted. The Court compared the invasiveness of blood draws to the non-invasiveness of breath tests. Justice Alito held that the search incident to an arrest doctrine permits law enforcement to conduct warrantless breath tests, but not blood tests, on suspected drunk drivers as a search incident to an arrest. Thus, a breath test can always be performed over a suspect's refusal, but a blood test requires special circumstances. The Court also held that "implied-consent laws that impose civil penalties and evidentiary consequences on motorists who refuse to comply" are permitted, but "motorists cannot be deemed to have consented to submit to a blood test on pain of committing a criminal offense."

BOX 10.16 *MITCHELL V. WISCONSIN* (2019) – BLOOD ALCOHOL TESTING

Gerald Mitchell was reported driving drunk, and he was soon found totally inebriated, wandering around a lake on foot near his car. A police officer arrested Mitchell for operating a vehicle while intoxicated. Mitchell was so inebriated that a breath test was not possible, nor was he able to give his consent for a blood test. Mitchell was taken to the hospital, where he passed out. Based on a Wisconsin implied-consent law, the officer directed the hospital staff to conduct a blood test. At trial, Mitchell moved to suppress the blood test, arguing it was taken without a warrant, but the prosecution responded that under the state implied-consent law, Mitchell gave his permission for the blood test by operating his vehicle on a state road. In addition to consent, the state also argued that a search incident to arrest and general reasonableness were applicable warrant exceptions. He was convicted, and the case was appealed to the U.S. Supreme Court. The Court, in a 5–4 decision without a single rationale, Judge Alito held that when a driver is unconscious and cannot be given a breath test, the exigent-circumstances doctrine almost always allows the police to order a warrantless blood test to measure the driver's blood alcohol concentration without offending the Fourth Amendment. Writing for the plurality, Justice Alito declared that exigency exists when (1) alcohol is metabolizing in the blood and (2) some other factor threatens a safety or law enforcement need that would take priority over a warrant application. Both conditions are met when a drunk-driving suspect is unconscious; permitting a warrantless blood draw is lawful in such a case. When the driver is unconscious, the police are likely to be saving other lives at the crash scene, rushing the driver to the hospital, and not having time to get a search warrant. The Court wrote, "In the emergency scenarios created by unconscious drivers, forcing police to put off other tasks for even a relatively short period of time may have terrible collateral costs." Further, an unconscious person was likely to have his blood drawn by the hospital personnel anyway as part of the driver's medical care. Justice Alito wrote:

> When police have probable cause to believe a person has committed a drunk-driving offense and the driver's unconsciousness or stupor requires him to be taken to the hospital or similar facility before police have a reasonable opportunity to administer a standard evidentiary breath test, they may almost always order a warrantless blood test to measure the driver's BAC without offending the Fourth Amendment. We do not rule out the possibility that, in an unusual case, a defendant would be able to show that his blood would not have been drawn if police had not been seeking BAC information and that police could not have reasonably judged that a warrant application would interfere with other pressing needs or duties.

This narrow holding applies only to cases where (1) the driver has been taken to a hospital, (2) the field breath test is unreliable, and (3) the police need more time to get a warrant. The Court did not strike down or uphold the state implied consent law.

BOX 10.17 MILESTONES IN THE HISTORY OF DRUNK DRIVING

1906	New Jersey passes first driving while intoxicatedlaw
1908	Henry Ford mass produced the Model T automobile
1910	New York made drunk driving unlawful
1920–1933	Prohibition era
1927	Emil Bogen described breath analysis for medicolegal purposes, documented 2,100 breath to 1 blood alcohol concentration
1936	Rolla Harger "Drunkometer" (wet chemistry)
1938	American Medical Association and National Safety Council recommends 0.15% blood alcohol concentration limit
1941	"Intoximeter," "Alcometer" (wet chemistry)
1954	Robert Borkenstein portable "Breathalyzer"
1957	*Breithaupt v. Abram*

1960s	Gas chromatogratphy becomes common lab instrument
1962	*Schmerber v. California*
1967	William Duce and Tom Parry Jones electronic breathalyzer
1970s–1990s	Enhancement of laws and penalties for drunk driving
1972	States begin to pass *per se* driving under the influence laws
1980	Candy Lightner founded Mothers Against Drunk Driving
1985	*Missouri v. McNeely*
Late 1980s/ early 1990s	Fifth- and sixth-generation instrumentation
1998	Pres Clinton recommends 0.08% blood alcohol concentration limit
2000	Pres Clinton requires states to lower blood alcohol concentration to 0.08%
2016	*Birchfield v. North Dakota*
2019	*Mitchell v. Wisconsin*

BOX 10.18 *SKINNER V. RAILWAY LABOR EXECUTIVES' ASSN* (1989); *NATIONAL TREASURY EMPLOYEES UNION V. VON RAAB (1989)* – DRUG TESTING IN THE WORKPLACE

In these companion cases, two federal employees' unions challenged mandatory workplace drug testing programs. *Skinner* involved federal regulations requiring the testing of railroad employees involved in major accidents and safety rules. *Von Raab* was involved in an employee drug-testing program for federal gun-toting customs officials involved in drug interdiction. In *Skinner*, the Court held that collecting biological samples, including blood, urine, and breath, is a search of the person subject to Fourth Amendment protections. The Court held in both cases that the suspicionless testing programs were permissible despite the absence of a warrant or probable cause because the programs were reasonable and furthered a substantial government interest. The Court recognized that such workers might imperil public safety if they were using illegal drugs.

- *WORKPLACE ALCOHOL AND DRUG TESTING* – although blood and supervised urine collection are intrusive bodily searches that would not generally be permissible for criminal prosecution purposes, they may be conducted in dangerous workplace settings where the blood draw is conducted for public safety purposes (*Skinner v. Railway Labor Executives' Assoc.*, 1989; *National Treasury Employees Union v. Von Raab*, 1989).

DNA Collection and Database Searching

The great power and promise of DNA testing for forensic purposes was recognized from the time it was initially developed in the 1990s. Accordingly, courts have been reluctant to exclude it. In *State v. Olivas* (1993), the Washington Supreme Court held that taking a DNA specimen was permissible under the sex offender law. The court held that the general privacy right of persons to be free from unjustified governmental intrusion should be balanced against the special needs beyond normal government law enforcement. In *Jones v. Murray* (1992), the Fourth Circuit held that taking a DNA specimen from a convicted offender to establish a DNA data bank for future use in prosecutions of recidivists was permissible due to a diminished right of privacy. In *U.S. v. Davis* (2012), the Fourth Circuit declared that police violated the Fourth Amendment by extracting DNA from lawfully seized clothing of a victim of a previous crime and retaining the resulting DNA profile in a database for use in other criminal investigations. However, the court admitted the evidence anyway because the police had acted in good faith. Courts have generally found the creation of forensic DNA profiles more analogous to fingerprinting (*Rise v. Oregon*, 1995; *Nicholas v. Goord*, 2005; *U.S. v. Amerson*, 2007). Indeed, as noted above, the U.S. Supreme Court in *Davis v. Mississippi* (1963) found that the collection of fingerprints did not constitute a search. It can be argued that since traces of DNA material remain on touched objects, like fingerprints, they are publicly exposed and abandoned.

The primary argument that DNA evidence is different from fingerprint evidence and deserves greater privacy protections is that DNA, unlike fingerprints, contains a vast treasure trove of personal genetic information that is contained in DNA. Indeed, legislatures have passed statutes to protect this information (e.g., Genetic Information Nondiscrimination Act [GINA], Health Insurance Portability and Accountability Act [HIPAA], state laws). To date, crime labs generally test DNA for individually identifiable markers (IIMs) that are not informative of anything other than identity (the so-called *nonsense DNA* or *junk DNA*), except Amelogenin as a gender marker. The crime labs have little incentive to mine the DNA for clinically relevant medical information. However, there is increasing research and actual use of ancestry informative markers (AIMs) and phenotype informative markers (PIMs). The possibility of behavior-associated markers is of more concern.

The first DNA case decided by the U.S. Supreme Court was *Maryland v. King* (2013). The Court concluded that the collection of DNA specimens from arrestees constitutes a search but is permissible because probable cause exists for arrest, the legitimate governmental interests are more significant than the minimal intrusiveness of collection, arrestees have a reduced expectation of privacy, and it is an administrative booking procedure like taking fingerprints and photographs. Thus, the Court looked at DNA through utilitarian spectacles and saw another form of fingerprint.

BOX 10.19 *MARYLAND V. KING* (2013) – DNA COLLECTION AND DATABASE SEARCH DURING BOOKING

Alonzo Jay King, Jr. was arrested for assault in 2009. Under the Maryland DNA Collection Act, a buccal DNA swab was taken from King at the time of his arrest and entered Maryland's database. The statute authorized police to take buccal swabs during booking from persons arrested for serious offenses. The DNA profile matched to an unsolved rape case in 2003. The DNA match was presented to a grand jury that indicted him for rape. The detective then obtained a search warrant to acquire a second buccal DNA sample that was used in his conviction for rape. The Supreme Court decided that

> when officers make an arrest supported by probable cause to hold for a serious offense, and they bring the suspect to the station to be detained in custody, taking and analyzing a cheek swab of the arrestee's DNA is, like fingerprinting and photographing, a legitimate police booking procedure that is reasonable under the Fourth Amendment.

The Court balanced legitimate state interests against individuals' interests in their bodily integrity and informational privacy. The Court concluded that it is constitutionally reasonable for the state to undertake the "negligible" physical intrusion of swabbing the inside of the legitimately detained arrestee's cheeks and using limited DNA profiling data to determine whether the individual might be associated with a crime scene or victim. Probable cause for arrest must exist. Arrestees have diminished rights and expectations of privacy. Routine administrative procedures at booking include fingerprinting, photographing, obtaining identifying information, and a strip search. The Court seemed little concerned about the vast amount of genetic information in the DNA specimen and was more impressed with its utility. The Court noted the limited identity testing involved and that it functions to exculpate suspects more than inculpate them. Justice Alito called DNA the fingerprint of the 21st Century. In his dissent, Justice Scalia worried about suspicionless searches that are not limited in scope and compared the cheek swabbings to general warrants. He declared, "I doubt that the proud men who wrote the charter of our liberties would have been so eager to open their mouths for royal inspection."

BOX 10.20 *RAYNOR V. STATE* (2014) – II

Raynor's case reached Maryland's highest court in 2014 (see Box 10.2). Although his counsel no longer disputed that the DNA from the armrests was lawfully obtained, he did argue that the analysis of the 13 identifying "junk" DNA loci was a Fourth Amendment search, noting that DNA contains "a massive amount of deeply personal information." In a split decision, the court found the analysis of the DNA lawful. DNA identity testing was only a targeted analysis of identifying loci and thus not dissimilar from fingerprint comparisons; it did not infringe on any reasonable expectation of privacy and, therefore, did not violate the Fourth Amendment. The U.S. Supreme Court denied certiorari.

Note: Maryland was the first state to pass legislative guardrails on forensic investigative genetic genealogy (FIGG).

Summary

Evidence collection is constitutionally regulated and, if impermissibly collected, may be held inadmissible. Items from a crime scene or death scene should be collected pursuant to a search warrant if practicable, but warrantless searches are not uncommon where the collection is in a public place, has been consented to, or has been abandoned. Items collected might consist of evidence, contraband, the fruits of a crime, or abandoned or personal property that must be returned.

Searches of people have greater protections, but collections of physical characteristics, such as fingerprints, signatures, or voice exemplars, do not implicate either the Fourth or Fifth Amendments. Invasive searches will generally require a search warrant. Warrantless breath analysis can be taken from drivers suspected of impaired driving, but not blood samples unless someone is too impaired to give a breath sample. Suspicionless collections of blood and urine for drug and alcohol testing can be taken from government employees in structured workplace programs for safety reasons. Fingerprints, photographs, and DNA samples may be collected during booking. A DNA sample left on a cup or armrest left behind from a suspect interview may be collected because it was abandoned.

Terms

Evidence – alleged facts presented to the factfinder to be weighed and considered to arrive at a verdict.

Personal Property – an individual's belongings, excluding any real estate property, including tangible and intangible assets.

Probative – having evidentiary value; helpful in proving a point in court.

Cases

Albrecht v. Treon, 617 F.3d 890 (6th Cir. 2010)
Birchfield v. North Dakota, 579 U.S. 438 (2016)
Breithaupt v. Abram, 352 U.S. 432 (1957)
Brotherton v. Cleveland, 923 F.2d 477 (6th Cir. 1991)
California v. Greenwood, 486 U.S. 35 (1988)
Camara v. Municipal Court, 387 U.S. 523 (1967)
City of West Covina v. Perkins, 525 U.S. 234 (1999)
Crocker v. Pleasant, 778 So.2d 978 (Fla. 2001)
Cupp v. Murphy, 412 U.S. 291 (1973)
Davis v. Mississippi, 394 U.S. 721 (1969)
Doe v. United States, 487 U.S. 201 (1988)
Florida v. Bostick, 501 U.S. 429 (1991)
Florida v. Royer, 460 U.S.491 (1983)
Friedman v. Commissioner of Public Safety, 473 N.W.2d 828 (Minn. 1991)
Griffin v. California, 380 U.S. 609 (1965)
Hayes v. Florida, 470 U.S. 811 (1985)
Jones v. Ashburnham, 102 Eng.Rep. 905 (1804)
Jones v. Murray, 962 F.2d 302 (4th Cir. 1992)
Lewis v. United States, 382 F.2d 817 (D.C. 1967)
Malloy v. Hogan, 378 U.S. 1 (1964)
Mapp v. Ohio, 367 U.S. 643 (1961)
Marshall v. Barlow's, Inc., 436 U.S. 307 (1978)
Maryland v. King, 569 U.S. 435 (2013)
Mincey v. Arizona, 437 U.S. 385 (1978)
Missouri v. McNeely, 569 U.S. 141 (2013)
Mitchell v. Wisconsin, 588 U.S. 840 (2019)
Moore v. Board of Regents of the University of California, 793 P.2d 479 (Cal. 1990)
National Treasury Employees Union v. Von Raab, 489 U.S. 656 (1989)
Nicholas v. Goord, 430 F.3d 652 (2d Cir. 2005)
People v. Roehler, 167 Cal. App.3d 353 (1985)
Pennsylvania v. Muniz, 496 U.S. 582 (1990)
Raynor v. Maryland, 29 A.3d 617 (Md. App. 2011) [*Raynor-I*]
Raynor v. Maryland, 99 A.3d 753 (Md. 2014) [Raynor-II]
Rise v. Oregon, 59 F.3d 1556 (9th Cir. 1995)
Rochin v. California, 342 U.S. 165 (1952)
Rodriguez v. United States, 575 U.S. 348 (2015)
Schmerber v. California, 384 U.S. 757 (1966)
See v. City of Seattle, 387 U.S. 541 (1967)
Shipley v. City of New York, 37 N.E.3d 58 (N.Y.Ct.App. 2015)
Skinner v. Railway Labor Executives' Association, 489 U.S. 602 (1989)

State v. Highland, 76 S.E. 140 (W. Va. 1912)
State v. Olivas, 856 P.2d 1076 (Wash.Sup.Ct. 1993)
Terry v. Ohio, 392 U.S. 1 (1968)
Timbs v. Indiana, 586 U.S. 146, (2019)
United States v. Amerson, 483 F.3d 73 (2d Cir. 2007)
United States v. Davis, 690 F.3d 226 (4th Cir. 2012)
United States v. Dionisio, 410 U.S. 1 (1973)
United States v. Edwards, 415 U.S. 800 (1974)
United States v. Fowlkes, 804 F.3d 954 (9th Cir. 2015)
United States v. Hook, 471 F.3d 766 (7th Cir. 2006)
United States v. Mara, 410 U.S. 19 (1973)
United States v. Patane, 542 U.S. 630 (2004)
United States v. Wade, 388 U.S. 218 (1967)
Vermont v. Garvey, 595 A.2d 267 (Vt. 1967)
Waeschle v. Dragovic, 576 F.3d 539 (6th Cir. 2009)
Whisenhunt v. State, Dept. of Public Safety, 746 P.2d 1298 (Alaska 1987)
Williams v. Schario, 93 F.3d 527 (8th Cir. 1996)
Wilson v. Wilson, 138 So.3d 1176 (Fla. Dist. Ct. App. 2014)
Winston v. Lee, 470 U.S. 753 (1985)
Woolverton v. Multicounty Grand Jury, 859 P.2d 1112 (Okl. Crim. App. 1993)

Statutes

Civil Action for Deprivation of Rights, 42 U.S.C. §1983 (1979)
Genetic Information Nondiscrimination Act (GINA), Pub. L. No. 110–233 (2008)
Health Insurance Portability and Accountability Act (HIPAA), Pub. L. No. 104–191 (1996)
Judicial Authorization Required for Forensic Genetic Genealogical DNA Analysis and Search, Md. Criminal Procedure Code §17–102 (2023)
Tucker Act, 28 U.S.C. §§1346(a) and 1491 (1887)

Thought Questions

1. Why has the Supreme Court flip-flopped on the constitutionality of blood draws?
2. Why couldn't the police officer just pull out the plastic bag sticking out of Fowlke's rectum?
3. Should police be able to use the DNA from a cup used by the defendant in the interrogation room without consent?

Further Readings

Gardner TJ, *Anderson TM, Criminal Evidence: Principles and Cases*, 9th ed, Cengage Learning, Boston, MA, 2016.

Maveety N, *Glass and Gavel: The U.S. Supreme Court and Alcohol*, Rowman & Littlefield Publishers, Lanham, MD, 2018.

Mozayani A, *Parish-Fisher C, Forensic Evidence Management: From the Crime Scene to the Courtroom*, CRC Press, Boca Raton, FL, 2017.

Chapter 11

Forensic Evidence II

Integrity and Preservation

Learning Objectives

After reading this chapter, students are expected to be able to:

- describe chain-of-custody requirements
- define spoliation and its implications for evidence storage.

Introduction

Forensic examinations and analyses are for naught if the evidence has not been properly collected and maintained. The integrity of the evidence is crucial. The scientific concepts of the transfer, persistence, prevalence, and recovery (TPPR) of evidence are relevant here to the maintenance, preservation, and potential cross-contamination of evidence.

Chain-of-Custody

Chain-of-custody (CoC) is the historical documentation of the custody and control of the evidence. It is a chronological paper trail that proves the evidence was in someone's physical possession or responsible for security from collection to forensic analysis or presentation in court.

DOI: 10.4324/9780429272455-11

Most evidence is not *self-authenticating* and will require CoC. A gun with a serial number, notarized documents, certified documents, and newspapers are examples of self-authenticating evidence that can be used in court without needing to prove its authenticity.

CoC is more than merely a paper trail. CoC is proof of the authenticity and origin of the evidence – its *provenance*. CoC is also proof of the integrity of the evidence. Unless the crime scene has somehow been manipulated or disturbed, the CoC proves that the evidence has not been tampered with, altered, or substituted. Thus, it ensures the court that the evidence is what it purported to be.

The CoC lays a proper foundation for the evidence and authenticates it. A forensic expert witness will not be allowed to testify until the proper CoC of the evidence tested, analyzed, or examined has first been established. Once the party proffering the evidence shows a proper CoC, the burden shifts to the opposition to prove that the chain has been broken. Failure to adequately establish the CoC will result in the evidence's exclusion. However, a weak or missing link in the chain is not necessarily fatal; in some cases, the evidence and the forensic expert's testimony may be put to the jury to weigh the credibility of this evidence.

BOX 11.1 *EX PARTE COLONE* (TEX. CRIM. APP. 2022) – EVIDENCE INTEGRITY

Joseph Colone, a 39-year-old with a long criminal history, was charged with the 2010 capital murder of a mother and her daughter to prevent them from reporting him to the police for armed robbery. A knit glove, a towel, and an undershirt were sent to a private lab. The items and DNA extracts were returned to the County and stored in a freezer. Subsequently, they were shipped to the TX DPS crime lab in a Styrofoam cooler with a sticker marked "refrigerate upon arrival." DPS staff received the evidence and the CoC submission form that failed to list the extracts or mention the need for refrigeration. The unopened cooler was placed in storage at room temperature.

Thirty days passed before Adam Vinson, a forensic biology screening analyst, opened the cooler and found five "damp and soggy" paper envelopes, a clear plastic bag, and melted ice packs with a foul-smelling liquid at the bottom of the cooler. Vinson documented the condition of the evidence and his presumptive serology and trace evidence testing in 47 pages of bench notes. He reported the results in his report but did not mention the condition of the evidence. A DNA analyst tested the materials and could not exclude Colone as the source. Nearly 3½ years later, Vinson, who then worked at another laboratory, was called to testify about the CoC and serological results. He testified to his usual procedures, but it came out that he did not recall the specifics of the case. The prosecutor showed him his report to refresh his memory. He declared that the envelopes were dry because the report did not mention any issues with the evidence. On cross-examination, Vinson stated that he would have to review the case file to answer questions about the time he worked on the case, but he declared that he did not have access to it [DPS would have shared it had he asked]. The condition of the evidence and the potential for cross-contamination was not brought out at trial, he was convicted and sentenced to death.

The problem with the evidence was later discovered by attorneys working on his appeal. In post-conviction proceedings. Vinson became defensive and maintained that he testified truthfully and that the irregularities did not affect the outcome of the testing. The Criminal Court of Appeals found the glove and towel were the centerpiece of the State's case and that Vinson's trial testimony was misleading, evasive, and false. Accordingly, the court set aside Colone's conviction.

The Texas Forensic Science Commission found Vinson to be professionally negligent when he appeared unprepared at trial. The Commission worked with the lab accrediting body to add a requirement for trial preparation.

Spoliation of Potentially Exculpatory Evidence

According to Black's Law Dictionary, *spoliation of evidence* is "the intentional, reckless, or negligent withholding, hiding, altering, fabricating, or destroying of evidence relevant to a legal proceeding." Like perjury, it can potentially change the fundamental factual basis of a case, and the courts take it very seriously.

- *DUTY TO PRESERVE EXCULPATORY EVIDENCE* – the government has a desire to preserve evidence that will be useful for prosecuting cases in court, but the government has a constitutional duty to preserve evidence it collects during criminal investigations that is "exculpatory." Exculpatory evidence is favorable to the defendant and material to either guilt or punishment. The *Brady* rule mandates prosecutors to disclose exculpatory material to the defense. That duty arises to protect a defendant's rights to due process and a fair trial under the Fourteenth Amendment.

  It is challenging for defendants to prove that the state violated its duty to preserve evidence and that the violation compromised the rights to due process and a fair trial. The defense must demonstrate that such evidence was exculpatory and material to the case. The defendant must establish that law enforcement officers had reason to believe it was exculpatory before they destroyed it, that the evidence cannot be replaced by other available evidence, and that it is material to proving innocence.

In *California v Trombetta* (1984), the defendants challenged their convictions for drunk driving by claiming the police did not retain their breath samples and, thus, argued that they were unable to refute the state's testing. The Court unanimously rejected this argument. Although due process rights compel the preservation of *known* exculpatory evidence where no alternative exists, due process does not compel the state to preserve *potentially* exculpatory evidence. The Court pointed out that the defense had other reasonable means to challenge the evidence.

BOX 11.2 *CALIFORNIA V. TROMBETTA* (1984) – DESTRUCTION/SPOLIATION OF POTENTIALLY EXCULPATORY EVIDENCE

The defendants were convicted in unrelated incidents for DUI based upon breath alcohol tests. Although it was technically feasible to preserve their breath samples, the arresting officers, as was their ordinary practice, did not do so. The defendants moved to suppress the testing based upon a failure to preserve their samples. In a unanimous decision, the Supreme Court held that the Fourteenth Amendment does not require law enforcement agencies to preserve breath samples as potentially exculpatory evidence. The loss or destruction of exculpatory evidence can deny a criminal defendant *due process* (*Brady v. Maryland*); therefore, the State must preserve exculpatory evidence. However, this duty is limited to (1) evidence with known exculpatory value and (2) where the defendant cannot obtain comparable evidence by other reasonably available means. The officers did not destroy the breath samples to circumvent the *Brady* requirement. In failing to preserve breath samples for respondents, the officers here acted "in good faith and in accord with their normal practice." The chances that preserved samples would have been exculpatory were extremely low. The breath samples were obtained as raw data for the Intoxilyzer. The evidence presented at trial was not the breath itself but the Intoxilyzer results obtained from the breath samples. The defendants could have submitted urine or blood samples for testing if they thought the Intoxilyzer was erroneous. The defendants, however, were not informed of the difference between the various testing procedures when they were asked to select among the three available methods of testing blood alcohol concentrations. The defendants could have also raised issues of faulty instrumentation at trial.

- *BAD FAITH REQUIREMENT* – good faith of police at the time of spoliation of the evidence can cure the violation. Thus, the defendant must prove the destruction was done in bad faith. It is not enough to show that the state was careless or negligent when it destroyed the evidence; the defense must prove willful, deceitful, or malicious intent.

In *Arizona v. Youngblood* (1985), the defendants challenged their conviction by claiming the police did not refrigerate the clothing of a boy who was sexually assaulted, which might have preserved DNA on them that might have shown someone else committed the crime. The Court held that a criminal defendant must show bad faith on the part of the police for failure to preserve potentially exculpatory evidence to constitute a denial of due process. The Court noted that the defendants would not have to prove bad faith if the evidence was known to be exculpatory; in such cases, good or bad faith is irrelevant.

BOX 11.3 *ARIZONA V. YOUNGBLOOD* (1988) – DESTRUCTION/SPOLIATION OF POTENTIALLY EXCULPATORY

A ten-year-old boy was abducted at a carnival, molested, and sodomized by a middle-aged man, whom the boy identified as Larry Youngblood. Swabbings of blood and semen from a sexual assault kit were preserved, but the police failed to refrigerate the clothing that had biological evidence. Testing on the swabs proved inconclusive as to identity. Two years after the crime, the clothing was tested using blood grouping and a P-30 protein molecule test, which indicated that only a small quantity of semen was present and did not identify the perpetrator. Defense experts testified that Youngblood might have been exonerated by timely testing of properly preserved semen samples on the clothing. Youngblood was convicted of child molestation, sexual assault, and kidnapping.

The Supreme Court held that the State did not have a duty to preserve the semen samples even though they might have been potentially exculpatory. Unless a criminal defendant can show bad faith by the police, failure to preserve potentially useful evidence is not a denial of due process of law. The police's failure to refrigerate the clothing and test the semen was, at worst, negligent. None of this information was concealed from the respondent at trial; the respondent's expert could have tested the clothing. There was no suggestion of the police's bad faith. Also, the State's failure to perform a newer P-30 test was not a violation of Due Process; they do not have a constitutional duty to perform any particular test.

Justice Stevens, in his concurring opinion, stated,

> In my opinion, there may well be cases in which the defendant is unable to prove that the State acted in bad faith but in which the loss or destruction of evidence is nonetheless so critical to the defense as to make a criminal trial fundamentally unfair.

More than a decade later, in 2000, the clothes were retested using newer DNA technology, which exonerated Youngblood. The new profile matched Walter Cruise, a Texas inmate who was convicted of the crime and sentenced to an additional 24 years in prison.

In *Illinois v. Fisher* (2004), the defendant challenged his conviction after police disposed of the evidence after ten years of storage according to their regular police policies, despite a discovery request to retain all evidence in the case made shortly after its acquisition but before the defendant became a long-term fugitive. The Court held that the conviction withstood the challenge because the police did not show bad faith.

BOX 11.4 *ILLINOIS V. FISHER* (2004) – DESTRUCTION/SPOLIATION OF POTENTIALLY EXCULPATORY

During a traffic stop, police arrested Fisher after observing him attempting to conceal a plastic bag containing a white powdery substance, later found to be cocaine, and was charged with possession. Fisher failed to appear in court and remained a fugitive for over ten years. Eventually, he was detained on an unrelated matter, and the cocaine possession charge was reinstated. However, the police, per established procedures, had destroyed the evidence the previous month. He was convicted but appealed based on the State's destruction of evidence. The Court declared:

> We have held that when the State suppresses or fails to disclose material exculpatory evidence, the good or bad faith of the prosecution is irrelevant: a due process violation occurs whenever such evidence is withheld. In Youngblood, by contrast, we concluded that the failure to preserve this 'potentially useful evidence' does not violate due process 'unless a criminal defendant can show bad faith on the part of the police.'... The substance seized from respondent was the sort of 'potentially useful evidence' referred to in Youngblood, not material exculpatory evidence... the applicability of the bad-faith requirement in Youngblood depended not on the centrality of the contested evidence to the prosecution's case or the defendant's defense, but on the distinction between 'material exculpatory' evidence and 'potentially useful' evidence... the substance destroyed here was, at best, 'potentially useful.'

Several states have rejected this federal rule requiring a showing of bad faith, the *Youngblood standard.* The federal test involves no consideration of the materiality of the missing evidence, and some argue that it is too broad – thus, a defendant could challenge the state despite the immateriality of the evidence. It is also argued that it is too narrow because it applies only to cases in which a defendant can demonstrate bad faith, not cases of gross negligence or reckless disregard that may critically prejudice a defendant. Moreover, it is suggested that defendants face a practical near impossibility of proving bad faith on the part of the police. There have been a few post-Youngblood cases finding bad faith. (See *Pena v. Texas* (2009) for a discussion of the states that have not followed *Youngblood*.)

Biological Evidence

The federal government and most States have enacted laws that specifically require the preservation of biological evidence, which refers to biological material – such as hair, tissue, bones, teeth, blood, semen, or other bodily fluids – or evidence items containing biological material. The motivation for these laws comes from the power of DNA to inculpate defendants and exculpate suspects, even after many years.

The federal legislation (18 U.S.C. §3600A, excerpt) states:

a. In General.—

Notwithstanding any other provision of law, the Government shall preserve biological evidence that was secured in the investigation or prosecution of a Federal offense, if a defendant is sentenced to imprisonment for such offense.

b. Defined Term.—For purposes of this section the term "biological evidence" means—
   1. a sexual assault forensic examination kit;
   2. or semen, blood, saliva, hair, skin tissue, or other identified biological material.

c. Criminal Penalty.—

Whoever knowingly and intentionally destroys, alters, or tampers with biological evidence that is required to be preserved under this section with the intent to prevent that evidence from being subjected to DNA testing or prevent the production or use of that evidence in an official proceeding, shall be fined under this title, imprisoned for not more than five years, or both.

d. Habeas Corpus.—

Nothing in this section shall provide a basis for relief in any Federal habeas corpus proceeding.

An example of state legislation is that of Mississippi (Miss. Code Ann. §99-49-1, excerpt):

2(a) "Biological evidence" means the contents of a sexual assault examination kit or

any item that contains blood, semen, hair, saliva, skin tissue, fingernail scrapings, bone, bodily fluids or other identifiable biological material that was collected as part of the criminal investigation or may reasonably be used to incriminate or exculpate any person for the offense. This definition applies whether that material is catalogued separately, such as on a slide, swab or in a test tube, or is present on other evidence, including, but not limited to, clothing, ligatures, bedding or other household material, drinking cups, cigarettes or other items.

3(a) The state shall preserve all biological evidence:

i. That is secured in relation to an investigation or prosecution of a crime for the period of time that the crime remains unsolved or
ii. That is secured in relation to an investigation or prosecution of a crime for the period of time that the person convicted of that crime remains in custody.

Sample Consumption

Laboratories may consume evidence when they test it unless a state statute prohibits it. There is no constitutional or rule of evidence duty to preserve it unless it is known to be exculpatory. No specimen must be saved to allow the defense to test it unless a state law requires it. Nonetheless, it is generally good to keep a portion of the evidence for the defense to test it, but there are times when testing will consume the entire sample. Most states now have laws that specifically require the preservation of biological evidence. However, the laws vary by state, and only some prohibit consumption during testing.

The first case on the consumption of evidence was decided in the Federal District Court in *D.C. in U.S. v Anderson* (2016). The court allowed DNA testing to consume the evidence over the defendant's objection, with the proviso that if any specimen remained after testing, it would be turned over to the defense for possible further testing.

BOX 11.5 *U.S. V. ANDERSON* (2016) – CONSUMPTION OF THE EVIDENCE DURING TESTING

Anderson, a convicted felon, was charged with unlawful possession of a firearm and ammunition. The Government requested a court order for Anderson to provide a sample of his DNA to compare to any DNA recovered from the gun and magazine. Pursuant to protocol, the Government notified defense counsel that the United States Attorney's Office intended to authorize the consumption of all the swabs from the firearm and magazine in question. The defense filed a motion to preserve evidence. It was thought there would likely be a DNA extract left over, but the lab could not guarantee it; the Government was willing to provide any remaining extract not consumed during testing to the defense. Anderson argued that the Government should be required to prove that consumption of the entire sample is necessary to produce scientifically reliable results; however, if the Government is not able to make this showing, then the swabs should be split in half before the extraction of the DNA and that one half be reserved for potential defense use. The Government opposed this request, arguing that Anderson's proposed protocol is not scientifically advisable and that there is no legal support for Anderson's position on the swabs. The Court held that there was no due process violation because the evidence was untested and, therefore, had no apparent exculpatory value. Federal Rules of Evidence Rule 16 does not impose on the government any duty to preserve portions of evidence for defense testing, but the lab must keep unused extract. The Court denied Anderson's Motion and permitted the Government to extract DNA from the swabs at issue without first splitting them in half, but any remaining extract not consumed during testing shall be provided to the defense.

Summary

Chain-of-custody documentation is required for evidence in forensic testing and examination to prove the provenance of the evidence and that it was not tampered with.

Forensic science laboratories have a constitutional duty to keep exculpatory evidence, not inculpatory evidence or potential exculpatory evidence. In federal courts, defendants claiming wrongful spoliation of evidence must show bad faith by the lab, not merely that the destruction of the evidence was recklessly accidental. However, several states do not require such a showing.

Most states have a specific statutory requirement to retain a biological specimen to allow later DNA testing if needed.

Laboratories have been allowed to consume the total specimen while testing evidence.

Terms

Spoliation of Evidence – the intentional, reckless, or negligent withholding, hiding, altering, fabricating, or destroying of evidence relevant to a legal proceeding.

Cases

Arizona v. Youngblood, 488 U.S. 51 (1988)
Brady v. Maryland, 373 U.S. 83 (1963)
California v. Trombetta, 467 U.S. 479 (1984)
Ex parte Colone, No. WR-89 538-01 (Tex. Crim. App. 2022)
Illinois v. Fisher, 540 U.S. 544 (2004)
Pena v. Texas, 285 S.W.3d 459 (Tex.Crim.App. 2009)
United States v. Anderson, 169 F.Supp.3d 60 (D.D.C. 2016)

Statutes

Preservation and Accessibility of Biological Evidence (Miss. Code Ann. §99-49-1, 2017)

Preservation of Biological Evidence §3600A (2016)

Thought Questions

1. How strict is the duty to preserve evidence really?

Further Readings

Biological Evidence Preservation: Considerations for Policy Makers, NISTIR 8048, 2015, accessible at: https://nvlpubs.nist.gov/nistpubs/ir/2015/NIST.IR.8048.pdf

Report of the Texas Forensic Science Commission report on Adam Vinson, accessible at: https://www.txcourts.gov/media/1455421/fr_colone-12052022-1.pdf

Chapter 12

Scientific Evidence I

The Science

Learning Objectives

After reading this chapter, students are expected to be able to:

- define science
- discuss criticisms of science
- discuss criticisms of forensic science.

Introduction

Forensic science is often defined as the application of science to courts' questions of interest. Prosecutions based on forensic science are a relatively recent development. Like other sciences, forensic science evolves and improves with time.

Historical Background

The history of science is the record of the replacement of ignorance with knowledge. The word *science* comes from the Latin *scientia*, meaning knowledge. In English, it meant collective knowledge by the late 14th century and included seeking, systematizing, and sharing knowledge. Those trying to understand

DOI: 10.4324/9780429272455-12

the natural world were called *natural philosophers*, which is the basis for the philosophy doctorate (Ph.D.) degree. We now call those people *scientists*, a term coined by William Whewell (1794–1866) in 1833. The scientific method is said to have been invented by Aristotle (384–322 BCE) and put into practice in medieval times by Ibn al-Haytham (965–1039), who is regarded as the "father of the scientific method" due to his emphasis on experimentation and reproducibility. Johannes Gutenberg's (1400–1468) development of a printing press with metal moveable type set in 1440 enabled the first information revolution that made books affordable to the public. Francis Bacon (1561–1626), an Attorney General and Lord Chancellor of England, has been called the "father of empiricism" for his emphasis on inductive reasoning and methodic skepticism, whereby scientists aim to avoid misleading themselves. Baconian scientific inquiry formed the philosophical underpinnings of the so-called European *Scientific Revolution* of the late Renaissance period and early modern period of the 16th and 17th centuries, in which developments in mathematics, physics, astronomy, biology, and chemistry transformed the views of society about nature. The Scientific Revolution traditionally began with the Copernican Revolution in 1543 and ended with Isaac Newton's publication of his *Principia* in 1687. The "new science" helped spark the intellectual social movement known as the Enlightenment of the 17th and 18th centuries, which was followed by the Industrial Revolution and the current Information Revolution. Scientific knowledge has been increasing at an ever-accelerating rate and is now said to be doubling daily.

Science

Science is difficult to define. It is conceived as a body of knowledge, method, or process. Science is fundamentally an exercise in skepticism and inquiry. It is a pursuit of knowledge acquisition, and over time, the confidence and breadth of knowledge increase. Science is dynamic and, as Tomas Kuhn notes in his *The Structure of Scientific Revolutions*, sometimes disruptively evolves, with examples of fault lines and paradigm shifts.

Science is often contrasted with mysticism and faith. Karl Popper postulated that the difference between them is that scientific theories can be empirically tested and falsified. Non-science, such as the existence of God, is non-testable and cannot be proven false.

The scientist wants objective, empirical evidence to prove a point and often asks, "Show me the data!" It is a rebuke to mere assertion, assumption, or opinion and a de-emphasis of reason and experience. It is said that the language of science is mathematics, which defines natural phenomena (i.e., $E = mc^2$) and is at the heart of statistical proofs and modeling. This is very different from language-based law, which emphasizes reason and experience.

The scientific method (aka hypothesis-driven science or experimental science) involves observation, forming a hypothesis or question, and testing the hypothesis through experimentation. Discovery science involves revelations of new science based upon observations or mining new patterns or correlations from large data sets. New science is often developed from new technology that enables previously impossible experiments and observations.

Experimentation is a formalized method of hypothesis testing, usually involving measurements, controls, dependent variables, and a single independent variable. Classically, this is thought to apply inductive reasoning, but alternatively, it can be considered empirical falsification because the experiment can disprove a hypothesis but cannot prove it.

Research and investigation are broader terms that may involve experimentation. The HHS Common Rule (45 CFR 46 Subpart A; §46.102(l)) defines research as:

> A systematic investigation, including research development, testing and evaluation, designed to develop or contribute to generalizable knowledge. Activities that meet this definition constitute research for purposes of this policy, whether or not they are conducted or supported under a program considered research for other purposes. For example, some demonstration and service programs may include research activities. For purposes of this part, the following activities are deemed not to be research: (1) Scholarly and journalistic activities.... (2) Public health surveillance activities.... (3) Collection and analysis of information, biospecimens, or records by or for a criminal justice agency for activities authorized by law or court order solely for criminal justice or criminal investigative purposes. (4) Authorized operational activities (as determined by each agency) in support of intelligence, homeland security, defense, or other national security missions.

The *philosophy of science* is the branch of philosophy concerned with the foundations, methods, and implications of science, and *epistemology* is the overlapping branch of philosophy concerned with the theory of knowledge. Among other things, philosophers will argue the distinctions between knowledge, justified beliefs, and truths.

The U.S. Supreme Court in *Daubert v. Merrell Dow Pharmaceutical, Inc.* (1993), discussed below, declared: "Of course, it would be unreasonable to conclude that the subject of scientific testimony must be "known" to a certainty; arguably, there are no certainties in science... Scientific conclusions are subject to perpetual revision."

General Sciences

Some science is weaker, and some is stronger. Good science is characterized by support through well-designed experiments with ample data, verified by multiple others, corroborated by its fit within what is known and a significant consensus within the scientific community of interest; weak science is found when these are lacking. Good science has an explanatory power and a predictive power.

Erroneous scientific findings have been published in the scientific literature. Retraction of scientific journal articles is not so uncommon. Common problems include a lack of controls, inadequate or biased data, improper statistics, poorly designed experiments, and failure to acknowledge limitations. The *publish-or-perish* paradigm strongly pressures academics to discover new findings, and they sometimes resort to fraudulent publications in hopes of maintaining their careers.

Basic scientists who study fundamental understandings without regard to practical application often point to the peer-review process as a filter to keep out bad science. Still, peer review has clearly been shown to be an imperfect system. Bogus articles have been intentionally published to expose problems in this system. This system is undermined by a new publishing paradigm in which authors pay to publish their papers.

Science is self-correcting. A lead investigator becomes an advocate for their claim, but with time, a novel scientific theory will be supported by other research, debunked, or modified by further research. A typical pattern involves an initial enthusiasm for a new finding, leading to excessive claims and the rise of an uncritical group of supporters who hope to benefit from the purported new finding (bandwagon effect). This early support is followed by research with opposing results and criticisms, including overly broad statements before a consensus that involves new but more realistic understandings emerges. The general scientific community sometimes rejects and suppresses new ideas that challenge the orthodoxy, but eventually the truth will win out. The process is imperfect and forensic science should be validated before application. Good science is like cream in a milk can – it rises to the top. The solution to bad or weak science is more science!

Science usually evolves slowly. The court's problem is the need to resolve a dispute now, but science does not have an answer now – it may take years before science becomes settled.

This example of reports of measurements of the speed of light shows that with time, the data becomes more precise and more accurate.

Foster, Huber, Judging Science: Scientific Knowledge and the Federal Courts, 1999

Henrion, Fischoff, Assessing uncertainty in physical constants. Am J Phy (1986) 54(9):791–798

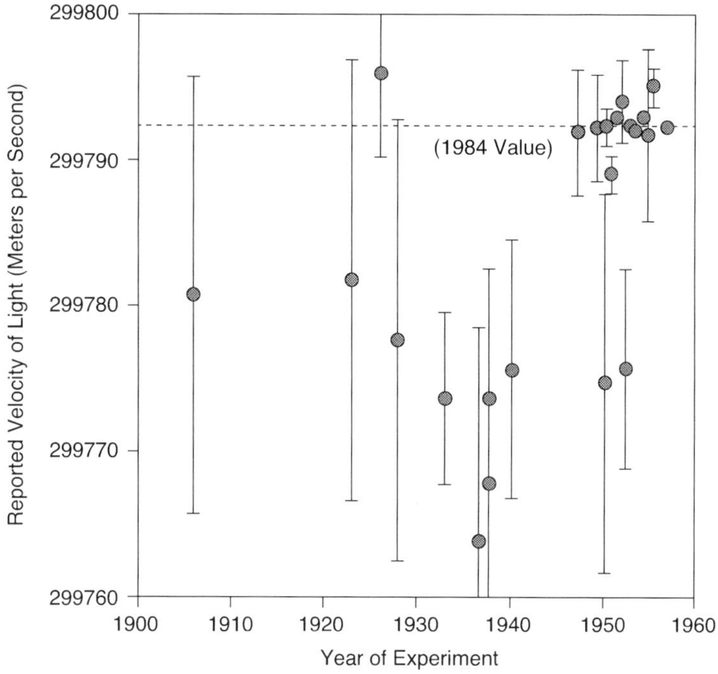

FIGURE 12.1 Scientific Self-Correction.

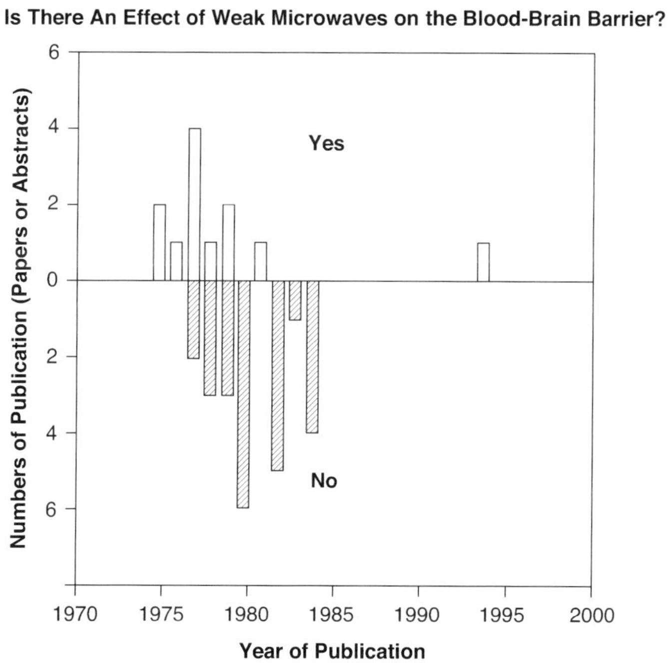

FIGURE 12.2 Scientific Self-Correction.

> This example of the effect of microwaves on the brain began with primarily confirmatory papers, the "bandwagon effect," and then shifted to papers that rejected such an association.
>
> Foster, Huber, Judging Science: Scientific Knowledge and the Federal Courts, 1999

Forensic Science

On the one hand, forensic science is no different from other sciences in that there is stronger and weaker science. On the other hand, the criticism seems louder than in other sciences. Perhaps the level of criticism reflects the consequences of getting it wrong.

Thousands of forensic scientists work daily to perform good science and offer valuable evidence. They do not go to work to perform shoddy work. Today's workforce is better educated than before, subjects themselves to proficiency testing, works in accredited laboratories, and uses better instrumentation. Forensic scientists worldwide conduct forensic science the same way because there is a global consensus on the benefits and methods of forensic science. In most cases, evidence of various types generally corroborates each other and the known history. If forensic science were as problematic as the pundits suggest, one would expect to see hundreds of appeals nationwide.

Critics inappropriately generalize and conflate various forensic science disciplines in "forensic science" as an indictment of all when it should be an indictment of only a few specific areas of forensic science, i.e., arson legacy folklore, bitemark identifications, and microscopic hair comparisons. Furthermore, critics conflate genuine forensic fraud (i.e., dry labbing), junk science (i.e., arson myths), weak science, and exaggerated claims (i.e., bitemark identifications). Finally, these critics also conflate bad or weak science with improper application or interpretation of the science. In other words, a wrongful conviction may result from fraud, negligence, improper testing, wrong interpretation, misleading testimony, or bad science.

The critics are virtually all, but not all, from outside the forensic science community itself. They often assert more knowledge and understanding of the field than they have. Participants in our American adversarial system include defense experts paid to be critical of the prosecution's forensic science. Moreover, the critics seem to operate in an echo chamber, where they garner support from each other and reference each other's works.

The media and the critics tend to point to exceptional problematic cases rather than most non-problematic cases. Moreover, they tend to point to old cases. Modern DNA testing has displaced the serology testing on which several of the early wrongful convictions were based. The Mayfield case, which involved a clear mistake in a problematic partial latent print comparison, resulted in significant reforms in the FBI's fingerprint practice.

Both the technologies of forensic science and laboratory practices in crime laboratories have improved substantially. Wrongful convictions based on forensic science have considerably decreased.

However, significant mistakes have been made, and many criticisms have kernels of truth. Forensic scientists have tended to be reactive, defensive, dismissive, and not open to constructive criticism. The adversarial system tends to polarize the participants rather than allow meaningful discussion. The forensic science community must continue to strive to address legitimate criticisms and educate those whose criticisms miss the mark.

BOX 12.1 ANNIE DOOKHAN – EVIDENTIAL FALSIFICATION

Annie Dookhan was a forensic chemist in Massachusetts who admitted to fabricating evidence ("dry labbing") and, in some cases, adding cocaine to some samples that did not initially contain cocaine. She was hired as a forensic chemist in 2003, but her fraudulent activities were not noticed until 2011, after the lab had been transferred from the Department of Health to the State Police forensics unit. Since her employment lasted more than eight years, the scandal affected up to 34,000 cases. In 2012, she was charged with obstruction of justice, tampering with evidence, perjury, and falsifying her credentials, and in 2013, she was sentenced to three to five years imprisonment but was paroled after 2½ years. A 2014 report of the state Inspector General investigation found that Dookhan acted alone, and the Inspector General made recommendations, particularly about employee training and managerial oversight. In 2015, the State Supreme Court ruled that defendants could pursue retrials, and in 2017, charges were dropped against 21,000 low-level drug criminal charges. This case is not about bad forensic science, but rather, it is about an employee who intentionally subverted the system and a laboratory that was not an accredited forensic laboratory and had inadequate oversight and quality assurance mechanisms.

BOX 12.2 BRANDON MAYFIELD – INTERPRETATIVE ERROR

In May of 2004, the FBI arrested Brandon Mayfield for the 2004 Madrid train bombings due to an erroneous fingerprint match. Mayfield was an attorney in Oregon and a former U.S. Army officer who married an Egyptian immigrant and converted to Islam shortly after that. The fingerprint match was made on a poor-quality partial latent print of a single fingertip. Mayfield turned up as a close match on a search of the IAFIS. The latent print examiner identified Mayfield, verified by another examiner, who knew that a match had been made. The defendant's own expert, a retired FBI latent print examiner, also identified the latent print as Mayfield's. The Spanish authorities contested the match and later matched the print to another, an Algerian national, Ouhnane Daoud, who was later convicted of the crime. There was, in fact, an unusual similarity in the fingerprint pattern of Mayfield and Daoud, but they were not identical; ten points of similarity of 15 that were used to identify Mayfield were also used to identify Daoud. Although Mayfield was never charged, he was held for over two weeks. The case was resolved with a formal apology from the U.S. government and a $2 million settlement. The incident was reviewed by an international panel and investigated by the Office of the Inspector General (OIG). The OIG reported that the examiners were dismissive of discrepancies, found level three minutiae that were absent, and concluded that the misidentification could have been prevented by a more rigorous application of fingerprint examination principles. There was speculation that Mayfield's religion had biased the examiners, but the OIG found that the match had been made before their knowledge of his religion. However, it might have affected the subsequent verification and review. Numerous changes were made in response to recommendations following the incident, including implementing blind verification. Claims of the infallibility of fingerprint evidence are no longer made. This incident should be seen as a faulty application of science, not bad forensic science.

BOX 12.3 FBI HAIR ANALYSIS – ERRONEOUS TESTIMONY

Three wrongful convictions (Santae A. Tribble, Kirk L. Odom, Donald E. Gates) based upon the FBI's microscopic hair comparison evidence were overturned when subsequent mitochondrial DNA testing of the hairs proved the matches wrong. FBI examiners in those cases had testified that the hairs "matched in all microscopic characteristics," "the samples were indistinguishable… [indistinguishable only] eight or ten times in the past ten years, while performing thousands of analyses." This trio of cases led to a review of the FBI hair analysis in 2012. Eventually, up to 17 cases were overturned. In 2015, news releases reported that a review conducted by DOJ, FBI, Innocence Project, and the National Association of Criminal Defense Lawyers lawyers of microscopic hair comparison analysis laboratory reports and testimony of approximately 500 cases (of 21,000) before 2000 in which a positive association had been made revealed that they contained "erroneous statements" in at least 90% of the cases. Reviewers deemed "errors" to involve statements that exceeded the limits of science or overstated the conclusions that may be appropriately drawn from a "positive association" between an evidentiary hair and a known hair. If the analyst merely stated that the hair was "consistent with" reference hairs of the defendant and was not further qualified with a statement of probability, then this was judged to be an "error." By 2002, the FBI began routinely using mitochondrial DNA testing where hairs appear similar. DOJ now requires using Uniform Language for Testimony and Reports (ULTRs). This occurrence is more about overstatements that went beyond the bounds of weak science.

NAS Report

Congress authorized and funded the National Academy of Sciences (NAS) to produce a report on the status and needs of the forensic community in late 2005. In 2009, the National Research Council (NRC) of the NAS issued a report entitled *Strengthening Forensic Science in the United States: A Path Forward*. The report was co-chaired by D.C. Circuit Judge Harry T. Edwards and Brown University statistician Constantine Gatsonis, who wrote in the Preface:

> The forensic science system, encompassing both research and practice, has serious problems that can only be addressed by a national commitment to overhaul the current structure that supports the forensic science community in this country.

In the Summary, they wrote:

> The term "forensic science" encompasses a broad range of forensic disciplines, each with its own set of technologies and practices. In other words, there is wide variability across forensic science disciplines with regard to techniques, methodologies, reliability, types and numbers of potential errors, research, general acceptability, and published material. Some of the forensic science disciplines are laboratory based (e.g., nuclear and mitochondrial DNA analysis, toxicology and drug analysis); others are based on expert interpretation of observed patterns (e.g., fingerprints, writing samples, toolmarks, bite marks, and specimens such as hair). … the committee found substantial evidence indicating that the level of scientific development and evaluation varies substantially among the forensic science disciplines.

The NAS report was highly publicized, widely discussed, and perhaps the most broadly impactful report on the forensic sciences. It was cited by a few courts, including by Justice Scalia in *Melendez-Diaz v Massachusetts* (2009), but did not have a discernable impact on criminal court decisions. It led to a serious legislative reform effort that did not result in the passage of any legislation. The executive branch's first significant response was forming a Subcommittee on Forensic Science (SoFS) within the White House's Office of Science and Technology Policy (OSTP) that operated from 2009 to 2012 and issued a report in 2014. This was succeeded by the DOJ/National Institute of Standards and Technology (NIST) National Commission on Forensic Sciences (NCFS), which operated from 2014 to 2017, and the DOJ/NIST Organization of Scientific Area Committees for Forensic Science (OSAC), which began working in 2015 and continues to the present. Still, other important initiatives were started in the years that followed the report.

It can be argued that many of the 13 recommendations of the NAS report have come to fruition. The report's number one recommendation was the creation of a National Institute of Forensic Science (NIFS); it was never seriously considered by Congress. Criticism of the then-existent DOJ Scientific

Working Groups (SWGs) was remedied by replacing them with the NIST OSAC. The OSAC has facilitated the generation of protocols and established a national registry of OSAC-approved protocols (Recommendation #6). The OSAC has also developed a list of standard terms (Recommendation #2). The NCFS wrote a National Code of Professional Responsibility (Recommendation #9), which the DOJ adopted with some modifications. Laboratories have begun publishing their quality assurance documents on their websites. They have also taken steps to minimize cognitive bias. Most publicly funded laboratories are accredited, and certification of forensic scientists has become more widespread (Recommendation #7).

BOX 12.4 SUMMARIZED NAS RECOMMENDATIONS

1. Independent National Institute of Forensic Science
2. Standardized Terminology and Reporting
3. Research on Accuracy, Reliability, and Validity
4. Independence of laboratories from police agencies
5. Cognitive Bias
6. Standardized Testing
7. Accreditation of Laboratories and Certification of Personnel
8. Quality Assurance and Quality Control
9. National Code of Ethics
10. Funding of Graduate Education Programs
11. Medical Examiner Office replacement of Coroners
12. Fingerprint identification systems interoperability
13. Homeland Security Preparedness

PCAST Report

In 2016, the President's Council of Advisors on Science and Technology (PCAST) issued a report entitled *Forensic Science in Criminal Courts: Ensuring Scientific Validity of Feature-Comparison Methods*. Eric Lander was the driving force behind the study.

PCAST sought to establish the scientific validity of some forensic sciences. The authors noted that extensive "experience" in casework cannot substitute for empirical studies of scientific validity because casework cannot reliably estimate error rates. They asserted that in casework, the examiner does not have independent knowledge of the "ground truth" or "right answer."

The authors established their own criteria and coined the terms "foundational validity" and "validity as applied" but provided no references for their approach. Foundational validity required at least two "black box" studies documenting the method's error rate published in the peer-reviewed literature. Validation as applied, depends upon proficiency testing and refers to individual error rates.

PCAST limited its review to:

> forensic feature-comparison methods' to refer to the wide variety of methods that aim to determine whether an evidentiary sample (e.g., from a crime scene) is or is not associated with a potential source sample (e.g., from a suspect) based on the presence of similar patterns, impressions, features, or characteristics.

PCAST chose to review the forensic examinations of DNA single-source and simple-mixture samples, DNA complex-mixture samples, bitemarks, latent fingerprints, firearms, and footwear impressions. The PCAST also reviewed the supporting literature for hair analysis but did not undertake a complete evaluation of its scientific validity. PCAST then purported to review the scientific literature to assess whether these disciplines were scientifically validated.

PCAST specifically concluded that fingerprint examinations had achieved foundational validity, albeit with a substantial false positive rate, and that single-source and simple-mixture DNA analyses are objective and whose foundational validity has been properly established. However, PCAST declared that firearms analysis, complex DNA mixture testing, bitemark evidence, footwear examinations, and microscopic hair analysis had not yet been scientifically validated. Overall, the report was a plea for more empirical data on error rates. NIJ and NIST have noted this and have funded more research to address this issue. The criticism of complex mixtures involving probabilistic genotyping has largely been addressed. The authors suggested that judges should not admit forensic science that has not been scientifically validated. PCAST challenges in court have largely not been fruitful.

BOX 12.5 PCAST KEY TERMS

- By "repeatable," we mean that, with known probability, an examiner obtains the same result, when analyzing samples from the same sources.
- By "reproducible," we mean that, with known probability, different examiners obtain the same result, when analyzing the same samples.
- By "accurate," we mean that, with known probabilities, an examiner obtains correct results both (1) for samples from the same source (true positives) and (2) for samples from different sources (true negatives).
- By "reliability," we mean repeatability, reproducibility, and accuracy.

- By "scientific validity," we mean that a method has shown, based on empirical studies, to be reliable with levels of repeatability, reproducibility, and accuracy that are appropriate to the intended application.
- By an "empirical study," we mean test in which a method has been used to analyze a large number of independent sets of samples, similar in relevant aspects to those encountered in casework, in order to estimate the method's repeatability, reproducibility, and accuracy.
- By a "black-box study," we mean an empirical study that assesses a subjective method by having examiners analyze samples and render opinions about the origin or similarity of samples.

BOX 12.6 PCAST SCIENTIFIC CRITERIA FOR SCIENTIFIC VALIDITY OF A FORENSIC FEATURE-COMPARISON METHOD

1. **Foundational validity**. To establish foundational validity for a forensic feature-comparison method, the following elements are required:

   a. a reproducible and consistent procedure for
      i. identifying features in evidence samples;
      ii. comparing the features in two samples; and
      iii. determining, based on the similarity between the features in two sets of features, whether the samples should be declared to be likely to come from the same source ("matching rule"); and

   b. empirical estimates, from appropriately designed studies from multiple groups, that establish
      i. the method's false positive rate – that is, the probability it declares a proposed identification between samples that actually come from different sources and
      ii. the method's sensitivity – that is, the probability it declares a proposed identification between samples that actually come from the same source.

   Scientific validation studies should satisfy a number of criteria:

   c. they should be based on sufficiently large collections of known and representative samples from relevant populations;
   d. they should be conducted so that the examinees have no information about the correct answer;
   e. the study design and analysis plan should be specified in advance and not modified afterward based on the results;
   f. the study should be conducted or overseen by individuals or organizations with no stake in the outcome;

g. data, software, and results should be available to allow other scientists to review the conclusions; and
h. to ensure that the results are robust and reproducible, there should be multiple independent studies by separate groups reaching similar conclusions.

Once a method has been established as foundationally valid based on adequate empirical studies, claims about the method's accuracy and the probative value of proposed identifications, in order to be valid, must be based on such empirical studies.

- **For objective methods**, foundational validity can be established by demonstrating the reliability of each of the individual steps (feature identification, feature comparison, matching rule, false match probability, and sensitivity).
- **For subjective methods**, foundational validity can be established only through **black-box studies** that measure how often many examiners reach accurate conclusions across many feature-comparison problems involving samples representative of the intended use. In the absence of such studies, a subjective feature-comparison method cannot be considered scientifically valid.

Foundational validity is a sine qua non, which can only be shown through empirical studies. Importantly, good professional practices – such as the existence of professional societies, certification programs, accreditation programs, peer-reviewed articles, standardized protocols, proficiency testing, and codes of ethics – cannot substitute for empirical evidence of scientific validity and reliability.

2. **Validity as applied**. Once a forensic feature-comparison method has been established as foundationally valid, it is necessary to establish its validity as applied in a given case.
   Validity as applied requires that:

a. the forensic examiner must have been shown to be capable of reliably applying the method, as shown by appropriate proficiency testing, and must actually have done so, as demonstrated by the procedures actually used in the case, the results obtained, and the laboratory notes, which should be made available for scientific review by others; and
b. assertions about the probative value of proposed identifications must be scientifically valid – including that examiners should report the overall false positive rate and sensitivity for the method established in the studies of foundational validity; demonstrate that the samples used in the foundational studies are relevant to the facts of the case; where applicable, report probative value of the observed match based on the specific features observed in the case; and not make claims or implications that go beyond the empirical evidence.

Historicity

A significant difference between forensic science and most other general sciences is *historicity* (historical actuality). Forensic science often tries to prove something in the past. This is also true of anthropology and cosmology. The problem is that we cannot go back in time to know what happened (even where a confession is made) – forensic scientists cannot measure their efforts against a gold standard. The identification of someone through DNA may not pose a problem of historicity, such as in sexual assault cases where the issue is whether the sexual act was rape or by consent. Forensic scientists may use abductive reasoning when reconstructing the crime scene, in which an incomplete set of facts and data are used to infer a likely explanation for a group of observations. In other words, forensic scientists may be using a set of observations of the present to infer what happened in the past.

Wrongful Convictions

As of 2024, the National Registry of Exonerations (NRE) had listed nearly 3,500 total DNA and non-DNA exonerations in the United States since 1989.

It should be recognized that most convictions are still achieved based on confessions and eyewitness testimony, which are now acknowledged to be far more fallible than previously thought and account for many more wrongful convictions than forensic science evidence. Other non-forensic science factors, such as inadequate legal defense, dishonest jailhouse snitches, and police and prosecutorial misconduct, also account for wrongful convictions.

Forensic science has brought more justice to bear than before its introduction. Forensic scientific evidence frequently exonerates the innocent and supports the prosecution of the actual perpetrators, who might otherwise go unrecognized or unconvicted. Scientific evidence is generally considered to be neutral and objective. Nonetheless, faulty forensic science or forensic science misapplied has resulted in wrongful convictions.

In an interim report in late 2022, the NRE and IP found that false or misleading forensic evidence occurs in approximately one-quarter of exonerations and that this proportion has remained stable over time. The overall number of exonerations has increased over the past three decades, although the number of DNA exonerations has declined. This increase in exonerations may reflect the increased resources and attention devoted to this effort and perhaps greater openness to exoneration by courts. However, the authors conclude that the "report has said little about what all of this means about the state of forensic science in the United States and how it can improve."

Not all forensic scientists would agree with the definitions and interpretations of the IP and NRE, which are generally critical of the forensic science community. Gerald LaPorte, then at NIJ, published a report in 2017 critical

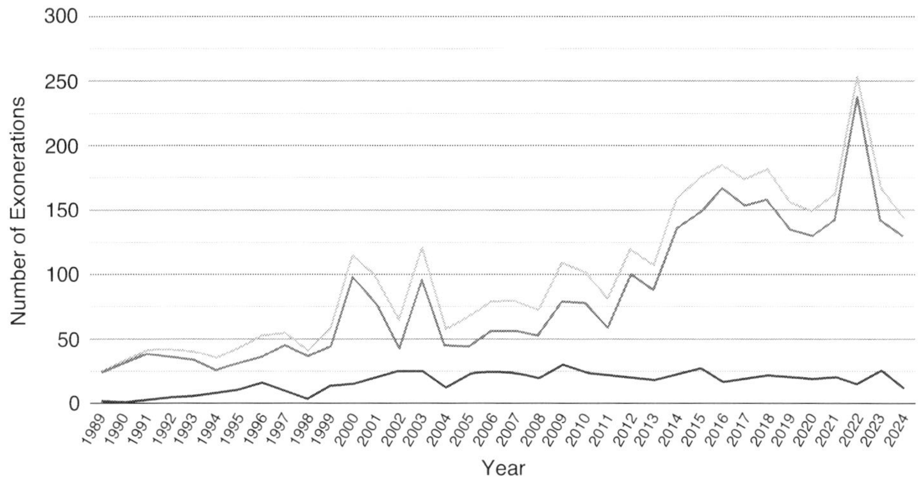

FIGURE 12.3 Exonerations by Year: DNA and Non-DNA Cases.

National Registry of Exonerations, current as of 1/4/2024.

https://www.law.umich.edu/special/exoneration/Pages/Exoneration-by-Year.aspx.

of their findings and noted discrepancies between their data. He declared that 83% of forensic-contributed DNA exonerations occurred after 1991 and only two after 2000. Although other exonerations from this period came to fruition, it did cause the IP and NRE to coordinate and reevaluate their own data.

More recently, John Morgan was funded by the NIJ to examine these cases further. He studied 732 exonerations that the NRE found associated with false or misleading forensic evidence and reported his findings in late 2023. He found that of the 732 cases, only 635 cases included a case error associated with forensic evidence, and 97 cases did not. He developed an error typology to categorize errors of individualization or classification (incorrect interpretation), reporting, testimony, use in court, and evidence handling. The most common errors were errors by officers of the court, including inadequate defense. The increasing complexity of scientific evidence may be exacerbating this problem. Errors associated with accredited public labs are declining. When forensic scientists made errors, they were often associated with incompetent or fraudulent examiners, disciplines with an inadequate scientific foundation, or organizational deficiencies in training, management, governance, or resources. He also found that forensic reports or testimony often miscommunicated results, did not conform to established standards, or failed to provide appropriate limiting information. He concluded, "In approximately half of wrongful convictions analyzed, improved technology, testimony standards, or practice standards may have prevented a wrongful conviction at the time of trial."

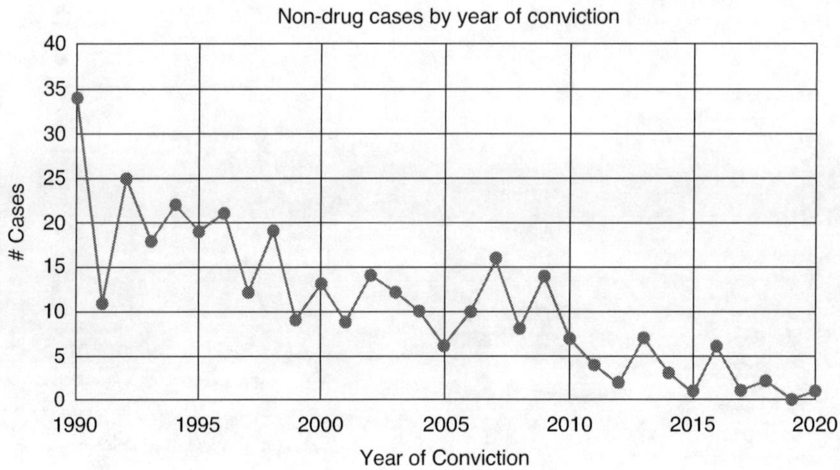

FIGURE 12.4 Exonerations by Year: Non-drug Cases False/Misleading Forensic Evidence Cases. J Morgan, Forensic Testimony Archaeology.

https://www.ojp.gov/pdffiles1/nij/grants/306259.pdf.

Morgan found, in contrast to the NRE, that forensic-evidence-associated cases have declined when viewed by year of conviction or year of exoneration. He believes that this is due to advances in standards and in new technologies, such as DNA replacing serology. However, he recognizes that errors are not inevitable and when they occur they reflect breakdowns in systems. Systems should be continually improving. Also, they should be used appropriately by the criminal justice system, which implies that police, attorneys, and judges must be constantly educated on forensic science.

Statistical Interpretation

Forensic scientists have also been criticized for making assertions that are not statistically supported. Critics were particularly inflamed by assertions that the examiner did not make mistakes or that, in their experience, out of the thousands of exams they have done, they have never seen one with these characteristics that was not a match. Furthermore, it is suggested that forensic scientists report their results as probabilistic rather than *categorical statements* (deterministic statements), e.g., identified, excluded, inconclusive.

DNA analysts have generally reported their results as *probabilistic statements* (graded statements), i.e., 1 in 4 quadrillion of a random match, rather than declaring an identification. Alleles were manually called from electropherograms, but now probabilistic genotyping software assigns probabilities to peak calling. Fingerprint examiners generally report identifications; however, the Department of Defense's Defense Forensic Science Center (DFSC) reports a statistical strength of the fingerprint identification based upon a similarity metric. NIST has developed statistical methods for comparing cartridge cases (congruent matching cells) and bullets (congruent matching profile segments) that are anticipated to be used in casework within the next few years. NIST is also working on statistical approaches to footwear and tire impressions. Statistical interpretation incorporates a sense of certainty lacking in a categorical expression. The military has successfully used probabilistic statements on reports for a few years. Even toxicologists, for their chemical identifications, now determine the certainty of their analysis.

There are two basic approaches to statistical statements: (1) frequentist and (2) Bayesian. The frequentist approach is essentially a counting method and applies to data. Random match probabilities are derived from allele frequencies and are both frequentist statements of facts. The Bayesian approach considers uncertainties and applies them to hypotheses. Forensic evidence that tends to prove or disprove the defendant's guilt involves uncertainties and the hypothesis that the defendant did or did not perpetrate the crime. This is expressed as a likelihood ratio, a Bayesian notion, in which the probability of guilt is divided by the probability of innocence – a likelihood ratio of one then means that the chances are equal, and a ratio of two means that the probability of guilt is twice as high as of innocence.

However, the likelihood ratio will depend upon the starting assumption of guilt – the "prior probability" (prior odds). To explain this concept, consider a laboratory test for Covid that is 94% sensitive, and 87% sensitive will have a positive predictive value of the test that depends upon the prevalence of Covid in the population tested – where the incidence is high, the false positives will be less and false negatives low, but the reverse will occur when the incidence is low. Typically, in forensics, the prior probability is assumed to be one – that the probability of guilt is equal to the probability of guilt before the testing. Concerns raised about the Bayesian approach include the speculative estimate of the prior probability and the difficulty of jurors in grasping the Bayesian concept.

The prosecutor's fallacy (base rate fallacy) is the assumption that a positive test that has a very high specificity is necessarily strong evidence of the defendant's guilt. The U.S. Supreme Court in *McDaniel v. Brown* (2010) recognized it as:

> The prosecutor's fallacy is the assumption that the random match probability is the same as the probability that the defendant was not the source of the DNA sample… ("Let P equal the probability of a match, given the evidence

genotype. The fallacy is to say that P is also the probability that the DNA at the crime scene came from someone other than the defendant").

It is a fallacy because it neglects the prior probability of guilt. If facial recognition software is 99% accurate, the vast majority of identifications will be false negatives in surveilling a population of a million people – 9,999 false positives and one true positive. The defense attorney's fallacy is the opposite – that a relatively poor test is not valuable.

In *People v. Collins* (1968), a mathematics teacher testified to the probability that the defendants matched the witness's description of a black male with a beard and mustache, and a Caucasian female with a blond ponytail, who were fleeing in a yellow car. The expert assumed the probabilities were independent and used the product rule. The appellate court set aside the conviction for the expert ignoring the possible dependencies, i.e., bearded men often also have moustaches, and for the mistaken inference that a random defendant has a specific combination of traits with the chance that the defendant is innocent – the prosecutor's fallacy. Instead, the correct statistical inference would be the probability that no other couple who could have committed the crime had the same traits given that at least one couple had the witnessed traits.

Similarly, Sally Clark was convicted of murder when a second infant son died of the Sudden Infant Death Syndrome (SIDS), and a pediatrician testified that the chance of two SIDS cases in one family was one in 73 million, since the prevalence of SIDS was 1 in 8,500. This calculation ignored the possibility of common genetic and environmental factors. This was again a misuse of statistics involving an inappropriate base rate, a lack of independence of variables, and the Prosecutor's fallacy. That the second infant had an infection also later came out. Her conviction was overturned, but she died a few years later of alcohol poisoning.

In 2015, NIST funded the Center for Statistics and Applications in Forensic Evidence (CSAFE) to "infuse statistical thinking and rigorous, science-based standards into forensic practice." They have created numerous helpful educational materials on statistics that are freely available on their website.

It can be anticipated that as objective instrumental measurements replace human interpretations, statistical analyses will become prevalent in forensic science.

Funding

The solution to weak or bad science is more science. Arguing legal admissibility does not address the underlying fundamental concerns. The amount of funding spent on forensic science research is paltry and fragmented.

TABLE 12.1 U.S. Research and Development Funding

FY2020 Federal R&D Outlays	$M	(%)
Department of Defense	66,695.0	39.8
Health and Human Services	60,005.7	35.8
Department of Energy	13,453.0	8.0
NASA	10,537.8	6.3
National Science Foundation	6,351.2	3.8
Department of Veterans Affairs	1,565.1	0.9
Department of Justice	96.4	>0.1
Other agencies	8,698.6	5.2
Total	167,402.8	99.8

https://ncses.nsf.gov/pubs/nsf22323.

The National Science Foundation (NSF) funds basic research, not applied research. DOJ spends less than 0.1% of the federal funding on research and development, and not all of that on forensic research. Furthermore, the intramural-to-extramural funding ratio is heavily out of balance compared to other areas of science funding. There are insufficient funds from the National Institutes of Justice to fund even a single academic research career. Although there are a few Ph.D. opportunities in Interdisciplinary Science, Forensic Chemistry, and Forensic Molecular Biology, there are only two Ph.D. programs in forensic science per se (Sam Houston State University, West Virginia University). Those who complain about the lack of good science in forensics and the lack of an adequate science research culture should lobby Congress for more funding for forensic science research. Without this funding, such criticism will continue.

Summary

Scientific knowledge evolves and, despite fits and starts, improves over time. Commentators have found fault with aspects of forensic science, and defendants have challenged its application in court. Courts have been used to categorical scientific results but are increasingly facing statistical evidence. Forensic scientists face a problem that other scientists generally do not face – a lack of a gold standard due to the historicity problem.

Wrongful convictions have been based upon faulty science, faulty application of the science, faulty interpretation of the results, or faulty testimony. The forensic science community is reacting and improving, but the anecdote to poor science is more science, and, therefore, there should be more funding for forensic research.

Terms

Categorical (Deterministic) Statement – a declarative statement of belief that a datum falls into one category or another.
Probabilistic (Graded) Statement – a statistical statement of belief that a datum has a certain likelihood of truth.
Research – a systematic investigation designed to develop or contribute to generalizable knowledge.
Science – a body of knowledge and a method of acquiring knowledge.

Cases

Daubert v. Merrell Dow Pharmaceuticals, Inc., 509 U.S. 579 (1993)
McDaniel v. Brown, 558 U.S. 120 (2010)
Melendez-Diaz v. Massachusetts, 557 U.S. 305 (2009)
People v. Collins, 68 Cal.2d 319 (Cal. 1968)
Regina v. Sally Clark, EWCA Crim 1020 (Eng 2003)

Other Authorities

Center for Statistics and Applications in Forensic Evidence (CSAFE) website, available at: https://forensicstats.org/

Code of Federal Regulations, Part 46—Protection of Human Subjects, Subpart A—Basic HHS Policy for Protection of Human Subjects, §46.102 Definitions for purposes of this policy, (l) *Research*, available at: https://www.ecfr.gov/cgi-bin/retrieveECFR?gp=&SID=83cd09e1c0f5c6937cd9d7513160fc3f&pitd=20180719&n=pt45.1.46&r=PART&ty=HTML#se45.1.46_1102

Edwards HT, Gatsonis C, et al., National Research Council (NRC), National Academy of Sciences (NAS), Committee on Identifying the Needs of the Forensic Sciences Community, *Strengthening Forensic Science: A Path Forward*, National Academies Press, Washington, DC, 2009, available at: https://www.ncjrs.gov/pdffiles1/nij/grants/228091.pdf

Ensuring Scientific Validity of Feature-Comparison Methods, President's Council of Advisors on Science and Technology, Sep 2016, available at: https://obamawhitehouse.archives.gov/sites/default/files/microsites/ostp/PCAST/pcast_forensic_science_report_final.pdf

The Impact of False or Misleading Forensic Evidence on Wrongful Convictions, NIJ webpage, Nov 28, 2023, available at: https://nij.ojp.gov/topics/articles/impact-false-or-misleading-forensic-evidence-wrongful-convictions

Thought Questions

1. Should we speak of forensic science or the forensic sciences?
2. Should forensic science be treated by the courts any differently than other sciences?
3. The Bureau of Labor Statistics categorizes crime laboratory analysts as forensic science technicians; should they be considered professional scientists or technicians?

Further Reading

ABS Group, Root and Cultural Cause Analysis of Report and Testimony Errors by FBI MHCA Examiners, Aug 2018, https://vault.fbi.gov/root-cause-analysis-of-microscopic-hair-comparison-analysis/root-cause-analysis-of-microscopic-hair-comparison-analysis-part-01-of-01/view

Audi R, *Epistemology: A Contemporary Introduction to the Theory of Knowledge*, 3rd ed, Routledge, New York, NY, 2010.

Bromwich Group, Looking Back to Move Forward: The Houston Police Department Crime Laboratory's Implementation of the Independent Investigator's 2007 Recommendations, Jan 29, 2014, https://www.bromwichgroup.com/wp-content/uploads/2014/04/Final-report.pdf

Clunie S, No One Left to Lie To: The Case of Annie Dookhan and the Importance of Scientific Ethics in the Criminal Justice System. Thesis, Oct 9, 2024, file:///C:/Users/weedn/Downloads/Clunie_S_CHEM300_No_one_left_2024.pdf.pdf

Cole SA, Meterko V, Chu S, Cooper G, Paredes JW, Possley M, Otterbourg K, The Contribution of Forensic and Expert Evidence to DNA Exoneration Cases: An Interim Report (National Registry of Exonerations and Innocence Project), Dec 2023, https://n2t.net/ark:/88112/x2g890

Fisher J, The Forensic Hall of Shame, website, Aug 28, 2022, https://jimfishertruecrime.blogspot.com/2013/06/forensic-science-hall-of-shame-experts.html

Foster KR, Huber PW, *Judging Science: Scientific Knowledge and the Federal Courts*, MIT Press, Cambridge, MA, 1997.

Frederic Whitehurst Exposed Widespread Misconduct and Fraudulent Scientific Practices within the FBI Crime Lab, Kohn, Kohn, & Colapinto website, 2024, https://kkc.com/whistleblower-case-archive/frederic-whitehurst/

Haack S, *Defending Science - Within Reason: Between Scientism and Cynicism*, Prometheus, Amherst, NY, 2011.

Ioannidis JPA, Limitations Are Not Properly Acknowledged in the Scientific Literature, *Journal of Clinical Epidemiology* 60(4):324–329, 2007.

Ioannidis JPA, Why Most Published Research Findings Are False, *PLOS Medicine* 2(8):e124, 2005. https://doi.org/10.1371/journal.pmed.0020124

Ioannidis JPA, Why Science Is Not Necessarily Self-correcting, *Perspectives on Psychological Science* 7(6):645–654, 2012. https://doi.org/10.1177/1745691612464056

Jasanoff S, *Science at the Bar: Law, Science, and Technology in America*, Harvard University Press, Cambridge, MA, 1995.

Macrina FL, *Scientific Integrity: Text and Cases in Responsible Conduct of Research*, 4th ed, ASM Press, Washington, DC, 2014.

Morgan J, Forensic Testimony Archaeology: Analysis of Exoneration Cases and Its Implications for Forensic Science Testimony and Communication, Feb 20, 2023, NCJRS, award #GS10F0114L/OJP2002BF.

Morgan JS. Current State of Forensic Science Improvement in the United States: Lessons from Wrongful Convictions. *Forensic Science Review* 36(1):41–54, 2024, http://forensicsciencereview.com/Abstract/36(1)-2%20(web).pdf

Stacey RB, Report on the Erroneous Fingerprint Individualization in the Madrid Train Bombing Case. *Historian* 404:294–647, 2005, https://www.ojp.gov/ncjrs/virtual-library/abstracts/report-erroneous-fingerprint-individualization-madrid-train-bombing

US DOJ OIG, A Review of the FBI's Handling of the Brandon Mavfield Case, Mar 2006, https://oig.justice.gov/sites/default/files/legacy/special/s0601/final.pdf

Chapter 13

Scientific Evidence II

Admissibility

Learning Objectives

After reading this chapter, students are expected to be able to:

- explain what is meant by the admissibility of scientific evidence
- define validity, reliability, and relevancy
- discuss the *Frye* and the *Daubert* trilogy decisions
- recite the *Daubert* factors
- explain the Federal Rules of Evidence on expert testimony.

Introduction

Courts require science to be valid, reliable, and relevant, but how do they know? This is a much broader issue than forensic science; it applies to all science introduced into court. This topic was not often litigated until the 20th Century, when prosecutors began using science to convict defendants.

Frye Standard for Admission of Novel Scientific Evidence

Like all evidence, forensic science evidence undergoes scrutiny in court at two levels: admissibility as a *matter of law* by the judge and weight as a

DOI: 10.4324/9780429272455-13

matter of fact by the jury or the judge in bench trials. The judge's role is to decide whether the evidence should be presented to the trier of fact, while the jury or judge in bench trials evaluates the evidence's credibility and significance.

The problem for the courts is whether to admit novel science into evidence that has not yet become well-established. As a generality, during the 1st century and a half of American jurisprudence, scientific evidence was admitted if an expert was willing to support it. There was little jurisprudential discussion or doctrine to exclude unsound scientific evidence until 1923.

In 1923, the Court of Appeals of the District of Columbia squarely addressed the issue of novel scientific evidence in *Frye v. U.S.* and declared:

> Just when a scientific principle or discovery crosses the line between the experimental and demonstrable stages is difficult to define. Somewhere in this twilight zone the evidential force of the principle must be recognized, and while the courts will go a long way in admitting experimental testimony deduced from a well-recognized scientific principle or discovery, the thing from which the deduction is made must be sufficiently established to have gained general acceptance in the particular field in which it belongs.

The *Frye* test asks if the novel science has gained *general acceptance* within the relevant scientific community. In other words, it looks for a general consensus of the experts in the field.

After the *Frye* decision, the general acceptance test was adopted by virtually all courts across the United States and became settled law for 70 years. It opened the door for the use of scientific evidence and expert witness testimony but was, at least initially, thought to keep out *junk science*. The decision established the scientific field as the validator of legal admissibility. It did not require close scrutiny of the science by the court or the attorneys because it deferred to the scientific community. Once the scientific evidence is admitted after a *Frye* hearing in a jurisdiction, it need not be reconsidered in future cases because it has been accepted.

The *Frye* test has been criticized as a popularity contest, requiring the process of counting scientific noses. It has also been criticized as rigid, austere, and slow for its intolerance of new, emerging, or cutting-edge scientific theories and methods. It takes time for a new scientific theory to become known and garner general acceptance. It has also been criticized as static, whereas science is dynamic and evolving.

From a practical standpoint, when experts are asked if their novel scientific method has gained general acceptance in the field, they often must speculate on what the relevant field is and what the field thinks without a poll being taken.

BOX 13.1 *FRYE V. UNITED STATES* (DC CIR. 1923) – NOVEL SCIENTIFIC EVIDENCE

James Alphonso Frye confessed to shooting Dr. R.W. Brown during a robbery in 1920. A year later, he was caught and questioned for an unrelated robbery, but after arrest, he retracted his confession. He claimed innocence and that he had falsely confessed to sharing the reward money with the detective. William Moulton Marston invented the systolic blood pressure deception test (an early polygraph) in 1915 and was approached by Frye's defense attorneys to use it in their case. While in jail, Marston performed the test on Frye and determined that he was telling the truth about his innocence. The defense moved to introduce this evidence into court to prove his innocence, but the judge excluded it. Frye's defense contended that Frye was told if he confessed to the murder, then the robbery charge would be dropped, and the murder charge would not stick with his alibi. The defense attempted to get Dr. Marston to testify to his systolic deception detection examination performed, which would corroborate Frye's testimony. Chief Justice Walter I. McCoy would not allow Dr. Marston's testimony:

> We do not bring experimental matters into court, but when it is established that scientific development has reached such a point as to become a matter of common knowledge as to its results, we allow the results to be shown in court.

Frye was convicted of second-degree murder. The defense appealed to the Court of Appeals for the District of Columbia (now the D.C. Circuit Court), arguing that excluding this exculpatory scientific evidence was improper. The court held that the scientific testimony was properly excluded, and the conviction was upheld. In so doing, Associate Justice Van Orsdel announced a *general acceptance* test in a now-famous passage. James Alphonse Frye served over 18 years for his crime and made multiple appeals for pardons even after his release. He died in 1953 and was buried in Arlington National Cemetery.

BOX 13.2 NOTES ON FRYE

William Moulton Marston had a Ph.D. in psychology and a JD from Harvard and was a professor at American University at the time of the Frye trial. Marston claimed that the jury reduced the charge from first-degree to second-degree murder from the knowledge that the Lie Detector had proved Frye's story truthful. Marston's systolic blood pressure deception test was later eclipsed by the more advanced polygraphs of John Larson and August Vollmer in Berkeley and Leonarde Keeler of Northwestern. Larson acknowledged that Marston was the first inventor, but he took credit for the police application. John Henry Wigmore, Dean of the Northwestern Law School and the leading expert on evidence, was skeptical of a technology that might replace juries but suggested that juries be permitted to form their own opinions of the blood pressure tracings – a notion that Marston rejected as he thought interpretation should be made only by trained and experienced experts. Eventually, Marston came to work for DC Comics, where he created the Wonder Woman comic-book action hero, who first appeared in 1941. Marston equipped her with her infallible lie detector, the "Golden Lasso of Truth."

BOX 13.3 *BAREFOOT V. ESTELLE* (1983) – QUESTIONABLE EXPERT TESTIMONY

The Supreme Court considered the expert testimony of two psychiatrists who would testify to the *future dangerousness* of defendants and their likelihood to pose a continued threat to society as required by a Texas death penalty statute. In this habeas corpus appeal, both psychiatrists called Barefoot a sociopath and claimed that his past behavior was a predictor of future behavior. The American Psychiatric Association submitted an amicus brief in support of the defendant, declaring that there is no scientific evidence to support such claims and no testimony could be given with any reasonable degree of certainty. Nevertheless, in a 6–3 decision, the Court refused to exclude the expert opinion of the psychiatrists and denied the stay of execution. The Court held that as a constitutional matter, Barefoot's claim raised the issue of the weight of the testimony, not its admissibility, and could have been challenged by other experts.

Federal Rules of Evidence

After a ten-year effort, Congress passed the Federal Rules of Evidence (FRE) in 1975 and has since been revised to govern the introduction of evidence in civil and criminal cases in federal trial courts. Most States adopted or revised their own rules in general conformance with the FRE.

The FRE codified the common law of evidence and made changes that were thought to make trials fairer. They eliminated ambushes and surprises so that the trial was more about substance and less about tactics. The drafters also overcame a historical mistrust of jurors and the limitations that had developed to keep them from receiving the evidence; they relaxed standards to liberally favor the admission of evidence and permit jurors to weigh the evidence. The rules make judges "gatekeepers" and give them broad discretion and duty to decide all preliminary questions, such as the admissibility of evidence and whether an expert is qualified. Unless prohibited by law, all relevant evidence is admissible, and irrelevant evidence is inadmissible. The judge may exclude relevant evidence if she finds the probative value of the evidence to be substantially outweighed by a danger of prejudice, confusion, misleading the jury, or duplicative of other evidence. Anyone is competent to be a witness in criminal cases, but state laws govern competency to testify in civil cases. Ordinary witnesses testify only to personal knowledge relevant to the case and their opinions about such knowledge. However, an expert has great latitude to express opinions where the testimony is in the expert's scope of expertise and relevant to the case. Attorneys are no longer limited to hypothetical questions when presenting their expert witnesses.

Nowhere in the federal rules can a requirement of general acceptance in the relevant community be found for the admissibility of scientific evidence. Judges could admit novel scientific evidence if it were found to be relevant and reliable, regardless of whether it has been generally accepted, although general acceptance may play a factor in the court's admissibility determination.

BOX 13.4 FEDERAL RULES OF EVIDENCE

- Rules 101–106, and 201, establish general provisions regarding rulings on evidence and judicial notice,
  - Rule 104(a) establishes the court as a "gatekeeper," requiring the court to determine the qualifications of witnesses and the admissibility of evidence Rules 301 and 302 establish presumptions in civil cases
- Rules 401–415 establish rules on the admissibility of relevant evidence
  - Rule 401 holds evidence is relevant if it has a tendency to make a fact more or less probable and is of consequence (material)
  - Rule 402 holds relevant evidence is admissible, irrelevant is not admissible
  - Rule 403 allows the judge to exclude evidence that is prejudicial, confusing, a waste of time, or for other reasons
- Rules 501–504 establish privileges, particularly on attorney-client and work product privileges
- Rules 601–615 establish rules on witnesses
  - Rule 601 holds anyone is competent to testify, except state law provides qualifications in civil cases
  - Rule 602 holds lay witnesses must have personal knowledge of the matter
- Rules 701–706 establish rules on opinion and expert testimony
  - Rule 701 holds lay witnesses may give an opinion if rationally based upon the witness's perception, helpful to explain the testimony, and not an area requiring expertise
  - Rule 702 allows a judge to permit a qualified expert witness to give an opinion on scientific, technical, or other specialized knowledge if based upon sufficient facts or data, the product of reliable principles and methods, and reliably applied

    - Rule 703 allows the expert to base an opinion on either personal knowledge or that they have been made aware of, and such bases need not be admissible
    - Rule 704 holds an expert may express an opinion that "embraces an ultimate issue," except the expert may not express an opinion about the mental state that constitutes an element of the crime charged or its defense
    - Rule 705 holds an expert may state an opinion without first testifying to the underlying facts or data but may be required to disclose them during cross-examination
    - Rule 706 allows the court to appoint an expert witness
- Rules 801–807 establish hearsay rules
- Rules 901–903 establish rules for authentication and identification of evidence
- Rules 1001–1008 establish rules for written documents, recordings, and photographs
- Rule 1101 establishes the applicability of the FRE.

BOX 13.5 RULE 702 – TESTIMONY BY EXPERT WITNESSES

A witness who is qualified as an expert by knowledge, skill, experience, training, or education may testify in the form of an opinion or otherwise if the proponent demonstrates to the court that it is more likely than not that:

a. the expert's scientific, technical, or other specialized knowledge will help the
   the trier of fact to understand the evidence or to determine a fact in issue;
b. the testimony is based on sufficient facts or data;
c. the testimony is the product of reliable principles and methods; and
d. the expert's opinion reflects a reliable application of the principles and methods to the facts of the case.

Daubert Standard for Admission of Scientific Evidence

The U.S. Supreme Court directly addressed whether or not the FRE incorporated or superseded the *Frye* rule in the 1993 case *Daubert v. Merrell Dow Pharmaceuticals, Inc.* [The plaintiffs pronounced their name as *Dow-Burt* rather than use the French pronunciation *Dough Bear*]. The case involved the use of Bendectin as a morning sickness pill that allegedly caused limb reduction birth defects. The scientific foundation of the allegation was questionable. The case held that the adoption of the FRE (particularly FRE Rule 702) superseded *Frye* and that "general acceptance" is not a necessary finding for the admissibility of scientific evidence. Justice Blackmun wrote for the Court, "a rigid 'general acceptance' requirement would be at odds with the 'liberal thrust' of the Federal Rules that were intended to relax traditional barriers to 'opinion' testimony." The liberal thrust of the FRE favors admissibility but also undermines the judge's gatekeeping role.

The Court stated that "The subject of an expert's testimony must be 'scientific ... knowledge.' The adjective 'scientific' implies a grounding in the methods and procedures of science. Similarly, the word 'knowledge' connotes more than subjective belief or unsupported speculation." The Court further stated, "there are important differences between the quest for truth in the courtroom and the quest for truth in the laboratory." In Footnote 9, the Court declared "In a case involving scientific evidence, *evidentiary reliability* will be based upon *scientific validity*."

Justice Blackmun set forth a set of four or five factors (depending upon how you count them), which he meant as suggested guidance for trial judges, as gatekeepers, to use in determining whether the scientific evidence is reliable and, therefore, should be admitted:

1. whether the expert's technique or theory can be or has been tested – that is, whether the expert's theory can be challenged in some objective sense;
2. whether the technique or theory has been subject to peer review and publication;
3. the known or potential rate of error of the technique or theory when applied;
4. the existence and maintenance of standards controlling the technique's operation; and
5. whether the technique or theory has been generally accepted in the scientific community.

The Court emphasized that these factors were neither exclusive nor dispositive and stated: "The inquiry envisioned by Rule 702 is, we emphasize, a flexible one."

The Court noted the two underlying concerns of the parties and the amici. The first concern was an "apprehension that abandonment of 'general acceptance' as the exclusive requirement for admission will result in a 'free-for-all' in which befuddled juries are confounded by absurd and irrational pseudoscientific assertions." The Court responded that the concern:

> seems to us to be overly pessimistic about the capabilities of the jury and of the adversary system generally. Vigorous cross-examination, presentation of contrary evidence, and careful instruction on the burden of proof are the traditional and appropriate means of attacking shaky but admissible evidence.

The second concern was "that recognition of a screening role for the judge that allows for the exclusion of 'invalid' evidence will sanction a stifling and repressive scientific orthodoxy, and will be inimical to the search for truth." The Court responded:

> We recognize that, in practice, a gatekeeping role for the judge, no matter how flexible, inevitably on occasion will prevent the jury from learning of authentic insights and innovations. That, nevertheless, is the balance that is struck by Rules of Evidence designed not for the exhaustive search for cosmic understanding but for the particularized resolution of legal disputes.

In his dissent, Chief Justice Rehnquist expressed concern that the new standard made trial judges "amateur scientists."

Daubert was not a new approach in federal court; it is consistent with the FRE approach that evidence must be relevant and probative and outweigh its potential prejudicial impact. Scientific methods that are sufficiently well established may still be subject to judicial notice – even under Daubert/FRE 702.

The theory of the FRE and Daubert is that it is helpful to have a screen or filter of scientific evidence to be considered by the jury. This presumes that the juries cannot always adequately weigh the scientific evidence. Although both judges and juries have difficulty assessing scientific testimony, the insertion of judicial scrutiny improves performance because of (1) the structured reasoning process in a Daubert inquiry, (2) judges repeat their decision-making task, often with feedback, and (3) judges are accountable to higher courts.

BOX 13.6 *DAUBERT V. MERRELL DOW PHARMACEUTICALS, INC.* (1993) – SCIENTIFIC EVIDENCE

Jason Daubert and Eric Schuller were born with severe birth defects after their mothers had used Bendectin for morning sickness during their pregnancies. The two minor children and their parents brought a product liability suit against the drug manufacturer. The United States Health and Human Services news (No. P80-45, Oct. 7, 1980) reported that every published study had concluded that Bendectin was not a human teratogen. The plaintiffs' eight experts did not deny this but concluded that Bendectin can cause birth defects based on animal studies, studies of similar chemicals, and "reanalysis" of previously published epidemiological studies. The trial court granted the respondent's summary judgment because the plaintiffs' evidence did not meet the applicable "general acceptance" standard, and the appellate court affirmed – they were particularly skeptical that the evidence had been generated for trial. The U.S. Supreme Court held that the FRE superseded prior caselaw in federal trials. The Court declared that the trial judge is the "gatekeeper" of the evidence to be admitted. The judge must find that the proffered evidence is relevant and reliable to admit the scientific evidence to the jury. The Court suggested that among the factors for consideration in determining scientific validity, judges can look to:

1. whether the scientific theory is testable (falsifiable)
2. whether there is peer-reviewed literature supporting the claim
3. whether there is a known error rate of the scientific test or whether controlling standards exist
4. whether the scientific testing has been generally accepted within the field

The case was remanded for further consideration. On remand back to the Ninth Circuit Court of Appeals, Judge Kozinski confirmed the District Court's grant of summary judgment to the defendants and dismissed the plaintiff's case:

> Plaintiffs do not attempt to show causation directly, instead they rely on experts who present circumstantial proof of causation... California tort law requires plaintiffs to show not merely that Bendectin increased the likelihood of injury, but that it more likely than not caused their injuries... the strongest inference to be drawn for plaintiffs based on the epidemiological evidence is that Bendectin could possibly have caused plaintiffs' injuries.

BOX 13.7 NOTES ON DAUBERT

Daubert was only one, the most famous, of many *toxic tort* lawsuits that were led by celebrity plaintiff's attorney Melvin Belli, the "King of Torts."

The star witness for the case against Bendectin, William McBride, was a controversial Sydney obstetrician who had revealed the dangers of thalidomide in pregnant women.

He claimed other drugs, particularly morning sickness drugs, caused birth defects. Dr. McBride was discredited in the 1990s when he was found guilty of falsifying research on the teratogenic effects of drugs and was struck off the medical register in Australia.

Since 1956, "Bendectin" (Doxylamine/Pyridoxine) was widely used as the only effective drug for morning sickness (nausea and vomiting of pregnancy) until 1983 when production for the U.S. market was discontinued in the face of lawsuits alleging that the drug caused congenital malformations – despite use by millions of women, scientific literature indicating it was safe, and the Food and Drug Administration (FDA) continued approval of its use in pregnant women.

The removal of Bendectin from the United States market had several consequences:

- it left pregnant women without a safe medication that could be used for alleviating morning sickness, which in its most severe form (hyperemesis gravidarum) could be life-threatening and cause women to terminate their pregnancy

- it resulted in an immediate increase in the rates of hospitalization for pregnancy-related nausea and vomiting
- it resulted in the use of other less-studied drugs in pregnancy
- it caused drug companies to avoid developing medications for pregnant patients; only a few medicines have been approved by the FDA for obstetrical indications in the past several decades

In 2013, Bendectin, renamed Diclegis, won FDA approval in the United States as the first morning sickness drug in 30 years. It is also now marketed as Bonjesta. Recent research has revealed that the nausea and vomiting of the first trimester of pregnancy are primarily caused by a single hormone, Growth Differentiation Factor 15, which could lead to more targeted treatment.

Daubert Trilogy

The U.S. Supreme Court heard two further cases on the admissibility of scientific evidence within a few years, and together, they are known as the *Daubert* trilogy. In *General Electric Co. v. Joiner* (1997), the Court held that the proper standard for appellate review of trial court judges' gatekeeping decisions is abuse of discretion. In *Kumho Tire Co. v. Carmichael* (1999), the Court held that *Daubert* applies to all experts, including non-scientists, who testify to technical or other specialized knowledge – including experience. The Daubert factors, considering "the particular circumstances of the particular case at issue," are used in assessing the reliability of non-scientific expert testimony,

These two cases provided further clarity on the *Daubert* decision. For instance, in *Kumho,* Justice Scalia declared that courts have "discretion to choose among reasonable means of excluding expertise that is fausse and science that is junky." He re-emphasized that the *Daubert* factors are not a "definitive checklist" and that the inquiry is flexible. *Joiner* made clear that the trial court can examine the reliability of the expert's reasoning process: "Conclusions and methodology are not entirely distinct from one another… A court may conclude that there is simply too great an analytical gap between the data and the opinion proffered."

BOX 13.8 *GENERAL ELECTRIC CO. V. JOINER* (1997) – GATEKEEPING

Joiner was an electrician who worked around transformers for ten years. Although he had been a smoker for eight years, he sued his employer, GE, when he developed small cell cancer of the lung, claiming that his exposure to toxic PCBs from the dielectric fluids of the transformers promoted his cancer. GE contended that there was no evidence that Joiner had significant exposure to PCBs nor any reliable proof that PCBs caused cancer. GE removed the case to federal court and filed for summary judgment. The District Court agreed with GE and dismissed the case, but the Court of Appeals reversed. The U.S. Supreme Court held that abuse-of-discretion is the proper standard of review for determining whether expert testimony should be admitted. The Court reversed the Court of Appeals and reinstated the District Court's grant of summary judgment.

BOX 13.9 *KUMHO TIRE CO., LTD. V. CARMICHAEL* (1999) – OTHER SPECIALIZED KNOWLEDGE

Patrick Carmichael was driving his minivan when the right rear tire blew out, resulting in the death of one passenger and severe injuries to others. Carmichael sued the tire manufacturer, claiming that a manufacturing defect in the tire caused the accident. Carmichael's case rested on the testimony of a tire failure expert, who made certain observations about the tire. The manufacturer vigorously disputed the expert and moved to exclude his testimony. The District Court found the tire expert's methods unscientific and granted the motion to exclude his testimony, but the Circuit Court reversed, reasoning that *Daubert* did not apply to skill or experience-based observations. The U.S. Supreme Court held that *Daubert* applied to all experts, including experience-based witnesses, and the District Court properly performed its gatekeeping function. The Court noted that FRE Rule 702 makes no distinction between "scientific," "technical," or "other specialized knowledge." The Court stated that the distinction was not always clear, nor was there a need to draw a distinction. The expert had worked for Michelin for ten years, and his experience as a tire engineer was not a concern. Visual inspection of tires was considered a generally reliable method of determining a defect in the tire. However, the District Court found the expert's conclusion, that the defect caused the tire to explode because he did not see evidence of other causes, was problematic. The Court declared, "Nothing in either *Daubert* or the Federal Rules of Evidence requires a district court to admit opinion evidence that is connected to existing data only by the *ipse dixit* of the expert [by the statement of the expert himself]." In light of this concern, the district court acted within its discretion to exclude the proffered evidence.

Daubert Aftermath

Most states have adopted the Daubert standard, although some retain the *Frye* standard with additional requirements. (CA, IL, MN, NJ, NY, PA, WA), and a few have their own unique standard (NV, ND, VA). The District of Columbia, where the *Frye* rule originated, has itself converted to *Daubert*. Canada took note of the American jurisprudence and adopted the *Daubert* standard.

Federal Rule of Evidence 702 was amended in response to *Daubert* and the subsequent cases considering it. No attempt was made to "codify" the *Daubert* factors; instead, the rule was written sufficiently broad to permit consideration of any or all of the specific *Daubert* factors as appropriate. The amendment confirms the trial court's role as gatekeeper and provides guidance to assess the reliability and helpfulness of proffered expert testimony. Consistent with *Kumho*, the amended Rule applies to all types of expert testimony.

Judge Kozinski, when faced with the remand of the Daubert case from the Supreme Court (*Daubert v. Merrell Dow Pharmaceuticals, Inc.*, 9th Cir. 1995), declared that the judiciary faced a brave new world and stated:

> Federal judges ruling on the admissibility of expert scientific testimony face a far more complex and daunting task in a post-Daubert world than before. The judge's task under Frye is relatively simple: to determine whether the method employed by the experts is generally accepted in the scientific community. Under Daubert, we must engage in a difficult, two-part analysis. First, we must determine nothing less than whether the experts' testimony reflects "scientific knowledge," whether their findings are "derived by the scientific method," and whether their work product amounts to "good science." Second, we must ensure that the proposed expert testimony is "relevant to the task at hand," that it logically advances a material aspect of the proposing party's case. The Supreme Court referred to this second prong of the analysis as the "fit" requirement.

In truth, there has not been a dramatic shift in the admissibility of scientific evidence in the quarter century since the *Daubert* decision, as some had predicted. Judges who wanted to scrutinize scientific evidence had the power to screen the proffered scientific evidence both pre- and post-*Daubert*. *Daubert* has caused a change in the rhetoric. Perhaps it has affected civil practice more than criminal practice. Some commentators have declared that the discretion and flexibility granted to trial judges have led to erratic and contradictory holdings.

Daubert theoretically broadens the admissibility standard to allow for authentic scientific breakthroughs and cutting-edge technology. *Daubert* also theoretically narrows the admissibility standard by granting trial judges more leeway to exclude junk science. Many courts still tend to focus on expert qualifications rather than the underlying science. There has been some increase in the admission of scientific evidence in civil and criminal cases, but this may have occurred anyway. There also appears to be some increased scrutiny, but the rejection of expert testimony is still the exception rather than the rule.

Trial judges must find that proffered expert testimony is properly grounded, well-reasoned, and not speculative before allowing the testimony. The trial judge is primarily responsible for ensuring that the jury is properly influenced by reliable and relevant testimony and not by impressive credentials or persuasive but unfounded arguments. The focus of the trial judge should be on the principles and methodology, not on the conclusions, although they are not always distinct from each other. Ultimately, the key objective for the judge may be to weigh the harm of erring in favor of admission versus exclusion.

Many judges have been quick to admit the evidence and let the jury sort it out or of a mind to assert their responsibility to filter out the weak evidence. They rely on scrutiny by adversarial cross-examination and presentation of contrary evidence. Committee notes to the updated FRE 702 declare that

> many courts have held that the critical questions of the sufficiency of an expert's basis, and the application of the expert's methodology, are questions of weight and not admissibility. These rulings are an incorrect application of Rules 702 and 104(a).

In applying the *Daubert* standard, courts often use the *Daubert* factors as a checklist, requiring that all four/five factors be met instead of using them as suggested guidance as intended. In some cases, courts have found other factors than those articulated by Justice Blackmun that are relevant in determining admissibility. In *In re Paoli R.R. Yard PCB Litigation* (1994), the court noted that attorneys proffering experts

> do not have to demonstrate to the judge by a preponderance of the evidence that the assessments of their experts are correct, they only have to demonstrate by a preponderance of evidence that their opinions are reliable.... The evidentiary requirement of reliability is lower than the merits standard of correctness.

Judge Kozinski, in the Daubert case on remand, stated that experts might be permitted to testify if their methods comported with "a recognized minority of scientists in their field." In *Ruiz-Troche v. Pepsi Cola of Puerto Rico* (1998), the court stated,

> Daubert neither requires nor empowers trial courts to determine which of several competing scientific theories has the best provenance. It demands only that the proponent of the evidence show that the expert's conclusion has been arrived at in a scientifically sound and methodologically reliable fashion.

Despite the great latitude given to the trial judge, failing to determine reliability may be a prejudicial error requiring a new trial (*U.S. v. Velarde*, 2000). However, judges need not determine reliability if there is no objection (*U.S. v. Andrews*, E.D. Mich. 2024).

Pretrial *Daubert* hearings to determine admissibility are more frequent in civil than criminal cases. Under *Frye*, admissibility is settled once general acceptance is found, and hearings in further cases are unnecessary. Under

Daubert, the courts can take notice of the reliability of a scientific technique; however, hearings can recur in the same jurisdiction to ensure that the science is still reliable and properly applied in the case.

PCAST

The 2016 President's Council of Advisors on Science and Technology (PCAST) report entitled *Forensic Science in Criminal Courts: Ensuring Scientific Validity of Feature-Comparison Methods* (discussed above) made a series of recommendations, including that judges should admit scientific evidence only if it has been validated in ways that they suggested. They wrote:

> Rule 702 (c,d) of the Federal Rules of Evidence requires that (1) expert testimony must be the product of "reliable principles and methods" and (2) experts must have "reliably applied" the methods to the facts of the case. The Supreme Court has stated that judges must determine "whether the reasoning or methodology underlying the testimony is scientifically valid".

Nonetheless, the report has had little apparent effect on criminal cases in court. Sparked by the PCAST report, the Judicial Conference Advisory Committee on Evidence Rules held a forensic science symposium in 2017 to discuss whether the FRE should be modified in response to the PCAST report but had declined to do so. Although a rule specific to forensic science was not adopted, FRE 702 was minimally amended in 2023.

Summary

Courts want only relevant and reliable scientific evidence to be admitted into evidence for the jury to consider. Still, they struggle with applying the most up-to-date and reliable science. Under the Frye standard, the scientific community determines what science is reliable, but the legal community attempts to determine it under the newer Daubert standard.

Forensic scientists may be required to appear at a pretrial hearing to determine whether their forensic science is reliable and whether they will be allowed to testify at trial.

Terms

Admissible – referring to alleged facts or evidence that have been allowed by the judge to be assessed by the factfinder and made part of the court record in the case.

Daubert Factors – a set of suggestions articulated by the Court in *Daubert* that trial judges may use to determine the reliability of scientific evidence.

Daubert Standard – a flexible determination by the trial court for the admissibility of scientific evidence based on its relevancy and reliability.

Frye Rule – the general acceptance standard articulated by the Court in *Frye v. U.S.* to determine the admissibility of novel scientific evidence.

Relevant (in a legal sense) – information that aids the trier of fact and pertains directly to the case at hand, aligning with the specific inquiry being considered.

Reliable (in a legal sense) – evidence that the trial judge deems scientifically valid and appropriate for the jury to consider.

Cases

Barefoot v. Estelle, 463 U.S. 880 (1983)

Daubert v. Merrell Dow Pharmaceuticals, Inc., 509 U.S. 579 (1993)

Daubert v. Merrell Dow Pharmaceuticals, Inc., 43 F.3d 1311 (9th Cir. 1995)

Frye v. United States, 293 F. 1013 (D.C. Cir. 1923)

General Electric Co. v. Joiner, 522 U.S. 136 (1997)

In re Paoli R.R. Yard PCB Litigation, 35 F.3d 717 (3d Cir. 1994)

Kumho Tire Co., Ltd. v. Carmichael, 526 U.S. 137 (1999)

Ruiz-Troche v. Pepsi Cola of Puerto Rico, 161 F.3d 77 (1st Cir. 1998)

United States v. Andrews, Criminal Case No. 08–20652 (E.D. Mich. 2024)

United States v. Velarde, 214 F.3d 1204 (10th Cir. 2000)

Other Authorities

Ensuring Scientific Validity of Feature-Comparison Methods, President's Council of Advisors on Science and Technology, Sep 2016; HYPERLINK "https://nam02.safelinks.protection.outlook.com/?url=https%3A%2F%2Fobamawhitehouse.archives.gov%2Fsites%2Fdefault%2Ffiles%2Fmicrosites%2Fostp%2FPCAST%2Fpcast_forensic_science_report_final.pdf&data=05%7C02%7Cnandhineesekarsekar%40codemantra.com%7Cf42cf5f5ce15446f907f08ddbe52c4d5%7C5489968a40664cbdb7d64a81c75a4a93%7C0%7C0%7C638875985033907693%7CUnknown%7CTWFpbGZsb3d8eyJFbXB0eU1hcGkiOnRydWUsIlYiOiIwLjAuMDAwMCIsIlAiOiJXaW4zMiIsIkFOIjoiTWFpbCIsIldUIjoyfQ%3D%3D%7C0%7C%7C%7C&sdata=XvLM9vyoKuaB49xOoUgc1vi%2BZP6rQGyGKHDHFLL8buQ%3D&reserved=0"https://obamawhitehouse.archives.gov/sites/default/files/microsites/ostp/PCAST/pcast_forensic_science_report_final.pdf.

Authority for the Promulgation of Rules, 28 U.S.C. §§ 2072-2075 (1975)

Federal Rules of Evidence (FRE), U.S. Code Title 28, available at: HYPERLINK "https://nam02.safelinks.protection.outlook.com/?url=https%3A%2F%2Fwww.law.cornell.edu%2Frules%2Ffre&data=05%7C02%7Cnandhineesekarsekar%40codemantra.com%7Cf42cf5f5ce

15446f907f08ddbe52c4d5%7C5489968a40664cbdb7d64a81c75a4a93%7C0%7C0%7C638875985033951473%7CUnknown%7CTWFpbGZsb3d8eyJFbXB0eU1hcGkiOnRydWUsIlYiOiIwLjAuMDAwMCIsIlAiOiJXaW4zMiIsIkFOIjoiTWFpbCIsIldUIjoyfQ%3D%3D%7C0%7C%7C%7C&sdata=JXIaWrs5Znj%2F6MFMPvR%2F3uyT2MrNmmUihyKdwf3mkBU%3D&reserved=0"https://www.law.cornell.edu/rules/fre.

Federal Rule of Evidence (FRE) Rule 702, Testimony by Expert Witnesses.

Thought Questions

1. How do judges, often with little knowledge of science, assess scientific evidence?
2. Did the U.S. Supreme Court decide *Daubert* correctly?
3. Are scientific validity and reliability best determined by lawyers or scientists?
4. Are courts well suited to evaluate science?
5. Should experience be judged the same as scientific evidence?

Further Reading

Beecher-Monas E, *Evaluating Scientific Evidence: An Interdisciplinary Framework for Intellectual Due Process,* Cambridge Press, Cambridge, MA, 2007.

Foster KR, Huber PW, *Judging Science: Scientific Knowledge and the Federal Courts,* Cambridge, MA, 1999.

Moenssens A, DesPortes D, Kennedy R, *Scientific Evidence in Civil and Criminal Cases,* 8th ed, West Academic Publishing, St Paul, Minnesota, 2021.

Chapter 14

Scientific Evidence III

Weight

Learning Objectives

After reading this chapter, students are expected to be able to:

- explain the weight to be accorded scientific evidence
- describe how an expert might prove that a scientific method is reliable
- describe the NAS report on forensic science and its impact on the forensic science community
- describe the PCAST report on forensic science and its impact on the forensic science community

Introduction

Once scientific evidence is admitted into evidence, it will be weighed by the *trier of fact*, whether a judge or jury, as all other evidence in their deliberations to determine a verdict whether by a *preponderance of the evidence* in a civil trial or *beyond a reasonable doubt* in a criminal trial.

Historical Background

Most criminal convictions are based on confessions or eyewitnesses and occasionally by circumstantial proof – as they always have been, but now forensic

DOI: 10.4324/9780429272455-14

evidence has become another essential basis for convictions. This has been a relatively recent development, and criminal jurisprudence continues to try to adapt to this change. Although forensic medicine and toxicology are much older, most forensic sciences are dated to the turn of the 20th century. Criminalistics dates to 1893 when Hans Gustav Adolf Gross (Groß) published his *Handbuch für Untersuchungsrichter als System der Kriminalistik*. Edmond Locard (1877–1966) established the first crime lab in Lyon, France in 1910. In the first half of the 20th century, we witnessed the development of a forensic science workforce followed by the establishment of forensic professional organizations.

Fingerprints, crime scene photography, and trace evidence were the main tools of forensic scientists from the earliest days. The comparison microscope was introduced in 1927. Gas chromatography and gas chromatography-mass spectrometry became widespread in the 1970s. Forensic DNA typing entered casework in the 1990s. However, the true power of these forensic technologies is when they are coupled with electronic databases. The FBI's original automated fingerprint identification system (AFIS) was launched in 1974, the FBI's National DNA Index System (NDIS) in 1998, and the Bureau of Alcohols, Tobacco, Firearms, and Explosives' (ATF's) National Integrated Ballistics Information Network (NIBIN) in 1999.

Standards setting began in the last quarter of the 20th century and continues today. The Technical Working Group on DNA Analysis Methods (TWGDAM, later SWGDAM) was established in 1988, and various scientific working groups (SWGs) were created after that. The National Institute of Standards and Technology (NIST) replaced the management of the SWGs and established the Organization of Scientific Area Committees (OSAC) in 2014. Technically, the OSAC does not set standards but facilitates their creation and posts a Registry of OSAC-approved standards. Standards development organizations (SDOs), i.e., the American Academy of Forensic Sciences (AAFS) Academy Standards Board (ASB), the ASTM International formerly known as the American Society for Testing and Materials (ASTM), the National Fire Protection Association (NFPA), and the American Dental Association (ADA), promulgate standards, which the OSAC may decide to place on their Registry. The 2018 ASTM E2329-17, Standard Practice for Identification of Seized Drugs, was the first standard approved and placed on the OSAC Registry. At the time of this writing, there are 233 standards on the OSAC Registry of Approved Standards.

Proving Reliability

Courts and scientists are both truth finders, but the truth is an aspirational goal for each. The truths sought, and the process to find them are very different. A corollary of this is that the words the courts and scientists use in common may have somewhat different meanings and nuances.

When a party proffers an expert to testify, the party must prove to the trial judge by a preponderance of evidence that the proffered scientific testimony is *relevant* and *reliable*. The attorney proffering the expert must lay a foundation for the expert to be qualified as competent to testify as an expert. Beyond determining competency, trial judges, as gatekeepers, must exclude unreliable and irrelevant evidence. The trial judge's task is not to analyze what the experts say but their basis for saying it. The trial judge should be particularly skeptical when the research was conducted for the litigation.

As construed by the courts, the legal meaning of reliability conflates credibility, trustworthiness, robustness, precision, accuracy, and validity. Justice Blackmun, writing in *Daubert*, quoted law professor James Starrs; "the difference between accuracy, validity, and reliability may be such that each is distinct from the other by no more than a hen's kick," and then declared, "In a case involving scientific evidence, evidentiary reliability will be based upon scientific validity." To a scientist, *validity* might be defined as: "The degree to which the tests accomplish the purposes for which they are being used" and is akin to notions of accuracy (the degree to which a test consistently yields the correct result). To a scientist, *reliability* might be defined as: "The measure of how stable and consistent a test is in measuring the same thing each time" and is akin to notions of *reproducibility* (the ability to replicate the finding), *precision* (the degree to which the test consistently reproduces a result), and *robustness* (reproducibility in varying conditions).

FRE Rule 702(c) refers to reliable principles. Reliable principles are concepts generally accepted within the relevant scientific field based on robust research and evidence. Scientific principles must be well-established and supported by research vetted by the scientific community through peer review and publication, with further validation through independent studies that confirm or refute the theory in real-world applications, effectively transitioning from basic science to applied science.

FRE Rule 702(c) also refers to reliable methods. Scientific methods are often used as research becomes applied to real-world problems in a transition or adoption phase. Early adopters perform validation studies. It may be that a manufacturer has validation studies to share with the community. Every laboratory must conduct its own internal validation studies before it uses a new test in casework. Validation studies may consist of multiple independent components, such as sensitivity, precision, and linearity. Reference standards may be used as gold standards to assess accuracy.

FRE Rule 702(d) refers to the reliable application of the principles and methods to the facts of the case. When performing scientific laboratory tests, positive and negative controls help to validate the particular test performance. This is part of the quality control procedures that lend validity at a broader level. From a higher perspective, quality assurance involves administrative oversight, properly maintained equipment, and documentation of procedures, among other things. Personnel should have appropriate education and training and undergo competency assessment. The personnel should be kept current through continuing education, attending meetings, and performing proficiency testing to document their ability to perform the testing or examination properly. Ethics and professional responsibility training and pledges have their role in maintaining a proper work ethic. The certification of forensic scientists and accreditation of the laboratories act as independent verification that proper measures are being taken.

Forensic science testing has evolved over the years, is conducted generally the same way in all countries, and continues to undergo court challenges routinely. So, experience is one method of establishing reliability. Scientific studies, validation testing, and black-box studies can establish reliability. Standards in the field suggest consensus on how to test or examine evidence. Board certification and proficiency testing document an analyst's capability to perform the testing reliably. Accreditation can document that procedures were followed. Reliability has many facets and can be established in various ways.

Pattern-Matching Examinations

Many forensic disciplines involve visual descriptions and pattern comparisons, such as friction ridge prints, documents, footwear impressions, firearms, tool marks examinations, and the much-criticized bitemark and microscopic hair comparisons. Critics have complained that these are subjective determinations that arose in police departments and not from the basic sciences. One may ask if such constitutes a "scientific" analysis worthy of inclusion among the forensic sciences. However, much like radiologists, forensic examiners specifically apply scientific understandings and a systematic approach and focus on key characteristics that set them apart from mere layman. Studies have revealed that such examiners consistently outperform those without education and training. Many examiners with innate abilities are drawn into the field, but skills are also acquired with experience.

Often, these disciplines apply the "ACE-V" (analysis, comparison, evaluation, verification) method or approach that involves an initial assessment of the adequacy of the questioned specimen to form an opinion and concludes with a verification that might be blinded.

Examiners examine the class characteristics and *minutiae* or *randomly acquired characteristics* (RACs) of questioned items. The quantity and quality of information impact the ability of examiners to perform their examinations. Prints and impressions may be altered by deformation and distortion. Mental factors, such as sleep, emotions, and drugs, may also affect the examinations. Studies have also shown a susceptibility to cognitive bias. However, it should be noted that examiners are more likely not to draw a conclusion or to conclude a non-match than an erroneous match.

As pointed out in the PCAST report, error rates will be a focus of scrutiny in court.

Laboratory Test Validation

Validation studies should be performed on all forensic scientific tests to show that they yield the expected results. The underlying scientific concepts should be confirmed with empirical data. Developmental validation documents early test development, often involving each step of the test – such as sample preparation. Validation studies may include studies on accuracy and precision but also on specificity, sensitivity, linearity, stability, mixtures, and conditions that might affect the results. Furthermore, studies of robustness involving "real world-like" specimens exposed to varying environmental conditions are also important. However, it is impossible to anticipate all future challenges, and common sense applies here. The scientific literature should contain published and peer-reviewed studies of tests that can provide a form of scientific validation.

Laboratories should perform internal validation studies of their own in-house standard operating protocols (SOPs) and procedures. These studies are expensive to conduct, vary in rigor, and are often less extensive than developmental validation studies. They aim to document that the laboratory can reliably obtain similar results. These validation studies are usually discoverable by litigants, and laboratories should be ready to defend their studies.

Laboratories may adopt the procedures and protocols of others but should not make internal validation unnecessary. Usual and customary practice, which infers experience with and acceptance of the test, can be a basis for reliability, but there should be some concern that the same mistake is not being blindly repeated.

The legal community considers validation studies conducted specifically for courtroom presentations suspect due to the possibility of bias.

Standards

Standards should state a base level of operation to perform the function required. Best practices are normative statements of optimal practice and constitute guidelines. Community consensus standards have the community's buy-in and represent a community statement of appropriate practice. Standards are generally thought to be enforceable, and a "voluntary standard" is considered by some to be an oxymoron. Courts may recognize the use of such voluntary consensus standards as evidence of reliability and, as such, be considered as *de facto* or *ad hoc* standards. If a laboratory fails to use or deviate from such standards, they may be called to justify why this is so.

Voluntary community consensus standards exist for most forensic science areas, including common terminology, methods, reporting, and educational and training requirements. These are established through SDOs. Globally, the International Organization for Standardization (ISO) is dominant. For the forensic sciences, these include the AAFS Academy Standards Board (ASB), the ASTM E30 Committee, the NFPA, and the ADA.

Voluntary consensus standards set by U.S. SDOs will conform to the ANSI (American National Standards Institute) Essential Requirements that articulate due process requirements, including openness and balance of interest in the standards-setting process. The U.S. federal government favors voluntary consensus standards and demands that federal agencies adopt voluntary consensus standards wherever possible. This direction is set forth in the National Technology Transfer and Advancement Act of 1995 (NTTAA) and OMB Circular A-119 as the NIST Guidance on Federal Conformity Assessment Activities (15 CFR Part 287).

The NIST has maintained the OSAC to facilitate the promulgation and adoption of community protocols and procedures by SDOs. The U.S. federal government has the resources to bring experts together, which the SDOs generally do not. OSAC (and its SWG predecessors) have, in fact, greatly facilitated standards setting in the forensic field. OSAC maintains a *Registry of OSAC-Approved Standards*, which they intend to be the go-to resource for forensic standards. NIST also makes available resources to facilitate implementation.

These voluntary standards can become *de facto* standards through acceptance in a community as usual and customary practice. Legislation can require the standards to be followed, and a few states have done so. Office/agency policy can require compliance with standards. Accrediting bodies can require compliance with the standards. Of course, defense attorneys can ask if the testing or examination met the standards and why not if they are not followed. The legal community is becoming increasingly aware of these consensus standards.

Personnel Qualifications

Education and Training

Forensic science positions now universally require a solid forensic science or primary science education to enter the workforce. Education provides forensic scientists with background knowledge and an understanding of their work. Training provides them with specific skills to do their jobs. Experience imparts tacit knowledge that provides personal insights and unspoken knowledge beyond the explicit knowledge gained from formal means. Together these impart the specialized knowledge, beyond the ken of the lay public, that allows them to testify as experts in their field.

Competency Testing

After forensic scientists have undergone their initial on-the-job training tailored to the specific laboratory and before they start casework, they must successfully pass a *competency assessment* administered by the laboratory where they work. This may be followed by a probationary period of employment while performance at the bench and in court is overseen.

Proficiency Testing

Proficiency testing monitors performance through the periodic demonstration that a laboratory or individual can continue to obtain correct results. This is necessary because people grow older and fall out of practice, and methods and instrumentation change. It also allows inter- and intralaboratory performance comparisons. ISO-recognized proficiency testing programs implement International Laboratory Accreditation Cooperation (ILAC) P-9. Proficiency testing should not be used to measure error rates, as the errors may not be recurrent because corrective action should be taken after each discrepancy; also, many laboratories do not conduct the usual quality assurance checks on proficiency tests as they do in casework. Proficiency testing can be mandated by offices, state forensic science commissions, legislation, or certification or accreditation requirements. Larger laboratories have been able to institute blind proficiency testing, but most laboratories cannot feasibly institute blind proficiency testing and use open proficiency tests. Numerous proficiency test providers in the forensic sciences offer an array of proficiency kits for most forensic science disciplines and areas.

Existing proficiency testing programs have been criticized as not sufficiently difficult and real world-like, but such criticism misses the point. Most proficiency testing is done for regulatory purposes, and it should be expected that if a forensic scientist knows their job, they should be able to achieve a successful result in a straightforward case. Difficult cases are valuable as educational challenges but inappropriate for regulatory purposes. Difficult proficiency tests will result in some participants failing, losing their certification, and placing their laboratories at risk of losing accreditation.

Certification

Certification is a method of independent verification by a certifying body that an individual possesses the knowledge, skills, and abilities (KSA) for a job. Certification bodies in the forensic community are accredited by the Forensic Specialties Accreditation Board (FSAB) and other conformity assessment bodies, such as the ANSI, using ISO/IEC 17024 standards.

Certifying bodies in the forensic community include the American Board of Criminalistics (ABC), the Board of Forensic Documents Examiners (BFDE), the American Board of Forensic Documents Examiners (ABFDE), the American Board of Forensic Toxicology (ABFT), the American Board of Pathology (ABP), the American Board of Medicolegal Death Investigation (ABMDI), the American Board of Forensic Odontologists (ABFO), the American Board of Forensic Anthropology (ABFA), the American Board of Forensic Entomologists (ABFE), the Association of Firearms and Toolmarks Examiners (AFTE), the International Association for Identification (IAI), and the International Association of Forensic Nurse Examiners (IAFN).

Numerous authorities have long urged universal certification of forensic science personnel. Board certification by the ABP has become nearly universal for forensic pathologists, and the ABMDI is common among medicolegal death investigators. Certification in other disciplines is varied and becoming more common. Some laboratories have mandated certification, as have some state forensic science commissions and a few state legislatures. Many in the digital evidence community and some in other forensic specialties have contended that examiner certification should be sufficient without laboratory accreditation. Certification demonstrates that an individual can perform the examination or testing but does not guarantee that proper procedures were performed. Thus, certification is akin to saying, "Trust me." However, laboratory accreditation requires a demonstration that proper procedures are performed.

Ethical Codes

As responsible professionals, forensic scientists should exhibit the utmost honesty and integrity regardless of ethical codes. It can be argued that as participants in the criminal justice system, forensic scientists should adhere to a higher standard and moral compass than the general public. All forensic science professional associations, i.e., AAFS, American Society of Crime Laboratory Directors, AFTE and the ANSI National Accreditation Board (ANAB) – the most prolific laboratory accreditation program – have ethical codes that apply to their members and laboratories. These codes vary by organization, particularly to what extent they are specific to the association activities, to laboratory activity or broadly apply to working in the profession. The organizations vary in how effectively they police their members and enforce their codes. The AAFS has a defined procedure that provides due process for the subject of an ethics complaint and has expelled members.

In general, sanctions for ethical code violations are rare and generally occur over egregious violations.

In 2016, the National Commission on Forensic Science articulated a *National Code of Professional Responsibility for Forensic Science and Forensic Medicine Service Providers*, which the DOJ adopted with minor changes. It called for disclosing "all nonconformities or breaches of law or professional standards that adversely affect a previously issued report or testimony." Although the code does not apply to non-DOJ forensic scientists, it remains a statement of ethical behavior norms for the entire forensic science community.

The Bureau of Justice Statistics 2020 census of publicly funded crime laboratories found that 94% have a written code of ethics.

Professionalism and Culture

A professional attitude and culture are also important and overlap with ethical conduct. Forensic scientists should view themselves as professionals whose role is crucial to the criminal justice system. Instances of misconduct, often highly publicized, demonstrate the dangers of allowing personal issues to compromise professional responsibilities.

Forensic scientists should adopt a mindset of neutrality and objectivity, allowing evidence to guide their conclusions, following the evidence wherever it leads. Ethnographer Beth Bechky describes the culture within crime labs as a "culture of anticipation," where every action is taken with an awareness of potential courtroom implications.

Law Professor Jennifer Mnookin advocates for a research culture among forensic scientists that emphasizes empiricism, transparency, and a commitment to continuous critical evaluation. Some academics consider crime lab staff to be mere technicians due to their lack of PhD degrees and traditional research roles. The Bureau of Labor Statistics categorizes them as technicians. The term *forensic science practitioner* has become a substitute for forensic scientists. However, this view oversimplifies the complexity of their work. Bechky points out that the ability to interpret and convey scientific findings effectively in court is just as crucial as the technical skills employed in the laboratory. Nonetheless, whether scientists or not, they are professionals who must know and apply science.

Laboratory Qualifications

Management and Supervision

The office administration has the primary responsibility for hiring, training, supervising, and disciplining the staff and may be held liable for inadequacies in this regard (*Monell v. Dept. of Social Services*, 1978; *City of Canton v. Harris*, 1989; *Connick v. Thompson*, 2011; *Ashcroft v. Iqbal*, 2009). Forensic science laboratories will perform technical and administrative reviews of casework and reports. Infractions of any sort could result in employment penalties and possible termination. Furthermore, they may be a basis for impeachment in court. Personnel actions are perhaps the most significant tool for maintaining discipline in an office or laboratory.

Quality Management Systems

Laboratory management should ensure proper personnel, adequate resources, and appropriate oversight are in place to perform reliable forensic science examinations and analyses. Laboratory leadership accomplishes this through a quality management system (QMS). QMSs generally include a full-time quality manager, quality assurance measures, and the use of quality controls. Documentation of each step involved in the examination or analysis and document control are critical elements. If errors are discovered during technical and administrative reviews, then procedures are implemented that include corrective actions, and a root cause investigation may be launched for serious errors or non-conformities.

Laboratories are increasingly posting their quality manuals online and making them publicly available to attain transparency and preclude the need to respond to multitudes of defense discovery requests.

The Association of Forensic Quality Assurance Managers (AFQAM) has been established to support the advancement of quality and excellence in the forensic science community by promoting standardized practices, accuracy, professionalism, and ethical conduct in all aspects of forensic services.

Accreditation

Accreditation is a third-party attestation that the laboratory is competent to carry out the testing or analysis. A *scheme owner* is an organization or person responsible for developing and maintaining a certification or conformity assessment scheme. Accreditation involves a *conformity assessment body* (CAB) audit to verify that a laboratory is doing what it says it is. Requirements will emphasize documentation and quality assurance measures. Accreditation also requires a competent staff generally determined through proficiency testing of laboratories and/or certification of laboratory staff.

Conformance standards are voluntary guidelines or specifications that an organization chooses to follow, whereas *compliance standards* refer to mandatory rules and regulations set by external authorities that must be adhered to and are often legally enforceable. *Accrediting bodies* (ABs) will look to see if a laboratory conforms to its internal procedures and protocols, but supplemental requirements will require compliance with external community-specific standards. Compliance with legal requirements includes employment law, state and federal Occupational Safety and Health Administration (OSHA) requirements, and building and fire codes, but forensic accreditation is not focused on these.

Most forensic ABs have adopted the ISO system, headquartered in Geneva, Switzerland. This system is internationally recognized and broadly applied. Specifically, ISO/IEC 17025 standards are used for testing and calibration laboratory operations, and ISO/IEC 17020 standards are used for bodies performing inspections or investigatory operations.

In the forensic community, the primary ABs are the ANSI National Accreditation Board (ANAB) and the American Association for Laboratory Accreditation (A2LA). ANAB now administers the ABFT accreditation program. The National Association of Medical Examiners (NAME) and the International Association of Coroners and Medical Examiners (IACME) accredit medical examiner and coroner offices. The International Accreditation Forum (IAF) and ILAC use ISO/IEC 17011 to provide international recognition to accreditation bodies.

Numerous authorities have long urged universal accreditation of forensic science laboratories. Unless legislatively mandated or required by State Forensic Science commissions, accreditation within the forensic community is voluntary. Nearly all forensic laboratories are accredited, but a minority of medical examiner offices are accredited. Many federal grants to publicly funded forensic science laboratories require the recipient to be accredited or, in some cases, apply for accreditation within two years of receiving the grant. The Bureau of Justice Statistics 2020 census of publicly funded crime laboratories found that 90.4% of publicly funded laboratories were accredited, and of state laboratories, 98% were accredited.

However, DNA analysis is specifically subject to federal regulation as a discipline. The DNA Identification Act of 1994 established the DNA Advisory Board's (DAB's) Quality Assurance Standards (QAS) to issue standards for DNA profiling used in the FBI's NDIS (34 CFR Part A, §12591). Unlike other standards, DAB standards are statutorily mandated. These standards require, among other things, validation studies, quality assurance mechanisms, audits, proficiency testing, and corrective actions when errors arise. The proficiency testing requirement is for every forensic DNA analyst every 180 days. In 2017, Congress directed the FBI to issue standards and procedures for implementing and using Rapid DNA instruments and DNA analysis. The DAB has not issued any requirements for Investigative Genetic Genealogy, but in September 2019, the Department of Justice issued an Interim Policy on Forensic Genetic Genealogical DNA Analysis and Searching.

Forensic Science Boards and Commissions

Eleven states and the District of Columbia have legislatively created forensic science boards or commissions; another four states have similar bodies created by agencies. Five bodies provide oversight, and nine are advisory. They vary in their activity and focus. The four primary functions of these bodies are (1) prevention and mitigation of problems, (2) ensuring national practices are implemented, (3) improvement of cooperation between forensic science laboratories and stakeholders, and (4) improvement of funding that addresses areas of need or opportunities to implement technological innovations. These boards have had a significant salutary impact but vary significantly in their coverage, support, and activism. Recently, there has been an effort to coordinate their activities through the National Association of Forensic Science Boards (NAFSB).

Regulation of Reports and Testimony

Guidance and standards on writing reports and testifying have been developed to convey appropriate interpretations accurately and avoid overstatements.

The Department of Justice has issued discipline-specific Uniform Language for Testimony and Reports (ULTRs) to govern the language used by Federal Bureau of Investigation (FBI), Drug Enforcement Agency (DEA), and ATF forensic scientists. For instance, guidance for latent print examiners states explicitly that "a conclusion provided during testimony or in a report is ultimately an examiner's decision and is not based on a statistically derived or verified measurement or comparison to all other friction ridge skin impression features" and the examiner should only conclude that a given fingerprint is a "source identification," "source exclusion," or "inconclusive," and specifically should not assert the print is "unique" or purports "individualization."

Discipline-specific standards (i.e., DNA, toxicology) on the OSAC Registry also cover reports and testimony.

Administrative and technical reviews may detect and correct nonconformities in writing reports, but breeches in testimony cannot be corrected. They may spur cross-examination or opposing testimony, but only prejudicial overstatements of material facts may give rise to appeals. If they are enforced at all, reporting and testimony conformance are enforced through employment sanctions.

Court Treatment of Forensic Science Irregularities

Conformance with regulations or standard practices is not determinative of the admissibility of expert testimony unless addressed explicitly by legislation. Non-conformance may have disciplinary or other negative consequences, but for testimonial purposes, such a finding has generally been held to go to the weight of the evidence as judged by the trier of fact. FRE Rule 702, however, requires the court to find more likely than not that each of the reliability-based requirements of the rule has been met. The Notes of the Advisory Committee to Rule 702 found that "courts have held that the critical questions of the sufficiency of an expert's basis, and the application of the expert's methodology, are questions of weight and not admissibility. These rulings are an incorrect application of Rules 702 and 104(a)."

As discussed elsewhere, errors discovered in proficiency testing or casework review may constitute Brady or Giglio material that the prosecution must disclose to the defense.

In *State v. Langill* (2008), the trial judge excluded fingerprint evidence where the examiner failed to take bench notes as required by the laboratory's protocol to adequately document that the ACE-V method had been reliably applied, although this ruling was later overturned.

BOX 14.1 *STATE V. LANGILL* (2008) [*LANGILL I*; SEE *LANGILL II*, P. 273] – NONCONFORMITY

In 2004, Karen Katz's apartment was burglarized. Approximately $1200 in a roll of bills that included ten $100 bills were taken from a lockbox in her dresser drawer and roughly $5 in change from a plastic bottle. There was no evidence of forced entry. Circumstantial evidence pointed to Richard Langill. Langill lived in the same apartment complex as Katz. Langill was known to "stare" into her apartment if the blinds were open. When questioned, Langill answered nervously, slowly, and with difficulty; he also changed his story. The defendant purchased a car from a salvage yard the day after the robbery with two 100-dollar bills. Langill was thought to have used a set of master keys that the apartment manager had lost a few months earlier. Police lifted latent prints from the dresser, lockbox, and bottle and forwarded them to the state forensic laboratory. Fingerprint examiner Lisa Corson found only one identifiable print taken from the dresser. She identified the print as belonging to Langill but violated the laboratory's operating procedures by not taking contemporaneous bench notes.

Langill was indicted, and his attorney moved to exclude the fingerprint evidence. In 2006, Justice Patricia Coffey of the Rockingham County Superior Court held a Daubert hearing and granted the defendant's motion to exclude the fingerprint evidence. Although she found Corson qualified as an expert and the principles of fingerprint examination sound, she found Corson's application of the ACE-V was unreliable as a result of incomplete documentation that did not record how the protocols were adhered to and the verification was subject to confirmation bias because it was not blinded. Corson's failure to record bench notes according to protocol is a failure to apply reliable scientific principles and methods appropriately.

The state appealed to the New Hampshire Supreme Court (*Langill I*), arguing that the trial court exceeded its role as "gatekeeper" of scientific evidence and inappropriately imposed standards not established by the scientific community. The court reversed the decision to exclude Corson's testimony and remanded the case to the Superior Court. The court declared that the decision of whether the expert appropriately applied the ACE-V method should be left in the hands of the jury. The court noted that blind verification was being debated within the community, and the record showed no indication that non-blinded verification was unreliable in this case.

Cognitive Bias

Defense attorneys have long attempted to discredit or impeach forensic scientists because of *explicit bias* from working in law enforcement agencies, but *implicit cognitive bias* has been a focus of attention in recent years. Cognitive bias is a systematic error in our thinking processes and may occur anywhere judgment is required, from specimen collection to interpretation. There are different types of cognitive bias. *Confirmation bias* is the tendency to find information that confirms already held beliefs – we see what we expect to see. The Dunning-Kruger effect suggests that we are not a good judge of our own expertise. Recognizing the possibility of bias, forensic scientists have examined or analyzed questioned items ("Qs") before known items ("Ks") so that they are unaware of what result they might be looking for. However, when an examiner performs a pattern comparison of the Qs and Ks simultaneously, verification is needed – preferably blinded. It has been recommended that *non-domain relevant* information be withheld from examiners or presented in a *sequential unmasking* process. However, at least some information is often needed to understand the specimens to be collected or tested or to interpret the results. This is particularly true in certain disciplines, such as forensic toxicology and forensic pathology. The forensic science community continues to try to address issues of cognitive bias.

Greater automation will likely address many of the criticisms of pattern-matching's subjectivity. However, algorithmic biases are of concern, and challenges to the transparency of proprietary software can be anticipated.

Reasonable Scientific Certainty

The phrase "reasonable medical certainty" was developed in medical malpractice litigation but was soon generalized to "reasonable scientific certainty" or "reasonable [discipline] certainty" and adopted widely into routine use. The term is an artificial legal term without meaning in the scientific community. When an expert witness is asked at the end of his testimony, "Is your testimony to a reasonable degree of scientific certainty?" the expert is placed in the awkward position of answering "no" or assuming that the scientific community would consider it reasonable. Defense attorneys consider it bolstering an expert's testimony. The Federal Rules of Evidence do not require that witnesses testify to this standard, but some states require it, particularly in civil litigation.

In 2016, the National Commission on Forensic Science recommended dropping the question. The U.S. Attorney General adopted the recommendation and prohibited federal prosecutors' use of the phrase. However, attorneys and courts have become accustomed to the question, and caselaw in many states requires these "magic words." Attorneys could and should more directly ask experts how certain they are of their opinions.

Harmless versus Harmful Error

In most criminal cases brought to trial, multiple pieces of incriminating information will point to the guilt of the perpetrator. In such cases, a finding of error in any one piece of information might be considered *harmless* and not *prejudicial* – likely not to result in a different conclusion. However, a jury might perceive scientific evidence as more compelling than other evidence – as powerful and objective, perhaps conclusive and definitive. In *State v. Marquez* (2009), the New Mexico Court of Appeals held that the trial court erred when it admitted testimony of a police officer who was unqualified to testify to the scientific accuracy of the blood alcohol level but that the error was harmless. In his dissent, Judge Kennedy wrote, "I do not believe that the jury can separate a proper basis for finding guilt from the improper one presented by the State." The New Mexico Supreme Court agreed with the dissent and overruled the Court of Appeals:

> Although the evidence in the present case was sufficient to support Defendant's conviction without reference to Officer Enyart's scientific testimony, we nonetheless are compelled to conclude that there is a reasonable probability that this testimony impacted the jury's verdict. Accordingly, the evidentiary error was not harmless, and a new trial is required.

The Court in *U.S. v. Velarde* (2000) also found the introduction of unreliable scientific testimony to be prejudicial and remanded the case for a new trial.

The well-documented "CSI" effect (from the television show CSI [crime scene investigation]), in which jurors expect forensic science evidence and are doubtful of prosecutions without it, demonstrates scientific evidence's substantial impact on jurors.

"New Evidence"

Science is ever-changing and evolving. New studies, data, and revelations can lead to new scientific understandings. However, courts must resolve the cases based on the evidence presented during the trial. Still, new scientific discoveries may clash with the important legal notion of finality of judgment – that the defendant has had his day in court, and the judgement should not be endlessly appealed.

If the contrary science existed at the time of trial but was not presented, then potential postconviction relief rests upon a showing of ineffective assistance of counsel (*Hinton v. Alabama,* 2014)

Expert opinion is evidence, and a new opinion is new evidence. Courts treat the change of mind of an expert and subsequent findings of another expert to be "new evidence." Opinions of the original testifying forensic expert may change due to:

1. A new scientific discovery that bears on the forensic expert's thinking
2. Scientific research has invalidated or undermined the prior testimony
3. A new test has become available that might overturn prior conclusions
4. New facts have become available that alter a forensic expert's thinking
5. Reconsideration and change of mind of the forensic expert

Forensic scientists may bring forth their new opinions to correct wrongs and promote justice when the prior testimony is subsequently considered false evidence. But what does it take to establish new evidence? Is one new study sufficient? Is it enough that a forensic scientist may change their mind?

When such new evidence infers actual innocence or to have likely resulted in a different trial outcome, prosecutors may file for dismissal of the charges, or the defense may appeal the conviction, or if a direct appeal has been exhausted, file a state petition for a writ of habeas corpus and then if unsuccessful file a federal petition for writ of habeas corpus. Without specific legislation, material new evidence may not be considered sufficient to grant a *writ of habeas corpus* or a new trial if constitutional violation or no procedural issue, such as ineffective assistance of counsel, is presented (*Herrera v. Collins,* 1993, see pp. 400–401; *DA's Office for the Third Judicial District v. Osborne,* 2009, see pp. 64–65). States have passed postconviction relief legislation that permits a new trial based on new evidence in limited situations. However, it remains difficult to revisit factual matters, even when they are later proven false.

BOX 14.2 *BRYAN V. TEXAS* (2020) – RECANTED TESTIMONY

Joe D. Bryan was convicted in 1987 and then again at retrial in 1989 for the murder of his wife in 1985, based in part upon the testimony of a detective Thorman, who claimed expertise in blood spatter pattern analysis. His wife, Mickey Bryan, was found dead in her bedroom with four gunshot wounds. Blood stains were found in the bedroom and on a flashlight lens found in the trunk of the husband's car a week after the crime when the car had been out of his possession for four days. Three decades later, in 2018, Det. Thorman recanted his testimony, stating that some of his techniques, methods, and conclusions were wrong (but did not specify which were bad). In 2018, the Texas Forensic Science Commission declared that the analysis was flawed. Nonetheless, the Texas Court of Criminal Appeals denied the writ of habeas corpus that cited the faulty analysis without explanation in January 2020. Bryan remained in prison for 31 years until he was paroled in March 2020 and has always maintained his innocence.

Summary

Forensic scientists must be able to defend their science, their application of the science, and their interpretation in court. Subjective opinions, possibly subject to cognitive bias, may be scrutinized. Regardless, there are several things that a forensic scientist can refer to in attempting to show the science to be reliable, such as the literature, validation studies, quality assurance, proficiency testing, and laboratory accreditation.

Standards have been and continue to be established for forensic science testing and examination. Forensic boards and commissions have been set up to provide oversight of forensic laboratories.

Harmful error and new evidence may provide a basis for appeal of a conviction.

Terms

Material – relevant and critically important to prove or disprove a claim.

Prejudicial – evidence that would unfairly sway a jury's opinion and would likely result in a verdict that it would not have rendered without the evidence.

Probative – having evidentiary value; helpful in proving a point in court.

Relevant (in a legal sense) – information that aids the trier of fact and pertains directly to the case at hand, aligning with the specific inquiry being considered.

Reliable (in a legal sense) – evidence that the trial judge deems scientifically valid and appropriate for the jury to consider.

Test Accuracy – the degree to which a test consistently yields the correct result.

Test Precision – the degree to which the test consistently reproduces a result.

Test Validity – demonstrated ability to measure what the test is supposed to measure.

Weight – the credibility, gravity, and persuasiveness given to alleged evidence by the factfinder.

Cases

Ashcroft v. Iqbal, 556 U.S. 662 (2009)
Bryan v. Texas, 804 S.W.2d 648 (Tex. App. 1991); see: https://www.nytimes.com/2020/01/17/us/joe-bryan-texas.html
City of Canton v. Harris, 489 U.S. 378 (1989)
Connick v. Thompson, 563 U.S. 51 (2011)
District Attorney's Office for the Third Judicial District v. Osborne, 557 U.S. 52 (2009)
Herrera v. Collins, 506 U.S. 390 (1993)
Hinton v. Alabama, 571 U.S. 263 (2014)
Monell v. Dept. of Social Services, 436 U.S. 658 (1978)
State v. Langill, 945 A.2d 1 (N.H. 2008) [*Langill I*]
State v. Marquez, 238 P.3d 880 (N.M. 2009)
United States v. Velarde, 214 F.3d 1204 (10th Cir. 2000)

Other Authorities

ANSI Essential Requirements: Due Process Requirements for American National Standards, available at: https://share.ansi.org/Shared%20Documents/Standards%20Activities/American%20National%20Standards/Procedures,%20Guides,%20and%20Forms/2020_ANSI_Essential_Requirements.pdf
Brooks C, Publicly Funded Forensic Crime Laboratories, 2020, U.S. Department of Justice, Dec. 2023, available at https://bjs.ojp.gov/document/pffcl20.pdf
Edwards HT, Gatsonis C, et al., National Research Council (NRC), National Academy of Sciences (NAS), Committee on Identifying the Needs of the Forensic Sciences Community, Strengthening Forensic Science: A Path Forward, National Academies Press, Washington, DC, 2009, available at: https://www.ncjrs.gov/pdffiles1/nij/grants/228091.pdf
Federal Rule of Evidence (FRE) Rule 702. Testimony by Expert Witnesses
Holdren JP, Lander ES, et al., President's Council of Advisors on Science and Technology (PCAST), Forensic Science in Criminal Courts: Ensuring Scientific Validity of Feature-Comparison Methods
Memorandum from the Attorney General to Heads of Department Components, Sept. 9, 2016, https://www.justice.gov/opa/file/891366/download
National Technology Transfer and Advancement Act of 1995 (NTTAA), available at: https://www.nist.gov/standardsgov/national-technology-transfer-and-advancement-act-1995
NIST Guidance on Federal Conformity Assessment Activities (15 CFR Part 287), available at: https://www.nist.gov/standardsgov/nist-guidance-federal-conformity-assessment-activities-15-cfr-part-287

Office of Science and Technology Policy (OSTP), Washington, DC, 2016, available at: https://obamawhitehouse.archives.gov/sites/default/files/microsites/ostp/PCAST/pcast_forensic_science_report_final.pdf

OMB Circular A-119, available at: https://www.whitehouse.gov/wp-content/uploads/2017/11/Circular-119-1.pdf

Ropero-Miller J, LaPorte G, State Forensic Science Commissions, Forensic Technology Center of Excellence, Nov. 2016, available at: https://forensiccoe.org/private/5dd6ab125ce02

Stolorow M, Melson K, et al., Subcommittee on Forensic Science, National Science and Technology Council, Strengthening the Forensic Sciences, Office of Science and Technology Policy (OSTP), Washington, DC, 2014, available at: https://obamawhitehouse.archives.gov/sites/default/files/microsites/ostp/NSTC/forensic_science___may_2014.pdf

Thought Questions

1. How do jurors, who may have a high school education, weigh scientific evidence?
2. How do courts know the evidence was degraded before testing?
3. How do courts know that someone has not altered the evidence?
4. How do courts know that the appropriate testing was done?

Further Reading

Aitken C, Taroni F, Bozza S, *Statistics and the Evaluation of Evidence for Forensic Scientists,* 3rd ed, John Wiley & Sons, Ltd, Hoboken, NJ, 2021.

Betchky BA, *Blood, Powder, and Residue: How Crime Labs Translate Evidence into Proof.* Princeton University Press, Princeton, NJ, 2020.

Dror IE, Cognitive and Human Factors in Expert Decision Making: Six Fallacies and the Eight Sources of Bias. *Analytical Chemistry* 92(12): 7998–8004, 2020, https://doi.org/10.1021/acs.analchem.0c00704

Evett IW, Berger CEH, Buckleton JS, Champod C, Jackson G, Finding the Way Forward for Forensic Science in the US—A Commentary on the PCAST Report, *Forensic Science International* 278:16–23, 2017, https://doi.org/10.1016/j.forsciint.2017.06.018

Haack S, *Defending Science—Within Reason: Between Scientism and Cynicism,* Prometheus Books, Amherst, NY 2007.

Haack S, *Evidence Matters: Science, Proof, and Truth in the Law,* Cambridge Press, New York, 2014.

Jasanoff S, *Science at the Bar: Law, Science, and Technology in America,* Harvard University Press, Cambridge, MA, 1997.

Lucy D, *Introduction to Statistics for Forensic Scientists,* John Wiley & Sons, Ltd, Hoboken, NJ, 2013.

Mnookin JL, Cole SA, Dror IE, Fisher BA. The Need for a Research Culture in the Forensic Sciences. *UCLA Law Review* 58:725, 2010, https://www.pnas.org/doi/abs/10.1073/pnas.2301840120

Vosk T, Emery AF, *Forensic Metrology: Scientific Measurement and Inference for Lawyers, Judges, and Criminalists,* CRC Press, Boca Raton, FL, 2014.

Chapter 15
Sixth Amendment Confrontation

Learning Objectives

After reading this chapter, students are expected to be able to:

- recite the confrontation clause
- recognize hearsay
- explain the *Crawford* revolution
- discuss the application of the Confrontation Clause to forensic science
- list alternatives for the unavailability of a forensic scientist to testify.

Introduction

The Confrontation Clause of the Sixth Amendment of the U.S. Constitution, which forms the basis for the defense's ability to compel a forensic scientist to testify, is a crucial element in the U.S. legal system. It states:

> in all criminal prosecutions, the accused shall enjoy the right … to be confronted with the witnesses against him…

The defendant has the right to look the accuser in the eye and to query his or her accusations. In *Lilly v. Virginia* (1999), the U.S. Supreme Court quoted John H. Wigmore, the great evidence scholar, who wrote, "Cross-examination is the greatest legal engine ever invented for the discovery of truth." The U.S. Supreme Court held that the fundamental right to a fair trial includes the

DOI: 10.4324/9780429272455-15

Sixth Amendment right to compulsory process and the right to confront and cross-examine witnesses (*Estelle v. Williams*, 1976).

This Sixth Amendment right to confrontation applies to criminal trials but does not apply to civil cases or other proceedings. In *U.S. v. Jacoby* (1960), the Court held that the protection of the United States Constitution and federal laws apply to members of the armed forces "except those [protections] which are expressly or by necessary implication inapplicable," rendering the right applicable to military courts-martial.

Historical Background

The right to confront your accusers is not a new concept. It has deep historical roots, tracing back to ancient Roman law, and is even mentioned in the Bible: "It is not the manner of the Romans to deliver any man up to die before the accused has met his accusers face to face and has been given a chance to defend himself against the charges" (Acts of the Apostles 25:16). This right was recognized in early English law from the 1555 English Marian Acts, promulgated under Queen Mary, where sworn statements of the justices of the peace and from coroners, who had examined prisoners accused of a felony, were inadmissible unless the prisoner had been present during the examination or had an opportunity to cross-examine the officer. In his Commentaries (1765–1769), Blackstone described live testimony in court as "much more conducive to the clearing up of the truth than the private and secret examination taken down in writing before an officer."

Nonetheless, the colonists in America were subjected to the Tudor and Stuart practice of trial by affidavit and found it to be unfair and loathsome. In addition, beginning in the 1760s, the vice-admiralty enforced controversial customs laws, such as the Stamp Act, which did not allow confrontation of accusers or jury trials. Madison would have also known of the notorious trial of Sir Walter Raleigh in 1603, in which he was found guilty, seemingly on mere rumors. Thus, the confrontation clause of the U.S. Constitution was written to avoid trials by writs and affidavits where someone could swear that they had been wronged and the person prosecuted on that basis without an opportunity to cross-examine the complainant.

BOX 15.1 1603 TRIAL OF SIR WALTER RALEIGH

A sworn affidavit by Lord Cobham, possibly obtained under duress while he was being held prisoner in the Tower of London, led to Raleigh's conviction for treason for plotting the murder and overthrow of King James I. At the trial, Raleigh had a letter from Cobham recanting his statement, and Raleigh repeatedly demanded that Cobham be produced at the trial to clear him.

Cobham was available to testify. Raleigh was unaware that the prosecutors had a more recent letter from Cobham accusing Raleigh anew. Perhaps under oath and looking his friend in the eye, he would have retracted his statements rather than let him be executed. The allegation in the affidavit was corroborated by Dyer, a local fisherman, who had heard while in Portugal that Raleigh would cut the throat of James before he would be crowned, to which Raleigh asked what evidence it was. In his closing statement, Raleigh warned the jury that none of them was safe if one could be convicted of treason "by suspicions and presumptions… without the open testimony of a single witness."

Like other provisions of the Bill of Rights, the Confrontation Clause was rarely a subject of judicial consideration for more than a century because it only applied to the federal government. Cases began to appear more frequently after 1965 when the Supreme Court held that the clause applies to the states under the Fourteenth Amendment (*Pointer v. Texas,* 1965). After a few limited defense wins due to the lack of ability to confront and cross-examine witnesses, the Court began regularly rejecting defendants' challenges in the early 1970s.

Hearsay Rule

The right to confront your accusers is said to encapsulate the *hearsay rule*. Hearsay is a contraction of "I heard it said." The hearsay rule holds that out-of-court statements proffered for the truth of the matter asserted are not admissible as evidence in court, where the *declarant* (the person making the statement) is not in court and available to be cross-examined. These *ex parte* statements (made outside the defendant's presence) may simply be gossip; therefore, such statements are considered untrustworthy and unreliable and thus legally inadmissible. Hearsay is considered incompetent evidence because there is no ability to place the witness under oath for the judge or jury to observe the witness's demeanor or test the witness through cross-examination.

A prosecutor cannot put on John to say that he heard Mary say, "Frank did it!" if proffered as proof that Frank indeed did it. However, a court may allow John to testify that he heard Mary say, "Frank did it!" if proffered for the proposition that Mary knows Frank, that Mary can hear, or that Mary has auditory hallucinations –where it is not proffered for the proof of the matter asserted.

However, the hearsay rule is not absolute! There have always been exceptions to the hearsay rule. Most exceptions are allowed into evidence because they embody an inherent trustworthiness. For instance, excited utterances may be admitted for the truth of the utterance because they are made in reaction to some event without time to think. Statements made to a doctor for healthcare are assumed true because it should be in the patient's interest for their care to tell the doctor the truth; thus, they are allowed into evidence as an exception to the hearsay rule. Official government records and even ordinary business records are also hearsay exceptions and admitted into evidence for the truth of the matter asserted because of a presumption they are made in the regular course of doing business. Other exceptions are made where the declarant is unavailable.

The hearsay rule and many of these Common Law exceptions to the hearsay rule are embodied in the Federal Rules of Evidence (FRE) and the various state rules of evidence. Article VIII of the FRE is devoted to hearsay. They define "hearsay" and hold hearsay inadmissible but provide 23 exceptions.

BOX 15.2 FRE 801 – HEARSAY

"Hearsay" means a statement that:

1. the declarant does not make while testifying at the current trial or hearing; and
2. a party offers in evidence to prove the truth of the matter asserted in the statement.

Statements That Are Not Hearsay.

1. A Declarant-Witness's Prior Statement
2. An Opposing Party's Statement.

BOX 15.3 FRE 801 – THE RULE AGAINST HEARSAY

Hearsay is not admissible unless any of the following provides otherwise:

- a federal statute;
- these rules; or
- other rules prescribed by the Supreme Court.

BOX 15.4 FRE 803 – HEARSAY EXCEPTIONS: WHETHER OR NOT DECLARANT IS AVAILABLE

Hearsay is not admissible unless:

1. Presence Sense Impression
2. Excited Utterance
3. Then-Existing Mental, Emotional, or Physical Condition
4. Statement Made for Medical Diagnosis or Treatment
5. Recorded Recollection
6. Records of a Regularly Conducted Activity
7. Absence of a Record of a Regularly Conducted Activity
8. Public Records....

23 exceptions

Many of these hearsay exceptions have been recognized for centuries under English common law. Courts have found such exceptions to be non-violative of the Constitution's Sixth Amendment because they were in use when the Bill of Rights was written.

Dying declarations relating to the cause of death are exceptions to the hearsay rule. The Bruton Rule holds that a confession can only be used against the one who made it, not other co-defendants. Admissions of guilt are not admissible because there are no negative consequences to the confessor for covering for the actual perpetrator. Admissions and declarations against interest are not confessions of guilt but rather damaging statements other than that the declarant was the perpetrator of the crime. These admissions and declarations are hearsay exceptions because the declarant has negative consequences, although not as damaging as a confession.

Excited utterances and *spontaneous statements* are classic hearsay exceptions because the declarant has no time to think. Statements made by 911 callers are usually admitted into evidence as excited utterances. Statements made during and immediately after the crime are generally admitted as hearsay exceptions.

Prior inconsistent statements made out of court may be used against the witness to impeach the witness's credibility. These statements are not used to prove the matter asserted but instead go to the witness's truthfulness and thus are not hearsay. However, constitutional protections come into play if the defendant makes the statements without Miranda warnings or counsel. In *Harris v. New York* (1971), the Court held that an un-Mirandized statement could be used against the defendant on cross-examination, "the privilege cannot be construed to include the right to commit perjury." The same result was held in *Oregon v. Hass* (1975), "inadmissibility would pervert the constitutional right into a right to falsify." Similarly, statements made without opportunity for counsel can be used for impeachment purposes (*Kansas v. Ventris,* 2009). While such statements cannot be used directly, a prosecutor can use them when the defendant has made a false statement during testimony.

Business records are perhaps the most common hearsay exception. Any record generated in the normal course of operating a business, government, or other function is considered sufficiently trustworthy to constitute a hearsay exception because the record is not prepared for use in court. Justice Scalia has explicitly held that forensic science reports are prepared for use in court and, therefore, are not business record exceptions (*Melendez-Diaz v. Massachusetts*, 2009).

Furthermore, FRE 807 includes a "residual exception" rule for cases not otherwise specified where there is circumstantial evidence of its truthfulness. In such cases, the party offering the witness must give notice to the opposing party before the trial or hearing.

BOX 15.5 FRE 807 – RESIDUAL EXCEPTION

a. **In General**. Under the following circumstances, a hearsay statement is not excluded by the rule against hearsay even if the statement is not admissible under a hearsay exception in Rule 803 or 804:
   1. the statement is supported by sufficient guarantees of trustworthiness – after considering the totality of circumstances under which it was made and evidence, if any, corroborating the statement; and
   2. it is more probative on the point for which it is offered than any other evidence that the proponent can obtain through reasonable efforts.

b. **Notice**. The statement is admissible only if the proponent gives an adverse party reasonable notice of the intent to offer the statement – including its substance and the declarant's name – so that the party has a fair opportunity to meet it. The notice must be provided in writing before the trial or hearing – or in any form during the trial or hearing if the court, for good cause, excuses a lack of earlier notice.

Unavailability of a Witness

For hearsay purposes, FRE 804 defines when a declarant is unavailable, and the hearsay statement may be allowed into evidence.

BOX 15.6 FRE 804 – HEARSAY EXCEPTIONS; DECLARANT UNAVAILABLE

a. **Criteria for Being Unavailable**. A declarant is considered to be unavailable as a witness if the declarant:
   1. is exempted from testifying about the subject matter of the declarant's statement because the court rules that a privilege applies;
   2. refuses to testify about the subject matter despite a court order to do so;
   3. testifies to not remembering the subject matter;
   4. cannot be present or testify at the trial or hearing because of death or a then-existing infirmity, physical illness, or mental illness; or
   5. is absent from the trial or hearing, and the statement's proponent has not been able, by process or other reasonable means, to procure:
      A. the declarant's attendance, in the case of a hearsay exception under Rule 804(b)(1) or (6); or

B. the declarant's attendance or testimony, in the case of a hearsay exception under Rule 804(b)(2), (3), or (4).

But this subdivision (a) does not apply if the statement's proponent procured or wrongfully caused the declarant's unavailability as a witness in order to prevent the declarant from attending or testifying.

b. **The Exceptions**. The following are not excluded by the rule against hearsay if the declarant is unavailable as a witness:

1. Former Testimony. Testimony that:
   A. was given as a witness at a trial, hearing, or lawful deposition, whether given during the current proceeding or a different one; and
   B. is now offered against a party who had – or, in a civil case, whose predecessor in interest had – an opportunity and similar motive to develop it by direct, cross-, or redirect examination.
2. Statement under the Belief of Imminent Death. In a prosecution for homicide or in a civil case, a statement that the declarant, while believing the declarant's death to be imminent, made about its cause or circumstances.
3. Statement against Interest. A statement that:
   A. a reasonable person in the declarant's position would have made only if the person believed it to be true because, when made, it was so contrary to the declarant's proprietary or pecuniary interest or had so great a tendency to invalidate the declarant's claim against someone else or to expose the declarant to civil or criminal liability; and
   B. if offered in a criminal case as one that tends to expose the declarant to criminal liability, is supported by corroborating circumstances that clearly indicate its trustworthiness after considering the totality of circumstances under which it was made and any evidence that supports or undermines it.
4. Statement of Personal or Family History. A statement about:
   A. the declarant's own birth, adoption, legitimacy, ancestry, marriage, divorce, relationship by blood, adoption, or marriage, or similar facts of personal or family history, even though the declarant had no way of acquiring personal knowledge about that fact; or
   B. another person concerning any of these facts, as well as death, if the declarant was related to the person by blood, adoption, or marriage or was so intimately associated with the person's family that the declarant's information is likely to be accurate.

1. [Other Exceptions. Transferred to Rule 807.]
2. Statement Offered against a Party That Wrongfully Caused the Declarant's Unavailability. A statement offered against a party that wrongfully caused – or acquiesced in wrongfully causing – the declarant's unavailability as a witness, and did so intending that result.

It is generally in the interest of the criminal justice system that the forensic scientist who examined or analyzed the evidence is made available to testify in court. Employees who have left an office from retirement or moved to another job should realize they may still be required to testify in their old cases.

Nonetheless, a former employee may retire or leave the office and refuse to appear in court as an expert voluntarily. A federal subpoena will compel the analyst to appear wherever he or she is in the United States. However, a state subpoena is limited to the state's jurisdiction. However, prosecutors may still compel the witness to testify utilizing the *Uniform Act to Secure the Attendance of Witnesses from Without a State in Criminal Proceedings* or similar enabling state law. This process will take time and may delay the proceedings. A step-by-step guide to employing the act can be found at https://www.naag.org/attorney-general-journal/subpoenaing-out-of-state-witnesses/. The compelled witness might refuse to testify as an expert but only as a fact witness; courts only rarely compel testimony as an expert (*Kaufman v. Edelstein*, 2d Cir. 1976; *In Re World Trade Center Lower Manhattan Disaster Site Litigation*, 2d Cir. 1972).

Expert witnesses no longer employed by the state expect to be paid for their time and travel accommodation according to an agreement with the office or by the attorney demanding their service. If an expert is called as a fact witness to avoid expert fees, then the expert should not answer questions asking for an opinion when testifying. Employers should allow employees time off to comply without docking their pay or vacation leave.

Crime labs and prosecutors have few options when a witness is truly unavailable. Prosecutors may be able to obtain agreement from the defense to stipulate to the facts. Prosecutors might also be able to use hypothetical questions if they can separately prove the facts asserted in the hypothetical. Crime lab directors may be able to have the evidence retested or send a substitute to testify based on an independent analysis of the raw facts. The crime lab director may ask if the prosecution can prosecute the case using the report without the testimony of the analyst or use a surrogate (substitute) witness. The defense can do little if the evidence is retested, but otherwise, the defense can and probably will object to the absence of the forensic scientist who performed the examination or analysis. These issues are discussed below.

Notice-and-demand statutes have been upheld and provide a reasonable mechanism to deal with the issue of confrontation by requiring the prosecution to give notice before trial of the intent to admit a laboratory report into evidence and providing the defense the opportunity to demand the scientist to testify at trial; failure to demand the expert constitutes a waiver. The National Commission on Forensic Sciences recommended adopting such provisions.

Remote Video Testimony

Sometimes, a witness may be made available through remote live video testimony. Courts are reluctant to permit this because remote video does not fully capture all body movements nor the atmosphere of face-to-face confrontation.

In *Maryland v. Craig* (1990), the U.S. Supreme Court recognized a public policy exception to the Confrontation Clause. In that case, the Supreme Court held that the two-way video conferencing of a child witness who was the alleged subject of child abuse was an exception mandated by necessity, in that case, psychological trauma. The Court stated that:

> … a defendant's right to confront accusatory witnesses may be satisfied absent a physical, face-to-face confrontation at trial only where denial of such confrontation is necessary to further an important public policy and only where the reliability of the testimony is otherwise assured.

In *People v. Wrotten* (NY 2010), a case involving a physical medical condition, the New York Appellate Division upheld the trial court's finding "by clear and convincing evidence that [the complainant] is unavailable to travel to New York without seriously endangering his health." A concurring judge quoted *Craig*

> that live testimony via one-way closed-circuit television is permissible under the Federal Constitution, provided there is an individualized determination that denial of 'physical, face-to-face confrontation' is 'necessary to further an important public policy' and 'the reliability of the testimony is otherwise assured.'

Testimony using live two-way videoconferencing became common during the COVID-19 pandemic, based upon the public policy exception of *Maryland v. Craig* (1990). Courts seem to have become more tolerant after the pandemic but do not consider it routine.

If the witness is unavailable during the trial, arranging a prerecorded videotaped deposition with the parties' participation might be possible for later use at trial. However, the court may or may not accept this as a viable substitute in criminal cases unless agreed to by the parties because courts may view prerecorded videotapes as less acceptable than live two-way videoconferencing. The defense may invoke their confrontation rights and demand the witness's presence during the trial.

U.S. Supreme Court Case Law

A series of U.S. Supreme Court decisions define the evolving constitutional law on confrontation, culminating in *Smith v. Arizona* (2024). These decisions involve attempts to introduce reports or substitute witnesses but not the original analyst at trial over the defendant's objections. Although constitutional law supersedes federal and state evidentiary law, there are times when the state evidentiary rules or notice-and-demand procedures go further.

Ohio v. Roberts

The U.S. Supreme Court in *Ohio v. Roberts* (1980) attempted to broadly define the hearsay exceptions that could be admitted in criminal cases as out-of-court statements with a particularized guarantee of trustworthiness based upon "an indicia of reliability."

BOX 15.7 *OHIO V. ROBERTS* (1980) – INDICIA OF RELIABILITY

Roberts was charged with check forgery and theft of stolen credit cards. The victim's daughter had given Roberts her parents' checks and credit cards. She did not show up to testify despite five subpoenas. The State offered the transcript of the daughter's testimony from the preliminary hearing and the defense objected. The Court held that the daughter's statement did not violate the Confrontation Clause:

> when a hearsay declarant is not present for cross-examination at trial, the Confrontation Clause normally requires a showing that he is unavailable. Even then, his statement is admissible only if it bears adequate 'indicia of reliability.' Reliability can be inferred without more in a case where the evidence falls within a firmly rooted hearsay exception. In other cases, the evidence must be excluded, at least absent a showing of particularized guarantees of trustworthiness. In this case, an out-of-court statement under oath, with an opportunity for counsel to cross-examine the witness, provides an adequate 'indicia of reliability'.

An additional requirement is that the declarant is not available for testimony and cross-examination at trial.

Crawford v. Washington

The Roberts rule was the law for a quarter century, but it was abolished by *Crawford v. Washington* (2004), inaugurating the *Crawford revolution*. In *Crawford*, Justice Antonin Scalia, writing for the majority, gave a thorough history of the Confrontation Clause and concluded that it was directed at keeping "ex parte" examinations out of the evidentiary record and to avoid trial by writs, affidavits, and statements under oath. He expressed concern over the inconsistent results reached by courts under *Roberts*. To Justice Scalia, cross-examination of the witness is vital, and he declared:

> Dispensing with confrontation because testimony is obviously reliable is akin to dispensing with jury trial because a defendant is obviously guilty... Where testimonial statements are at issue, the only indicium of reliability sufficient to satisfy constitutional demands is the one the Constitution actually prescribes: confrontation.

The court held that the Confrontation Clause bars the admission of an absent witness's statements at trial unless the witness is unavailable, and the defendant had a prior chance to subject her to cross-examination. Specifically, the Clause applies to statements that are *testimonial* and introduced for the truth of the matter asserted (hearsay). Thus, *Crawford* changed the Sixth Amendment inquiry from a determination of *indicia of reliability* to whether a statement is *testimonial hearsay*.

BOX 15.8 *CRAWFORD V. WASHINGTON* (2004) – RIGHT TO CONFRONTATION

Crawford confronted Lee over an allegation that Lee had attempted to rape Crawford's wife, and then Crawford stabbed Lee. Crawford claimed self-defense as he believed Lee had picked up a knife, but Lee denied he had picked it up. Crawford's wife told the police that Lee had not picked up the weapon but otherwise corroborated Crawford's story. However, she did not testify against her husband due to marital privilege. The prosecutor attempted to introduce the tape-recorded statement to the police on the grounds of "indicia of reliability" due to partially corroborating statements. The defense objected on the Sixth Amendment grounds. The Court overruled the earlier *Roberts* general test of "adequate indicia of reliability," which, in that case, the prior opportunity to cross-examine the declarant was determined sufficient. The *Crawford* Court held that the Confrontation Clause applies to "witnesses" against the accused, meaning those who "bear testimony." Furthermore, testimonial statements of witnesses are not allowed where the declarant does not appear at trial unless he or she is unavailable to testify and the defendant had a prior opportunity for cross-examination. "Where testimonial statements are at issue, the only indicium of reliability sufficient to satisfy constitutional demands is the one the Constitution actually prescribes: confrontation."

Defense attorneys believe that the Confrontation Clause should mean they have a right to cross-examine experts who produce evidence for the prosecution about the science, the irregularities in the application of the science, and their interpretations. Within a few years, the U.S. Supreme Court applied the Confrontation Clause to forensic scientists' testimony, reports, and notes in a series of cases that have split the court – nor are all issues yet resolved.

Melendez-Diaz v. Massachusetts

In *Melendez-Diaz v. Massachusetts* (2009), the Court faced a case where a sworn "Certificate of Analysis" (COA) was substituted for the testimony of a forensic analyst. The Court held that this violated the defendant's Sixth Amendment right to confrontation, based upon *Crawford*. At the time, most states had laws that allowed the admission of lab reports without testimonial support using COAs. The Massachusetts law at that time did not contain a *notice-and-demand* provision that required notice to the defendant by the prosecution before the trial of the intention to introduce a report into evidence without the expert's testimony.

Justice Scalia held that notice-and-demand statutes are constitutional, but the admission of the COAs alone, without the analysts' testimony and opportunity to cross-examine them, violates the defendant's constitutional right to confrontation. The analyst who did the testing was a witness for purposes of the Confrontation Clause, and the COA was testimonial. It could not substitute for the analyst's testimony, even though the analyst had sworn under oath that they were true and accurate.

The Court rejected the argument that the COAs were business records, a recognized hearsay exception. Justice Scalia noted that most business records would escape Sixth Amendment scrutiny, not because they meet an exception to the hearsay rule, but because they are non-testimonial - they were not created for use at trial.

The Court rejected the argument that the COAs were non-accusatory. The COAs did not name the defendant; they simply reported the results of forensic analysis. Justice Scalia declared that evidence that proves an essential element of a crime is accusatory for purposes of the Confrontation Clause; "The text of the Amendment contemplates two classes of witnesses—those against the defendant and those in his favor...there is not a third category of witnesses, helpful to the prosecution, but somehow immune from confrontation."

The Court rejected the argument that the analysis was neutral and reliable scientific evidence; "Nor is it evident that what respondent calls 'neutral scientific testing' is as neutral or reliable as respondent suggests." Justice Scalia noted, "Forensic evidence is not uniquely immune from the risk of manipulation" and cited the 2009 National Academy of Sciences report and cases of forensic fraud. He found scientific reports inherently untrustworthy when not subjected to an opportunity for cross-examination; "The analysts are... subject to confrontation; we would reach the same conclusion if all analysts always possessed the scientific acumen of Mme. Curie and the veracity of Mother Theresa."

Justice Scalia also noted the role of cross-examination in testing the reliability of COAs. He wrote that "confrontation is one means of assuring accurate forensic analysis" and added that "there is little reason to believe that confrontation will be useless in testing an analyst's honesty, proficiency, and methodology—the features that are commonly the focus in the cross-examination of experts."

In his dissent, Justice Kennedy wrote,

> The court sweeps away an accepted rule governing the admission of scientific evidence. Until today, scientific analysis could be introduced into evidence without testimony from the "analyst" who produced it. This rule has been established for at least 90 years...The court dictates to the States, as a matter of constitutional law, an as-yet-undefined set of rules governing what kinds of evidence may be admitted without in-court testimony.

BOX 15.9 *MELENDEZ-DIAZ V. MASSACHUSETTS* (2009) – CERTIFICATE OF ANALYSIS

Melendez-Diaz was charged with possession and drug trafficking when 19 small plastic bags of white powder were found in the police car he was transported in after his arrest. The state crime lab tested the white powder, revealing cocaine.

The prosecution introduced three "certificates of analysis" (COAs) by analysts in the lab. COAs are affidavits reporting the lab results and are sworn under oath before a notary public that the certificate is true and accurate. A certificate reported the weight of the seized bags and stated that the bags had been "examined with the following results: The substance was found to contain Cocaine." The defense objected that the forensic analysts were not available to cross-examine.

In a 5–4 ruling, the court held that defendants have a right to cross-examine lab analysts and that using COAs without the opportunity to cross-examine the analyst violates the Sixth Amendment.

In amicus briefs filed in *Melendez-Diaz* and subsequent cases, forensic scientists complained that the right to confrontation might mean everyone touching the evidence would be called into court. They argued that the burden imposed upon already overburdened labs would be too much. This was mainly a concern of large laboratories performing batch testing. Justice Kennedy noted this concern in his dissent:

> "Consider how many people play a role in a routine test... One person prepares a sample of the drug... A second person interprets...a third person—perhaps an independent contractor—has calibrated the machine... Finally, a fourth person— perhaps the laboratory's director—certifies that his subordinates followed established procedures... the court cannot define with clarity who the analyst is." Justice Scalia responded to this in Footnote 1 of the majority opinion, "Contrary to the dissent's suggestion...we do not hold, and it is not the case, that anyone whose testimony may be relevant in establishing the chain of custody, authenticity of the sample, or accuracy of the testing device, must appear in person as a part of the prosecution's case...It is up to the prosecution to decide what steps...are so crucial as to require evidence."

However, this practical concern did not garner much traction with other Justices in the face of a fundamental Constitutional right. Nor has this concern materialized since *Melendez-Diaz*. Prosecutors do not need to call all possible witnesses, and judges or juries do not favorably look upon attempts to do so.

Forensic science labs may want to send a senior staff scientist who did not perform the testing or examination to testify for a more junior and less qualified staff member. However, the senior examiner or analyst may not know if procedures were followed, if a specimen was dropped, if contamination was possible, or if other irregularities existed.

Bullcoming v. New Mexico

In *Bullcoming v. New Mexico* (2011), the Court held that the State could not introduce one lab analyst's findings through the testimony of a surrogate (substitute) analyst.

BOX 15.10 *BULLCOMING V. NEW MEXICO* (2011) – SUBSTITUTE EXPERT

Bullcoming rear-ended a truck at an intersection and was subsequently arrested and charged with driving while intoxicated (DWI). After he refused a breath test, a blood sample was taken pursuant to a warrant. The resulting formal certified but unsworn toxicology report revealed a blood alcohol concentration (BAC) of 0.21 g/dL, well above the 0.16 g/dL threshold for aggravated DWI. The report was submitted to the court, and another scientist (not the supervisor), Gerasimos Razatos, testified to it, but not the analyst Curtis Caylor, who performed the testing. Caylor had "very recently" been put on unpaid leave for an undisclosed reason, was removed from his workstation, and was thus unavailable for trial. Razatos neither signed the COA nor performed or observed the testing, but he did have access to the gas chromatography-mass spectrometer raw data. The defense objected that they had a constitutional right to cross-examine the laboratory analyst who did the testing.

> The question presented is whether the Confrontation Clause permits the prosecution to introduce a forensic laboratory report containing a testimonial certification—made for the purpose of proving a particular fact—through the in-court testimony of a scientist who did not sign the certification or perform or observe the test reported in the certification. We hold that surrogate testimony of that order does not meet the constitutional requirement. The accused's right is to be confronted with the analyst who made the certification unless that analyst is unavailable at trial, and the accused had an opportunity, pretrial, to cross-examine that particular scientist.

In a decision divided 5–4, the Court held that this violated the defendant's Sixth Amendment right to confrontation.

Williams v. Illinois

In *Williams v. Illinois* (2012), a state DNA analyst testified to the DNA testing of the defendant and to the database match of a DNA profile of a rape victim produced by Cellmark Diagnostics, the commercial laboratory that performed the outsourced testing. The Cellmark DNA report was not introduced, and no one from Cellmark testified. The defense demanded the right to confront the Cellmark analyst.

A majority of Justices found that the State analyst had been a conduit for what another analyst had reported and that this "basis" of her testimony, the "underlying facts and data," was introduced to establish the truth of the matter asserted. Nonetheless, the court's plurality decision was that the Confrontation Clause was not violated because a majority of the justices did not find the Cellmark lab report to be testimonial.

Four Justices found the Cellmark report to be non-testimonial because it was not used as proof of the matter it asserted but rather merely as the "basis" for the expert opinion, as allowed under FRE 703. Justice Alito reiterated,

> under settled evidence law, an expert may express an opinion that is based on facts that the expert assumes, but does not know, to be true. It is then up to the party who calls the expert to introduce other evidence establishing the facts assumed by the expert. ... this form of expert testimony does not violate the Confrontation Clause because that provision has no application to out-of-court statements that are not offered to prove the truth of the matter asserted.

The four justices of the dissent found the Cellmark report to be testimonial because it was prepared for the primary purpose of being used as evidence against the defendant, even though the report was prepared before any suspect was identified, and the report only provided a profile and did not name the defendant. Accordingly, they believed the defendant was deprived of his right to confront the witnesses against him. Justice Kagan asked: "[h]ave we not already decided this case?"

Justice Thomas, who sided with the majority in *Melendez-Diaz* and *Bullcoming*, provided the swing vote because he believed the lab report was not sufficiently solemn. In his view, testimonial refers to sworn statements or statements certified as true and accurate – as the COAs in *Melendez Diaz* and *Bullcoming* were.

BOX 15.11 *WILLIAMS V. ILLINOIS* (2012) – STATEMENTS AS "BASIS" FOR OPINION

Sandy Williams was arrested for abduction, robbery, and rape of "LJ." L.J. survived the encounter and was taken to the hospital, where a sexual assault kit was obtained. Brian Haspack, working in the Illinois State Police (ISP) crime lab, confirmed the presence of semen on the vaginal swabs. Vaginal swabs were sent to Cellmark Diagnostics, a private contract laboratory, for DNA testing. Sandra Lambatos, in the ISP lab, then searched the National DNA Index System (NDIS) database using the Cellmark DNA profile. The profile matched a profile from a sample of William's blood that had been taken after he was arrested on subsequent, unrelated charges.

L.J. identified Williams in a line-up as the perpetrator. Williams was arrested. A new blood sample was tested by Karen Abbinanti of the ISP lab that matched the DNA profile of the semen on the vaginal swabs.

At the bench trial, Haspack testified that he found semen on the vaginal swabs; Abbinanti testified to the DNA testing of the reference blood specimen from Williams and the resulting DNA profile. Lambatos testified to the search of the DNA database, the DNA profile from the swabs, and the comparison of the profile from the swabs and the reference sample profile. She also testified to the chain of custody of the vaginal swabs sent to Cellmark and that Cellmark was an accredited laboratory, but she did not vouch for the accuracy of the profiles generated by Cellmark; nobody from Cellmark testified to the DNA testing that it performed, and its report was not submitted into evidence.

The defense objected to Lambatos's testimony for lack of foundation, arguing that the prosecution had offered "no evidence with regard to any testing that's been done to generate a DNA profile by another lab to be testified to by this witness."

Lambatos testified to the DNA database search and hit, but although she relied on the Cellmark report, she had not observed the DNA testing performed by Cellmark. Thus, she was not competent to testify to the Cellmark testing.

Justice Alito, writing for the plurality, noted,

> For more than 200 years, the law of evidence has permitted the sort of testimony that was given by the expert in this case. ... this form of expert testimony does not violate the Confrontation Clause because that provision has no application to out-of-court statements that are not offered to prove the truth of the matter asserted. When an expert testifies for the prosecution in a criminal case, the defendant has the opportunity to cross-examine the expert about any statements that are offered for their truth. Out-of-court statements that are related by the expert solely for the purpose of explaining the assumptions on which that opinion rests are not offered for their truth and thus fall outside the scope of the Confrontation Clause. Applying this rule to the present case, we conclude that the expert's testimony did not violate the Sixth Amendment.

The court held in a 5–4 plurality decision (Justice Thomas concurring in the judgment only) that the Cellmark DNA report was nontestimonial, and thus, there was no violation of the Confrontation Clause. The conviction was allowed to stand. However, there was no majority rationale for this holding.

Stuart v. Alabama

The Court had an opportunity to clarify its position but instead denied certiorari in the DUI case of *Stuart v. Alabama* (2018), in which the laboratory chief, not the laboratory analyst, testified. Justices Gorsuch and Sotomayor dissented from the denial, arguing,

> …our criminal justice system depends on adversarial testing and cross-examination. …This Court's most recent foray in this field, *Williams v. Illinois*, yielded no majority, and its various opinions have sown confusion in courts across the country. … [We] owe lower courts struggling to abide by our holdings more clarity than we have afforded them in this area.

Smith v. Arizona

In *Smith v. Arizona* (2024), the Court provided some clarity to this "muddle." The case involved a surrogate witness who testified to his own expert opinion and the notes and report of the testing analyst that served as the basis of his opinion. The Court held that when an expert presents another's statements as the "basis" for his opinion, he offers those statements for their truth. Thus, a surrogate witness testifying to another expert's "testimonial" statements violates the defendant's confrontation rights. The prosecution may not introduce the testimonial out-of-court statements of a forensic analyst at trial offered for the truth of the matter asserted (hearsay) unless she is unavailable and the defendant has had a prior chance to cross-examine her.

The Court unanimously overturned the state court ruling rejecting Smith's claim. However, although the majority reaffirmed that the primary purpose test should be used to determine if statements are testimonial, the other Justices were not fully convinced. Accordingly, the Court remanded the case for further consideration of this issue and whether it had been waived.

BOX 15.12 *SMITH V. ARIZONA* (2024) – BASIS TESTIMONY RECONSIDERED

Arizona officers executed a search warrant at a rural shed where drug activity was expected. Eleven individuals, including Jason Smith, were detained in the shed. The search revealed six pounds of marijuana on a drying shelf, marijuana in various containers, cannabis wax near the bed and in the refrigerator, a jacket with methamphetamine, and a meth pipe on the couch. Elizabeth Rast tested the materials and found they contained usable levels of methamphetamine, marijuana, and cannabis. Three weeks before the trial, she stopped working for the lab for unspecified reasons. The State provided Greggory Longoni as a substitute to provide his own independent opinion of the drug testing performed by Rast.

At trial, Longoni testified to what Rast's records revealed about her testing before providing his own "independent opinion." The actual report was not admitted into evidence. Smith was convicted, and the defendant appealed based on violation of his Sixth Amendment rights. The Arizona Court of Appeals upheld the conviction, holding that statements about Rast's work were only used as a basis for Longoni's independent expert opinion and not for their truth.

Justice Kagan, writing for the Court and joined by four others, held in favor of Smith,

> the State's basis evidence—more precisely, the truth of the statements on which its expert relied—propped up the whole case; yet the maker of the statements was not in the courtroom, and Smith could not ask her any questions.

She noted that Rast could have testified to her personal knowledge of how the lab typically functioned and to forensic guidelines and techniques generally or answer hypothetical questions, but "Here, the State used Longoni to relay what Rast wrote down about how she identified the seized substances."

In Section III, Justice Kagan wrote,

> What remains is whether the out-of-court statements Longoni conveyed were testimonial... To implicate the Confrontation Clause, a statement must be hearsay ("for the truth"), and it must be testimonial—and those two issues are separate from each other.... The latter focuses on the "primary purpose" of the statement, and in particular on how it relates to a future criminal proceeding... But that issue is not now fit for our resolution. ... But we offer a few thoughts,... First, the court will need to consider exactly which of Rast's statements are at issue. [her notes or final report]... In then addressing the statements' primary purpose—why Rast created the report or notes—the court should consider the range of recordkeeping activities that lab analysts engage in... After all, some records of lab analysts will not have an evidentiary purpose... lab records may come into being primarily to comply with laboratory accreditation requirements or to facilitate internal review and quality control... Or some analysts' notes may be written simply as reminders to self... In those cases, the record would not count as testimonial. To do so, the document's primary purpose must have a 'focus on court.'

Justice Thomas concurred with all but Section III. He wrote,

> I disagree with the Court's suggestion that the Arizona Court of Appeals should answer that question by looking to each statement's 'primary purpose.' I continue to adhere to my view that 'the Confrontation Clause is implicated by extrajudicial statements only insofar as they are contained in formalized testimonial materials, such as affidavits, depositions, prior testimony, or confessions.'

He then referred to the solemnity of the Marian examination practices in support of his view.

Justice Gorsuch also concurred with all but Section III. He found the Section gratuitous, and he was unsure of the Court's guidance regarding the definition of testimonial. He wondered if the primary purpose of the test was correct. He wondered if "witnesses" reach any person who gives or furnishes evidence or reaches all those who bear testimony or if a statement bears testimony if it explicitly or implicitly relates to a factual assertion or discloses information. He wondered if "testimony" could mean evidence and proof of some fact and a solemn declaration or affirmation to establish some fact. Does the primary purpose test focus on what an objective observer would think or the declarant's purpose, and how does the court discern the primary purpose? He closed with Chief Justice John Marshall's charge to the judiciary in *U.S. v. Burr* (1807) of "'be[ing] watchful of every inroad' on the accused's right to be confronted with the witnesses against him."

Justice Alito wrote a dissent that Chief Justice Roberts joined.

> Today, the Court inflicts a needless, unwarranted, and crippling wound on modern evidence law.... I think the Court has gone far astray...
>
> Expert testimony presents a challenge for a legal system like ours that restricts a fact-finder's ability to consider hearsay. This is so because an expert's opinion very often is based on facts that are not proved in court. As a modern treatise puts it, the value of experts lies in their ability to 'brin[g] to bear a body of knowledge largely extraneous to the facts of the particular case.'... courts in Great Britain and this country long ago recognized the value of expert testimony and concluded that they 'must ... accept this kind of knowledge from scientific men,' even if it meant allowing testimony based on facts of which the expert did not have firsthand knowledge....
>
> Throughout the 19th and into the 20th century, experts generally testified in the form of an opinion in response to a hypothetical question.... By the early-20th century, this form of testimony was scorned. In the second edition of his treatise, issued in 1923, Wigmore proclaimed the hypothetical question 'that feature which does most to disgust men of science with the law of Evidence'... This state of affairs sparked efforts to eliminate hypothetical questions as a requirement.... In 1937, the Commissioners on Uniform State Laws incorporated a provision in their Model Expert Testimony Act that permitted experts to give their opinions without preliminarily disclosing their underlying facts or data.... In 1972, the Federal Rules of Evidence followed suit with Rules 703 and 705, and many States made similar changes.... What replaced hypotheticals was the procedure exemplified by the Federal Rules of Evidence. Rule 703 provides that an expert's opinion may be based on 'facts or data in the case that the expert has been made aware of or personally observed.'... These facts or data need not be 'admissible' in evidence, and they are not admitted for the truth of what they assert. Fed. Rule Evid. 703. Instead, these facts or data may, under some circumstances, be disclosed to the jury for a limited purpose: to assist the jurors in judging the weight that should be given to the expert's opinion....
>
> The Court seems to think that all basis testimony is necessarily offered for its truth. This is just plain wrong. What makes basis evidence 'useful' is the assistance it gives the fact-finder in judging the weight that should be given to the expert's opinion....
>
> It is a routine matter for trial judges to instruct juries that evidence is admitted for only a limited purpose.... In such instances, courts use limiting instructions.... Our cases have recognized only one situation in which a limiting

> instruction is insufficient: where a defendant is directly incriminated by the extrajudicial statements of a non-testifying codefendant....
>
> As it happens, I agree with the Court that Longoni stepped over the line and at times testified to the truth of the matter asserted. The prosecution asked Longoni on several occasions to describe the tests that Rast performed or to swear to their accuracy, and Longoni played along.

The majority countered that the matter is a constitutional issue, not about rules of evidence.

Testimonial Statements

The Court did not fully resolve the question of what constitutes testimonial hearsay. In previous cases, the Court determined that statements made to police during interrogation are testimonial (*Davis v. Washington,* 2006) and statements made during an emergency are not testimonial (*Michigan v. Bryant,* 2011). Regarding forensic cases, Justice Kagan, writing for the majority, determined that it involved the statement's primary purpose. She did not mention that the statement needed to be directed at the defendant or that it needed to be solemn. She noted that courts should consider the range of recordkeeping activities that lab analysts engage in and that some records of lab analysts will not have an evidentiary purpose. She declared that records that "would not count as testimonial" are those created "to comply with record keeping activities," to comply with laboratory operating procedures, "primarily to comply with laboratory accreditation requirements," "to facilitate internal review and quality control," and as "notes ... written simply as reminders to self." Nor would "Raw data" be testimonial. While testimonial hearsay is inadmissible, it can be reviewed by an expert in forming an opinion, even if he cannot testify to it.

Autopsy reports and postmortem toxicology reports in homicide cases are arguably prepared for public health purposes and courts have split on whether they are testimonial or not. Similarly, courts may differ on whether the "V" (verification) in the Analysis, Comparison, Evaluation, and Verification (ACE-V) method is fundamentally part of the analysis and testimonial or merely quality control and non-testimonial (*State v. Langill,* 2010).

BOX 15.13 *STATE V. LANGILL* (2010) – *II* [SEE *LANGILL I*, P. 186] – THIRD-PARTY VERIFICATION

The apartment of Karen Katz was burglarized. Police lifted latent prints. Fingerprint examiner Lisa Corson found one identifiable print from the dresser, which she identified as belonging to Langill. After a Daubert hearing, the trial court excluded the fingerprint evidence. An appeal to the New Hampshire Supreme Court (*Langill I*) resulted in a reversal and remand.

After his conviction, the defense again appealed (*Langill II*). The prosecutor had asked Corson if her ACE-V work had been verified, and the defense objected that it was hearsay and violated his right to confrontation. The prosecutor responded that she was testifying to what was recorded in the paperwork. The trial court found it to be hearsay but overruled the objection based on a business record exception. Corson then testified that the initials "TJ" for Timothy Jackson were entered in the verification column. She could not say how Jackson verified her identification. Jackson did not testify. The New Hampshire Supreme Court held that the verification evidence was inadmissible hearsay and prejudiced the defendant. Thus, the trial court erred when denying the defendant's motion to strike Corson's testimony. In its opinion, the court explained that "the testimony that Jackson had verified Corson's conclusion is tantamount to testimony that Jackson had affirmed the truth of Corson's match and had concluded that the latent print matched the defendant's print..." The case was again reversed and remanded.

Independent Expert Opinion

A surrogate (substitute) witness may testify to their opinion of their own independent analysis or examination of the raw data. The testimony must reflect a genuine independent opinion and not merely become a conduit for the original analyst's findings (*Burns v. U.S.,* DC Ct App, 2020; *People v. Ortega,* 2023). This practice will be scrutinized, particularly after the *Smith v. Arizona* decision. The independent expert should avoid reviewing the opinions of the original examiner, if possible, to avoid an allegation that his or her opinion is not truly independent. Nonetheless, the expert is allowed to review testimonial evidence in forming an expert opinion, just not testify to it where the defense objects.

BOX 15.14 *BURNS V. U. S.* (D.C. CT APP, 2020) – INDEPENDENT OPINION

The defendant was convicted in the District of Columbia Superior Court of first-degree premeditated murder while armed and other offenses. The prosecution called Dr. Mitchell, the Washington, D.C. Chief Medical Examiner, to testify to the autopsy performed by a forensic pathologist, Dr. Topps, who had since left the Medical Examiner's Office. The Court summarized Dr. Mitchell's involvement as:

> Dr. Roger Mitchell, the Chief Medical Examiner, did not attend any part of the autopsy or have any involvement in the examination. Dr. Mitchell did sign the autopsy report in February 2016 as a reviewing official, but he took no notes in the case, did not otherwise participate in the drafting or review of the report, and made no edits to it.

The government asserted before the trial that Dr. Mitchell had reviewed the autopsy report, diagrams, and photographs and that his testimony would be based on those reviews. The Court overruled the defendant's objection to the testimony. However,

> Despite its pretrial assurances, the government elicited testimony from Dr. Mitchell at trial that far exceeded whatever independent opinions Dr. Mitchell might have held based solely on a review of the autopsy diagrams and photographs. The government sought repeatedly to bolster Dr. Mitchell's credibility before the jury by presenting his opinions as consistent with Dr. Tops's findings and conclusions and as supported by the entirety of the autopsy records of the case. In the process, Dr. Mitchell directly told the jury of several specific findings and conclusions made by Dr. Tops and indirectly suggested many others.

The D.C. Court of Appeals, on appeal by the defendant, found that the "government presented Dr. Mitchell to the jury far more as a 'transmitter' of the hearsay in the autopsy report and other [office] materials than as an expert communicating his own independent judgment," and reversed the convictions.

BOX 15.15 *PEOPLE V. ORTEGA* (NY, 2023) – INDEPENDENT OPINION

A nanny killed the two- and six-year-old children under her care. She pled not guilty by reason of insanity. The prosecution introduced the two autopsy reports and an expert witness, Dr. Susan Ely, who did not perform or observe the autopsies that were performed by Dr. James Hayes.

> Though the entirety of each report was available to the jury, the jury only viewed seven diagrams of the decedents' bodies… displayed during Dr. Ely's testimony.… we hold that the reports are testimonial under established Supreme Court precedent.… Here, we cannot be certain that any of Dr. Ely's conclusions were based on her independent review of primary data because such evidence was not elicited by the People. At times during her testimony, Dr. Ely appeared to be reading from the displayed diagrams or the autopsy reports themselves.… At other times, however, Dr. Ely offered what appeared to be independent conclusions. Specifically, two pieces of Dr. Ely's testimony do not appear in the autopsy reports and thus, at first glance, seem to be her conclusions alone… We are unable to discern whether Dr. Ely based this conclusion on Dr. Hayes's various conclusions, such as his characterizations of some stab wounds as "gaping" and the grouping and orientation of the varying wounds, or on an independent analysis of permissible primary data, such as the photographs' objective depiction of the wounds and their patterning… Nearly all of Dr. Ely's testimony was the type of "surrogate testimony" rejected by the Supreme Court in Bullcoming in that Dr. Ely simply "parrot[ed]" the autopsy reports… We thus conclude that all of Dr. Ely's testimony was improper under the Sixth Amendment.

Supervisor-Assistant/Teacher-Student

In *Malaska v. Maryland* (2014), the Court addressed an attending forensic pathologist testifying about an autopsy performed by his student forensic pathology fellow. The Court wrote:

> It is our view that the evidence established that both Dr. Weedn and Dr. Boggs were involved in the autopsy of Liller in their respective roles. However, because Dr. Weedn—and only Dr. Weedn—carried the responsibility and authority to make the ultimate determination as to the cause and manner of death, we conclude that he was a proper witness, for confrontation clause purposes… We have found no authorities—and *Malaska* cites to none—which suggest that, where a supervisor and an assistant are involved in their respective roles in performing a test or scientific procedure, or in contributing to a scientific report, the Sixth Amendment mandates that both be called to testify.

It should be recalled that in *Bullcoming*, the supervising toxicologist was not permitted to testify for the analyst who performed the testing. The difference may be the degree of supervisor involvement.

Practical Implications of Confrontation

The forensic scientist who examined or analyzed the raw data should testify when requested where possible. A mere co-signature will not be considered sufficient for testimony to the findings of a case. Evidence should not be totally consumed where possible, and the residual should be stored at least until a conviction is secured. Raw data documentation should be extensive and created to enable an independent opinion. In the case of autopsies, this particularly means copious photographs. Notes should be separated in the case file, perhaps in a folder entitled "notes to self." Facts and raw data should be separated from interpretations in final reports as much as possible with an eye toward possible redaction of opinions. Prosecutors may want to consider the testimony of separate fact and expert witnesses.

Summary

The Sixth Amendment provides a right to confrontation. Forensic scientists whose evidence is used by the prosecution are "accusers" and may be compulsorily called to testify in person against a defendant. When the forensic scientist is truly unavailable, retesting or using substitute independent examination or analysis of raw data must be considered.

Terms

Certificate of Analysis – a formal laboratory document, usually sworn, for court attesting to a test or examination results.

Confrontation Clause – the clause in the Sixth Amendment that gives a defendant the right to confront his accusers.

Declarant – the person who made the out-of-court statement.

Hearsay – an out-of-court statement introduced in court for the truth of the matter asserted.

Testimonial – the out-of-court statement of a witness or communicative document designed for court and offered to prove the truth of the matter asserted.

Cases

Bullcoming v. New Mexico, 564 U.S. 647 (2011)
Burns v. United States, 235 A.3d 758 (D.C. Ct. App. 2020)
Crawford v. Washington, 541 U.S. 36 (2004)
Davis v. Washington, 547 U. S. 813 (2006)
Estelle v. Williams, 425 U.S. 501 (1976)
Harris v. New York, 401 U.S. 222 (1971)
In Re World Trade Center Lower Manhattan Disaster Site Litigation, 474 F.2d 529 (2d Cir. 1972)
Kansas v. Ventris, 556 U.S. 586 (2009)
Kaufman v. Edelstein, 539 F.2d 811 (2d Cir. 1976)
Lilly v. Virginia, 527 U.S. 116 (1999)
Malaska v. Maryland, 88 A.3d 805 (Md Ct. Special App. 2014)
Maryland v. Craig, 497 U.S. 836 (1990)
Melendez-Diaz v. Massachusetts, 557 U.S. 30 5 (2009)
Michigan v. Bryant, 562 U. S. 344, (2011)
Ohio v. Roberts, 448 U.S. 56 (1980)
Oregon v. Hass, 420 U.S. 714 (1975)
People v. Ortega case, 203 N.Y.S.3d 868 (NY 2023)
People v. Wrotten, 901 N.Y.S.2d 265 (NY 2010)
Pointer v. Texas, 380 U.S. 400 (1965)
Smith v. Arizona, 602 U.S. ___ (2024)
State v. Langill, 13 A.3d 171 (N.H. 2010) [*Langill II*]
Stuart v. Alabama, 586 U.S. ___ (2018)
United States v. Burr (25 F. Cas. 187; CC Va. 1807)
United States v. Jacoby, 11 USCMA 428, 29 CMR 244 (1960)
Williams v. Illinois, 567 U.S. 50 (2012)

Statutes and Other Authorities

Federal Rule of Evidence (FRE) Rule 703. Bases of an Expert's Opinion Testimony

Federal Rule of Evidence (FRE) Rule 801. Definitions That Apply to This Article; Exclusions from Hearsay

Federal Rule of Evidence (FRE) Rule 802. The Rule against Hearsay
Federal Rule of Evidence (FRE) Rule 803. Exceptions to the Rule against Hearsay — Regardless of Whether the Declarant Is Available as a Witness
Federal Rule of Evidence (FRE) Rule 804. Hearsay Exceptions; Declarant Unavailable
Federal Rule of Evidence (FRE) Rule 807. Residual Exception
Uniform Act to Secure the Attendance of Witnesses from without a State in Criminal Proceedings, https://www.uniformlaws.org/committees/community-home?CommunityKey=69a013a1-5b59-4d8d-aee3-deb474a4a6b8

Thought Questions

1. If you were the defendant, who would you want to be able to cross-examine?
2. If you were the prosecutor, who would you want to put on the stand?
3. How would you have decided the *Williams* case?

Further Reading

Dale R, *Who Killed Sir Walter Raleigh?*, The History Press, Charleston, SC, 2011.
Fishman CS, *A Student's Guide to Hearsay*, 5th ed, Carolina Academic Press, Durham, NC, 2019.
Herrmann FR, Speer BM, Facing the Accuser: Ancient and Medieval Precursors of the Confrontation Clause, *Virginia Journal of International Law* 34(3):481–552, 1993.
Kirkpatrick L, The Admissibility of Forensic Reports in the Post-Justice Scalia Supreme Court, GW Law School Public Law and Legal Theory Paper No. 2019–40, https://ssrn.com/abstract=3429152
Kry R, Confrontation under the Marian Statutes – A Response to Professor Davies, *Brooklyn Law Review* 72(2):493–556, 2007.
Langbein JH, The Origins of Public Prosecution at Common Law, *American Journal of Legal History* 17(4):313–335, 1973, https://doi.org/10.2307/845098
Maliszewski B, The *Trial of Sir Walter Raleigh (1152–1618): Winchester Trial 1603*, CreateSpace Independent Publishing Platform, Scotts Valley, CA, 2013.
Marcus P, Duncan D, Miller T, Moreno J, *The Rights of the Accused under the Sixth Amendment: Trials, Presentation of Evidence, and Confrontation*, 2d ed, American Bar Association, Chicago, IL, 2016.

Chapter 16
Pretrial, Trial, and Appellate Procedures

Learning Objectives

After reading this chapter, students are expected to be able to:

- list pretrial procedures
- describe the differences between civil and criminal discovery
- know the requirements to testify as a civil or criminal expert
- define *Brady* and *Giglio* material
- name the participants in the courtroom
- describe the jury selection process
- describe the use of evidence in a trial
- recognize process crimes.

Introduction

Forensic scientists must have a comprehensive understanding of the judicial process. While only a few cases proceed to trial, and even fewer are appealed, knowledge of these procedures is essential. Despite the significant differences between civil and criminal procedures and variations between federal and state courts, they share commonalities that are important to grasp.

DOI: 10.4324/9780429272455-16

Historical Background

Before the modern jury system, Europe and England relied on Germanic legal traditions that used ritualistic practices as irrational proof of guilt. These methods, often brutal and arbitrary, were prevalent during times of weak governments and widespread superstition. One such practice, cruentation, involved bringing an accused person before a murder victim's body to see if it would bleed, a sign interpreted as guilt. Other widespread methods included *trial by ordeal* and *trial by combat* that sought "judgment by God" (*judicium Dei*), believing divine intervention would reveal innocence or guilt. These ordeals, often administered by clergy, were common in serious or unwitnessed cases.

- *Trial by fire* required walking across red-hot plowshares or enduring molten metal poured onto the body.
- *Trial by hot iron* involved carrying a red-hot iron over a distance.
- *Trial by hot water* required retrieving a stone from boiling water, with injuries examined after three days to determine guilt.
- *Trial by water*, used particularly in witch hunts, involved binding and throwing the accused into water – floating indicated guilt, sinking suggested innocence, though often fatal.

Trials by ordeal often coerced confessions, as many preferred admitting guilt to facing brutal tests. By the 13th century, skepticism of these barbaric practices led to their decline. In 1215, Pope Innocent III prohibited clergy from participating in trials by fire and water, promoting *trial by compurgation* instead, where a defendant could swear an oath and have 12 others vouch for their honesty. However, this, too, proved unreliable and prone to manipulation.

The reign of Henry II (1133–1189) transformed English law that competed with church law. Henry expanded the role of royal justice in England through the creation of local Royal courts (assizes) and traveling justices riding the circuit (the Eyre). The Assize of Clarendon (1166) particularly created reforms that established the beginnings of grand juries and jury trials, as well as prohibited trials by ordeal, except by water, and trials by compurgation. The *Treatise of Glanvill*, the earliest treatise on English law, summarized the law at the end of his reign.

Unlike today's, early jurors acted as witnesses and decision-makers, as no formal police existed. Jurors, drawn from the local community (vicinage rule), were expected to know the details of the case. Defendants had no legal representation and had to defend themselves.

Between the 13th and 16th centuries, judges formalized jury trials. Fixed courts replaced itinerant ones, and jurors were no longer appointed by the sheriff but selected by involved parties to ensure impartiality. However, accused individuals still had to represent themselves.

The role of lawyers expanded significantly during the 18th century as the Industrial Revolution began. Legal representation became more common, and lawyers began calling and examining witnesses, influencing trial outcomes. Judges transitioned from active managers to neutral umpires, ensuring procedural fairness. The establishment of formal rules of evidence further shaped the adversarial system in modern jury trials. Today, the jury system stands as a bulwark of fairness and justice, replacing medieval Europe's brutal and arbitrary practices.

Modern Court Procedures

Most civil and criminal cases are disposed of without a trial. Those cases that proceed to trial involve procedures in the following sequence: (1) pleadings, (2) discovery, (3) negotiations or plea agreements, (4) pretrial conferences and hearings, (5) pretrial motions, (6) trial, (7) adjudication, and (8) in criminal cases sentencing.

Pretrial Procedures

Pleadings

Pleadings are the initial documents filed with the court to begin a case. In criminal cases, prosecutors file charges (*indictment, information, or a warrant*) against the defendant. In civil cases, the plaintiff files a *petition* or *complaint* that states a cause of action against the defendant, and the defendant responds with pleadings of his own, called the answer. The civil defendant may also file a counterclaim. Notice of the civil filings must be served on all defendants, which is called service of process and usually must be performed by hand.

Discovery

Legal Discovery is the general term encompassing the processes and activities that parties employ in civil and criminal proceedings to gather information and factual data from each other before trial. Discovery is used to reveal the facts of the case, to assist in formulating the issues to be litigated, and to preserve evidence of witnesses who may not be available at trial. Formal discovery evolved during the 20th century to replace legal maneuvering, theater, surprise, and ambush with fairness and substantive deliberation. This does not mean that the opposing sides will disclose everything, but much of the evidence and the main points will be disclosed to permit the other side to prepare for trial adequately. Modern discovery is liberal in that it favors broad inclusion, rather than exclusion, of evidence proffered for admission into court, which has resulted in more fair and equitable resolutions of legal disputes and criminal proceedings.

Privileged communications are non-discoverable; FRE 501 declares that the Common Law generally governs claims of privilege. Examples of privileged communications include spousal, doctor-patient, spiritual advisor communications, medical risk management materials, and proprietary and patented processes. FRE 502 defines attorney-client and work product privileges. The communications between a client and an attorney are private and confidential and are not revealed by the attorney without the client's consent. The client can waive the privilege and disclose the information. Inadvertent disclosures and disclosures in state proceedings do not ordinarily constitute waivers of the privilege. Other than reports, communication between expert witnesses and the parties is privileged; similarly, communications of non-testifying expert consultants are non-discoverable. Furthermore, the work products of the attorneys are also privileged. The confidentiality of these materials continues even after the case has been litigated. Of course, *Brady* and *Giglio* material (discussed below) must still be disclosed in criminal cases.

Criminal defense attorneys are ethically bound to represent their clients, even when they believe them to be factually guilty. Factual guilt is not equivalent to legal guilt – which the prosecutor must prove. However, attorneys are court officers who cannot knowingly aid and abet the commission of crimes, which falls outside the privilege. For instance, the defense attorney cannot knowingly allow his defendant to commit perjury by lying under oath. If a client insists he will lie, the defense attorney usually asks the judge to be relieved or withdraw from the case or not participate in questioning the defendant on the stand.

Civil Discovery

Civil discovery aims to ensure a level playing field for all parties. No side should possess a procedural or technical evidentiary advantage. The rules of civil procedure promote reciprocity and equal access to evidence. Discovery in civil cases is often extensive.

The Federal Rules of Civil Procedure (FRCP) is the guide to federal civil procedures, and the states have their own rules that are generally similar. FRCP Rule 26 is the primary rule governing discovery.

FRCP rule 26(f) requires a conference between the parties to discuss the claims and defenses in good faith, the possibility for settlement or other resolution, and discovery, including preserving discoverable information. A discovery plan must be filed with the court within 14 days after the conference. Once the plan is filed, discovery exchanges can proceed without further need for court filing or judicial orders.

In most civil cases the duty to disclose some information is automatic (FRCP 26(a)), occurring without being requested. Each party litigant should provide the opposing party with all relevant documents, data, tangible information, any damages claimed, and a witness list. Non-automatic discovery must be requested.

- *Requests for production* (FRCP 34) are formal written requests to hand over specific physical evidence to the court or the opposing party.
- *Interrogatories* (FRCP 33) are formal written questions posed to the opposing party.
- *Admissions* (FRCP 36) are formal written requests for agreements of particular facts to facilitate pretrial negotiations and trial proceedings.

The FRCP gives opposing parties 30 days to respond to interrogatories, admissions, and requests for production. Where discovery is in dispute, motions to compel discovery may be filed and argued before a judge. During the trial, alleged discovery violations may be discussed with the judge outside the presence of the jury and spectators (*in camera*).

- *Subpoenas* (FRCP 45), issued by the court clerk, can be used to compel a person to appear and testify or to compel the production of items. Most commonly, a *subpoena testificandum* is served for an appearance at a deposition or in court to testify. A *subpoena duces tecum* is served to produce a document, electronic information, tangible items, or inspection before trial requires notice and a copy of the subpoena served to each party litigant. The federal rule specifies that subpoenas are valid: (1) within 100 miles of where a person resides, works, or regularly conducts business; (2) within the state for a party litigant or its officers; or (3) for attendance at a hearing, deposition or trial where the person would not incur substantial expense.
- *Depositions* (FRCP 30) involve sworn testimony of a party or witnesses taken outside of court, without the judge or jury, but with counsel of all sides and a court reporter. All expert witnesses in a case should expect to be deposed.

Federal Rule of Civil Procedure (FRCP) Rule 26 governs the use of expert witnesses in civil cases in federal courts. It requires that the attorney proffering a testifying expert must disclose to the opposing counsel the written report of an expert, the facts or data considered by the expert, the qualifications of that expert (typically the curriculum vitae), a list of all publications by the expert in the previous ten years, a list of all cases that the witness has testified in court or by deposition in the previous four years, the exhibits to be used by the expert in court, and a statement of compensation to be paid the expert. Testifying expert's written report must contain his or her opinions and the bases for the opinions.

BOX 16.1 FRCP RULE 26(A)2(B). WITNESSES WHO MUST PROVIDE A WRITTEN REPORT

Unless otherwise stipulated or ordered by the court, this disclosure must be accompanied by a written report – prepared and signed by the witness – if the witness is one retained or specially employed to provide expert testimony in the case or one whose duties as the party's employee regularly involve giving expert testimony. The report must contain:

i. a complete statement of all opinions the witness will express and the basis and reasons for them;
ii. the facts or data considered by the witness in forming them;
iii. any exhibits that will be used to summarize or support them;
iv. the witness's qualifications, including a list of all publications authored in the previous ten years;
v. a list of all other cases in which, during the previous four years, the witness testified as an expert at trial or by deposition; and
vi. a statement of the compensation to be paid for the study and testimony in the case.

Criminal Discovery

The legal framework for criminal discovery reflects a balance between ensuring a fair trial for the defendant and maintaining the prosecution's ability to prove its case without infringing on the defendant's constitutional rights. There is general reciprocity in criminal discovery between the prosecution and defendant; the FRCrimP 16(a) Government's Disclosure generally mirrors 16(b) the Defendant's Disclosure. Under FRCrimP Rule 16, the defendant is entitled to discovery of their own statements, testimony before the grand jury, and access to tangible evidence the prosecution intends to use at trial. The Jencks Act (18 U.S.C. §3500) requires federal prosecutors to disclose witness statements in the government's possession that relate to the subject of the witness's testimony, but only after the witness has testified on direct examination to ensure the defense can effectively cross-examine witnesses.

However, the prosecution's right to evidence from the defendant is constrained by the need to protect the defendant's Fifth Amendment privilege against self-incrimination. The defendant cannot be compelled to provide evidence that would incriminate themselves. The prosecution may be left not knowing the defense strategy. However, the defense is required to provide notice or evidence when raising certain affirmative defenses (i.e., insanity defense – FRCrimP 12.2 or an alibi defense – FRCrimP 12.1). In some jurisdictions (e.g., Florida), pretrial deposition of a criminal defense witness is permitted.

The Supreme Court has ruled that some evidence is required by the U.S. Constitution to be disclosed by federal and state prosecutors to defendants for a fair trial:

- *Brady* Material (*Brady v Maryland*): any exculpatory or potentially exculpatory material must be turned over to the defense, such as a forensic science report that tends to exonerate the defendant.
- *Giglio* Material (*Giglio v U.S.*): any material tending to impeach the character or testimony of a prosecution witness must be turned over to the defense, such as a failed proficiency test, disciplinary actions involving an expert, and criminal convictions.

Federal Rules of Criminal Procedure (FRCrimP) Rule 16 (G) Expert Witnesses governs the use of expert witnesses in federal courts in criminal cases. It requires the government, when requested by the defendant, to give the defendant a written summary of any expert testimony the government intends to use during its case-in-chief. The summary must describe the witness's opinions, the bases and reasons for those opinions, and the witness's qualifications. However, in 2017, the U.S. Department of Justice (DOJ) issued Supplemental Guidance to the Ogden Memo to federal prosecutors regarding discovery involving forensic evidence and forensic experts. The guidance directs U.S. Attorneys and Assistant U.S. Attorneys in criminal trials to routinely provide the defense with (1) forensic experts' laboratory reports, (2) a summary of intended expert testimony, (3) the laboratory's case file, and (4) the experts' qualifications. DOJ laboratories' quality assurance documents and procedures are available on DOJ's website. Thus, federal prosecutors should automatically provide broader discovery materials than the Federal Rules of Evidence require.

BOX 16.2 FRCRIMP RULE 16(F) AND (G)

(F) *Reports of Examinations and Tests*. Upon a defendant's request, the government must permit a defendant to inspect and to copy or photograph the results or reports of any physical or mental examination and of any scientific test or experiment if:

i. the item is within the government's possession, custody, or control;
ii. the attorney for the government knows – or through due diligence could know – that the item exists; and
iii. the item is material to preparing the defense or the government intends to use the item in its case-in-chief at trial.

(G) Expert Witnesses.

i. Duty to Disclose. At the defendant's request, the government must disclose to the defendant, in writing, the information required by (iii) for any testimony that the government intends to use at trial under Federal Rules of Evidence 702, 703, or 705 during its case-in-chief, or during its rebuttal to counter testimony that the defendant has timely disclosed under (b)(1)(C). If the government requests discovery under the second bullet point in (b)(1)(C)(i) and the defendant complies, the government must, at the defendant's request, disclose to the defendant, in writing, the information required by (iii) for testimony that the government intends to use at trial under Federal Rules of Evidence 702, 703, or 705 on the issue of the defendant's mental condition.

ii. Time to Disclose. The court, by order or local rule, must set a time for the government to make its disclosures. The time must be sufficient before trial to provide a fair opportunity for the defendant to meet the government's evidence.

iii. Contents of the Disclosure. The disclosure for each expert witness must contain:
   - a complete statement of all opinions that the government will elicit from the witness in its case-in-chief, or during its rebuttal to counter testimony that the defendant has timely disclosed under (b)(1)(C);
   - the bases and reasons for them; the witness's qualifications, including a list of all publications authored in the previous ten years; and
   - a list of all other cases in which, during the previous four years, the witness has testified as an expert at trial or by deposition.

iv. Information Previously Disclosed. If the government previously provided a report under (F) that contained information required by (iii), that information may be referred to, rather than repeated, in the expert-witness disclosure.

v. Signing the Disclosure. The witness must approve and sign the disclosure unless the government:
   - states in the disclosure why it could not obtain the witness's signature through reasonable efforts;
   - or has previously provided under (F) a report, signed by the witness, that contains all the opinions and the bases and reasons for them required by (iii).

vi. Supplementing and Correcting a Disclosure. The government must supplement or correct its disclosures in accordance with (c).

Federal subpoenas (FRCrimP 17) of a witness may be served at any place within the United States or in a foreign country in accordance with 28 U.S.C. §1783. Ignoring a subpoena without an adequate excuse may result in a contempt of court order.

Pretrial Conferences and Motions

Pretrial conferences involving both parties and the judge generally occur in civil cases after the discovery phase when both sides understand their case well. They are primarily aimed at disposing of the cases by settlement in civil cases and scheduling pretrial motions and trials, if necessary. The negotiation may have been worked out beforehand, but the judge must approve it. Competing and contested motions will be decided by the judge; unopposed motions will generally be approved. In criminal cases, the judge may not participate in plea negotiations.

Pretrial motions in civil cases are generally made to avoid trial through a summary judgment, in which the judge rules for one party or the other on the merits of the case, to narrow the scope of the issues to be tried, or to settle discovery issues.

Criminal pretrial conferences may be held to promote a fair and expeditious trial (FRCrimP 17.1). Both the defendant, his attorney, and the prosecution must be present. The court must prepare a memorandum of matters to which the parties agreed during the conference.

Pretrial hearings in criminal cases are generally held after filing a motion to work out some legal or evidentiary issues, such as discovery, requests for Bills of Particular, motions to suppress, or a Daubert Hearing to evaluate the admissibility of certain expert testimony. Not all pretrial motions require a hearing.

A *motion in limine* (Latin for "at the threshold") is a motion, generally a pretrial motion, filed by a party asking the court for an order or ruling excluding or limiting testimony or other evidence at trial because it is inflammatory, prejudicial, irrelevant, or inadmissible. The motion is discussed and decided outside the presence of the jury. It can also be used sometimes to preadmit evidence to prevent objections and discussion in front of a jury.

Trial Procedures

The order of trial procedures is as follows: (1) jury selection, (2) opening statements, (3) plaintiff's/prosecution's case-in-chief, (4) defense case-in-chief, (5) rebuttal, (6) closing arguments, (7) jury instructions, (8) jury deliberation and verdict, and (9) damages award/judicial orders/sentencing. Civil trials may involve multiple plaintiffs and defendants. Criminal trials may also have multiple defendants. However, the court may sever the defendants in the interest of justice and hold separate trials.

Participants

PARTIES: The opposing litigants in the case.

- Plaintiff – brings the lawsuit against the defendant (litigants) in civil trials. The plaintiff's attorney represents the plaintiff as his legal counsel. Plaintiff's attorneys are often referred to as trial attorneys. Plaintiffs may represent themselves—this is called *pro se*.

- Prosecutor – prosecutes the defendant in criminal trials. A U.S. Attorney (USA) or Assistant U.S. Attorney (AUSA) represents the government in federal cases. In state cases, a District Attorney (DA), a State's Attorney, a Commonwealth's Attorney, or an assistant, represents the government.
- Defendant – the person against whom the suit is brought in civil trials and the accused in criminal cases. A public defender, a court-appointed attorney, or a privately hired criminal defense lawyer represents the criminal defendant. Defendants in both civil and criminal cases may represent themselves.

JUDGE: The judge presides over the proceedings, rules on issues of law, renders the verdict in bench trials, and imposes a sentence on the defendant. The judge decides questions of law. The judge is called "Your Honor" or "The Court".

JURY: Weighs the evidence and renders the verdict and sometimes the punishment in a bifurcated (two-part) trial (e.g., death penalty). The jury decides on questions of fact. The foreperson of the jury speaks for the entire jury. This trial jury is also known as the *petit jury*, which distinguishes it from the *grand jury*, a larger panel not involved in trials. In federal and most state courts, a petit jury is comprised of 12 members. In Florida, non-capital cases may be tried with six members. The jury may vary from 6 to 12 members in federal civil courts. Bench trials are trials without a jury; the judge then takes on the additional role of the factfinder.

COURTROOM CLERK: The clerk helps with administrative duties and ensures orderly proceedings. The clerk keeps *the docket* and is responsible for all documents and evidence. The clerk swears in anyone who must be placed under oath before testifying.

COURT REPORTER: The court reporter is a stenographer responsible for generating an accurate record of everything said in the courtroom (transcripts; the "record"). The resultant permanent record of the trial is the basis for any appeals. Some courts use only an electronic recording that is transcribed in the case of an appeal.

BAILIFF: A Deputy Sheriff usually maintains order in the court. A Deputy U.S. Marshall serves this role in federal courts.

The Courtroom

Courthouses and courtrooms generally impose structures intended to impress upon the participants that they are places of solemn and formal proceedings. The judge is seated on an elevated *bench* in the center of the front of the room, surrounded by the clerk and court reporter. The *witness stand* is also next to the judge. The *judge's chamber* is behind the bench. The parties and their counsel are seated at tables inside the *bar* – a small fence

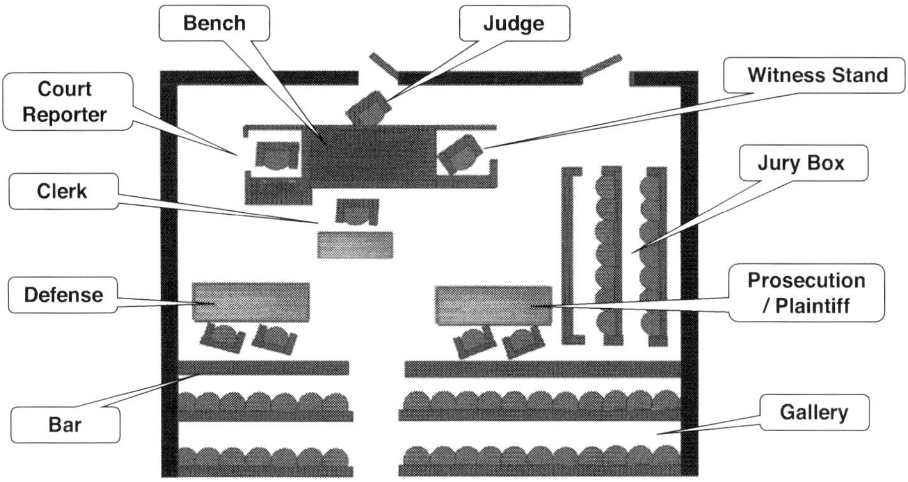

FIGURE 16.1 Courtroom Diagram.

to separate the onlookers from the participants in what is termed *the gallery*. The jury sits in the *jury box*, to the side and near the entrance to the *jury room*. There will likely be small anterooms for witnesses while waiting. A criminal defendant's holding area will be out of sight.

Jury Selection

The trial begins with the selection of the jury. A *petit jury*, generally of six jurors in civil cases and 12 jurors in criminal cases, is empaneled to hear jury trials. The general rule is that state court criminal juries have 12 members. Florida only requires six jurors, except in capital cases where 12 members participate. In *Williams v. Florida* (1970), the Supreme Court held that a "12-man panel is not a necessary ingredient of 'trial by jury' …" In Federal Courts, Rule 23 of the FRCrimP establishes as a general rule that a jury consists of 12 people. However, the Rule allows the parties to stipulate to a smaller jury.

The jury pool (the *venire*) is selected randomly from a variety of lists of citizens, such as voter registration, motor vehicle licenses, and tax documents. It is a civic duty to serve that can be enforced through contempt of court. The eventual jury panel is selected in a process known as *voir dire* (to speak the truth). Prospective jurors will be sent a written questionnaire and then further questioned in person by the judge and counsel. Each side will have the ability to make a limited number of peremptory challenges (cannot be used in a purely discriminatory fashion, e.g., to exclude all Blacks) and additionally, an unlimited number of for-cause challenges upon a sufficient showing of bias, rendering that person incapable of reaching a fair and impartial verdict. One or more alternate jurors may be selected as alternate jurors and will hear the case with other jurors, replacing any juror excused during the trial or deliberation. Alternate jurors not replacing a juror do not participate in deliberation. This process would eliminate the need for a stipulation for a smaller jury in Federal courts, as noted above. Rarely, particularly in highly publicized trials, the jury is sequestered to prevent tampering through undue persuasion, bribes, or threats. The jurors are sworn to try the case. In a criminal jury trial, when the jury is sworn, jeopardy attaches for purposes of the Fifth Amendment double jeopardy clause. In a non-jury trial, jeopardy attaches when the first witness is sworn to testify.

Opening Statements

The prosecutor or plaintiff's attorney, who bears the burden of proving the case, will make the first opening statement to the jury, giving an overview from their perspective of the case they intend to prove. The Defense counsel may then respond with their opening statement. However, the defense may elect not to make an opening statement at the beginning of the trial but reserve it for the beginning of the defense case-in-chief. Opening statements are not supposed to include persuasive arguments or discussions of the law, only a summary of what facts they intend to prove. Objections by opposing counsel are generally not favored during these opening statements. Opening statements are critical in creating a framework and setting the tone for the trial.

The Presentation of Evidence

After the opening statements, the factfinder will hear testimony from each side. The prosecution or plaintiff will first present their *case-in-chief*, and then the defense will be allowed to give its case-in-chief. Counsel will proffer evidence in the form of witnesses, documents, or tangible items to be accepted by the court as admissible evidence. The trial involves the presentation of evidence upon which the jury will render its verdict. Evidence can be categorized as:

- *Testimonial Evidence* – the oral responses of an ordinary or expert witness introduced into the record in a deposition or trial
- *Documentary Evidence* – written or electronic documents admitted into evidence
- *Physical (Real) Evidence* – physical objects that played an actual or direct role in the incident or transaction that gave rise to the civil or criminal case
- *Demonstrative Exhibit* – any item or device used to aid the trier of fact in understanding the issues at trial, such as the witness's PowerPoint slides

Evidence undergoes two levels of scrutiny: admission and weighing. A judge must first determine that the proffered evidence should be admitted for the jury to hear or see. This is a question of law. Then, the jury (or judge in lieu of a jury) weighs the evidence for its credibility and relative importance to the case. This assessment is a determination of fact.

When evidence is first proffered, a *foundation* must be laid to ensure that the evidence is admissible. Witnesses must be qualified as competent to testify. *Voir dire* refers to the process of examination of the background of a witness and fitness to give testimony on a given subject. A *Frye* or *Daubert* hearing may be held to determine if the science of an expert witness is reliable. Tangible things must be authenticated, usually by live testimony, called a chain of custody; for instance, a photograph must be found to be a true and accurate representation of what it purports to capture.

Proffered evidence must be relevant and reliable to be admitted into the record. Federal Rule of Evidence (FRE) 401 declares that evidence is relevant if (a) it has any tendency to make a fact more or less probable than it would be without the evidence and (b) the fact is of consequence in determining the action. Federal Rule of Evidence (FRE) 402 states that relevant evidence is admissible unless prohibited by law or the rules; irrelevant evidence is not admissible. *Materiality* is the significance of facts to the matter at hand; material facts bear on the decision of the case, and immaterial facts do not. In addition to relevancy, to be admitted, the proffered evidence must also be reliable, and the probative value of the proffered evidence must outweigh any prejudicial or inflammatory effect that such evidence may have or is confusing, misleading, cumulative, or a waste of time (FRE 403); for instance, a judge may find that the autopsy photographs are too inflammatory to present to the jury.

The *burden of proof* is the legal standard of sufficiency that a party seeking to prove a fact must satisfy. A criminal defendant must be convicted beyond a reasonable doubt (*Cochran and Sayre v. U.S.*, 1895); this is the burden of proof required of the jury or a judge for the factual finding of the ultimate question in their verdict. A civil defendant must be found liable by a preponderance of the evidence and sometimes to a clear and convincing standard.

BOX 16.3 HIERARCHY OF POSSIBLE BURDENS OF PROOF

- Beyond a Reasonable Doubt
- Clear and Convincing
- Preponderance
- Probable Cause
- Reasonable Suspicion

Prima facie evidence refers to evidence that is sufficient to establish a presumption of fact but can be rebutted by contrary evidence. The term "prima facie" comes from Latin, meaning "at first sight" or "on its face."

The admissibility of all expert testimony is governed by the principles of FRE Rule 104(a). This provision makes the judge, the gatekeeper. Under that Rule, the proponent has the burden of establishing that the pertinent admissibility requirements are met by a preponderance of the evidence.

Witnesses may be ordinary (lay) witnesses who have direct knowledge of the facts in the case. They may provide factual statements of what they saw, heard, or smelled. Ordinary witnesses may not give opinion testimony unless based on their perception; it is helpful to understand their testimony or determine a fact in issue (FRE 701). However, expert witnesses must have knowledge, skills, or experience beyond that of an ordinary layperson that is relevant to the particular case. Experts may give opinions. Each witness will be subjected to the following:

1. *Direct examination* by the proponent of the witness
2. *Cross-examination* by the opposing counsel
3. *Redirect* by the proponent of the witness
4. *Re-cross* by the opposing counsel

During testimony, the opposing counsel may object, suggesting fault with the question being asked of the witness or the witness's answer. Sometimes, the judge will excuse the jury so that the discussion between the attorneys and the judge, which might be prejudicial, is outside the jury's presence. Alternatively, the judge may play loud white noise to the jury so they cannot hear the discussions. The judge will then either *overrule* the objection and the objection will be disregarded by the jury and testimony will continue, or the judge will *sustain* the objection, thereby accepting the objection, striking the question and answer from the record, and telling the counsel to rephrase the question or move on to the next question. The court may instruct the jury to disregard the objectionable question and answer.

Each side will *rest its case* after exhausting its witnesses, ending its case-in-chief. Criminal defendants are not required to put on a defense case but often do. The prosecution may be able to present rebuttal evidence after the defendant rests its case.

Closing Arguments

Once the attorneys for both sides have presented their cases, they will each give a closing argument, also known as a *summation*. These are arguments, not statements, trying to persuade the factfinder of their view. This is their opportunity to summarize their cases for the jury and draw attention to the facts that support their side. The prosecutor or plaintiff has the burden of proof and the right to open and close the arguments. Thus, the plaintiff's or prosecutor's opening argument will be followed by the defendant, and then a rebuttal will be made by the prosecutor or plaintiff. The closing arguments are not evidence and may not go outside the proof presented during the trial. Attorneys sometimes stretch this rule and other rules, raising objections, but are rarely disciplined.

Jury Instructions

Jury instruction is a process in which the judge gives the jury a set of legal standards to decide whether the defendant is guilty or liable. Counsel for each side will be able to provide input before the judge delivers the instructions. The judge may also describe key concepts, such as "guilt beyond a reasonable doubt" or "clear and convincing evidence," and may define any crimes or torts the jury may consider. The case will then "go to the jury."

Jury Deliberation and Verdict

The jury deliberates to reach a verdict on the defendant's guilt or innocence in criminal cases or the liability involved in a civil case. Deliberation involves a private discussion of the case among the jurors, and it may last from hours to weeks. Depending on the court, the jury foreperson, clerk, or judge will announce the verdict in open court.

Federal and state courts require that a jury in a criminal case be unanimous in finding a defendant "guilty" or "not guilty" of a serious offense. In *Ramos v. Louisiana* (2020), the Supreme Court held that the Sixth Amendment right to a jury trial, as applied to the states by the Fourteenth Amendment, requires a unanimous verdict to convict a defendant of a serious offense. If the jury cannot come to a unanimous decision, they are a "hung" jury, a "mistrial" is declared, and the case will be dismissed or retried. A criminal verdict can only be guilty or not guilty on each charge. The defendant may be found guilty on some charges and not guilty on others. Verdicts may also be rendered on "aggravating factors" in some cases.

When defendants are found not guilty, they are acquitted and free to go. They cannot be tried again in the same sovereign for the same crime due to the Fifth Amendment protection from Double Jeopardy. When they are found guilty, they are convicted. The federal government is a separate sovereign from the states, so the same criminal acts may be charged in both federal and state courts, and a conviction or acquittal in one sovereign does not prevent prosecution in the other.

A civil verdict in federal court must be unanimous unless otherwise stipulated. However, most states allow non-unanimous civil verdicts. Civil verdicts can be much more complicated, including whether the defendant's actions or lack of action caused injury to the plaintiff and, if so, the compensation or penalty the defendant must pay.

Penalty

If a plaintiff in a civil case wins, the judge or jury will assess damages and other relief. If a prosecutor in a criminal case wins, the judge will impose a judgment of conviction and sentence.

In federal court, a criminal defendant who has been found guilty or voluntarily pled guilty is scheduled for a sentencing hearing approximately 90 days after the verdict.

Between conviction and sentencing, a presentence report will be prepared by a probation officer based on an investigation into the criminal and life history of the convicted person and any extenuating circumstances that may mitigate the harshness of the sentence. Punishment can include imprisonment, house arrest, supervised release, substance abuse treatment, counseling, educational training, payment of fines, or restitution. Federal judges use the advice of U.S. Sentencing Guidelines when assigning the appropriate punishment. States often have their own advisory sentencing guidelines for state judges. For some crimes, federal law sets a mandatory minimum sentence. The federal system has abolished parole, as have about 16 states; elsewhere, imprisonment is often followed by a period of supervised release, in which a probation officer will supervise the offender while living back in the community.

Post-Trial Motions

Post-trial motions are frequently filed in civil cases. After the verdict has been returned by a civil jury or a judge in a bench trial, the court formalizes the judgment, often with input from the prevailing party. The motions may be for a new trial because of an error occurring during the trial, a motion for judgment notwithstanding the verdict (*non obstante veridicto*, NOV), or a motion to amend or nullify the decision.

In criminal cases, the convicted defendant might also file a motion for a new trial, a motion for judgment of acquittal, or a motion to correct a clerical error in the judgement or an order. Collateral motions such as the discovery of new evidence or prosecutorial misconduct can be filed. There are few post-trial motions that a prosecutor files. However, at the time of sentencing, the government may request the court to remand the defendant to the custody of the United States Marshal or the sheriff in state court pending an appeal.

Appeals

When the post-trial motions have been resolved, the losing civil party or the criminal defendant will consider whether to appeal the judgment or the sentence. The government cannot appeal an acquittal of a defendant, although it can cross-appeal on legal issues if the defendant appeals. While the state and federal court structures are similar, there is an overlap between the two systems. In both systems, there is an appeal of right from a judgment in a court of record to a first-level appellate court. An appeal from a conviction or civil judgment in the U.S. District Court will be to the Court of Appeals (an intermediate appellate court) in the circuit in which the district court sits. Most states also have intermediate appellate courts, variously named. Appeals can only be taken on issues raised and objected to during the trial. That rule ensures that the trial judge can consider and rule on the objections in the context of the ongoing trial.

The intermediate appellate courts usually sit in panels of three judges. They will rule on the appeal on the papers (the pleadings submitted to the court) or after oral argument, which is allowed only in a small minority of cases. From the intermediate court of appeals, there may be a further appeal to the court of last resort, the U.S. Supreme Court, or the state's highest court. See Chapter 3 for further discussion on the appellate process and collateral attacks to convictions.

Process Crimes

Process crimes involve subversion of the judicial process:

- *Failure to Appear* – the offense when a defendant or respondent fails to appear at the stated time before a tribunal as directed in a summons.
- *Making False Statements* – the offense defined for federal courts by 18 U.S.C. §1001 as knowingly and willfully making false or fraudulent statements or concealing information in any matter within the federal government's jurisdiction. In *Brogan v. U.S.* (1998), the Supreme Court held that a mere denial of guilt (an "exculpatory no") by a suspect when questioned by a federal agent is a false statement under the statute. However, the DOJ's policy is not to charge a violation where a suspect, during an investigation, merely denies guilt in response to questioning.
- *Obstruction of Justice* – the offense of interference with the orderly administration of law and justice, including evidence tampering, witness intimidation, or threatening officials. The federal crime is embodied at 18 U.S.C. §§1501–1521. At common law, it is the perverting the course of justice. Title 18 U.S.C. §1512 applies to overt coercion of court or government officials by threats or actual physical harm and the obstruction, influencing or impeding of an official proceeding. The Supreme Court held in *Fischer v. U.S.* (2024) that the defendant, who invaded the U.S. Capitol building during the January 6, 2020, insurrection was improperly charged with obstruction and impeding an official action under 18 U.S.C. §1512(c)(2), writing that the section of the statute in question applies only when

the defendant impairs the "availability or integrity for use in an official proceeding of records, documents, objects, or other things used in an official proceeding, or attempting to do so."

- *Contempt of Court* – the offense of showing disobedience or disrespect toward the court of law and its officers from in-court behavior that opposes or defies the court's authority, justice, or dignity or failing to obey a court order.
- *Perjury* – the offense of willfully making a false statement or misrepresentation under oath or affirmation to tell the truth, whether spoken or in writing, concerning matters material to an official proceeding.

Summary

Cases begin by filing charges by a prosecutor or a petition or complaint by a plaintiff's attorney, followed by discovery. Discovery is fulsome in civil cases and less so in criminal trials. Prosecutors must disclose exculpatory (*Brady* and *Giglio*) materials, but the defense does not have to disclose information due to the defendant's privilege against self-incrimination. After discovery, attorneys will make pretrial motions and hold pretrial meetings, usually concerning the presentation of evidence. At this stage, forensic scientists should review their testimony with the attorneys. Daubert or Fry hearings may be held to establish the admissibility of scientific evidence.

The trial begins with jury selection, in which each side voir dires potential jurors. Attorneys make opening statements, present their evidence, and then give their closing arguments. The jury receives instructions and then deliberates to reach a verdict. If the plaintiff or prosecution prevails, the penalty or sentencing phase begins.

Post-trial motions or an appeal may follow the trial. Fraud or subversion of these proceedings, such as failure to appear, perjury, and contempt of court, are known as process crimes.

Terms

Bailiff – the law enforcement officer in the courtroom to provide security and maintain order.

Bar – the small court fence separating the trial participants from the spectators.

Bench – the place where the judge sits; often a term used for a trial by a judge alone (bench trial).

Brady Material – exculpatory or potentially exculpatory information that must be turned over to the defense by the prosecution.

Burden of Proof – the task required of a party to prove a claim.

Court Clerk – an administrative assistant of the judge who keeps the docket.
Court Reporter – a stenographer responsible for creating a written record of the trial.
Discovery – the legal process of obtaining information from the opposing side.
Giglio Material – information that could be used to impeach the prosecution's witnesses that must be turned over to the defense by the prosecution.
Motion in Limine – a pretrial motion or a motion filed with the judge, discussed outside the jury's presence, to request that certain evidence be excluded and not referred to in trial.
Pleadings – initial filings with the court that sets the trial in motion; the court papers in which the parties to a case explain their positions.
Process Crimes – crimes involving subverting the judicial process.
Service of Process – legal notice of the court actions.
Voir Dire – questioning jurors or witnesses for their qualifications or competency to serve.

Cases

Brady v. Maryland, 373 U.S. 83 (1963)
Brogan v. United States, 522 U.S. 398 (1998)
Cochran and Sayre v. United States, 157 U.S. 286 (1895)
Fischer v. United States, 603 U.S.___ (2024)
Giglio v. United States, 405 U.S. 150 (1972)
Ramos v. Louisiana, 590 U.S. 83 (2020)
Williams v. Florida, 399 U.S. 78 (1970)

Statutes and Other Authorities

Federal Rule of Civil Procedure (FRCP) Rule 26. Duty to Disclose; General Provisions Governing Discovery; (B) Proceedings Exempt from Initial Disclosure
Federal Rules of Civil Procedure (FRCP) Rule 30. Depositions by Oral Examination
Federal Rules of Civil Procedure (FRCP) Rule 33. Interrogatories to Parties
Federal Rules of Civil Procedure (FRCP) Rule 34. Producing Documents, Electronically Stored Information, and Tangible Things, or Entering onto Land for Inspection and Other Purposes
Federal Rules of Civil Procedure (FRCP) Rule 36. Requests for Admissions
Federal Rules of Criminal Procedure (FRCrimP) Rule 16. Discovery and Inspection; (G) Expert Witnesses
Federal Rule of Evidence (FRE) Rule 104. Preliminary Questions
Federal Rule of Evidence (FRE) Rule 401. Test for Relevant Evidence

Federal Rule of Evidence (FRE) Rule 402. General Admissibility of Relevant Evidence
Federal Rule of Evidence (FRE) Rule 403. Excluding Relevant Evidence for Prejudice, Confusion, Waste of time, or Other Reasons
Federal Rule of Evidence (FRE) Rule 501. Privilege in General
Federal Rule of Evidence (FRE) Rule 502. Attorney-Client Privilege and Work Product; Limitations on Waiver
Federal Rule of Evidence (FRE) Rule 701. Opinion Testimony by Lay Witnesses
Jencks Act, 18 U.S.C. §3500 (1957)
Obstruction of Justice, 18 U.S.C. §§1501–1521
Statements or Entries Generally, 18 U.S.C. §1001 (1948)
Subpoena of Person in Foreign Country, 28 U.S.C. §1783 (1948)
Tampering with a Witness, Victim, or an Informant, 18 U.S.C. §1512 (1982)

Thought Questions

1. Why shouldn't a prosecutor be allowed to use argument in her opening statement?
2. What is the difference between deposition and trial testimony?
3. What is the difference between interrogatories and admissions?

Further Reading

Baker JH, *An Introduction to English Legal History*, 4th ed, Oxford Univ Press, Oxford, 2011.

Curry MS, *Trial Fundamentals: A Concise and Practical Handbook on Courtroom Evidence, Procedure, & Trial Tactics*, CreateSpace Independent Publishing Platform, Scotts Valley, CA, 2019.

Langbein JH, Shaping the Eighteenth-Century Criminal Trial: A View from the Ryder Sources, *Univ of Chicago Law Review* 50(1):1–136, 1983, https://doi.org/10.2307/1599383

Langbein JH, The Criminal Trial before the Lawyers, *Univ of Chicago Law Review* 45(2):263–316, 1978, https://doi.org/10.2307/1599166

Langbein JH, *The Origins of Adversary Criminal Trial*, Oxford Univ Press, Oxford, 2010.

Langbein JH, The Origins of Public Prosecution at Common Law, *American Journal of Legal History* 17(4):313–335, 1973, https://doi.org/10.2307/845098

Langbein JH, *Torture and the Law of Proof: Europe and England in the Ancient Regime*, Univ of Chicago Press, Chicago, IL, 2012.

Langbein JH, Lerner RL, Smith BP, *History of the Common Law: The Development of Anglo-American Legal Institutions*, Aspen Publishers, New York, 2009.

Maitland FW, Montague FC, *A Sketch of English Legal History*, The Lawbook Exchange, Ltd, Clark, NJ, 2010.

Manuel TA, *Trial Techniques and Trials*, 10th ed, Wolters Kluwer, Frederick, MD, 2017.

Chapter 17
Expert Testimony

Learning Objectives

After reading this chapter, students are expected to be able to:

- explain the difference between an ordinary witness and an expert witness
- explain what qualifies a witness to be an expert
- describe how an attorney lays a foundation for an expert
- recite the federal rules of evidence that govern expert testimony
- discuss the necessary bases of an expert opinion
- recite the order of examination of a witness
- describe an effective expert witness.

Introduction

Less than 5% of criminal cases go to trial. Forensic toxicologists commonly testify in driving under the influence cases, and forensic pathologists commonly testify in homicides, but other forensic scientists testify less frequently. Nonetheless, testimony is a vital skill for a forensic scientist. Forensic scientists must not only analyze evidence that may be used in court but also be able to explain it in court. Expert witnesses are responsible for fairly presenting their science without advocating for a side; they speak as a voice for the evidence.

DOI: 10.4324/9780429272455-17

A failure to discharge this responsibility may result in a miscarriage of justice. A problematic testimony may cost a forensic scientist his or her career.

Historical Background

The principal case that established the role of the expert witness is the celebrated *Folkes v. Chadd* (1781–1783), also known as the Wells Harbor case. This was a time when law and science were undergoing dramatic change; courts were becoming adversarial, and the Industrial Revolution was beginning. In *Folkes*, partisan expert testimony was key, and Lord Mansfield ruled that it was essential that men of science should be able to give their opinions. This was a shift from traditional expertise based upon experience to a new breed of expert, the bookish natural philosophers who based their opinions on their privileged knowledge of the laws of nature.

John Wigmore has written that:

> the general recognition by the end of the 1700s that there was a class of persons, i.e., those skilled in matters of science, who, though they personally knew nothing about the circumstances of the particular case, might yet, perhaps by way of exception, give their testimony on the matter.

BOX 17.1 *FOLKES V. CHADD* (1781–1783) – SCIENTIFIC OPINION TESTIMONY

Wells Harbour is a port in Norfolk, England. It was surrounded by marshlands with no major river flowing into it, scoured by the ebb and flow of the North Sea. In the 1720s, it silted in and could no longer be used as a port. The locals blamed the deterioration of the harbor on embankments on the side of the channel that property owners had placed to farm the marshlands; they thought the embankments greatly weakened the body of backwater available for scouring the harbor. In 1780, the harbor commissioners decided to cut the embankment of Sir Martin Browne Folkes, the largest and thought to be the most harmful, to restore the harbor.

Folkes sued to enjoin the commissioners from proceeding with their plan and hired Robert Mylne, a father figure in civil engineering but an outsider to Norfolk, as their expert. He conducted studies of the harbor and wrote a report, based upon his calculations, indicating that natural forces were responsible, and the embankment had little, if any, effect. At the trial in the Norfolk assizes, Mylne testified without objection and impressed the jury, who found for Folkes. The commissioners appealed from their complete inability to counter this expert, claiming that they were surprised by his testimony and declared, "In matters of science, the reasoning of men of science can only be answered by men of science." They needed to call their own expert. A new trial was granted.

For the second trial, Folkes employed John Smeaton, the only expert with a better reputation than Mylne, although arrogant and difficult. Like Mylne, Smeaton was also an outsider and a natural philosopher. He performed his own studies of the harbor and wrote a detailed report based on scientific principles and calculations. The commissioners hired four experts, including civil engineers, but practical men were concerned with only what they could observe and measure. At the Court of Common Pleas trial, the commissioners' lawyer objected to Smeaton's speculative opinion and lack of personal knowledge. Justice Gould agreed and declared that Smeaton's testimony "could be no foundation for the jury's verdict," consistent with the Common Law notion that opinions must be based upon personal knowledge, and he was not allowed to testify. The jury found for the commissioners, and Folkes appealed to the King's Bench, arguing that Smeaton should have been allowed to testify.

Lord Mansfield, the most influential judge of the 18th century and Chief Justice of the King's Bench, overruled Justice Gould and declared that Smeaton could testify in a now-famous passage:

> The question is, to what has this decay been owing? The defendant says to this bank, Why? Because it prevents the backwater. That is a matter of opinion; the whole question is a matter of opinion, from facts agreed upon. ...It is objected to that Smeaton is going to speak, not as to facts, but as to opinion. That opinion, however, is deduced from facts which are not disputed—the situation of the banks, the source of tides and winds, and the shifting of sands. His opinion, deduced from all these facts, is that, mathematically speaking, the bank may contribute to the mischief, but not sensibly. Mr. Smeaton understands the construction of harbors, the causes of their destruction, and how remedied. In matters of science no other witness can be called. ...On certain matters, such as those of science or art, upon which the court itself cannot form an opinion, special study, skill or experience being required for the purpose, 'expert' witnesses may give evidence of their opinion.

In the third trial, the public heard all the experts in open court who were subjected to vigorous cross-examination. The jury found the embankment to be injurious to the harbor in accord with public sentiment and against Smeaton's "speculative doctrines, scientific opinions, and visionary conjectures."DF

Ordinary and Expert Witnesses

Ordinary witnesses, also known as lay witnesses, fact witnesses, or percipient witnesses, must have direct knowledge of the facts in the case. Ordinary witnesses may provide factual statements of what they saw (eyewitness), heard (ear-witness), or smelled (nose witness) or opinions reasonably drawn from their perceptions.

BOX 17.2 FEDERAL RULES OF EVIDENCE ON LAY WITNESSES

FRE 601 – Competency to Testify in General

Every person is competent to be a witness unless these rules provide otherwise. But in a civil case, state law governs the witness's competency regarding a claim or defense for which state law supplies the rule of decision.

FRE 602 – Need for Personal Knowledge

A witness may testify to a matter only if evidence is introduced sufficient to support a finding that the witness has personal knowledge of the matter. Evidence to prove personal knowledge may consist of the witness's own testimony. This rule does not apply to a witness's expert testimony under Rule 703.

FRE 701 – Opinion Testimony by Lay Witnesses

If a witness is not testifying as an expert, testimony in the form of an opinion is limited to one that is: (a) rationally based on the witness's perception; (b) helpful to clearly understanding the witness's testimony or to determining a fact in issue; and (c) not based on scientific, technical, or other specialized knowledge within the scope of Rule 702.

The role of witnesses is to provide the factfinder, whether judge or jury, with helpful information for deliberation in the case. The factfinder weighs the various facts, opinions, and other evidence items to arrive at a verdict. Although witnesses should not be advocates, they are proffered by one side or another and thus considered partisan by the court.

Some witnesses provide dual testimony, testifying to facts and expert opinions. This is particularly true of forensic scientists who may testify to the scene, evidence, laboratory procedures, and interpretative opinion. However, if called as a fact witness, the expert should refrain from answering questions that call for an expert opinion.

Fact witnesses are not paid, but expert witnesses are paid for their time if they do not work for the state.

Expert Witnesses

In contrast to ordinary witnesses, expert witnesses may give opinion testimony about things within their area of expertise despite lacking personal knowledge of the case's underlying facts. A witness is qualified as an expert when the witness has specialized knowledge or experience that is not within common knowledge and is relevant to the particular case.

BOX 17.3 FRE 702 – TESTIMONY BY EXPERT WITNESSES

A witness who is qualified as an expert by knowledge, skill, experience, training, or education may testify in the form of an opinion or otherwise if the proponent demonstrates to the court that it is more likely than not that:

a. the expert's scientific, technical, or other specialized knowledge will help the trier of fact to understand the evidence or to determine a fact in issue;
b. the testimony is based on sufficient facts or data;
c. the testimony is the product of reliable principles and methods; and
d. the expert's opinion reflects a reliable application of the principles and methods to the facts of the case.

Federal Rules of Evidence (FRE) 702 declares that witnesses' *expertise* is due to *scientific, technical, or other specialized knowledge* that is beyond the ken of laypersons.

FRE 702 establishes that expert witnesses are *qualified* as competent to testify in the form of an opinion based on their *knowledge, skill, experience, training, or education*. In laying a foundation for the expert, the attorney proffering the expert will begin by asking the expert about his or her qualifications as listed above. The opposing attorney may then *voir dire* the witness before the judge is asked to accept the witness as an expert.

FRE 702 allows the qualified expert to testify in the form of an opinion or otherwise if the testimony meets the four requirements of the rule. Ordinary witnesses may not offer opinions beyond their personal knowledge of the case. However, experts may opine on issues within their expertise despite having no personal knowledge of the facts or cause of action. Further, the testimony does not have to be given explicitly in the form of an opinion. The notes to the rule state: "The expert may give a dissertation or exposition of scientific or other principles relevant to the case, leaving the trier of fact to apply them to the facts."

Experts are no longer required to testify to *hypothetical questions*. The requirement that the bases for an expert opinion is grounded in a hypothetical question has been abandoned, *Rabata v. Dohner* (1969). Traditionally, experts were asked to opine on *hypothetical questions*. The question posed would contain all the facts in evidence needed for the opinion, and assuming that they are true, the expert witness could form an opinion and, if so, state it. The legal requirement for this highly structured format was eliminated when the Federal Rules of Evidence were promulgated. Hypothetical questions are unnecessary where the expert testifies from his knowledge of facts disclosed in his testimony.

FRE 702 was amended in response to *Daubert v. Merrell Dow Pharmaceuticals, Inc.* (1993). The *Daubert* factors were not incorporated into the rule; instead, the rule was written sufficiently broadly to permit appropriate gatekeeping by the trial judge. FRE 702 allows a qualified expert to provide testimony on their specialized knowledge where it is helpful to the trier of fact, based on sufficient facts or data produced from reliable principles and methods that have been reliably applied in the particular case. In short, the testimony must be relevant and reliable.

FRE 702 declares that the facts and data that form the basis of the expert opinion must be *sufficient*, but this is not further defined. FRE 703 allows broad consideration of any facts or data that other experts in the particular field would reasonably rely upon. The witness either personally observed the facts or data [direct knowledge] or was made aware of the facts or data [indirect knowledge]. The notes to Rule 703 explain this, which means that the facts or data may be derived from firsthand observation of the witness, presentation at the trial (as in a hypothetical question), or from outside to the court. The notes state that this third source broadens the basis for expert opinions to bring judicial practice in line with the experts' practice of forming their opinions from numerous disparate sources.

Bases of an Expert

FRE 703 states that the facts or data need not be admissible if they are of the kind that *other experts in the field would reasonably rely upon*. The rationale is that if other experts would reasonably rely on the information to form their opinions, there should be no need for further courtroom scrutiny. The notes to FRE 702 state:

> There has been some confusion over the relationship between Rules 702 and 703. The amendment makes clear that the sufficiency of the basis of an expert's testimony is to be decided under Rule 702. Rule 702 sets forth the overarching requirement of reliability, and an analysis of the sufficiency of the expert's basis cannot be divorced from the ultimate reliability of the expert's opinion. In contrast, the "reasonable reliance" requirement of Rule 703 is a relatively narrow inquiry. When an expert relies on inadmissible information, Rule 703 requires the trial court to determine whether that information is of a type reasonably relied on by other experts in the field. If so, the expert can rely on the information in reaching an opinion. However, the question whether the expert is relying on a *sufficient* basis of information—whether admissible information or not—is governed by the requirements of Rule 702.

BOX 17.4 FEDERAL RULES OF EVIDENCE ON BASES OF EXPERT OPINION

FRE 703 – Bases of an Expert

An expert may base an opinion on facts or data in the case that the expert has been made aware of or personally observed. If experts in the particular field would reasonably rely on those kinds of facts or data in forming an opinion on the subject, they need not be admissible for the opinion to be admitted. But if the facts or data would otherwise be inadmissible, the proponent of the opinion may disclose them to the jury only if their probative value in helping the jury evaluate the opinion substantially outweighs their prejudicial effect.

FRE 705 – Disclosing the Facts or Data Underlying an Expert

Unless the court orders otherwise, an expert may state an opinion – and give the reasons for it – without first testifying to the underlying facts or data. But the expert may be required to disclose those facts or data on cross-examination.

FRE 703 permits an expert to base opinions on any relevant information of a type reasonably relied on by other experts in the field, regardless of admissibility, although otherwise inadmissible facts cannot be disclosed to a jury unless "their probative value in helping the jury evaluate the opinion substantially outweighs their prejudicial effect." FRE 705 allows the opposing party, during cross-examination, to compel disclosure of the facts or data underlying the opinion. Where the jury is allowed to hear the hearsay that is the basis of an expert opinion, the judge must give a limiting instruction to the jury, and not to do so is error.

Qualifying an Expert Witness

A qualified expert has been found competent to testify to an area of expertise by the judge after a sufficient foundation and *voir dire* challenge.

The trial judge is the gatekeeper who rules what is admitted into evidence. FRE 104(a) states: "The court must decide any preliminary question about whether a witness is qualified… or evidence is admissible."

Before a witness takes the stand, and often before trial, the opposing counsel may make a motion *in limine* to exclude the testimony of a witness, e.g., to shield the jury from unfair prejudice. This will result in a discussion outside of the jury's presence. A *Frye* or *Daubert* hearing, without the jury, may be held if the basis or reliability of the expert opinion is challenged. This is usually a scheduled hearing to allow both sides to prepare.

FRE 603 states: "Before testifying, a witness must give an oath or affirmation to testify truthfully. It must be in a form designed to impress that duty on the witness's conscience." Oaths and affirmations are jurats attesting to the truth of the information given; oaths involve reference to God, while affirmations are without such references.

The attorney tendering an expert must lay a foundation to qualify the witness as an expert. Typically, the attorney will ask witnesses about their education, training, work experience, publications, personal certification in their discipline, whether they were unsuccessful in any proficiency test, and if they have testified before, and if so, whether they have ever been rejected as an expert by a court. The proponent will usually seek to admit the witness's curriculum vitae into evidence, after which the proponent will ask the judge to accept the witness as competent to testify as an expert.

The opposing attorney then may waive any objections to the expert's qualifications and accept the witness as an expert, object to the expert and state the grounds for the objection, or *voir dire* the witness and challenge the competency of the witness to testify in the case. The expertise or credibility of the witness will be questioned. For example, the witness may be queried about cognitive bias, such as receiving non-domain information from the police. The argument over the expert's qualifications may be made after the jury has been excused or *in camera* in the judge's chamber, so the jury does not hear the argument.

Under FRE 104(a), the court decides any preliminary questions about whether the witness is qualified as an expert. If the witness is found not qualified, then the witness is excused. If the witness is qualified, testimony will normally proceed immediately after that. The expert is qualified in an area of expertise, and testimony outside that area of expertise is objectionable.

Some courts and jurisdictions do not inform the jury that a qualified witness is testifying as an "expert" and prohibit both parties from using the term "expert" at trial to avoid inadvertently placing the court's imprimatur of authority on a witness's opinion.

Once a witness is qualified as an expert in a particular field, the next question under FRE 104(a) is whether the evidence he or she is about to give meets the requirements of FRE 702(a)–(d). The proponent of the evidence has the burden of establishing that the pertinent admissibility requirements are met by a preponderance of the evidence (more likely than not); see *Bourjaily v. U.S.* (1987). As the Court stated in *In re Paoli R.R. Yard PCB Litigation* (1994), proponents

> do not have to demonstrate to the judge by a preponderance of the evidence that the assessments of their experts are correct, they only have to demonstrate by a preponderance of evidence that their opinions are reliable… The evidentiary requirement of reliability is lower than the merits standard of correctness.

BOX 17.5 SAMPLE VOIR DIRE QUESTIONS

- Please say and spell your name for the record.
- What is your occupation?
- What is your educational background?
- Where do you work?
- What is your work title?
- How long have you worked there?
- Are you a member of any professional associations?
- Have you published any peer-reviewed articles?
- Have you testified in court before?
- …Your honor, I proffer the witness as an expert in the field of xxx.

Examining an Expert Witness

The judge is ultimately responsible for the courtroom proceedings and has some control over the attorneys and the witnesses. FRE 611(a) codifies this when it declares:

> The court should exercise reasonable control over the mode and order of examining witnesses and presenting evidence so as to 1) make those procedures effective for determining the truth; 2) avoid wasting time; and 3) protect witnesses from harassment or undue embarrassment.

The notes to the rule indicate:

> It covers such concerns as whether testimony shall be in the form of a free narrative or responses to specific questions, ... the order of calling witnesses and presenting evidence, ... the use of demonstrative evidence, ... and the many other questions arising during the course of a trial which can be solved only by the judge's common sense and fairness in view of the particular circumstances.

Examination of witnesses follows a structured order, consisting of (1) direct examination by the proponent, (2) cross-examination by the opposing party, (3) redirect by the proponent, and (4) re-cross by the opposing party. This order of examination is used whether the proponent of the witness is the prosecutor, plaintiff's attorney, or defense counsel. A judge will rarely allow further back-and-forth sessions. It is not uncommon that an attorney will waive the opportunity to examine the witness further. The attorney might not want to emphasize the witness by calling further attention to the witness or allowing the witness to continue speaking. If the examination is too harsh and overly critical, the line of questioning may backfire – attorneys should pick their battles.

Through the *direct examination* of the witnesses called to testify, the prosecution, complainant, or the defense will establish the elements of their case-in-chief. The direct examination may be a series of questions with short answers, often including yes-or-no and closed questions, in which the proponent maintains focus and control, but more often, the direct examination consists of open-ended questions to allow the expert to educate the court. Witnesses are given much latitude on direct examination. FRE 611(c) declares:

> Leading questions should not be used on direct examination except as necessary to develop the witness's testimony. Ordinarily, the court should allow leading questions: 1) on cross-examination; and 2) when a party calls a hostile witness, an adverse party, or a witness identified with an adverse party.
>
> *HOSTILE WITNESSES* – A *hostile (adverse) witness* is a trial witness whose testimony on direct examination is either openly antagonistic or appears contrary to the legal position of the party who called the witness yet still wants to prove some facts. The witness may be known to be hostile from the outset or may unexpectedly turn hostile during their testimony. The attorney

examining the witness may request the judge's permission to treat the witness as hostile, and if the judge agrees, then the attorney is permitted to cross-examine the witness and ask leading questions (FRE 611(c)). Attorneys cannot ask leading questions of their own non-hostile witnesses, except to develop the witness's testimony.

The *cross-examination* is generally designed to impeach or disqualify, discredit, expose faults in the expert's reasoning, or otherwise undermine or limit the expert's testimony. Cross-examination is limited in scope to credibility and matters testified to on direct examination unless the judge permits more. Specifically, FRE 611(b) states: "Cross-examination should not go beyond the subject matter of the direct examination and matters affecting the witness's credibility. The court may allow inquiry into additional matters as if on direct examination." Witnesses are generally given far less latitude to explain answers during cross-examination. Questions are often in a yes-or-no format. Leading questions are allowed during cross-examination.

A witness may be impeached by attacking the witness' honesty through prior inconsistent statements, integrity through prior criminal acts or immoral behavior, bias through prior words or actions, competence through faulty bases of opinion, or inability to answer questions that such experts should know or a showing of a bad reputation.

If a defendant testifies in her own defense at trial to the case's merits, then he has waived his privilege against self-incrimination. If the defendant at a pre-trial suppression hearing testifies to such preliminary matters as the validity of a search and seizure or the admissibility of a confession, he will not have waived his right against self-incrimination as to the merits of the case, but his pre-trial testimony may be used to impeach the defendant if testifying at trial.

During *redirect examination*, the proponent will attempt to rehabilitate the witness with questions intended to allow the witness to correct misimpressions that the jury may have taken from the cross-examination. The proponent's questions must stay within the scope of the cross-examination but, with the court's permission, may also ask questions that he or she forgot to ask previously.

The *re-cross* is used to rebut the impressions left by the proponent from his redirect examination. The opposing counsel must also stay within the narrower scope of redirect examination but, with the court's permission, may also ask questions that he or she forgot to ask previously.

Refreshing Memory

Present recollection refreshed is the legal term for refreshing the memory of a witness who forgot something while on the witness stand and under oath. The witness's memory may be refreshed by the attorney examining the witness by showing the witness personal notes, a photograph, or anything else – but whatever it is that is shown is only supposed to jog the witness's memory and not substitute for it. Once the witness's recollection is refreshed, the document is removed, and the next question is asked, which may be, "Does that refresh your recollection?" If it does, then the witness may answer the original question. If the memory is not refreshed, the attorney must move on to another line of questioning. FRE 612 and 613 cover writings used to refresh a witness's memory. The document or object does not have to be admissible. Opposing counsel must be able to examine it, cross-examine the witness about it, and introduce relevant parts of it.

However, if the witness is not able to recall the memory and cannot testify fully and accurately to a matter she once knew about, then FRE 803(5) declares a writing made at or about the time, while the matter was fresh in the witness's mind, that accurately reflects the witness's knowledge – a *past recollection recorded* – may be read into the record, but only the opposing counsel may introduce it.

Objections

Examination of the witness may be interrupted by objections from the opposing counsel. The objections may be to the form or nature of the question and requesting the court to strike the question or the answer. The attorneys must, on the record, object to permit appeal. The judge will sustain or overrule the motion.

Common Objections

Objections to Questions	Objections to Answers
Leading question	Vague and ambiguous answer
Question calls for a narrative	Answer lacks relevance
Argumentative question	Answer is speculative
Question already asked and answered	Hearsay
Question is vague and ambiguous	

SIDEBAR – a sidebar discussion is a discussion between the attorneys and the judge at the bench during a trial but outside the ability of the jury to hear it. White noise may be played to ensure that the conversation is not overheard.

Challenges to the Testimony

IMPEACHMENT AND REHABILITATION – an opposing attorney may choose to impeach a witness through cross-examination that attacks his credibility. The attorney may employ logic, prior inconsistent statements, contradicting facts, or introduce extrinsic evidence that reflects negatively on the witness's truthfulness or knowledge. Rehabilitation is a process used at trial after a witness's credibility has been attacked through impeachment to rehabilitate the witness's credibility. A witness is rehabilitated either by introducing evidence of the witness's good character for truthfulness and honesty or by introducing evidence of a prior consistent statement made by the witness. Usually, a witness's credibility can only be rehabilitated after their credibility has been attacked. The introduction of evidence of a witness's credibility by the proponent before his or her credibility is attacked is considered bolstering and is not permitted.

REBUTTAL EVIDENCE – rebuttal evidence, usually in the form of rebuttal testimony, is presented to contradict or nullify other evidence that an adverse party has presented. The rebuttal witness must be confined solely to the subject matter of the evidence to be rebutted.

Opinion on the Ultimate Issue

Traditionally, experts could not opine on an ultimate issue in the case because it was considered to be an invasion of the province of the jury. This prohibition was generally eliminated by FRE 704(a), "An opinion is not objectionable just because it embraces an ultimate issue." The drafters of the Federal Rules of Evidence, as explained in the notes to the rule, noted that the common law strictures preventing an expert from testifying on an ultimate issue were found to be "unduly restrictive, difficult of application, and generally served only to deprive the trier of fact of useful information."

However, the new rule was designed to help the trier of fact, not replace them. The rule does not allow the admission of opinions that would merely tell the jury what result to reach. While an expert "may opine on an issue of fact within the jury's province," he or she "may not give testimony stating ultimate legal conclusions based on those facts" *U.S. v. Bilzerian* (1991). Expert witnesses should narrow their testimony so that the fact finder can still reach its own factual/legal conclusion.

Testimony should not communicate a legal standard, explicit or implicit, to the jury, as this would compete with the judge's functions of instructing the jury on the law (*Hygh v. Jacobs* (1992)), i.e., legal expert in a civil rights case stating that a "search" was conducted of plaintiffs' residence (*Specht v. Jensen* (1988)); testimony in a worker's products liability case which uses the terms "defective" or "unreasonably dangerous" when describing a machine (*Perez v. Townsend Engineering Co.* (2008)); testimony stating defendants violated a statute imposing a certain standard of care (*Iacangelo v. Georgetown University* (2008)).

FRE 704(b) carves out a single specific exception to an opinion on an ultimate issue:

> In a criminal case, an expert witness must not state an opinion about whether the defendant did or did not have a mental state or condition that constitutes an element of the crime charged or of a defense; those matters are for the trier of fact alone.

The expert opinion that "most people" in a group have a particular mental state is not an opinion about the "defendant" and thus does not violate the rule (*Diaz v. U.S.*, 602 U.S. ___ 2024)

The mental state exception was mandated by an act of Congress in 1984 in response to the 1982 trial of John Hinckley Jr., who attempted to assassinate President Reagan by shooting him. Hinckley was found not guilty by reason of insanity after the court allowed contradictory expert opinions that some criticized for confusing the jury into rendering that verdict. The amendment to Rule 704 that added section (b) was passed in response to that criticism. In *U.S. v. Kristiansen* (1990), the Court recognized that the purpose of the rule "is to prevent a jury adjudicating an insanity claim from becoming thoroughly confused by medical experts' testimony about the ultimate legal issues."

Congress intended this exception to apply only to psychiatric testimony; however, some courts have held that it applies to all opinions as to whether a defendant possessed the requisite mental state to commit the crime. In *U.S. v. Newman* (1988), the Court declared an expert "may not offer an opinion on the ultimate issues of whether the defendant was in fact induced to commit the crime or lacked predisposition."

Introducing Physical Evidence

AUTHENTICATION – attorneys use witnesses to authenticate documents, photographs, and other items to authenticate them prior to their admission into evidence.

BOX 17.6 INTRODUCING AN EXHIBIT

1. Mark Exhibit : Please mark this as State's Exhibit 17 ... hand it to the clerk for labeling.
2. Show the Opposing Counsel and the Judge: Let the record reflect that I am showing Exhibit 38 to ...
3. Approach: Your Honor, may I approach the witness?

4. Show the Witness: Show the witness the exhibit. I am handing you State's Exhibit #17. Do you recognize it?
5. Authentication (Lay the Foundation): Is this the knife you found at the scene? Or if a photograph, Is this a fair and accurate representation of ...
6. Move for Admission: I tender this exhibit into evidence.
7. Objection: The judge will ask the opposing counsel for any objection.
8. Admission: The judge declares "Admitted."

FRE 901(a) declares the general rule: "To satisfy the requirement of authenticating or identifying an item of evidence, the proponent must produce evidence sufficient to support a finding that the item is what the proponent claims it is." Testimony that an item is what it is claimed to be satisfies this requirement. This rule is the predicate for the chain of custody requirement for physical evidence seized from a crime scene or a victim or defendant and then analyzed by a forensic scientist.

FRE 902 lists documents, records, and data that are self-authenticating and do not require a witness to authenticate, such as certified copies of public records, official publications by a public authority, and newspapers and periodicals. The opposite party, however, is not foreclosed from disputing their authenticity.

BOX 17.7 FRE 902 DECLARES THE FOLLOWING DOCUMENTS, RECORDS, AND DATA ARE SELF-AUTHENTICATING AND DO NOT REQUIRE AUTHENTICATION BY A WITNESS

- Domestic public documents that are sealed and signed
- Domestic public documents that are not sealed but are signed and certified
- Foreign public documents
- Certified copies of public records
- Official publications
- Newspapers and periodicals
- Trade inscriptions and the like
- Acknowledged documents
- Commercial paper and related documents
- Presumptions under a federal statute
- Certified domestic records of a regularly conducted activity
- Certified foreign records of a regularly conducted activity
- Certified records generated by an electronic process or system
- Certified data copied from an electronic device, storage medium, or file

While some of the categories of self-authenticating documents authenticate the document, the contents of the document may be objectionable on hearsay or relevance grounds and, in criminal cases, the right to confrontation. For example, statements by third parties in a newspaper, records generated by an electronic process or system, and material copied from an electronic storage medium may be objected to by the opposing party as statements by an out-of-court, non-party declarant.

FRE 1006 allows witnesses to use a summary to prove the content of voluminous writings, recordings, or photographs. The contents must be so voluminous that they cannot be examined in court. They can be presented in the form of a chart, summary, or calculation. The evidence presented in this way is to be considered by the fact finder, unlike exhibits used only as illustrative aids under FRE 107.

FRE 1002 codifies the *best evidence rule* and declares, "An original writing, recording, or photograph is required to prove its content unless these rules or a federal statute provides otherwise." The notes to this rule state:

> The assumption should not be made that the rule will come into operation on every occasion when use is made of a photograph in evidence. On the contrary, the rule will seldom apply to ordinary photographs. In most instances, a party wishes to introduce the item, and the question raised is the propriety of receiving it in evidence.

In most instances, the witness will identify a photograph as a true and correct representation of the scene or object depicted therein and use the photograph to illustrate his or her testimony. In these cases, the best evidence rule does not apply.

LEARNED TREATISES – FRE 803(18) establishes statements in learned treatises, periodicals, or pamphlets as an exception to the hearsay rule. The statement is called to the attention of an expert witness on cross-examination or relied upon by the expert on direct examination. The publication is established as a reliable authority by the expert's admission or testimony, by another expert's testimony, or by judicial notice. The statement may be read into evidence, but the treatise may not be admitted as an exhibit. This exception is often employed to contradict an expert by the statement in the publication contrary to the testimony by the in-court expert.

Jury Evaluation of Witnesses

Many commentators have pointed to the inability of jurors to comprehend science and claim that jurors merely adopt the expert's view or form judgments based on the emotional appeals of the lawyers. For example, Peter Huber, in his book *Galileo's Revenge: Junk Science in the Courtroom*, asserts that "junk science is currently offered to incompetent juries who make superficial judgments about experts, and whose intellectual inadequacies are compounded by juries' alleged natural sympathies...." However, studies of juries have generally disproved this claim.

One of the earliest and most controversial studies of jury deliberations was known as the Chicago Jury Project and published in part in *The American Jury* by Professors Kalven and Zeisel. Legal scholars and social scientists at the University of Chicago conducted various studies, including juror surveys, post-verdict interviews, and mock jury experiments. It also included microphone recordings in the jury room of six Wichita, Kansas, cases that became a national scandal. Their study of 3,576 criminal jury trials found that judges and juries were in complete agreement in 15 of 20 cases; in one, the jury would have been hung, and in four, they reached a different verdict. The jury was seven times more likely to acquit the defendant where they disagreed. The disagreements were primarily on the weight of the evidence, facts known only to the judge, disparity of counsel, and the sentiments of the jury toward the law or the defendant.

Social science studies have since found that jurors are active information processors. Juries actively evaluate conflicting claims, process them rationally, and construct a narrative framework that provides a plausible interpretation of the evidence. Post-trial interviews show that jurors spend considerable deliberation time discussing the nature of the expert's testimony and sanctioning other jurors who interject personal or legally irrelevant information. Deliberating jurors are found to have an excellent collective memory of trial information but poor comprehension of some information, particularly the judge's instructions.

In reacting to everyday life problems, laypersons use reasoning skills, but they have difficulty applying them to new domains with which they are unfamiliar. The attorneys' job is to help jurors understand the information and distill it down to issues they can relate to.

The *Story Model* is widely accepted as a general description of how jurors process information and reach conclusions. The various trial inputs, including the testimony of experts, are not viewed in isolation but instead are integrated into "stories." Because the information received usually involves contradictory accounts, jurors make sense of the discrepant information by engaging in an explanation-based decision process involving constructing a narrative framework that provides a plausible interpretation of the evidence. Two basic cognitive processes are used to integrate information: (1) central processing, which involves careful scrutiny of the message and the quality of the arguments being made, and (2) peripheral processing, which involves heuristic shortcuts to assess the information.

As active information processors, jurors attend to more than just the evidence and legal guidelines. Peripheral cues such as witnesses' credibility or legal actors' attractiveness affect them. Cognitive factors that may come into play include cognitive dissonance and attempts to find compatibility with a worldview, thin-slicing or snap judgments, and anchoring in which reference is made to an initial or primed expectation. The CSI effect is an expectation that they will see a lot of forensic evidence and may find the prosecutions lacking where their expectation goes unfulfilled. Jurors may experience *juror stress*. Group thinking and group dynamics are also influential.

Psychological research has revealed two styles of jury deliberation: (1) verdict-driven or (2) evidence-driven. Verdict-driven juries take an early vote and then structure their discussions around the verdict options. Evidence-driven juries evaluate the evidence and attempt to discern truth from the data.

Effective Testimony

Aristotle (384–322 BC) wrote his *Rhetoric* two millennia ago when public speaking was very important in classical Athens. He described the qualities of a speaker and three modes of persuasion a speaker can use to appeal to an audience: ethos, pathos, and logos. People are more likely to believe in a person with good morals, goodwill, and good sense.

ETHOS – Witnesses must appear credible. They should come to court dressed up and with a professional appearance. They should maintain professional bearing. They should be prepared and know the matters upon which they testify. They should be sincere.

PATHOS – Witnesses must appear appropriately motivated. They should not be flippant or arrogant. They should want to educate the jury about what they have to say and attempt to create an emotional connection with the jury. They should not speak down to the jury or up to the jury but rather to the jury as peers. They should not testify in an unemotional monotone but should show interest and, perhaps, at appropriate times, passion. However, they should not be advocates but instead be impartial and show objectivity as neutral reporters of science. Witnesses must not get angry or lose their cool.

LOGOS – Witnesses must appear to be believable and reasoned. They should possess knowledge of their area of expertise and be able to explain it in simple, logical descriptions. Jargon and technical terms should be avoided. Explanations should seem reasonable and sensible. It helps to explain not just what but also why. Analogies and examples are particularly useful.

The expert witness should be prepared and understand his or her role in the big picture. The expert should meet with the attorney before trial to make sure that the expert knows what the attorney will ask and that the attorney understands what the expert will say. The expert should know the case material and review it prior to court, as well as relevant scientific literature. The expert should also check his or her curriculum vitae to ensure dates of employment. The expert should know what he or she wants to convey to the jury and how it must be organized. Practicing a presentation using demonstrative evidence and answering questions with the attorney is good.

The *demeanor* of the witness is important. The expert must not talk up to or down to the jury. The expert witness should be knowledgeable, confident, and likable. The expert must be understandable and use plain language rather than technical jargon. The expert will appear credible if he or she is clear and forthright rather than hesitating or equivocal. The expert should be engaged in the dialogue – show some emotion and not be dry and robotic. It is essential that the expert witness remains calm and does not become upset and lose his or her cool. The witness should generally face and address the jury when answering questions but not stare at the jury nor ignore the attorney asking the questions.

BOX 17.8 CARDINAL RULES OF TESTIMONY

1. Listen to the question
2. Think about an answer
3. Answer the question
4. Stop

Witnesses must pay close attention to questions and make sure they allow the questioner to complete their question and that they understand the question posed. The witness should not be afraid to ask the questioner to repeat or rephrase the question. It is good for witnesses to pause and think about their answers before answering. The witness should answer the question being asked and not avoid the question or argue with the questioner. Particularly on cross-examination, the witness should be aware of compound questions. If the proponent of the witness does not object to the form of the question, then the witness should make sure to answer each part of the question to avoid confusion or conflation of the answer.

The expert must stay within the limits of his or her expertise and not give an opinion beyond the expert's qualification. When appropriate, the expert should say, "I don't know," "That is beyond my expertise," or "That would call for speculation on my part." The expert should never guess or speculate on the answer to a question during testimony.

Attorneys wanting to control the narrative, particularly the opposing attorney during cross-examination, will ask yes-or-no questions. The witness should avoid answering a question that is equivocal or that the witness is unsure of. The witness may respond "I can't answer the question as phrased." The attorney proffering the witness may object to the question or be able to rehabilitate the witness upon redirect or re-cross.

When testifying, the expert witness must remember that the record must be preserved and that words, not gestures or images, are recorded. The witness should think about what the transcript will read. The witness should not simply nod their head in assent to the question but instead say "yes." When explaining a photograph, the witness should say something like, "Referring to Exhibit 72, an autopsy photograph of the decedent, I am pointing to the gunshot wound on the temple…"

A surprising amount of communication is non-verbal, and juries are expected to weigh the tone, demeanor, fidgeting, and squirming of witnesses to discern who is and is not telling the truth. Therefore, it is incumbent on the witness to maintain a professional bearing and be attentive to their non-verbal cues. Witnesses should remain relaxed, be open and not defensive, lean toward the questioner as appropriate, appear attentive, and make eye contact with the questioner and the jury.

Courtroom Etiquette

The court is a formal place, and the decorum of the courtroom is taken seriously. Participants must show respect for the judge, their courtroom, and the system. Appropriate clothing should be worn. Cellphones should be left behind. Participants should arrive on time. Participants should rise when the judge and the jury enter and exit the courtroom. The judge should be addressed as "Your Honor." The attorneys often start, "May it please the court," Yes-no questions should be answered yes or no, followed by Sir or Ma'am. Direct all concerns and remarks to the bench and not the opposing counsel. Good manners, courtesy, politeness, proper behavior, and orderly conduct are demanded, and serious infractions can result in a *Contempt of Court* charge.

BOX 17.9 EXCERPT FROM THE MOVIE *MY COUSIN VINNY*, 1992

This fictional excerpt illustrates the testimony of an expert witness:

Prosecutor Trotter: Your Honor, I object to this witness – improper foundation. I'm not aware of this person's qualifications. I want to *voir dire* this witness as to the extent of her expertise.
Judge Haller: Granted. Mr. Trotter, you may proceed.
Q: Miss Vito, what's your current profession?
A: I'm an out-of-work hairdresser.
Q: Out-of-work hairdresser. Now, in what way does that qualify you as an expert in automobiles?
A: It doesn't.
Q: Well in what way are you qualified?

A: Well, my father was a mechanic. His father was a mechanic. My mother's father was a mechanic. My three brothers are mechanics. Four uncles on my father's side are mechanics…

Q: Miss Vito, your family is obviously qualified, but have you ever worked as a mechanic?

A: Yeah, in my father's garage, yeah.

Q: As a mechanic? What did you do in your father's garage?

A: Tune-ups, oil changes, brake relining, engine rebuilds; rebuilt some tranny's, rear end…

Q: Ok, ok. But does being an ex-mechanic necessarily qualify you as being an expert on tire marks?

A. Vito: No. Thank you. Good-by.

Judge Haller: Sit down and stay there until you're told to leave.

Vincent Gambini: You're Honor, Miss Vito's expertise is in general automotive knowledge. It is in this area that her testimony will be applicable. Now if Mr. Trotter wishes to *voir dire* the witness at to the extent of her expertise in this area, I'm sure that he is gonna be more than satisfied.

Judge Haller: Ok.

Q: Alright, alright. Now Miss Vito, being an expert on general automotive knowledge, can you tell me what would be the correct ignition timing be on a 1955 Bellaire Chevrolet with a 327 cubic engine and a 4-barrel carburetor?

A: It's a bullshit question.

Q: Does that mean you can't answer it?

A: It's a bullshit question. It's impossible to answer.

Q: It's impossible to answer because you don't know the answer!

A: Nobody could answer that question!

Prosecutor Trotter: Your Honor, I move to disqualify Miss Vito as an expert witness.

Judge Haller: Can you answer the question?

A: No. It is a trick question.Judge Haller: Why is it a trick question?A: 'Cause Chevy didn't make a 327 in '55. The 327 didn't come out til '62. And it wasn't offered in the Chevy Bel Aire with the 4-barrel carburetor til '64. However, in 1964 the correct ignition timing would be 4 degrees before top dead center.

Prosecutor Trotter: Well, uh, she's acceptable your Honor.

…

A: …there is no way that these tire marks were made by a 1964 Buick Skylark. These marks were made by a 1963 Pontiac Tempest. …

When the left tire mark goes up on the curb and the right tire mark stays flat and even? Well, the '64 Skylark had a solid rear axle, so when the left tire would go up on the curb, the right tire would tilt out and ride along its edge. But that didn't happen here. The tire mark stayed flat and even. This car had an independent rear suspension. Now, in the 1960's, there were only two other cars made in America that had positraction, and independent rear suspension, and enough power to make those marks. One was the Corvette, which could never be confused with the Buick Skylark. The other had the same body length, height, width, weight, wheelbase, and wheel track as the '64 Skylark, and that was the 1963 Pontiac Tempest.

Note: despite Ms. Mona Lisa Vito's apparent confidence, three cars could have made those marks, the third being the Chevy Corvair.

Summary

Federal Rules 703 and 704 govern expert testimony in federal courts, and similar state rules govern expert testimony in state and local courts. These rules grant deference to expert witnesses to give opinions in their field of specialized knowledge. A foundation must be laid during a *voir dire* examination for the judge to qualify a forensic scientist as competent to give expert testimony. The judge, as gatekeeper, should ensure that the testimony is relevant, based on sufficient data and facts, and grounded on the application of reliable science.

The witness may be asked to authenticate documents or items as exhibits for the record.

Forensic scientists should look and act professionally and respect court decorum. They should also listen to the questions, answer them, and stop talking. They should speak to the jury, not above or below them, with integrity, compassion, and intelligence.

Terms

Affirmation – a formal, solemn declaration affirming the truth, made without reference to God, to which the penalty of perjury applies; this serves as a non-religious equivalent of an oath.

Authentication – the process to prove that an item or exhibit is what it is purported to be.

Competency – a determination by a judge that a witness has the authority to testify in the case.

Expert – a witness with scientific, technical or other specialized knowledge, beyond the ken of lay persons, acquired through knowledge, skill, experience, training, or education, who is allowed to testify to an opinion based on that specialized knowledge.

Impeachment – the attempt by the opposing attorney to disqualify, discredit, or undermine a witness's testimony.

Material – relevant and critically important to prove or disprove a claim.

Oath – an oath is a formal vow invoking a divine witness to speak the truth, to which the penalty of perjury applies.

Objection – a motion made by the opposing attorney to the judge to strike a question or answer that they believe is improper.

Past Recollection Recorded – a memory that a witness once had but can no longer be recalled, that was documented in writing or otherwise.

Prejudicial – evidence that would unfairly sway a jury's opinion and would likely result in a verdict that it would not have rendered without the evidence.

Present Recollection Refreshed – a memory that a witness can recall after some reminder.

Probative – having evidentiary value; helpful in proving a point in court.

Proffer – a request to the court that a witness or item be admitted into evidence for consideration by the factfinder and to be made part of the record.

Proponent – the attorney who proffers evidence, including witness testimony, for admission into evidence for consideration by the factfinder.

Qualification – the determination by the court that the expert witness has the appropriate background and basis to give an expert opinion on the topic.

Rehabilitation – the attempt by the proponent of a witness during redirect examination to correct or overcome the impeachment attempt by opposing counsel during their cross-examination of the witness.

Voir Dire – the examination of a witness by the opposing attorney to challenge the witness's qualification or competency to testify in the case.

Cases

Bourjaily v. United States, 483 U.S. 171 (1987)
Daubert v. Merrell Dow Pharmaceuticals, Inc., 509 U.S. 579 (1993)
Diaz v. U.S., 602 U.S. ___ (2024)
Folkes v. Chadd, 3 Doug. 157, 99 Eng. Rep. 589 (1782)
Hygh v. Jacobs, 961 F.2d 359 (2d Cir. 1992)
Iacangelo v. Georgetown University, 560 F.Supp.2d 53 (D.D.C. 2008)
In re Paoli R.R. Yard PCB Litigation, 35 F.3d 717 (3d Cir. 1994)
Perez v. Townsend Engineering Co., 562 F. Supp. 2d. 647 (M.D. Pa. 2008)
Rabata v. Dohner, 172 N.W.2d 409 (1969)
Specht v. Jensen, 853 F.2d 805 (10th Cir. 1988)
United States v. Bilzerian, 926 F.2d 1285 (2d Cir. 1991)
United States v. Kristiansen, 901 F.2d 1463 (8th Cir. 1990)
United States v. Newman, 849 F.2d 156 (5th Cir. 1988)

Other Authorities

Federal Rules of Evidence, https://www.uscourts.gov/rules-policies/current-rules-practice-procedure/federal-rules-evidence
Federal Rule of Evidence (FRE) Rule 104. Preliminary Questions

Federal Rule of Evidence (FRE) Rule 601. Competency to Testify in General
Federal Rule of Evidence (FRE) Rule 602. Need for Personal Knowledge
Federal Rule of Evidence (FRE) Rule 603. Oath or Affirmation to Testify Truthfully
Federal Rule of Evidence (FRE) Rule 611. Mode and Order of Examining Witnesses and Presenting Evidence
Federal Rule of Evidence (FRE) Rule 612. Writing Used to Refresh a Witness's Memory
Federal Rule of Evidence (FRE) Rule 613. Witness's Prior Statement
Federal Rule of Evidence (FRE) Rule 701. Opinion by Lay Witnesses
Federal Rule of Evidence (FRE) Rule 702. Testimony by Expert Witnesses
Federal Rule of Evidence (FRE) Rule 703. Bases of an Ultimate Issue
Federal Rule of Evidence (FRE) Rule 704. Opinion on an Ultimate Issue
Federal Rule of Evidence (FRE) Rule 705. Disclosing the Facts or Data Underlying an Expert's Opinion
Federal Rule of Evidence (FRE) Rule 803. Exceptions to the Rule Against Hearsay — Regardless of Whether the Declarant Is Available as a Witness
Federal Rule of Evidence (FRE) Rule 901. Authenticating or Identifying Evidence
Federal Rule of Evidence (FRE) Rule 902. Evidence That Is Self-Authenticating
Federal Rule of Evidence (FRE) Rule 1002. Requirement of the Original
Federal Rule of Evidence (FRE) Rule 1006. Summaries to Prove Content

Thought Questions

1. Should the expert be able to testify to a legal conclusion if it is within the purview of his or her expertise?
2. How should an expert respond when asked a "yes or no" question on cross-examination that cannot be answered in that fashion?
3. Should experts relying on technical skill and experience be held to the same standard of admissibility as experts relying on a scientific-based method of analysis?
4. As an expert, would you testify to your opinion in which you have a reasonable degree of certainty? Is that any different than saying you have high confidence in your opinion?

Further Reading

Babitsky SB, Mangraviti JJ, *How to Become a Dangerous Expert Witness: Advanced Techniques and Strategies,* SEAK, Inc., Falmouth, MA, 2005.
Bailey FL, Fishman KJ, *Excellence in Cross-Examination,* Thomson Reuters, Eagan, MN, 2017.

Bornstein BH, Greene E, *The Jury under Fire: Myth, Controversy, and Reform*, Oxford Univ Press, Oxford, 2017.

Devine DJ, *Jury Decision Making: The State of the Science,* New York Univ Press, New York, 2012.

Golan T, *Laws of Men and Laws of Nature: The History of Scientific Expert Testimony in England and America,* Harvard University Press, Cambridge, MA, 2004.

Houck MM, Funk C, Feder HA, *Successful Expert Testimony,* CRC Press, Boca Raton, FL, 2018.

Kalven H, Zeisel H, *The American Jury,* University of Chicago Press, Chicago, IL, 1971.

Kovera MB, *The Psychology of Juries,* American Psychological Association, Washington, DC, 2017.

Lubet S, Boals EI, *Expert Testimony*, 4th ed, National Institute for Trial Advocacy/Wolters Kluwer Law, Boulder, CO, 2020.

Matson JV, *Effective Expert Witnessing,* 5th ed, Taylor & Francis/CRC Press, Boca Raton, FL, 2012.

Pozner L, Todd RJ, *Cross-Examination: Science and Techniques,* 3rd ed, LexisNexis, New York, 2018.

Shapiro BJ, *Beyond Reasonable Doubt and Probable Cause: Historical Perspectives on the Anglo-American Law of Evidence,* Univ of California Press, Berkeley, CA 1991.

Smith FC, *A Guide to Forensic Testimony: The Art and Practice of Presenting Testimony as an Expert Technical Witness,* Addison-Wesley Professional, Hoboken, NJ, 2002.

Younger I, *The Art of Cross-Examination,* ABA, Chicago, IL, 1976.

Glossary

Actus Reus – criminal conduct.
Admissible – referring to alleged facts and evidence that have been allowed by the judge to be assessed by the factfinder and made part of the court record in the case.
Affiant – the officer who requests the warrant in an affidavit.
Affirmation – a formal, solemn declaration affirming the truth, made without reference to God, to which the penalty of perjury applies; this serves as a non-religious equivalent of an oath.
Amicus Brief – a brief of a non-party as a friend of the court.
Appeal of Right – an appeal that a court must hear.
Arraignment – a hearing before the trial judge to obtain the defendant's plea of guilty or not guilty.
Attenuation – lessening of impact; gradual loss; where the connection between the evidence challenged and the illegal activity is so remote as to allow it to be admissible.
Authentication – the process to prove that an item or exhibit is what it is purported to be.
Bail – money or property posted to guarantee a later appearance in court.
Bailiff – the law enforcement officer in the courtroom to provide security and maintain order.

Bar – the small court fence separating the trial participants from the spectators.
Bench – the place where the judge sits; often a term used for a trial by a judge alone (bench trial).
Bench Trial – a trial conducted without a jury.
Bill of Rights – the first ten Amendments to the U.S. Constitution.
Binding Precedent – prior published opinions of appellate judges controlling the present case.
Brady Material – exculpatory or potentially exculpatory information that must be turned over to the defense by the prosecution.
Branches of Law – areas of legal specialization.
Burden of Proof – the task required of a party to prove a claim.
Case Law – legal doctrine developed through judicial decisions rather than law based on constitutions, statutes, or regulations.
Castle Doctrine – laws that permit using force to defend oneself within a home without retreat.
Categorical (Deterministic) Statement – a declarative statement of belief that a datum falls into one category or another.
Certificate of Analysis – a formal laboratory document, usually sworn, for court attesting to a test or examination results.
Civil Law – the system of jurisprudence derived from Roman law and based on legal codes; it is also used as a term for non-criminal branches of law.
Civil War (Reconstruction) Amendments – the Thirteenth, Fourteenth, and Fifteenth Amendments of the U.S. Constitution.
Code of Federal Regulations – the compilation of federal regulations.
Common Law – legal doctrine developed in early English case law.
Competency – a determination by a judge that a witness has the authority to testify in the case.
Complaint – a formal request for police intervention by a citizen.
Concurring Opinion – an independent opinion that supports the majority holding.
Confrontation Clause – the clause in the Sixth Amendment that gives a defendant the right to confront his accusers.
Contracts – legally recognized agreements involving reciprocal promises.
Court Clerk – an administrative assistant of the judge who keeps the docket.
Court of Last Resort – the highest appellate court available to a party.
Court Reporter – a stenographer responsible for creating a written record of the trial.
Curtilage – the zone of habitation beyond the dwelling that includes a reasonable expectation of privacy.
Damages – injuries for which a defendant is liable.

Daubert Factors – a set of suggestions articulated by the Court in *Daubert* that trial judges may use to determine the reliability of scientific evidence.

Daubert Standard – a flexible determination by the trial court for the admissibility of scientific evidence based on its relevancy and reliability.

Declarant – the person who made the out-of-court statement.

Discovery – the legal process of obtaining information from the opposing side.

Dissenting Opinion – an opinion contrary to the majority or plurality holding.

Diversion Program – a program that takes a defendant out of the system in an attempt for rehabilitation.

Due Process – the right to a fair legal process and respect for individual rights.

Evidence – alleged facts presented to the factfinder to be weighed and considered to arrive at a verdict.

Exclusionary Rule – the prohibition of illegally obtained evidence in a criminal trial.

Execution – the service of a warrant.

Exigency – an urgent need.

Expert – a witness with scientific, technical, or other specialized knowledge, beyond the ken of lay persons, acquired through knowledge, skill, experience, training, or education, who is allowed to testify to an opinion based on that specialized knowledge.

Federal Diversity – a basis of federal jurisdiction based upon citizenship from different states or international citizenship.

Federal Preemption – the supremacy of federal statutes over state laws.

Federal Register – a daily publication of Presidential documents, proposed federal regulations, and other information of the federal government to be made public.

Felony – traditionally a crime punishable by a year or more in prison.

Foreign Intelligence Surveillance Court (FISC) – hears requests for surveillance warrants of foreign agents, lone wolves, and terrorists.

Franks Hearing – a motion *in limine* filed by the defendant to challenge a warrant issued because the affiant knowingly made false or misleading statements.

Frisk – a quick pat down of a person for weapons.

Fruit of the Poisonous Tree – secondary evidence that was obtained after police conduct that violated the defendant's rights.

Frye Rule – the general acceptance standard articulated by the Court in *Frye v. U.S.* to determine the admissibility of novel scientific evidence.

General Intent – the intent to commit the crime.
Giglio Material – information that could be used to impeach the prosecution's witnesses that must be turned over to the defense by the prosecution.
Good Faith – well-intentioned police conduct used in the context of an honest mistake or reliance.
Grand Jury – secret hearing by a panel of citizens to determine probable cause to charge the defendant or to investigate criminal activity.
Habeas Corpus – a collateral federal or state proceeding alleging wrongful detention or imprisonment.
Hearsay – an out-of-court statement introduced in court for the truth of the matter asserted.
Impeachment – the attempt by the opposing attorney to disqualify, discredit, or undermine a witness's testimony.
Inchoate Crime – incomplete, incipient, or anticipated crime.
Indictment – a charging document issued by a grand jury.
Individualized Suspicion – the notion that the suspicion is of a particular person.
Intentional Torts – non-accidental harm caused by a tortfeasor.
Joint and Several Liability – liability of any and all tortfeasors for tortious conduct.
Judicial Review – the power of the courts to interpret, enforce, and strike down legislation.
Jurisdiction – the power of a court to hear a case.
Law – the set of rules promulgated by competent authorities and enforceable by the government.
Material – relevant and critically important to prove or disprove a claim.
Mens Rea – a culpable mental state.
Misdemeanor – traditionally a crime punishable by less than a year in prison.
Motion in Limine – a pretrial motion or a motion filed with the judge, discussed outside the jury's presence, to request that certain evidence be excluded and not referred to in trial.
Negligence – accidental harm caused by a tortfeasor.
Oath – an oath is a formal vow invoking a divine witness to speak the truth, to which the penalty of perjury applies.
Objection – a motion made by the opposing attorney to the judge to strike a question or answer that they believe is improper.
Open Fields – a legal euphemism for the private land that extends beyond the curtilage.
Open View – visible from a constitutionally non-protected area.
Particularity – reasonable specificity in the description of places, items, and persons as the basis for issuance of a warrant.

Past Recollection Recorded – a memory that a witness once had, but can no longer be recalled, that was documented in writing or otherwise.

Penal Codes – comprehensive and ordered statutes defining crimes in a jurisdiction.

Personal Jurisdiction – the court's power to hear the parties' case.

Personal Property – an individual's belongings, excluding any real estate property, including tangible and intangible assets.

Plain View – visible from a constitutionally protected area, where an officer has a legal right to be.

Plea Colloquy – the exchange between the judge and the defendant, in which the defendant pleads guilty or not guilty.

Pleadings – initial filings with the court that sets the trial in motion; the court papers in which the parties to a case explain their positions.

Plurality Opinion – an opinion in a case without a majority opinion that received the most support.

Police Power – the constitutional power reserved to the states to regulate and enforce their inhabitants' health, safety, morals, and general welfare.

Prejudicial – evidence that would unfairly sway a jury's opinion and would likely result in a verdict that it would not have rendered without the evidence.

Preliminary Hearing – a public hearing by a magistrate to determine probable cause to proceed.

Present Recollection Refreshed – a memory that a witness can recall after some reminder.

Probabilistic (Graded) Statement – a statistical statement of belief that a datum has a certain likelihood of truth.

Probable Cause – more than a mere reasonable suspicion but less than a preponderance, substantial chance of criminal activity; the standard required for arresting someone, for issuing a warrant, and for bringing someone to trial; it is based upon the totality of the circumstances.

Probative – having evidentiary value; helpful in proving a point in court.

Process Crime – a crime to subvert the judicial process.

Proffer – a request to the court that a witness or item be admitted into evidence for consideration by the factfinder and to be made part of the record.

Proponent – the attorney who proffers evidence, including witness testimony, for admission into evidence for consideration by the factfinder.

Protective Sweep – a quick search of a limited area for weapons and dangerous instrumentalities.

Qualification – the determination by the court that the expert witness has the appropriate background and basis to give an expert opinion on the topic.

Qualified Immunity – bars suits against government officials acting in their official capacity in good faith.

Reasonable Articulable Suspicion – a suspicion that is more than a hunch but less than probable cause that can be clearly stated; it is an objective standard that reasonable persons would also find suspicious given the same information.

Rehabilitation – the attempt by the proponent of a witness during redirect examination to correct or overcome the impeachment attempt by the opposing counsel during their cross-examination of the witness.

Reasonable – sound judgment, appropriate or fair; in a judicial sense, it is the objective notion of what an ordinary person of sound judgment would do or think if in the same circumstance.

Reasonable Expectation of Privacy – an expectation of privacy deemed reasonable in public norms.

Relevant (in a legal sense) – information that aids the trier of fact and pertains directly to the case at hand, aligning with the specific inquiry being considered.

Reliable (in a legal sense) – evidence that the trial judge deems scientifically valid and appropriate for the jury to consider.

Remand – to order back to the lower court for further proceedings or a new trial.

Remedies – judicially ordered relief, e.g., restitution, specific performance, injunction.

Rescission – cancellation of a contract.

Research – a systematic investigation designed to develop or contribute to generalizable knowledge.

Respondeat Superior – the doctrine of vicarious liability of the supervisor for the employee.

Science – a body of knowledge and a method of acquiring knowledge.

Search – to look for something; in a constitutional sense, it is looking for something within the zone of Fourth Amendment protection.

Service of Process – legal notice of the court actions.

Sources of Law – the various methods by which law is promulgated.

Sovereign Immunity – traditional immunity for government actions.

Specific Intent – the intent to cause a specific harm.

Spoliation of Evidence – the intentional, reckless, or negligent withholding, hiding, altering, fabricating, or destroying of evidence relevant to a legal proceeding.

Stand-Your-Ground Law – laws that permit the use of force to defend oneself or others without having to retreat in places where one has a lawful right to be.
Stare Decisis – the doctrine of legal precedent.
Statute of Limitations – statutorily defined period within which someone can be sued or prosecuted for a crime.
Subject Matter Jurisdiction – the court's power to hear the case's subject matter.
Strict Liability – legal imposition of responsibility without regard to fault.
Test Accuracy – the degree to which a test consistently yields the correct result.
Test Precision – the degree to which the test consistently reproduces a result.
Test Validity – demonstrated ability to measure what the test is supposed to measure.
Testimonial – the out-of-court statement of a witness or communicative document designed for court and offered to prove the truth of the matter asserted.
Third-party Disclosure – revealing information to others not party to the original communication.
Tortfeasor – a person, group, or entity that commits a tort, a wrongdoer.
Torts – personal injury suits.
Trier of Fact – the jury in a jury trial; the judge in a bench trial.
Unconscionable Contracts – contracts that are so unfair as to be unenforceable.
United States Code – the compilation of federal statutes.
Vicarious Liability – imputed liability from the actions of others.
Voir Dire – the process of questioning potential jurors to assess their suitability to serve on a jury or questioning witnesses to determine their competency to testify in a particular case.
Weight – the credibility, gravity, and persuasiveness given to alleged evidence by the factfinder.
Writ of Capias – an arrest warrant issued by a court upon the return of an indictment.

Case Index

Adams v. Williams, 407 U.S. 143 (1972) 178
Aguilar v. Texas, 378 U.S. 108 (1964) 34, 161
Air Pollution Variance Board v. Western Alfalfa Corp., 416 U.S. 861 (1974) 189
Alabama v. White, 496 U.S. 325 (1990) 178
Albrecht v. Treon, 617 F.3d 890 (6th Cir. 2010) 201
Alden v. Maine, 527 U.S. 706 (1999) 80
Almeciga v. Center for Investigative Reporting, Inc., 121 F. Supp. 3d 379 (S.D.N.Y. 2015) 82
Arizona v. Evans, 514 U.S. 1 (1995) 122
Arizona v. Gant, 556 U.S. 332 (2009) 181, 183
Arizona v. Hicks, 480 U.S. 321 (1987) 173
Arizona v. Johnson, 555 U.S. 323 (2009) 179
Arizona v. Youngblood, 488 U.S. 51 (1988) 225, 226
Ashcroft v. al-Kidd, 563 U.S. 731 (2011) 81
Ashcroft v. Iqbal, 556 U.S. 662 (2009) 277
Atwater v. City of Largo Vista, 532 U.S. 318 (2001) 180

Bailey v. United States, 568 U.S. 186 (2013) 154
Baker v. Carr, 369 U.S. 186 (1962) 57
Barefoot v. Estelle, 463 U.S. 880 (1983) 256
Barron v. City of Baltimore, 32 U.S. (7 Pet.) 243 (1833) 28, 128
Batson v. Kentucky, 476 U.S. 79 (1986) 117
Beck v. Alabama, 447 U.S. 625 (1980) 93
Benton v. Maryland, 385 U.S. 784 (1969) 35
Birchfield v. North Dakota, 579 U.S. 438 (2016) 180, 210, 212, 214
Bivens v. Six Unknown Federal Agents, 403 U.S. 388 (1971) 79, 81
Blockburger v. United States, 284 U.S. 299 (1932) 94
Board of Educ. of Indep. Sch. Dist. No. 92 of Pottawatomie County. v. Earls, 536 U.S. 822 (2002) 188
Boyd v. United States, 116 U.S. 616 (1886) 129
Bowers v. Hardwick, 478 U.S. 186 (1986) 37
Bourjaily v. United States, 483 U.S. 171 (1987) 340
Brady v. Maryland, 373 U.S. 83 (1963) 224, 319
Bravo v. City of Santa Maria, Nos. 14-55557, 14-55687. (9th Cir. 2016) 155
Breithaupt v. Abram, 352 U.S. 432 (1957) 209, 210, 213
Brendlin v. California, 551 U.S. 1 (2007) 179, 183
Brigham City, Utah v. Stuart, 547 U.S. 398 (2006) 157, 185–187
Brinegar v. United States, 338 U.S. 160 (1949) 150

Bristol-Myers Squibb Co. v. Superior Court of San Francisco County, 582 U.S. 255 (2017) 49
Brogan v. United States, 522 U.S. 398 (1998) 329
Brotherton v. Cleveland, 923 F.2d 477 (6th Cir. 1991) 201
Brower v. County of Inyo, 489 U.S. 593 (1989) 180
Brown v. Board of Education, 347 U.S. 483 (1954) 34, 59
Brown v. Mississippi, 297 U.S. 278 (1936) 31
Brown v. Ohio, 432 U.S. 161 (1977) 94
Bryan v. Texas, 804 S.W.2d 648 (Tex. App. 1991) 284
Bullcoming v. New Mexico, 564 U.S. 647 (2011) 301
Bumper v. North Carolina, 391 U.S. 543 (1968) 175
Burns v. United States, 235 A.3d 758 (D.C. Ct. App. 2020) 308
Burrage v. United States, 571 U.S. 204 (2014) 92
Byrd v. United States, 584 U.S. 395 (2018) 132

Cady v. Dombrowski, 413 U.S. 433 (1973) 184
California v. Acevedo, 500 U.S. 565 (1991) 184, 185
California v. Carney, 471 U.S. 386 (1985) 185
California v. Ciraolo, 476 U.S. 207 (1986) 173, 174
California v. Greenwood, 486 U.S. 35 (1988) 198
California v. Trombetta, 467 U.S. 479 (1984) 224
Camara v. Municipal Court, 387 U.S. 523 (1967) 167, 189, 200
Caniglia v Strom, 593 U.S. 194 (2021) 183–184
Carlson v. Green, 446 U.S. 14 (1980) 79
Carpenter v. United States, 585 U.S. 296 (2018) 140–142
Carroll v. United States, 267 U.S. 132 (1925) 184, 185
Chambers v. Maroney, 399 U.S. 42 (1970) 184
Chandler v. Miller, 520 U.S. 305 (1997) 189
Chevron v. Natural Resources Defense Council, 467 U.S. 837 (1984) 15
Chimel v. California, 395 U.S. 752 (1969) 35, 139, 180–182
City of Canton v. Harris, 489 U.S. 378 (1989) 67, 277
City of Indianapolis v. Edmond, 531 U.S. 32 (2000) 188
City of Ontario v. Quon, 560 U.S. 746 (2010) 172
City of West Covina v. Perkins, 525 U.S. 234 (1999) 197
Clark v. City of San Antonio, 714 F. App'x 446 (5th Cir. 2018) 157
Cochran and Sayre v. United States, 157 U.S. 286 (1895) 325
Cohen v Beneficial Industrial Loan Corp., 337 U.S. 541 (1949) 117
Collins v. Virginia, 584 U.S. 586 (2018) 133
Colonnade Catering Corp. v. United States, 397 U.S. 72 (1970) 190
Colorado v. Bertine, 479 U.S. 386 (1987) 183
Commonwealth v. Sadari, 752 A.2d 393 (Pa. 2000) 188
Coolidge v. New Hampshire, 403 U.S. 443 (1971) 148, 184
Connick v. Thompson, 563 U.S. 51 (2011) 277
County of Riverside v. McLaughlin, 500 U.S. 413 (1991) 178
Crawford v. Washington, 541 U.S. 36 (2004) 297–298
Crocker v. Pleasant, 778 So.2d 978 (Fla. 2001) 200
Cruzan v. Missouri Department of Health, 497 U.S. 261 (1990) 58
Cupp v. Murphy, 412 U.S. 291 (1973) 209

Daimler AG v. Bauman, 571 U.S. 117 (2014) 49
Dalia v. United States, 441 U.S. 238 (1979) 155
Daubert v. Merrell Dow Pharmaceuticals, Inc., 43 F.3d 1311 (9th Cir. 1995) 264
Daubert v. Merrell Dow Pharmaceuticals, Inc., 509 U.S. 579
(1993) 82, 233, 258–266, 271, 321, 337
Davis v. Mississippi, 394 U.S. 721 (1969) 180, 204–206, 215
Davis v. Passman, 442 U.S. 228 (1979) 79
Davis v. Washington, 547 U. S. 813 (2006) 307
Delaware v. Prouse, 440 U.S. 648 (1979) 178
DeShaney v. Winnebago County Department of Social Services, 489 U.S. 189 (1989) 21
Diaz v. United States, 602 U.S. ___ (2024) 345
District Attorney's Office for the Third Judicial District v. Osborne, 557 U.S. 52
(2009) 38, 40–41, 210, 284
District of Columbia v. Heller, 554 U.S. 570 (2008) 15
Dobbs v. Jackson Women's Health Organization, 597 U.S. 215 (2022) 8–9, 37
Doe v. Calumet City, 641 N.E.2d 498 (IL 1994) 181
Doe v. United States, 487 U.S. 201 (1988) 204
Donovan v. Dewey, 452 U.S. 594 (1981) 190
Draper v. United States, 358 U.S. 307 (1959) 151
Duncan v. Louisiana, 391 U.S. 145 (1968) 35
Durham v. United States, 214 F.2d 862 (D.C. Cir. 1954) 103

Egbert v. Boule, 596 U.S. 482 (2022) 79
Entick v. Carrington, 95 Eng. Rep. 807 (C.P. 1765) 20

Escobedo v. Illinois, 378 U.S. 478 (1964) 34, 113
Estelle v. Williams, 425 U.S. 501 (1976) 289
Ex parte Colone, No. WR-89 538-01 (Tex. Crim. App. 2022) 222–223
Ex parte Young, 209 U.S. 123 (1908) 80

Ferguson v. City of Charleston, 532 U.S. 67 (2001) 189
Fernandez v. California, 571 U.S. 292 (2014) 176
Fisher v. United States, 425 U.S. 391 (1976) 130
Fischer v. United States, 603 U.S.___ (2024) 329
Fitzpatrick v. Bitzer, 427 U.S. 445 (1976) 80
Florence v. Board of Chosen Freeholders, 566 U.S. 318 (2012) 181, 189
Flores v. City of Mount Vernon, 41 F. Supp. 2d 439 (S.D.N.Y. 1999) 181
Florida v. Bostick, 501 U.S. 429 (1991) 175, 202
Florida v. Harris, 568 U.S. 237 (2013) 174
Florida v. Jardines, 569 U.S. 1 (2013) 133, 134
Florida v. Jimeno, 499 U.S. 934 (1991) 176
Florida v. J.L., 529 U.S. 266 (2000) 178
Florida v. Riley, 488 U.S. 445 (1989) 173, 174
Florida v. Royer, 460 U.S. 491 (1983) 175, 178, 202
Florida v. Wells, 495 U.S. 1 (1989) 183
Folkes v. Chadd, 3 Doug. 157, 99 Eng. Rep. 589 (1782) 334–335
Frank v. Maryland, 359 U.S. 360 (1959) 166
Franks v. Delaware, 438 U.S. 154 (1978) 156
Friedman v. Commissioner of Public Safety, 473 N.W.2d 828 (Minn. 1991) 206
Frisbie v Collins, 342 U.S. 519 (1952) 180
Frye v. United States, 293 F. 1013 (D.C. Cir. 1923) 253–256, 265

Gamble v. United States, 587 U.S. 678 (2019) 13
General Electric Co. v. Joiner, 522 U.S. 136 (1997) 262–263
Georgia v. Randolph, 547 U.S. 103 (2006) 176
Gideon v. Wainwright, 372 U.S. 335 (1963) 31, 34, 58, 59
Giglio v. United States, 405 U.S. 150 (1972) 319
Gitlow v. New York, 268 U.S. 652 (1925) 31
Greenman v. Yuba Power Products, Inc., 377 P.2d 897 (1963) 72, 73
Griffin v. California, 380 U.S. 609 (1965) 35, 202
Griffin v. Wisconsin, 483 U.S. 868 (1987) 189
Griswold v. Connecticut, 381 U.S. 479 (1965) 35, 37, 129
Groh v. Ramirez, 540 U.S. 551 (2004) 153

Hallock v. Bonner, 387 F.3d 147 (2d Cir. 2004) 117
Hans v. Louisiana, 134 U.S. 1 (1890) 80
Harlow v. Fitzgerald, 457 U.S. 800 (1982) 81
Harris v. New York, 401 U.S. 222 (1971) 292
Harris v. United States, 331 U.S. 145 (1947) 126, 127, 181
Hayes v. Florida, 470 U.S. 811 (1985) 177, 205
Herrera v. Collins, 506 U.S. 390 (1993) 38, 39–40, 284
Herring v. United States, 555 U.S. 135 (2009) 122, 155, 180
Hiibel v. Sixth Judicial District Court of Nevada, 542 U.S. 177 (2004) 178
Hinton v. Alabama, 571 U.S. 263 (2014) 284
Hoffa v. United States, 385 U.S. 293 (1966) 175
Horton v. California, 496 U.S. 128 (1990) 173
Howe v. State, 916 P.2d 153 (Nev. 1996) 175
Hudson v. Michigan, 547 U.S. 586 (2006) 156
Husty v. U.S., 282 U.S. 694 (1931) 184
Hygh v. Jacobs, 961 F.2d 359 (2d Cir. 1992) 344

Iacangelo v Georgetown University, 560 F. Supp. 2d 53 (D.D.C. 2008) 345
Illinois v. Fisher, 540 U.S. 544 (2004) 226
Illinois v. Gates, 462 U.S. 213 (1983) 150, 152–153
Illinois v. Krull, 480 U.S. 340 (1987) 122
Illinois v. Lafayette, 462 U.S. 640 (1983) 183
Illinois v. McArthur, 531 U.S. 326 (2001) 186
Illinois v. Rodriguez, 497 U.S. 177 (1990) 177
Illinois v. Wardlow, 528 U.S. 119 (2000) 178
In the Matter of a Search of a Residence in Oakland, California, 354 F. Supp. 3d 1010 (N.D. Cal. 2019) 143
In the Matter of the Search of a White Google Pixel 3XL Cellphone in a Black Incipio Case, 398 F. Supp. 3d 785 (D. Idaho 2019) 143
In re Gault, 387 U.S. 1 (1967) 35
In re Paoli R.R. Yard PCB Litigation, 35 F.3d 717 (3d Cir. 1994) 265, 340
In Re World Trade Center Lower Manhattan Disaster Site Litigation, 474 F.2d 529 (2d Cir. 1972) 295
Ingram v. City of Columbus, 185 F.3d 579 (6th Cir. 1999) 188

Johnson v. United States, 333 U.S. 10 (1948) 148, 185
Jones v. Ashburnham, 102 E.R. 905 (1804) 200
Jones v. Murray, 962 F.2d 302 (4th Cir. 1992) 215

Kahler v. Kansas, 589 U.S. 271 (2020) 104
Kansas v. Glover, 589 U.S. 376 (2020) 178
Kansas v. Ventris, 556 U.S. 586 (2009) 292
Katz v. United States, 389 U.S. 347 (1967) 35, 130, 141, 172
Kaufman v. Edelstein, 539 F.2d 811 (2d Cir. 1976) 295

Kentucky v. King, 563 U.S. 452 (2011) 186
Ker v. California, 374 U.S. 23 (1963) 180
Kisor v. Wilkie, 588 U.S. 558 (2019) 15
Klayman v. Obama, 957 F.Supp.2d 1 (D.D.C 2013) [Klayman I] 165–166
Klopfer v. North Carolina, 386 U.S. 213 (1967) 35
Knowles v. Iowa, 525 U.S. 113 (1998) 180, 182
Kumho Tire Co., Ltd. v. Carmichael, 526 U.S. 137 (1999) 262, 263
Kyllo v. United States, 533 U.S. 27 (2001) 173, 175

Lake County Estates v. Tahoe Regional Planning Agency, 440 U.S. 391 (1979) 80
Lee v. State, 2 P.3d 517 (Wyo. 2000) 155
Lee v. United States., 343 U.S. 747 (1942) 175
Lewis v. United States, 385 U.S. 206 (1966) 175, 206
Lilly v. Virginia, 527 U.S. 116 (1999) 288
Lochner v. New York, 198 U.S. 45 (1905) 37, 58
Loper Bright Enterprises v. Raimondo, 603 U.S. ___ (2024) 15
Loving v. Virginia, 388 US 1 (1967) 37

Malaska v. Maryland, 88 A.3d 805 (Md Ct. Special App. 2014) 310
Malley v. Briggs, 475 U.S. 335 (1986) 81
Malloy v. Hogan, 378 U.S. 1 (1964) 34, 207
Mapp v. Ohio, 367 U.S. 643 (1961) 32–34, 121, 128, 207, 209
Marbury v. Madison, 5 U.S. (1 Cranch) 137 (1803) 14
Marshall v. Barlow's, Inc., 436 U.S. 307 (1978) 167, 200, 306
Maryland v. Buie, 494 U.S. 325 (1990) 182
Maryland v. Craig, 497 U.S. 836 (1990) 296
Maryland v. Garrison, 480 U.S. 79 (1987) 158
Maryland v. King, 569 U.S. 435 (2013) 189, 215, 216
Maryland v. Pringle, 540 U.S. 366 (2003) 183
Maryland v. Wilson, 519 U.S. 408 (1997) 179, 182
Massachusetts v. Sheppard, 468 U.S. 981 (1984) 122
Mayfield III v. Dalton, 109 F.3d 1423 (9th Cir. 1997) 50
McBoyle v. United States, 283 U.S. 25 (1931) 9
McDaniel v. Brown, 558 U.S. 120 (2010) 247
McGirt v. Oklahoma, 591 U.S. __ (2020) 13
McQuiggin v. Perkins, 569 U.S. 383 (2013) 57
Melendez-Diaz v. Massachusetts, 557 U.S. 305 (2009) 239, 292, 299–301
Michigan Dept. of State Police v. Sitz, 496 U.S. 444 (1990) 178, 188
Michigan v. Bryant, 562 U. S. 344, (2011) 307
Michigan v. Clifford, 464 U.S. 287 (1984) 189
Michigan v. Long, 463 U.S. 1032 (1983) 179
Michigan v. Summers, 452 U.S. 692 (1981) 154
Michigan v. Tyler, 436 U.S. 499 (1978) 167, 189
Mincey v. Arizona, 437 U.S. 385 (1978) 182, 186, 197
Minnesota v. Dickerson, 508 U.S. 366 (1993) 173, 178
Miranda v. Arizona, 384 U.S. 436 (1966) 35, 58, 113, 175, 185
Missouri v. McNeely, 569 U.S. 141 (2013) 180, 210–212, 214
Mitchell v. Wisconsin, 588 U.S. 840 (2019) 210, 212–214
Monell v. Dept. of Social Services, 436 U.S. 658 (1978) 67, 277
Monroe v. Pape, 365 U.S. 167 (1961) 79
Moore v. Board of Regents of the University of California, 793 P.2d 479 (Cal. 1990) 201
Muehler v. Mena, 544 U.S. 93 (2005) 154
Murphy v. National Collegiate Athletic Association, 584 U.S. 453 (2018) 12
Murray v. United States, 487 U.S. 533 (1988) 122

Nardone v. United States, 308 U.S. 338 (1939) 122
National Treasury Employees Union v. Von Raab, 489 U.S. 656 (1989) 189, 214
Nelson v. McMullen, 207 F.3d 1202 (10th Cir. 2000) 181
New Jersey v. T.L.O., 469 U.S. 325 (1987) 188, 189
New York v. Belton, 453 U.S. 454 (1981) 183
New York v. Burger, 482 U.S. 691 (1987) 189, 190
New York v. P.J. Video, Inc., 475 U.S. 868 (1985) 150
Nicholas v. Goord, 430 F.3d 652 (2d Cir. 2005) 215
Nix v. Williams, 467 U.S. 431 (1984) 121, 123

Obama v. Klayman, 800 F.3d 559 (D.C.Cir.2015) [Klayman II] 165–166
Obergefell v. Hodges, 576 U.S. 644 (2015) 37
O'Connor v. Ortega, 480 U.S. 709 (1987) 188, 189
Ohio v. Roberts, 448 U.S. 56 (1980) 297
Ohio v. Robinette, 519 U.S. 53 (1996) 176, 179
Oklahoma v. Castro-Huerta, 597 U.S. 629 (2022) 13
Oliver v. United States, 466 U.S. 170 (1984) 132, 134
Olmstead v. United States, 277 U.S. 438 (1928) 130
Oregon v. Hass, 420 U.S. 714 (1975) 292

Parker v. Gladden, 385 U.S. 363 (1966) 35
Palko v. Connecticut, 302 U.S. 319 (1937) 2, 31, 37
Palsgraf v. Long Island Railroad Co., 162 N.E. 99 (1928) 72
Payton v. New York, 445 U.S. 573 (1980) 154, 173
Pearson v. Callahan, 555 U.S. 223 (2009) 81
Pena v. Texas, 285 S.W.3d 459 (Tex. Crim. App. 2009) 226
Pennsylvania v. Labron, 518 U.S. 938 (1996) 184
Pennsylvania v. Mimms, 434 U.S. 106 (1977) 179
Pennsylvania v. Muniz, 496 U.S. 582 (1990) 204
People v. Keta, 593 N.E.2d 1328 (NY 1992) 190
People v. Kuhn, 306 N.E.2d 777 (NY 1973) 188
People v. Materon, 107 A.D.2d 408 (N.Y. App. Div. 1985) 188
People v. Ortega case, 203 N.Y.S.3d 868 (NY 2023) 308, 309
People v. Ramey, 545 P.2d 1333 (Cal 1976) 185
People v. Randolph, 4 P.3d 477 (Colo. 2000) 156
People v. Roehler, 167 Cal. App.3d 353 (1985) 199–200
People v. Smith, 46 Cal. App.5th 375 (2020) 186
People v. Wells, 202 P.2d 53 (Cal. Sup. Ct. 1949) 103
People v. Wrotten, 901 N.Y.S.2d 265 (NY 2010) 296
Perez v. Townsend Engineering Co., 562 F. Supp. 2d. 647 (M.D. Pa. 2008) 345
Pierce v. Society of Sisters, 268 U.S. 510 (1925) 37
Planned Parenthood of Southeastern Pennsylvania v. Casey, 505 U.S. 833 (1992) 8
Pointer v. Texas, 380 U.S. 400 (1965) 35, 290
Powell v. Alabama, 287 U.S. 45 (1932) 31, 32, 59
Powell v. Texas, 392 U.S. 514 (1968) 90
President Riverboat Casino, Inc. v. Missouri Gaming Commission, 13 S.W.3d 635 (Mo. 2000) 11, 119

Rabata v. Dohner, 172 N.W.2d 409 (1969) 337
Ramos v. Louisiana, 590 U.S. 83 (2020) 248
Raynor v. Maryland, 29 A.3d 617 (Md. App. 2011) [*Raynor-I*] 198–199
Raynor v. Maryland, 99 A.3d 753 (Md. 2014) [*Raynor-II*] 217
Regina v. Dudley and Stephens, 15 Cox C.C. 624, 117 Eng. Rep. 101 (QB. 1844) 104
Regina v. M'Naghten (8 ER 718, Rep 229, England, 1843) 102, 103
Richards v. Wisconsin, 520 U.S. 385 (1997) 167
Riley v. California, 573 U.S. 373 (2014) 138–140, 180
Rise v. Oregon, 59 F.3d 1556 (9th Cir. 1995) 215
Robertson v. Commonwealth, 82 S.W.3d 832 (Ky. 2002) 92
Robinson v. California, 370 U.S. 660 (1962) 34, 90
Rochin v. California, 342 U.S. 165 (1952) 206, 207
Rodriguez v. United States, 575 U.S. 348 (2015) 178, 202
Roe v. Wade, 410 U.S. 113 (1973), 8
Ruiz-Troche v. Pepsi Cola, 161 F.3d 77 (1st Cir. 1998) 265

Samson v. California, 547 U.S. 843 (2006) 189
Samuels v. LeFevre, 885 F. Supp. 32 (N.D.N.Y, 1998) 67
Saucier v. Katz, 533 U.S. 194 (2001) 81
Schmerber v. California, 384 U.S. 757 (1966) 35, 181, 202, 203–204, 209–211, 214
Schneckloth v. Bustamonte, 412 U.S. 218 (1973) 175, 176
Securities and Exchange Commission v. Jarkesy, 603 U.S. ___ (2024) 15
See v. City of Seattle, 387 U.S. 541 (1967) 167, 189, 200
Shipley v. City of New York, 37 N.E.3d 58 (NY. Ct. App. 2015) 201
Silverthorne Lumber Co. v. United States, 251 U.S. 385 (1920) 122
Skilling v. United States, 561 U.S. 358 (2010) 16
Skinner v. Oklahoma, 316 U.S. 535 (1942) 14
Skinner v. Railway Labor Executives' Association, 489 U.S. 602 (1989) 189, 214
Slaughter-House Cases, 83 U.S. (16 Wall) 36 (1872) 29
Smith v. Arizona, 602 U.S. ___ (2024) 304–308
Smith v. Maryland, 442 U.S. 735 (1979) 138, 140, 144, 166
South Dakota v. Opperman, 428 U.S. 364 (1976) 183
Specht v. Jensen, 853 F.2d 805 (10th Cir., 1988) 344
Spinelli v. United States, 393 U.S. 410 (1969) 35, 151–153
State v. Andrews, 234 A.3d 1254 (N.J. 2020) 143
State v. Boretsky, 894 A.2d 659 (N.J. 2006) 185
State v. Highland, 76 S.E. 140 (W. Va. 1912) 201
State v. Langill, 13 A.3d 171 (N.H. 2010) [*Langill II*] 307–308
State v. Langill, 945 A.2d 1 (N.H. 2008) [*Langill I*] 281–282
State v. Marquez, 238 P.3d 880 (N.M. 2009) 283
State v. Olivas, 856 P.2d 1076 (Wash. Sup. Ct. 1993) 215
State v. Patterson, 758 So.2d 955 (La. 2000) 177
State v. Sullivan, 16 S.W.2d 551 (Ark. 2000) 180

State v. Thompson, 693 So.2d 282 (La. 1997) 157
State v. Timberlake, 726 N.W.2d 509 (Minn. Ct. App. 2007) 173
State v. Williams, 516 So.2d 1081 (Fl. Dist. Ct. 1987) 181
Steagald v. United States, 451 U.S. 204 (1981) 154
Stoner v. California, 376 U.S. 483 (1964) 176
Strickland v. Washington, 466 U.S. 668 (1984) 31, 54
Stuart v. Alabama, 586 U.S. ___ (2018) 304

Terry v. Ohio, 392 U.S. 1 (1968) 35, 177, 202
Texas v. Brown, 460 U.S. 730 (1983) 173
Thomas v. Bauman, 835 F. App'x 5 (6th Cir. 2020) 157
Thompson v. Louisiana, 469 U.S. 17 (1984) 182
Thornton v. United States, 541 U.S. 615 (2004) 183
Timbs v. Indiana, 586 U.S. 146, (2019), 197
Torres v. Madrid, 592 U.S. 306 (2021) 180
Trump v. United States, 603 U.S. ___ (2024) 5, 82
Trupiano v. United States, 334 U.S. 699 (1948) 179, 182
Turner v. State, 754 A.2d 1074 (Md. Ct. Spec. App. 2000) 176

United States v. Amerson, 483 F.3d 73 (2d Cir. 2007) 215
United States v. Anderson, 154 F.3d 1225 (10th Cir. 1998) 186
United States v. Anderson, 169 F.Supp.3d 60 (D.D.C. 2016) 228–229
United States v. Andrews, Criminal Case No. 08-20652 (E.D. Mich. 2024) 265
United States v. Arvisu, 534 U.S. 266 (2002) 153
United States v. Banks, 540 U.S. 31 (2003) 157
United States v. Bates, 522 U.S. 23 (1997) 151
United States v. Bilzerian, 926 F.2d 1285 (2d Cir. 1991) 344
United States v. Biswell, 406 U.S. 311, (1972) 190
United States v. Bramble, 103 F. 3d 1475 (9th Cir. 1996) 175
United States v. Brawner, 471 F.2d 969 (D.C. Cir. 1972) 103
United States v. Brigham, 382 F.3d 500 (2004) 177
United States v. Burr, 25 F. Cas. 187; CC Va. 1807) 306
United States v. Carey, 172 F.3d 1268 (10th Cir. 1999) 174
United States v. Carolene Products, 304 U.S. 144 (1938) 14
United States v. Chadwick, 433 U.S. 1 (1977) 129, 182, 184
United States v. Chatrie, 107 F.4th 319 (4th Cir. 2024) 142–143
United States v. Cortez, 449 U.S. 411 (1981) 178
United States v. Davis, 588 U.S. 445 (2019) 16
United States v. Davis, 690 F.3d 226 (4th Cir. 2012) 215
United States v. Dawkins, 17 F.3d 399 (D.C. Cir.1994) 186
United States v. Dionisio, 410 U.S. 1 (1973) 203–205
United States v. Dorman, 435 F.2d 385 (D.C. Cir. 1970) 186
United States v. Drayton, 536 U.S. 194 (2002) 175–176
United States v. Dunn, 480 U.S. 294 (1987) 133
United States v. Edwards, 415 U.S. 800 (1974) 181, 202, 203
United States v. Fowlkes, 804 F.3d 954 (9th Cir. 2015) 208
United States v. Freitas, 800 F.2d 1451 (9th Cir. 1986) 155
United States v. Fuentes 105 F.3d 487 (9th Cir. 1997) 176
United States v. Gomez, 633 F.2d 999 (2d Cir. 1980) 186
United States. v. Gray, 369 F.3d 1024 (8th Cir. 2004) 176
United States v. Grubbs, 547 U.S. 90 (2006) 155
United States v. Guevara-Martinez, 262 F.2d 751 (2001) 180
United States v. Havens, 446 U.S. 620 (1980) 123
United States v. Hensley, 469 U.S. 221 (1985) 177
United States v. Herzbrun, 724 F.2d 773 (11th Cir. 1984) 176
United States v. Hook, 471 F.3d 766 (7th Cir. 2006) 204
United States v. Houston 813 F.3d 282 (6th Cir. 2016) 135–136
United States v. Hubbell, 530 U.S. 27 (2000) 153
United States v. Hudson and Goodwin (11 U.S. (7 Cranch) 32, 1812) 87
United States v. Hython, 443 F.3d 480 (6th Cir. 2006) 154
United States v. Jacoby, 11 USCMA 428, 29 CMR 244 (1960) 289
United States v. Jones, 565 U.S. 400 (2012) 136–137
United States v. Kirschner, 823 F.Supp.2d 665 (E.D. Mich. 2010) 143
United States v. Knotts, 460 U.S. 276 (1983) 137
United States v. Kristiansen, 901 F.2d 1463 (8th Cir. 1990) 345
United States v. Leon, 468 U.S. 897 (1984) 122, 155

United States v. Mara, 410 U.S. 19 (1973) 203–205
United States v. Martinez-Fuerte, 428 U.S. 543 (1976) 188
United States v. Mathis, 357 F.3d 1200 (10th Cir.2004) 154
United States v. Matlock, 415 U.S. 164 (1974) 175
United States v. McConney, 728 F.2d 1195 (9th Cir. 1984) 185
United States v. Melgar, 927 F. Supp. 939 (E.D. Va. 1996) 182
United States v. Mendenhall, 446 U.S. 544 (1980) 177
United States v. Montoya de Hernandez, 473 U.S. 531 (1985) 178
United States v. Newman, 849 F.2d 156 (5th Cir. 1988) 345
United States v. Pampinella, 131 F. Supp. 595 (N.D. Ill. 1955) 180
United States v. Patane, 542 U.S. 630 (2004) 206
United States v. Pulido-Baquerizo, 800 F.2d 899 (9th Cir. 1986) 176
United States v. Rabinowitz, 339 U.S. 56 (1950) 172, 181
United States v. Ramirez, 523 U.S. 65 (1998) 157
United States v. Ray, No. 06-4747 (4th Cir. 2007) 151
United States v. Rich, 992 F.2d 502 (5th Cir. 1993) 176
United States v. Richard, 994 F.2d 244 (5th Cir. 1993) 186
United States v. Roach, 582 F.3d 1192 (10th Cir. 2009) 150, 154
United States v. Robinson, 414 U.S. 218 (1973) 181
United States v. Ross, 456 U.S. 798 (1982) 184, 185
United States v. Ross, 263 F.3d 844 (8th Cir. 2001) 176
United States v. Santana, 427 U.S. 38 (1975) 188
United States v. Segura, 663 F.2d 411 (2d Cir. 1981) 186
United States v. Seslar, 996 F.2d 1058 (10th Cir. 1993) 177
United States v. Sharpe, 470 U.S. 675 (1985) 178
United States v. Sokolow, 490 U.S. 1 (1989) 153
United States v. Spriggs 827 F. Supp. 372 (E.D. Va. 1993) 176
United States v. Thriftimart, Inc., 429 F.2d 1006 (9th Cir. 1970) 189
United States v. Velarde, 214 F.3d 1204 (10th Cir. 2000) 265, 283
United States v. Verdugo-Urquidez, 494 U.S. 259 (1990) 128
United States v. Wade, 388 U.S. 218 (1967) 206
United States v. White, 401 U.S. 745 (1971) 135
United States v. Wong, 334 F.3d 831 (9th Cir. 2004) 174
Utah v. Strieff, 579 U.S. 232 (2016) 123

Vermont v. Garvey, 595 A.2d 267 (Vt. 1967) 206
Vernonia School District 47J v. Acton, 515 U.S. 646 (1995) 188
Village of Arlington Heights v. Metropolitan Housing Development Corp., 429 U.S. 252
(1977) 14
Virginia v. Moore, 553 U.S. 164 (2008) 180

Waeschle v. Dragovic, 576 F.3d 539 (6th Cir. 2009) 201
Warden v. Hayden, 387 U.S. 294 (1967) 149, 185, 187
Washington v. Chrisman, 455 U.S. 1 (1982) 173
Washington v. Texas, 388 U.S. 14 (1967) 35
Weeks v. United States, 232 U.S. 383 (1914) 121, 179
Welsh v. Wisconsin, 466 U.S. 740 (1984) 156
West Virginia v. Environmental Protection Agency, 597 U.S. 697 (2022) 15
Whisenhunt v. State, Dept. of Public Safety, 746 P.2d 1298 (Alaska 1987) 206
Whren v. United States, 517 U.S. 806 (1996) 178
Wickard v. Filburn, 317 U.S. 111 (1942) 12
Williams v. Florida, 399 U.S. 78 (1970) 323
Williams v. Illinois, 567 U.S. 50 (2012) 302–304
Williams v. Schario, 93 F.3d 527 (8th Cir. 1996) 204
Wilson v. Arkansas, 514 U.S. 927 (1995) 156
Wilson v. Wilson 138 So.3d 1176 (Fla. Dist. Ct. App. 2014) 200
Winston v. Lee, 470 U.S. 753 (1985) 180, 202, 207, 208
Wolf v. Colorado, 338 U.S. 25 (1949) 31, 33, 121
Wong Sun v. United States, 371 U.S. 471 (1963) 123
Wooley v. Maynard, 430 U.S. 705 (1977) 60
Woolverton v. Multicounty Grand Jury, 859 P.2d 1112 (Okl. Crim. App. 1993) 203
Worcester v. Georgia, 31 U.S. 515 (1832) 12
Wyoming v. Houghton, 526 U.S. 295 (1999) 185

Ybarra v. Illinois, 444 U.S. 85 (1979) 154

Zap v. United States, 328 U.S. 624 (1946) 175
Zinermon v. Burch, 494 U.S. 113 (1990) 37
Zurcher v. Stanford Daily, 436 U.S. 547 (1978) 154

Statutory Authorities

Additional Grounds for Issuing Warrant, 18 U.S.C. § 3103a (2001) 156
Administrative Warrants, 49 U.S.C. § 32707 166
Americans With Disabilities Act (ADA), 42 U.S.C. §§ 12101, et seq. (1990) 79
Antiterrorism and Effective Death Penalty Act (AEDPA), 28 U.S.C. § 2254 (1996) 57
Assimilative Crimes Act (ACA), 18 U.S.C. § 13 (1825) 12
Authority for the Promulgation of Rules, 28 U.S.C. §§ 2072-2075 (1975) 256

Breaking Doors or Windows for Entry or Exit, 18 U.S.C. § 3109 (1995) 157

Cell-Site Simulators, 18 U.S.C. § 3119 (2023) 144
Civil Action for Deprivation of Rights, 42 U.S.C. § 1983 (1979) 36–37, 41, 67, 78–79, 81, 198
Civil Rights of Institutionalized Persons Act (CRIPA), 42 U.S.C. §§ 1997–1997j (1980) 79
Computer Fraud and Abuse Act (CFAA), 18 U.S.C. § 1030 (1984) 99–100
Consumer Product Safety Act (CPSA) 15 U.S.C. §§ 2051-2089 (1972) 77
Continuing Criminal Enterprise Act (CCE), 21 U.S.C. § 848 (1970) 99
Counterfeit Goods Trafficking, 18 U.S.C. § 2318 (1962), § 2320 (1984) 100
Crimes, 18 U.S.C. §§ 1 – 2725 87, 98–100
Criminal Infringement of a Copyright, 17 U.S.C. § 506(a) (1976) & 18 U.S.C § 2319 1982) 100
Criminal Procedure, 18 U.S.C. §§ 3001 – 3772 110–118

Deprivation of Rights Under Color of Law, 18 U.S.C. § 242 (1996) 37, 78, 79
Digital Millennium Copyright Act, 17 U.S.C. §§ 1201-1205 (1998) 100
Diplomatic Relations Act, 22 U.S.C. § 254 (1978) 82

Electronic Communications Privacy Act (ECPA), 18 U.S.C. §§ 2510-2523 (1986) 100, 138

Fair Debt Collection Practices Act (FDCPA), 15 U.S.C. §§1692-1692p (1977) 77–78
Federal Intelligence Surveillance Act (FISA), 50 U.S.C. §§ 1801-1885c (1978) 164–166

Federal Rules of Evidence, https://www.uscourts.gov/rules-policies/current-rules-practice-procedure/federal-rules-evidence 256–258
Federal Tort Claims Act (FTCA), 28 U.S.C. **§1346(b) and** §§ 2671-2680 (1946) 68, 80–81
Federal Trade Commission Act (FTC Act), 15 U.S.C. §§ 41-58 (1914) 77
Federal Wiretap Act, 18 U.S.C. § 2511 (1968) 100, 138
Foreign Sovereign Immunities Act (FSIA), 28 U.S.C. §§ 1330, 1332, 1391(f), 1441(d), and 1602–1611 (1976) 82
First Step Act of 2018, Pub. L. No. 115-391 88

Genetic Information Nondiscrimination Act (GINA), Pub. L. No. 110-233 (2008) 215
Grounds for Issuing Search Warrant, 18 U.S.C. § 3103 155

Health Insurance Portability and Accountability Act (HIPAA), Pub. L. No. 104-191 (1996) 215
Honest Services Fraud, 18 U.S.C. § 1346 (1988) [voided] 16
Hobbs Act, 18 U.S.C. § 1951 (1946) 99
Hobbs Act, 18 U.S.C. § 924(c) (1951) 16, 99

Insanity Defense, 18 U.S.C. §17 (1984) 104

Jencks Act, 18 U.S.C. § 3500 (1957) 318
Judicial Authorization Required for Forensic Genetic Genealogical DNA Analysis and Search, Md. Criminal Procedure Code § 17-102 (2023) 217

Major Crimes Act, 18 U.S.C. § 1153 (1885) 13

Obstruction of Justice, 18 U.S.C. §§ 1501-1521 329–330
Offenses not capital, 18 U.S.C. §3282 (1948) 101

Pen Register Act, 18 U.S.C. §§ 3121-3127 (1986) 137, 144
Post-Conviction DNA Testing, 18 U.S.C. § 3600-3600A (2016) 38, 227
Preservation and Accessibility of Biological Evidence, Miss. Code Ann. § 99-49-1 (2017) 227–228
Preservation of Biological Evidence § 3600A (2016) 227
Protection of Human Subjects, Definitions for purposes of this policy, Research, 45 C.F.R. §46.102(l) 233

Racketeer Influenced and Corrupt Organizations Act (RICO), 18 U.S.C. §§ 1961-68 (1970) 99

Second Chance Act of 2007, Pub. L. No. 110-199 88
Statements or entries generally, 18 U.S.C. § 1001 (1948) 329
Stored Communications Act (SCA), 18 U.S.C. §§ 2701-2712 (1986) 100, 138, 165
Subpoena of person in foreign country, 28 U.S.C. § 1783 (1948) 320

Tampering with a witness, victim, or an informant, 18 U.S.C. §1512 (1982) 329–330
Tucker Act, 28 U.S.C. §§ 1346(a) and 1491 (1887) 81

Uniform Act to Secure the Attendance of Witnesses from Without a State in Criminal Proceedings 295
Uniting and Strengthening America by Providing Appropriate Tools Required to Intercept and Obstruct Terrorism Act of 2001 (USA PATRIOT Act), Pub. L. No. 107-56 155, 165
United States Code (U.S.C.), https://www.govinfo.gov/app/collection/uscode 17

Violent Crime Control and Law Enforcement Act (VCCLEA), Police Pattern or Practice (34 U.S.C. §12601 (1994) 79

Subject Index

§ 242 37, 78, 79
§ 1983 36, 37, 41, 67, 78–79, 81, 198

abandoned property 91, 197, 198, 215
abuse of discretion 53, 55, 262
accreditation 240, 243, 272, 278–279
ACE-V 272, 281–282, 307–308
actual innocence 38–41
actus reus 90, 98
administrative law 19
administrative searches 166–167, 189–190
administrative warrants 166–167, 168
admissible 120–123, 201, 253–266, 321
affiant 149–150, 156–157
affirmation 5, 150, 330, 339
aggravated assault 89, 93, 97
alcohol testing 203, 209–214
alternative dispute resolution 19–20
American Law Institute (ALI) 68, 72, 87
amicus brief 54, 300
Annie Dookhan 237
anticipatory warrants 154–155
appeals 44, 52–55, 117, 118, 328–329
appellant 45, 53
appellee 46, 53
arraignment 114–115
arrest 108, 112–113, 154, 157, 166, 180
arson 98
assault 69, 97–98
Assimilative Crimes Act 12
assumption of risk 70
attempt 93
attenuation 123
attorney-client privilege 316
Auer deference rule 15
authentication 258, 345–347
automobile exception 184–185

bail 113–114, 120, 198
bailiff 56, 322
bar 322, 323
bases of an expert 338–339
battered wife problem 102
battery 69, 97
bench 54, 322, 343, 351
bench trial 52, 117, 254
bill of attainder 87, 119, 120
Bill of Rights 17, 25, 27–28, 30–35
binding precedent 6, 7
Bivens claim 79, 81
biological evidence laws 227–228
bitemarks 241
black box studies 240, 242
blood spatter pattern analysis 284–285

bodies 93, 199–201
booking 113
Brady material 319
branches of law 19–20
Brandeis brief 54
Brandon Mayfield 237–238
burden of proof 65, 69–70, 115, 179, 325
burglary 89, 98
business records 291, 292, 299

capital offense 88, 93
Carroll doctrine 184, 185
case or controversy 49, 50
case law 6–7, 18, 45–46
castle doctrine 102
categorical statements 246
causation 68, 71–72, 90, 92
cause of action 64, 67, 79, 315
cellphones 138–144
cell site location information (CSLI) 140, 142
cell-site simulators 144
cert. 52, 55
certificate of analysis 299–301
certification 240, 272, 276
chain-of-custody 221–222, 300
charging 111
Chevron doctrine 15
civil law (branch) 19, 44, 63–83
Civil Law (Roman) 5–6
Civil Rights Act 36–37, 41, 67, 78–79, 81
civil rights movement 34
Civil War amendments 29–30
clearly erroneous 53
Code of Federal Regulations (C.F.R.) 18
cognitive bias 240, 273, 282
collateral attack 53–54, 57, 118
comity 13
Commerce Clause 12
Common Law 5–7, 45, 46
comparative negligence 70
compelling state interest 14
compensatory damages 65
competency 73, 257, 272, 275, 336, 340
competency testing 275
complaint 71, 110, 111
compliance 278
concurring opinion 55
confidential informant 151–153
conflict of law 18–19
conformance 276–277, 279, 280
Confrontation Clause 288–289, 290
consent 175–177
conspiracy 79, 90, 93, 94
consumption of evidence 228–229
constitutions 18
contraband 131, 149, 153
contracts 73–78, 80
contributory negligence 70
corpus delicti 93
corpus juris civilis 5
court clerk 317, 322, 323
court of last resort 47, 48
court reporter 45, 46, 317, 322, 323
courtroom etiquette 351
Crime Data Explorer 89
criminal defenses 101–104
criminal law 19, 64–65, 86–100
criminal negligence 94, 95
cross-contamination 221, 223
curtilage 132–133, 134, 198

damages 65–66, 70, 72
Daubert factors 259, 262, 264, 265, 337
Daubert standard 258–260, 263–266
Daubert trilogy 262–263
declarant 290
defendants' rights revolution 34
defense attorney's fallacy 248
depositions 296, 317, 319
detention 35, 57, 69, 154, 175, 177–179
dicta 7
diminished capacity 103
discovery 116, 315–320, 321
discretionary appeal 52
dissenting opinion 55
diversion 115
diversity 50–51
DNA 38, 40–41, 50, 198–199, 215–217, 225–229, 241, 244–246, 270, 279
double jeopardy 13, 28, 35, 52, 94, 116, 120, 324
dog sniff 134, 174, 178, 202

elements of a crime 90–93
en banc opinion 48, 54, 55
epistemology 233
ethical codes 272, 276–277
evidence 117, 131, 149, 324–326
exclusionary rule 32–33, 120–123
execution of a warrant 156–157
exigency 157, 172, 185–187
exonerations 244–246
ex parte 57, 290, 297
expert witness 295, 317–320, 333–340
ex post facto 14, 87, 119, 120

fact witness 295, 335–336
FBI hair analysis 238
federal diversity 50–51
federal preemption 11–13
federal question 50
Federal Register 18

Federal Rules of Evidence (FRE) 256–258
Federal Tort Claims Act (FTCA) 68, 79, 80–81
federalism 9–10
felony 89, 108
felony murder 94, 95
Feres doctrine 80
finality of judgment38, 52, 284
fingernail scrapings 209, 227
fingerprints 143, 180, 198, 203, 204, 205–206, 241, 270, 272–273, 281–282, 307–308
firearms 183–184, 241, 270, 272–273
First Step Act 88
FISA warrants 164–166
footwear 241, 247
forensic science boards/commissions 279–280
forum 49
foundation for evidence 222, 325, 337, 339
Franks hearing 156
fraud 16, 69
FRCP rule 26 316–318
FRCrimP rule 16 318–320
FRE 104(a) 257, 265, 281, 326, 339, 340
FRE 702 257, 258, 264, 266, 271–272, 281, 337–338
FRE 703 258, 302, 304–307, 338–339
frisk 177–179, 202
fruit of the poisonous tree 122, 197
fruits of a crime 131, 149, 173, 197
Frye rule 253–256, 258, 263, 325, 339
fundamental fairness 25, 30, 31, 206
funding of forensic science 248–249

gatekeeping. 259, 260, 262–263, 265, 326, 339
general acceptance 239, 254, 255, 257, 258–259
general damages 65
general intent 91
general jurisdiction 49
general warrants 119, 127–128, 148, 171
geofence warrants 142–143
Giglio material 281, 316, 319
good faith 81, 122, 141, 142, 156, 158, 180, 224, 316
grand jury 28, 34, 111–112, 115

habeas corpus. 45, 53, 54, 57, 118, 119, 120
hair analysis 227, 236, 238, 241, 272–273
Hammurabi's code 2, 26
handwriting 82, 203, 204–205
harmful error 53, 283
hearsay 258, 290–293, 297–298
historicity 244
Hobbs Act 16, 99
holding of a case 7
homicide 89, 92, 94–96
hostile witness 341–342
hot pursuit 185, 187–188
hue and cry 109
human rights 2–4

impeachment 48, 292, 344
IMSI-catchers 144
in forma pauperis 59, 114
inchoate crimes 93–94
independent contractor 66
indictment 111–112, 114, 119, 315
individualized suspicion 177, 189, 203, 205
independent expert opinion 308–309
ineffective assistance of counsel 53–54, 284
inevitable discovery 122–123
injunctions 66
Innocence Protection Act 38
insanity defense 102–104, 345
instrumentality 149
intentional torts 68–70
interlocutory appeal 52, 117
international law 18
inventory searches 183

Jencks Act 318
joint and several liability 52
judicial activism 57–60
judicial restraint 58
judicial review 14–16, 87
jurisdiction 48–51
jury instructions 117, 327
jury selection 323–324
justice of the peace 148, 188

knock and announce rule 156–157

larceny 89, 91, 93, 98
law 1–4, 17–20, 64
lay witness 326, 335–336
least restrictive means 14
legal reporter 45–47
lesser-included offense 93
likelihood ratio 247
limited jurisdiction 49
Lochnerize 58
Louis Brandeis 6, 54, 129

Magna Carta 26, 27, 30
Major Crimes Act 13
Major Questions Doctrine 15
malice 94, 95
manslaughter 95–96
Marian Acts 289, 305
materiality 226, 325
medicolegal death investigation 199–201

mens rea 90–92, 98
Miranda warning 35, 113, 175, 185, 292
misdemeanor 89
M'Naghten rule 102
Model Penal Code 87, 90, 101, 103
motion *in limine* 321, 339
murder 94–95

NAS report 239–240
natural law 2–4
Necessary and Proper Clause 10, 12
necessity 101, 104
negligence 71–72
new evidence 38–41, 57, 283–285
no-knock warrants 157
nolo contendere 115
nonconformity 275, 278, 280–282
notice and demand laws 295, 297, 299

oath 5, 74, 149, 150, 314, 330
objection 53, 326, 343
obstruction of justice 329–330
Oliver Wendell Holmes, Jr. 6, 7, 68
open fields 132, 134
open view 135, 172–173
ordinances 18, 79
ordinary witness 257, 326, 335–336
original jurisdiction 49

particularity 150, 153–154, 155
past recollection recorded 343
pattern matching 240–243, 247, 272–273, 282
PCAST report 240–243, 266
pen registers 137–138, 144
penal codes 17, 87, 84
per curiam opinion 55
percipient witness 335
perjury 330
personal injury suits 67–73
personal jurisdiction 48–49
personal property 98, 197, 201
persuasive argument 7
petit jury 117, 322, 323
physical characteristics 143, 203–206, 211
plain view exception 172–175, 182, 186
plea agreement 44, 61, 109, 116
plea colloquy 114
pleadings 45, 54, 315, 329
plurality opinion 55
police power 11, 98, 119, 126
positive law 4
posse comitatus 109
postconviction remedies 118
post-trial motions 117
preliminary hearing 112, 115–116, 124
prejudicial 53, 257, 260, 265, 283
present recollection refreshed 342–343
presentment 114
pretrial conference 116
prima facie 326
principle of legality 14
Privileges and Immunities Clause 13, 29–30
probabilistic statements 246–248
probable cause 35, 36, 111–113, 115–116, 119, 150–151, 153, 154, 180
probable cause hearing 115–116
probative 117, 197, 260, 325
procedural due process 36
process crimes 329–330
proffer 336, 337, 349, 350
proficiency testing 272, 275, 281
proponent 326, 337, 340, 341–342, 346
prosecutor's fallacy 247–248
protective sweep 179–183
provenance 222
psychiatric testimony 256, 345
public invitation 134
punitive damages 65, 66

qualifications 257, 264, 274–277, 317, 319, 320, 337, 340, 350
qualified immunity 81–82
quality management systems 278

rape 89, 97
rational basis test 14
reasonable expectation of privacy 129–144, 174, 182, 198–199
reasonable scientific certainty 282–283
reasonable suspicion 35, 177–179, 191, 202
reasonableness 126–128, 189
Reasonableness Clause 126, 128, 171–172
reception statutes 7
refreshing memory 342–343
regulations 15, 18, 19
rehabilitation of a witness 344
relevant evidence 256, 257, 260, 264, 271, 321, 325
reliable evidence 236–246, 257, 259, 265–266, 270–280, 283, 298
remand 54, 118
remedies 65–66
research 233, 248–249
respondeat superior 66, 277–278
rescission 78
restorative justice 88
retreat laws 102
retributive justice 88
RICO 99
ripe 49
robbery 89, 93, 98

Roberts Rule 297
rule of law 4–5, 7, 25

science 231–236
scientific validation 240–243, 271, 273
Scottsboro boys 31–32
search 132–144, 149, 111, 117, 140, 156–157, 179–184, 189–190, 196–217
search incident to arrest exception 179–184
Second Chance Act 88
seized goods 197
selective incorporation doctrine 30–33
self-authenticating 222, 346–347
self-defense 101–102
sentencing 103, 117–118, 328
service of process 315
sexual assault 97
Sharia law 5
Shepardize 47
sneak and peak warrants 155
solicitation 93, 94
sources of law 17–18
sovereign immunity 80
special courts 47, 49
special damages 65
special needs doctrine 188–189
specific intent 91
specific performance 66, 74
speedy trial 28, 114, 120
spoliation of evidence 223–226
staleness 49, 154
standards 270, 273–274
standing 49, 155, 166, 183
stand-your-ground law 102
stare decisis 7, 8
state action 20, 21, 36, 128, 131
statistical interpretation 246–248
statute of limitations 38, 49, 57, 67, 79, 80, 101
statute of repose 67
stipulation 295, 318, 323, 324, 327
stored communications act 100, 138, 140
strict liability 72–73, 75, 91, 92
strict scrutiny 14
subject matter jurisdiction 49, 50
subpoenas 28, 120, 202, 295, 317, 320
substantive due process 31, 36–38
Supremacy Clause 11
Supreme Court 47–48, 52, 55–56
surgery 207, 208
surveillance 130, 135–144
suspect class 14

temporary restraining order 66
test accuracy 241, 271, 273
test precision 271, 273
test validity 240–243, 259, 261, 271
testimonial 143, 204, 298, 304–309
theft 89, 91, 93, 98
third-party disclosure 135, 138–140
tortfeasor 66, 67, 68, 71
torts 67–73, 79
totality of the circumstances 81, 151–153
trap and trace device 137
treaties 6, 10, 11, 17, 18, 50
trial 34, 44, 51–52, 117, 314–315, 321–328
trial by ordeal 314–315
trial record 54
trier of fact 51–52, 117, 254, 281
trier of law 51–52, 265

ultimate question 52, 325, 344–345
unavailability 293–295
unconscionable contracts 76
undue burden test 14
Uniform Commercial Code (UCC) 17, 74, 76
Uniform Language for Testimony and Reports (ULTRs) 238, 280
United States Code (U.S.C.) 17
Universal Declaration of Human Rights 4

validation 240–243, 271–272, 273
vehicle search 139, 181, 183–185, 189
venue 49, 51
verdict 52, 117, 327
verification 272, 281–282, 282, 307–308
vicarious liability 66–67, 90, 91–92
video testimony 296
voice 204
voir dire 117, 323, 325, 337, 339–340, 351–352

Walter Raleigh 289–290
Warrant Clause 128, 148, 171–172
Warren Court 34–35
weight 253–254, 256, 265, 348
writ of capias 112
writ of certiorari 52, 55
writ of habeas corpus 57, 78, 118, 119, 120, 227, 284
wrongful convictions 236–238, 244–246
wrongful death 65, 69, 70

zone of privacy 129–130

Made in the USA
Las Vegas, NV
19 September 2026

666b7518-a27c-4ef9-96f5-9f3ea9cebc38R02